"Take Up the Black Man's Burden"

Charles E. Coulter

"Take Up the Black Man's Burden"

Kansas City's African American Communities 1865–1939

University of Missouri Press
Columbia

University of Missouri Press, Columbia, Missouri 65211
Printed and bound in the United States of America

First paperback printing, 2016

Library of Congress Cataloging-in-Publication Data

Coulter, Charles E. (Charles Edward), 1954–
Take up the Black man's burden : Kansas City's African American communities, 1865–1939 / Charles E. Coulter.
p. cm.
Summary: "Examines the people and institutions that shaped Kansas City's Black communities from the end of the Civil War until the outbreak of World War II, blending rich historical research with first-person accounts that allow participants in this historical drama to tell their own stories of struggle and accomplishment"—Provided by publisher.
Includes bibliographical references and index.
ISBN: 978-0-8262-1649-6 (hardcover)
ISBN: 978-0-8262-2112-4 (paperback)
1. African Americans—Missouri—Kansas City—History. 2. African Americans—Missouri—Kansas City—Social conditions. 3. African American neighborhoods—Missouri—Kansas City—History. 4. Kansas City (Mo.)—Race relations—History. 5. Kansas City (Mo.)—Social conditions. I. Title.
F474.K29N43 2006
977.8'4110496073—dc22 2005032000

♾™ This paper meets the requirements of the American National Standard for Permanence of Paper for Printed Library Materials, Z39.48, 1984.

Text design: Foley Design
Cover design: Susan Ferber
Typeface: ITC Usherwood Book

Cover art courtesy of Missouri Valley Special Collections, Kansas City Public Library, Kansas City, Missouri

to Maureen, Michael, and MaryAlice Rose,
children of love;

to Paul, Martin, Malcolm, and Trane,
men of soul and vision;

and to Mary Hunter Coulter,
who first taught me to read

It is beside the point to ask whether we form a real race. Biologically we are mingled of all conceivable elements, but race is psychology, not biology; and psychologically we are a unified race with one history, one red memory and one revolt.

—William Edward Burghardt Du Bois,
"The Negro College"

Contents

Acknowledgments

THIS WORK BEGAN as the germ of an idea for a dissertation project in 1995, shortly after the 1920 manuscript census records were first made available to the public. It has resisted redefinition, modification, trimming, or just plain obliteration. It after all turned out to be what it was meant to be: a snapshot look at a community that had been long ignored.

As always, a number of people were involved in making this project a success, and it is impossible to mention them all. But some folks deserve special mention. Dr. Dennis Merrill of the History Department at the University of Missouri–Kansas City (UMKC) started out as adviser for this project and along the way became a friend as well. Professors Lou Potts, Pat Peebles, William Worley, Barbara Ryan, and Tanya Price of UMKC added their special expertise and encouragement as well. Dr. Pat Hovis, assistant dean of graduate studies, also encouraged me to make my wild dream a reality. Dave Boutros, Betty, Jennifer, and Marilyn at Western Historical Manuscripts–UMKC were incredibly patient and helpful, as was Bill Livingston at the Black Archives of Mid-America.

The exigencies of work and family life interrupted the scholarly process, forcing me to take a nontraditional route to the completion of this work. Help came from many an unexpected source. Along the way I received encouragement and support from an eclectic bunch of folks: Marie, James, Deborah, Cheryl, Ron, Carrie, and all of the Hunters and Coulters for starters. Author Colson Whitehead showed me how to laugh.

Many people contributed to bringing the manuscript into the hands of readers. Thanks go to Christopher Reed, professor of history at Roosevelt University, and the other anonymous reader for the University of Missouri Press. They both offered valuable insights and bolstered the accuracy of the text with their comments.

The *Kansas City Star,* editor Mark Zieman, and Miriam Pepper were more than gracious with their help and support. Monroe Dodd offered valuable insights and suggestions for honing the manuscript. Artist Eric Craven went above and beyond.

This also gives me a chance to say thanks to the people who have made a difference in my life: Edwin and Linda Berger, Fathers John Schuele and Don Farnan, Sisters Helen Flemington and Judy Warmbold, Joyce VanCrum and Dottie Pfannenstiel, Carol Brady, Rudena Mallory, Kenneth Bobb and Renee Goodeau-Bobb, Don and Jo LePore, Fred Brown, and all of my friends at St. Therese Little Flower, especially the members of the choir. I'd also like to thank the wildest inner sanctum: Terri, Geri, Bob and Toni, Karen Lipschuetz, June, Karen H., Shirl, Chris, Cliff, Rick, Terrell, and Sam. Big thanks go to Kati, Dody, and the three best children in the world: Maureen, Michael, and MaryAlice Rose. And thanks to the disc jockeys and staff at KMJK-FM (107.3) of Lexington and Kansas City, whose music kept me going when all else failed.

As always, all errors of omission, commission, and interpretation are completely mine. Peace.

"Take Up the Black Man's Burden"

Introduction

"Lift Every Voice and Sing"

I believe it to be true,
You see,
Tomorrow belongs to me.

—LANGSTON HUGHES, "NOTE,"
UNDATED POEM

ON JANUARY 29, 1919, more than eight thousand residents of the two Kansas Cities and the surrounding communities filed into Convention Hall for a remarkable celebration. The occasion: the three hundredth anniversary of the first reported landing of people of African descent on American soil. The celebration, loosely timed to coincide with the anniversary of the Emancipation Proclamation, was seen by the organizers—members of the black elite on both sides of the state line—as more than an opportunity to pay homage to those forgotten ancestors; it was a chance to celebrate the remarkable accomplishments of the descendants of those Africans and of the millions brought to American shores since 1619.[1] Even more so, the celebration in Convention Hall that Wednesday evening served as the culmination of a day of festivities within the two Kansas Cities, festivities that served to link the disparate elements of the African diaspora: descendants of

1. Descriptions of the planning of the celebration and of the celebration itself are drawn from the *Kansas City Sun* weekly editions of January 4, January 25, February 1, and February 8, 1919. The significance of the celebration is attested by its lingering place in black Kansas City's collective memory. Nathan B. Young and William H. Young, in *Your Kansas City and Mine*, a compilation of black life in the late 1940s, include two references.

slaves and free black men and women; natives of the United States and other elements of the black Atlantic.[2] It was a day full of accolades and inspired ovations. "Magnificently Glorious," proclaimed the *Kansas City Sun,* a black weekly, in its report a week later. These festivities pointed both to a glorious past and toward a brighter future.

The ideals of the festival drew from two concurrent themes prevalent in black Kansas City in the period between the two world wars. One was a growing African American assertiveness, in which pleas for equality had been replaced by a *demand* for social justice. Mixed with these sharply defined demands was a developing sense of racial pride, in which a form of black nationalism intertwined with the political ideals of the greater American society. Although specific details of segments of the 1919 festival are lacking, the milestones highlighted in the pageant parallel those of other cultural expressions of what would soon be universally known as the outlook of the "New Negro": from Ada Crogman's musical pageant *Milestones* to Carter G. Woodson's majestic work of scholarship, *The Negro in Our History.*

The Kansas City festivities started with a parade from the city's six-year-old Union Station, where the celebration's featured speakers arrived by train. From Union Station, a procession of automobiles began a round of visits to the African American schools and public institutions of the two Kansas Cities. The first stop was at Lincoln High School at Nineteenth and Tracy on the Missouri side. The students and faculty of the school rendered a rousing reception for the visiting dignitaries. The chairman of the celebration committee, noted black politician and editor Nelson C. Crews, introduced the visitors, each of whom then gave a brief address. The same routine was followed at all-black Sumner High School in Kansas City, Kansas, and Western University in Quindaro, the predominantly black settlement tucked away between northwestern Kansas City, Kansas, and the south bank of the Missouri River. From there, the delegation proceeded on the customary automobile tour of the boulevards of Kansas City, Missouri, before retiring to Crews's home at 2624 Highland Street for dinner and a brief social hour.

Then it was on to Convention Hall for the celebration. Music instructor R. G. Jackson of Western University led a chorus in two selections, and the Reverend D. A. Holmes, at the time the pastor of Metropolitan

2. Paul Gilroy, an Afro-Brit, uses the phrase "Black Atlantic" to describe the sphere of African resettlement, whether forced or voluntary. It includes people of color in North America, the Caribbean, South America, and Europe.

Baptist Church in Kansas City, Kansas, offered the invocation.[3] The Reverend H. B. Parks, former pastor of Allen Chapel African Methodist Episcopal (AME) Church and presiding bishop of the AME district, then offered a "soul-stirring" address on the reasons for the celebration. After the opening ceremonies, a procession mounted the stage. Members of the Knights of Pythias, a black fraternal order, and the Building Laborers Professional Union of America (the strongest black labor organization in the two Kansas Cities) opened with a portrayal of "Africa in 1619." No real description of the portrayal exists, yet given the tone and atmosphere of the rest of the program and the growing interest among African Americans in black history in the first two decades of the twentieth century, it is likely that the performance reflected an Africa ruled by military and economic black elites. Although the names of the Songhay and Mali empires were not commonplace in the greater American culture, their accomplishments had begun to attain a certain cachet within the growing African American professional class.[4]

Then came a delegation of Boy Scouts piloting a "Dutch vessel" bringing the first Africans to Virginia. Again, no real description survives. Scholar Françoise Charras argues that from the early nineteenth century until 1944, the horrors of the Middle Passage had been effectively buried in the collective consciousness of the African American public. Yet it is worth noting that historian Carter G. Woodson, writing in 1923, described the slave trade thus: "One must bear in mind that for every slave imported into America at least four or five others had to meet death in the numerous wars, in the inhuman drive to the coast, and in *the cruel shipment in unsanitary ships hardly suitable for importing hogs.*"[5]

Members of Bethel AME Church followed with a portrayal of black men and women working in a southern cotton field, while within a

3. Jackson, a graduate of the Music Department at the University of Kansas, founded the Jackson Jubilee Singers, a musical touring company similar to the Fisk Jubilee Singers of Fisk University. See Susan O. Greenbaum, *The Afro-American Community in Kansas City, Kansas: A History,* 72.

4. The second decade of the twentieth century saw a dramatic surge in interest among African Americans in their history. African Americans in urban communities in the North and Midwest organized literary clubs to study the growth and achievements of African civilizations as well as the accomplishments of noted men and women of color. In 1915, historian Carter G. Woodson organized the Association for the Study of Negro Life and History; a year later, he published the first issue of the *Journal of Negro History* and argued for the setting aside of one day a year to celebrate black history. That day in February eventually evolved into Black History Month. See in particular August Meier and Elliott Rudwick, *Black History and the Historical Profession, 1915–1980,* 1–71.

5. Woodson and Charles H. Wesley, *The Negro in Our History,* 69 (emphasis in original).

southern cabin the ladies of the Woman's Self-Government Club demonstrated how African Americans stealthily obtained the key of knowledge. With knowledge in hand, African Americans then gained liberty. The Intercity Lawyers Club drew up the documents, and "Abraham Lincoln" (in a dark portrayal by noted black lawyer L. Amasa Knox) issued the Emancipation Proclamation of 1863, ending slavery in the states then in rebellion. Following emancipation came Reconstruction, aptly portrayed by the men and women of the Second Baptist Church, the oldest black church in Kansas City, Missouri. It is likely, foreshadowing the seminal work of black historian W. E. B. Du Bois twenty years later, that Reconstruction was portrayed this night as a period of black achievement. D. W. Griffith's movie classic *The Birth of a Nation*—with its racist stereotypes, demeaning images, and distorted view of Reconstruction—had been released four years earlier; it had been shown at the Globe Theater in downtown Kansas City without any protest of note. By 1919, however, the National Association for the Advancement of Colored People (NAACP) had organized vehement protests against the movie, and it is probable that the pageant's adult organizers, many of whom were no more than a generation or so removed from slavery and emancipation, seized the opportunity to offer a ringing rebuttal to Griffith's movie.

There was yet more to the festival. The pageant was advertised as a "comprehensive display of the achievements and production" of African Americans. The remaining displays in the procession were a tribute to the organizations and institutions that had developed in black Kansas City. After a performance by a high school cadet band (led by noted music instructor N. Clark Smith), the girls auxiliaries of the Young Women's Christian Association (YWCA), the Boy Scouts, representatives of the Red Cross, the black chapter of the Women's Christian Temperance Union (their presentation was titled *The Death of John Barleycorn*), the Poro Club, Old City Hospital, and various other black fraternal and charitable organizations processed across the stage. All were, the *Sun* noted, magnificently attired in uniforms or appropriate dress.

Pinkie Osborne, wife of pastor William T. R. Osborne of Ebenezer AME Church and manager of the pageant, then offered "Tri-Centennial Ode" composed by C. B. Johnson, a black teacher in Kirksville, Missouri. Nelson Crews then introduced the guest speaker, Col. Frank Denison, who commanded the Eighth Illinois (an all-black regiment) in Europe during the First World War. Denison's remarks, the *Sun* reported, had the crowd of eight thousand "standing on [its] feet, cheering like mad" and turned the great auditorium into "an ocean of white handkerchiefs, flags and pennants." When Denison finished his remarks, the ovation intensified, and when the band struck up "See the Conquering Hero Comes," the tumult intensified. It was then time to pay homage to Kansas City's own "conquering heroes." John Lynch, a major in the U.S. Army, then introduced the other black Kansas Citians who had fought in Europe. Among them would have been Lincoln teacher Hugh O. Cook, who was blinded temporarily by a gas attack during the war; salesman Homer B. Roberts; and several members of Allen Chapel AME's congregation who had served with the Ninety-second Infantry Division (an all-black unit).[6]

Those spectators who lost interest in the proceedings could take time to tour the numerous exhibits on display in the auditorium. All were part of the festival's theme, reflecting the ingenuity and creativity of African Americans. Some are worth noting: Among the exhibits was a handmade quilt stitched by a slave one hundred years previously and passed down from generation to generation. A group of black women from Manhattan, Kansas, contributed a quantity of handmade items. A number of aspiring artists from the two Kansas Cities also placed their handiwork on display. The all-black universities in the two states—Western University and Lincoln University in Jefferson City, Missouri—also provided exhibits.

The final part of the program was an appeal by Lincoln principal John R. E. Lee for racial loyalty. Lee was an ardent fund-raiser and activist, and his brief message likely dealt with the need for support of the various organizations, institutions, and industries reflected in the daylong pageant. Lee kept his remarks brief, possibly because of the makeup of his audience. According to the *Sun,* a number of whites were included in the crowd; at least on this occasion there was no Jim Crow in evidence at Convention Hall. The crowd also reflected the various dimensions of Kansas City's African American communities. Many of the spectators were members of the growing black middle class in the two Kansas Cities. The crowd also included African Americans from surrounding "villages and communities." By the second decade of the twentieth century, the African American communities of Kansas City were the "central city" for black residents of western Missouri and northeastern Kansas. Lincoln High School drew students from parts of Platte County, Excelsior Springs, and even Liberty. Sumner was the only high school for African American students in northeastern Kansas. Black

6. Among the other black Kansas Citians to see action in Europe were Cpls. John Graves and Will Knox. Both served with the 366th Ambulance Company attached to the all-black Ninety-second Division. *Kansas City Sun,* January 4, 1919.

boys and girls from South Park, Merriam, and even Olathe joined its student body. Western University, which had begun as Freedman's University in 1867, attracted students from across the region and the nation.

The participants and spectators for the tricentennial celebration represented a significant slice of this far-flung community. Representatives of the major churches, fraternal organizations, and schools joined with packinghouse workers, railroad porters, domestics, and common laborers to celebrate African American achievement. The festival served to link African Americans from Kansas City's West Side, the Church Hill area east of downtown, the West Bottoms, and the East Side with their friends, relatives, and peers on the Kansas side and from the rural communities in the cities' hinterlands. This festival reflected many aspects of life in the African American communities around Kansas City in the interwar period. By using the festival as a starting point, this study aims to examine the world of Kansas City's African Americans between the end of the First World War and the start of the Second World War in Europe. It was a world shaped by a myriad of social forces familiar to students of the period: urbanization, migration, industrialization and modernization, and, not least of all, racial segregation and discrimination. African American community building in this period occurred within a framework shaped by these forces, but just as historian Stephanie Shaw notes in her examination of African American women during the Jim Crow era, this study "looks past oppression" to investigate what African American men and women in Kansas City could and did do in constructing their community and their sense of identity in the 1920s.[7]

Historian Darlene Clark Hine maintains that the development of parallel communities (one white and one black), with parallel institutions and organizations, created a safe haven for African Americans in the first half of the twentieth century.[8] In their own community, Hine notes, African Americans then developed strategies to attack those forces that made the creation of parallel communities necessary. The development of separate black churches, businesses, and professional organizations was not an acquiescence to segregation; rather, these groups were essential elements in the fight to integrate African Americans into the mainstream of American society. This study embraces Hine's model on African American community development and highlights the agency

7. See Shaw, *What a Woman Ought to Be and to Do: Black Professional Women Workers during the Jim Crow Era*.

8. Hine, "Black Professionals and Race Consciousness: Origins of the Civil Rights Movement, 1890–1950," 1279–94.

of Kansas City's African Americans in developing organizations and institutions that sustained their communities.

The present investigation, though indebted to both popular and the few scholarly analyses of various aspects of Kansas City's African American communities, attempts to carry the story a lot further. Drawing from a variety of sources (manuscript census records, organizational records, memoirs, newspaper accounts, statistical studies, oral histories, popular fiction, poetry, and popular histories), it seeks to re-create the world of African Americans in Kansas City, Missouri, in the years between the two world wars. It seeks to illustrate how African Americans saw themselves and the world in which they lived, while at the same time acting upon and reacting to the social and economic structures that lined their world. Though recognizing that segregation and discrimination were a part of that world, this volume attempts to move beyond a race-relations model and show how African Americans defined and created a world of their own in the first four decades of the twentieth century.

The festival of January 29, 1919, offers a unique window into the world of Kansas City's African American community. Among the organizers and participants in the festival were some of Kansas City's most prominent black men and women. But the festival would not have been a success if it had relied on the work of a few elite members of the community; Kansas City's less prominent Africans Americans played a vital role as well. The festival gives us a glimpse of the world black Kansas Citians created for themselves.

The twenty-one years between the First and Second World Wars, particularly the decade 1919–1929, were important ones for Kansas City's black residents. In those years are the roots of the careers of many of the prominent individuals and of the institutions that sustained the African American communities. In 1919, the Paseo Young Men's Christian Association (YMCA) was just six years old, while the YWCA for black women was still a year away. The fight for a new Lincoln High School gained momentum, and the area around Eighteenth and Vine began its transformation into the economic cornerstone of the community. St. Stephens and Vine Street Baptist Churches emerged as rivals in prominence and popularity to mainstays Allen Chapel and Second Baptist. The fledgling National Association for the Advancement of Colored People worked to gain a foothold in Kansas City in 1919, but Ida M. Becks was just beginning her campaign to bring the Urban League to town. Both organizations would compete in Kansas City in the 1920s with an active branch of Marcus Garvey's United Negro Improvement

Association (UNIA) and other activist organizations. Theron B. Watkins would emerge as a political force, while L. Amasa Knox was just beginning his legal and political career. Chester Franklin started the *Kansas City Call* in 1919; eighty-one years later it was still going strong. Roy Wilkins began his journalism career, and Minnie Crosthwaite led Kansas City's black club women into a long career of social service. The new modern General Hospital No. 2, the first black-run public hospital in the country, opened to much acclaim in 1930. And lest we forget, Kansas City's Monarchs ruled black baseball in the 1920s, while the clubs along Twelfth and Eighteenth Streets provided a sounding board for Kansas City's contribution to the American art form known as jazz.

The foundations for the political and economic success for black elites lay in the trials and triumphs of the black working class. After all, only 3 percent of the African American population in the two Kansas Cities could claim even middle-class status. The black working class, with the exception of a few isolated blocks in the two Kansas Cities, made up the vast majority in most neighborhoods. Their pennies and nickels provided working capital for black-owned businesses. Such venerable institutions as Smith's Drugstore and the Eblon Theater relied on the black working class to succeed.

Black labor, in a sixty-year span, helped fuel the growth of Kansas City from a way station on the road west into a thriving metropolis. The Hannibal Bridge—the first across the Missouri River—was completed in 1869 and opened Kansas City's hinterlands to the markets of the East. Although their precise roles can never be determined, black men undoubtedly contributed their labor to the construction of the bridge. African Americans found jobs throughout the two Kansas Cities. Joined by Irish and eastern European immigrants, African Americans provided the difficult, tedious, and sometimes dangerous work that helped transform Kansas City. It was an exciting world, shaped in part by the conflicting aspirations of African Americans and the inconsistent nature of Missouri's versions of Jim Crow. It was a world few white Kansas Citians saw or recognized. It is a world too often obscured from our historical viewpoint by the crack of the bat and the blare of the trumpet.

For African Americans living on the Great Plains, Kansas City was a nexus through which information, ideas, and people were moved and sometimes transformed. Kansas City stood at the center of a web of African American communities; its influence was felt throughout northwestern Missouri, eastern Kansas, and as far south as Oklahoma. Admittedly, Kansas City's influence was weak at some points along this web, but its allure attracted thousands of African Americans after World War I.

Not all African Americans, of course, saw Kansas City as their ultimate destination. Black Kansas City also served as a way station—a transition point between North and South—throughout the interwar period. Activist Florence Kennedy and jazz musician Charlie Parker, for example, both grew up in the Kansas City area; both believed it necessary to head to New York to achieve their life dreams. Other luminaries—activist Roy Wilkins, artists Aaron Douglas and Henry Ossawa Tanner, musician William "Count" Basie, and writers Melvin Tolson and Langston Hughes among them—made forays into Kansas City before moving on to greater heights. This is not to disparage those who came and stayed or those who never left; countless African Americans enriched the city with their labor, their creativity, and their quest for social justice.

This study documents the artistic and intellectual contributions of people of color to Kansas City's culture in the seventy years after the Civil War. In the pages of three black weeklies—the *Kansas City Sun* and later the *Kansas City Call* and *Kansas City American*—African Americans articulated the concerns, grievances, and practical remedies of black America in general and black Kansas City in particular. Kansas City's African Americans also contributed to a variety of national publications; their writings appeared in black weeklies from Baltimore to Utah and in magazines such as *Crisis, Voice of the Negro, Opportunity,* and others. Granted, these publications tapped only a privileged few among Kansas City's African American professional class, but their concerns reflected those of a much broader base. Black professionals spoke of the needs and aspirations of a wide range of African Americans. Equally important was the diversity of opinion reflected in these articulations. Black Kansas Citians also left a valuable legacy in the arts. In addition to creating the city's rich jazz tradition, black Kansas Citians offered valuable additions to America's classical and secular music history. Moreover, the work of some of black America's earliest artists was filtered through at least a brief exposure to Kansas City's environment.

Fortunately for the purposes of this book, the articulations of black professionals are not the only surviving descriptions of the lives and thoughts of Kansas City's African Americans. Oral histories of black workers as well as the memoirs of those African Americans who made the successful transition from working class to professional also offer valuable insights into our re-creation of that time and place. This volume offers a venue for describing the African American men and women who constructed communities in Kansas City, Missouri. It delves into the lives of lawyers and laborers, saints and sinners, those highly educated and those illiterate, men and women, young and old. It seeks to give voice to those whose lives remain at best on the fringes of our historical memory.

This study accepts, as a given, that the components of the identity triad—race, class, and gender—are each socially constructed. That is, each of these so-called fixed categories in reality unfolds as the consequence of economic, social, and political forces. I, however, follow the lead of historian Ira Berlin, who argues that race is a particular kind of social construction—a historical construction. The social category of race, according to Berlin, cannot exist outside of time and place. "Race, no less than class," Berlin says, "is the product of history, and it only exists on the contested social terrain in which men and women struggle to control their destinies." This contested terrain is multidimensional and multifaceted. Anthropologist Leela Fernandes, in fashioning her study of female workers in the jute mills of Calcutta, holds that the boundaries of any social category are constantly in flux and are produced in relation to other social categories or identities. In Fernandes's view, no social construction can exist independently.[9] This volume examines the intersection of race, class, gender, and community as they played out in the construction of black Kansas City in the period 1919–1941.

Concepts of "blackness" and "whiteness"—particularly in a border city such as Kansas City—were consistent sources of tension, with *each* set of historical actors fighting to set the limits of both categories. I argue, in contrast to much of the work in "whiteness" studies, that the construction of race was or is at least a two-way street. Although white Americans could attempt to set the boundaries for racial categories, African Americans and other "racial minorities" constantly asserted their own ideas of identity and community. I maintain that African Americans in Kansas City created their own sense of racial identity through social and cultural practices both urban and rural, southern and northern, modern and traditional.

It should also be noted that African American history does not exist within a vacuum. This study recognizes that the trinal forces of industrialization, urbanization, and commercialization—forces that shaped

9. Berlin, *Many Thousands Gone: The First Two Centuries of Slavery in North America*, 1 (Berlin draws on the pioneering work of British historian Edward P. Thompson, particularly his influential study of British laborers, *The Making of the English Working Class*); Fernandes, *Producing Workers: The Politics of Gender, Class, and Culture in the Calcutta Jute Mills*, xiii.

nineteenth- and twentieth-century American society—did not bypass African American communities. The movement of African Americans to the cities in the half century after the Civil War coincided with a nationwide trend, as the United States became less of a rural, agricultural society and more urban and commercial. Changes in American society in the 1920s and 1930s were not restricted to the white middle class. Black Kansas Citians, in particular, were caught in the same tensions between city and country, modern and traditional, that marked American society in the years before the Second World War.[10]

African Americans in the two Kansas Cities also influenced and were influenced by trends and issues within greater black America. The "New Negro," a term in usage since the 1890s to describe the more politicized, more assertive, and more militant African Americans, readily described many of the men and women who drove black Kansas City in the first three decades of the twentieth century.[11] The debates over the development of black business and over segregated public facilities were played out in the homes and churches and on the street corners of black Kansas City. The debate between Booker T. Washington and W. E. B. Du Bois over the direction of black education was refashioned within Kansas City's schools.

Finally, this study is part of an attempt to rethink African American history. It emphasizes the enabling aspects of African Americans' lives rather than the disabling ones. It attempts, as Ira Katznelson suggests, "to inquire after the social processes that produced the landscape we see, and about the various social relationships" that bound African Americans in the "factory, the office, the neighbourhood, the park, and the other arenas of city life."[12] This work assesses the prevalence of kinship, occupational, and geographical bonds within the African American communities spread throughout the two Kansas Cities. Family linkages, of course, were important, but it becomes apparent that employment and state of origin also made up threads of the mosaic of life in Kansas City in the 1920s. But members of these communities more often than

10. Historians have often commented on the plethora of advertisements in the black-controlled press for skin lighteners and hair-straightening products, but they have overlooked the equally pervasive number of ads for the newest iceboxes, washing machines, Victrolas, and other appliances. See Ralph Ellison's illuminating essay "The Something or Another" in his *Shadow and Act*.

11. Howard University professor Alain Locke forever linked the term to 1920 African American culture with his anthology of poetry and prose originally published in *Survey Graphic* in 1925 and then in book form. See Locke, *The New Negro: Voices of the Harlem Renaissance*.

12. Katznelson, *Marxism and the City*, 27.

not gave primacy to their racial identity. Black men and women in Kansas City were determined to define race on their own terms; they would play a vital role in determining how race would be constructed in their lives.

Chapter One describes the historical foundations of the African American communities before 1920. It examines the people, institutions, and economic and social forces that shaped those communities. Chapter Two discusses the working lives of black men and women in Kansas City, particularly the everyday workers whose hard work and wages were the underpinnings of the community in the interwar years. Chapter Three examines the careers of the men and women who had gained a measure of status in black Kansas City in the period, and Chapter Four looks at the institutions they developed to lift up the community and to fight the restrictions of Jim Crow. The state of black education in Kansas City is the focus of Chapter Five. Education, in its various components, remained essential to black Kansas Citians, and most sought the greatest expansive learning opportunities possible for their children. But the schools were more than tools for education; they were symbols of community. Schools were gathering places for community organizations, and they promoted community-oriented events. More than any other institution in black America, schools symbolized the community's present and its future. Chapter Five also examines the role of the church within Kansas City's black community. As has been well documented, the church was the other foundation on which African American communities rested in the first half of the twentieth century. Chapter Six looks at leisure and play. By the second decade of the twentieth century, opportunities for leisure in this country had expanded beyond the activities of a privileged few. Whether professional or working class, male or female, African Americans in Kansas City enjoyed a variety of recreational activities. New movie theaters offered the latest from the booming Hollywood movie industry, as well as the work of black filmmaker Oscar Micheaux. Middle-class African Americans could enjoy the spas of Excelsior Springs or join their counterparts from across the nation in the cabins at Idlewild, Michigan. Like the rest of the country, black Kansas Citians were learning to enjoy leisure. Chapter Seven examines housing, the most problematic component of existence for African Americans in the 1920s. Housing was, at least on the Missouri side, the arena in which most of the conflicts between whites and blacks occurred. Violence by whites directed at blacks occurred most frequently when African Americans attempted to transgress some symbolic geographical boundary (most often Twenty-seventh Street) along the Troost-

Vine corridor. Chapter Eight probes how African Americans in Kansas City coped with the difficulties brought on by the Great Depression. Chapter Nine provides a glimpse at the African American community in 1939, a decade after the start of the Great Depression and just months before a second war would break out in Europe. The foundations for Kansas City's African American community in the twentieth century were laid in those first three decades.

Local Scholarship

Where is our historian to give us our side view. . . of Negro history, to teach our people our own history?

—ARTHUR A. SCHOMBURG, "RACIAL INTEGRITY"

The scholarly literature on African Americans in Kansas City has been scattered, limited, and often written without a real understanding of the processes, people, and institutions that made up black Kansas City before World War II. One exception is the work of Asa Martin, an employee of Kansas City's Board of Public Welfare, who surveyed the African American community of Kansas City in the 1910s and subsequently drew together his findings for a master's thesis at William Jewell College in Liberty. His work was eventually published as *Our Negro Population: A Sociological Study of the Negroes of Kansas City, Missouri.* Martin's sociological description of the black community, motivated by Progressive Era sentiments, is tainted at times by the racial proscriptions of the period, and some of his statistical information is open to challenge. Nevertheless, *Our Negro Population* provides the first real glimpse of the lives of African Americans on the Missouri side.

Martin's work remained the only completed scholarly treatment of African Americans in Kansas City for almost the next seventy years. In 1982, graduate student Dwayne Martin used the 1880 manuscript census to develop a statistical and comparative analysis of black Kansas City in the late nineteenth century. In his master's thesis, "The Hidden Community: The Black Community of Kansas City, Missouri, during the 1870s and 1880s," Martin sought to challenge some of the prevailing sociological paradigms of the twentieth century concerning family and social life among African Americans. Echoing the work of historian Herbert Gutman on the black family and challenging the arguments of political scientist Daniel Patrick Moynihan, Dwayne Martin found that stable two-parent families were the rule, rather than the exception, in the "hidden community" in the 1880s.[13] Because of a paucity of sources available at the time, Martin painted in broad strokes. In his hands, the "hidden community" is reduced to a series of numbers. The individual, the living, breathing human being, is almost as invisible in his hands as the larger community became to historians in the decades that followed. Biographical sketches of five prominent black men are included in Martin's final chapter, but for the most part, they and other individuals remain exterior to his analysis.

Prominent individuals and institutions are the theme for two popular histories of black Kansas City. Nathan B. Young and William H. Young's *Your Kansas City and Mine,* published in 1950, is poorly organized and undocumented. It even lacked, until 1997, any kind of an index. Yet it contains a wealth of information on institutions and individuals in the African American community. The criteria for inclusion in the volume are unclear, however. James Crews, a postal worker and prominent member of the National Association for the Advancement of Colored People, is given a three-sentence biographical sketch; his brother, Nelson, owner of the *Kansas City Sun* for ten years, prominent member of the Republican Party, and supporter of most of the endeavors in the black community in his lifetime, does not merit a mention. The volume is, though, much more useful than Elvis Gibson's *Kansas City: Mecca of the New Negro.* Gibson has put together a variety of photos, newspaper clippings, and other primary sources with little thought to organization or documentation. Some of the newspaper clippings, in fact, are undated or run without the name of the newspaper from which they were drawn.

The volumes by Young and Young and Gibson, however, do serve to fill a void left by traditional scholars. The first scholarly analysis of the impact of the Pendergast machine on Kansas City (William M. Reddig's *Tom's Town: Kansas City and the Pendergast Legend*) makes no mention of African Americans, although black Kansas Citians were beneficiaries of the Pendergast machine's largess and proved to be some of its strongest supporters. A. Theodore Brown and Lyle W. Dorsett in *K.C.: A History of Kansas City, Missouri* ignore the African American community with the exception of a limited discussion of the impact of the 1875 Civil Rights Act and an attempt by black political hopefuls to form a

13. Moynihan, an architect of Lyndon Johnson's War on Poverty in the 1960s, contended in the 1970s that single-parent families, that is, female-headed households, were a direct legacy of slavery and had been the norm for African American families since. Martin, Gutman, and other students of the late nineteenth and early twentieth centuries successfully demonstrated that female-headed households were truly an exception within African American communities until after the Great Depression.

third party in the 1880s. Sherry Lamb Schirmer and Richard D. McKinzie attempted, in *At the River's Bend: An Illustrated History of Kansas City, Independence and Jackson County,* to include African Americans in their social history of Kansas City, but, again, the scarcity of available sources limits their discussion.

The contributions of African Americans to Kansas City's rich history in music and sports have been more thoroughly researched. Janet Bruce's history of the Kansas City Monarchs, one of the original franchises in the Negro National League, attempts to be more than an account of games and the men who played them. Bruce delves into the role the Monarchs played in the community, but beyond a few references to well-known institutions, she does not shed any new light on the formation of the African American community. Nathan W. Pearson's *Goin' to Kansas City* is an oral history of the jazz community. Pearson allows the musicians and patrons of the city's many jazz clubs to describe the promiscuously vibrant world of Kansas City jazz, and he allows them to give witness to the major vices (gambling, narcotics, and prostitution) that were prevalent in their world. His description of Kansas City outside of the jazz "scene," however, is limited to the corruption, inner workings, and confrontations of the two major political factions—that of Tom Pendergast and that of Joe Shannon—within the Democratic Party. In this discussion, African Americans become lost, with the exception of known gamblers Felix Payne and Piney Brown. The African Americans who remained attached to Kansas City's Republican Party, as impotent as it was, and those who did not frequent, follow, or openly support the world of the jazz musicians are omitted from Pearson's history. Pearson demonstrates how "wide open" Kansas City was between the two world wars, but "wide open" often applied to just a minority of the city's African American residents.

Sherry Lamb Schirmer's work *A City Divided: The Racial Landscape of Kansas City, 1900–1960* examines the spatial boundaries between black and white Kansas Citians in the first six decades of the twentieth century. In assessing the attempts by the two groups to determine the limits of community, Schirmer emphasizes the tensions and conflicts that separated African Americans and whites, particularly on the East Side. Schirmer is particularly interested in what might be best described as the pathology of Kansas City's African American community. White middle-class reformers argued for the eradication of vice in Kansas City but settled for erecting a cordon sanitaire around the neighborhoods in which saloons, brothels, and gambling joints thrived. The prevalence of these dens of iniquity in primarily African American communities then had a twofold impact. First, reformers' efforts helped reinforce spatial segregation in housing in the years before World War II. By linking vice and black residents in popular perceptions, reformers provided more ammunition for white segregationists to distance their homes from those of African Americans. Second, Schirmer asserts, "vice became a fact of life, not only for the black men and women who engaged in those enterprises, but *for every resident of the black eastside,* regardless of station or personal values."[14] In other words, there was no way for the majority of Kansas City's African Americans to avoid the deleterious effects of the criminal actions of a relatively few black men and women. The work of institutions such as churches and schools seems incidental, as do collective political and social organizations. Schirmer, in fact, gives little attention to the agency of African Americans in the creation of their communities. Aside from brief discussions of the lives of noted "race" men and women such as Chester Franklin and Minnie Crosthwaite, Schirmer takes every opportunity to describe the futile attempts by African Americans to assert themselves in twentieth-century Kansas City. The unveiling of General Hospital No. 2, considered by many in the African American community to be a milestone event, in Schirmer's view is overshadowed by the political machinations and scandal that surrounded the construction and operation of the facility in its early years. In fact, in addition to several minor errors of fact, Schirmer displays little sensitivity to the collective consciousness of African Americans in Kansas City, and she made little use of the available sources, including *Your Kansas City and Mine* and Urban League records.[15] Despite its shortcomings, however, Schirmer's study offers important glimpses of the political and economic landscape of Kansas City as the city matured.

In the past several years, historian Gary R. Kremer has extended our knowledge of some aspects of the social history of black Kansas City with two articles in the *Missouri Historical Review.* One article, written by Kremer and Evan P. Orr, describes the development of Lake Placid, an Ozarks resort for black Missourians, by a black Kansas City doctor. Lake Placid was founded in the late 1930s, so much of Kremer's discussion deals with the post–World War II era. Kremer's second article describes the lives of black residents in the Leeds district, a semirural area on the eastern edge of Kansas City. Both of these articles have

14. Schirmer, *City Divided,* 126 (emphasis added).

15. For example, Hugh O. Cook was vice principal of Lincoln High School until after World War I (Young and Young, *Your Kansas City and Mine,* 55, 90), and Theron B. Watkins was firmly ensconced in Kansas City before 1918 (149).

made solid contributions to our knowledge of black Kansas City and have been useful for this volume.[16]

Each of the works discussed above provides a portion of the history of African Americans within the Kansas City area, but this study is the first to take a broad-based, scholarly approach to the lives of black men and women in Kansas City. Much of this history has been available, though scattered in a number of sources. This volume attempts to bring all of these various pieces into one mosaic depicting life in Kansas City's African American communities.

16. See Kremer and Orr, "Lake Placid: A Recreational Center for Colored People in the Missouri Ozarks"; and Kremer, "'Just Like the Garden of Eden': African-American Community Life in Kansas City's Leeds."

One

The Souls of Black Folk

Kansas City. . . can neither be [a] termed Southern nor Northern city. There is no doubt, however, about the prevailing atmosphere being definitely Southern.

—FRAYSER T. LANE, EXECUTIVE SECRETARY OF THE KANSAS CITY URBAN LEAGUE, 1925

IN THE SPRING OF 1920, a black laborer with the wonderful name of John X. Brown purchased a new home in the 1300 block of Garfield through Samuel Hopkins's Square Deal Realty. It was a symbol of success for Brown, a thirty-one-year-old native of Missouri, and his wife, Armeda, twenty-eight. In their previous home, on Washington Street on the west side of downtown, the Browns had shared their home with twelve other adults: two brothers (Burl and Roland Williams, who both worked as waiters in a restaurant); a husband and wife (Terrance, a laborer, and Fannie); a twenty-three-year-old mechanic (George Weathers, who had moved to the area from Florida); two unemployed women (Cordelia Sanford, age thirty-eight, and Della Nicholson, age twenty-five); a twenty-two-year-old chauffeur (George Howard); and four laborers of various points of origin (Oklahoma, Louisiana, Missouri, and Texas).[1]

We know little else about John X. and Armeda Brown beyond what is available in the manuscript census. They left no personal papers or

1. U.S. Department of Commerce, Bureau of the Census, Fourteenth Census of the United States (1920).

diaries. The Browns are, however, representative of the changing nature of black Kansas City in the 1920s. The move to the Garfield Street residence was a step up from the overcrowded housing conditions faced by many of Kansas City's African Americans on the West Side and elsewhere. More important, the Browns' move also foreshadowed the changing geographical limits of Kansas City's African American communities. The Browns would be in the first wave of African Americans to leave the West Side, the West and East Bottoms, and the downtown area and to settle in the East Side. Garfield, twenty-one blocks east of Main Street, sits between The Paseo and Prospect Avenue. It is about ten blocks east of Troost. The Browns' new home would sit at the northern edge of a two hundred–square-block area that by 1940 would contain 94 percent of Kansas City's black residents.

The Beginning

Kansas City's history, and the history of its African American community, has been profoundly shaped by the peculiarities of its geography. Present-day Kansas City wraps over and around the Missouri River, which serves only briefly as part of its boundary. Its downtown, located just southeast of the confluence of the Kaw (or Kansas) and Missouri Rivers, spreads southward and eastward from the bluffs that overlook the river and its floodplain. The rest of the city's boundaries, particularly the state line on its western edge, are arbitrary, points on a map dictated by surveyors and diplomats. No physical feature separates much of Kansas City, Missouri, from Kansas City, Kansas, or the rest of the Kansas suburbs. The result has been, historically, a blurring of the lines of community. Particularly in the African American community, the boundary between the two Kansas Cities consistently appeared permeable.

One of the first persons of African descent to venture into the Kansas City region was York, the personal slave of Capt. William Clark. In 1804, Clark accepted an offer from U.S. Army captain Meriwether Lewis to serve as a cocommander of what would become an eight thousand–mile exploratory journey from St. Louis up the Missouri River and through the newly purchased Louisiana Territory to the Pacific Ocean—and back. On June 26, 1804, the expedition reached the mouth of the Kansas River, the future site of Kansas City. The expedition spent four days there, examining the rivers and the land around them and repacking their supplies, but York's specific role or activities at this point can never be determined with any certainty. None of the surviving documents of the trip appear to elaborate on York's role this early in the journey.[2]

The next African Americans to enter the region also likely were slaves. Although Kansas City would never match the slave population of cross-state St. Louis, the region would attract a number of slaveholders. Slaves were brought into Jackson and Clay Counties; by the 1860s, Jackson County held 3,944 slaves, most of them in the communities of Independence and Westport.[3] For example, black men, most if not all of them slaves, are credited with building the first courthouse of Jackson County, in Independence. Under the direction of one Samuel Shepherd, the men felled the trees and hewed the logs for the two-story log building. The area also boasted 70 free blacks, including Hiram Young, an Independence artisan who helped build the yokes for many of the wagons that went westward to New Mexico and Oregon, and Emily Fisher, who ran a boardinghouse. Fisher's establishment is considered the first hotel in Independence.[4]

The end of the Civil War brought the end of slavery in Missouri. Although many of the former slaves would remain in agricultural pursuits after the war, some—particularly young African American males—would be attracted to urban settings. The lure in many cases was the chance for gainful employment, but many of the young freedmen in the area known as Little Dixie would be frustrated in their attempts to find work.[5] In postwar Missouri, small towns such as Lexington and Chillicothe had many more black job hunters than they had jobs. Eventually, many of these young men would either return to farmwork or head west to the two Kansas Cities, drawn in part by the railroads and the development of the great stockyards and packinghouses that straddled the state line.

2. Bernard DeVoto, ed., *The Journals of Lewis and Clark*, 9; Stephen E. Ambrose, *Undaunted Courage: Meriwether Lewis, Thomas Jefferson, and the Opening of the American West*, 147–49. A bronze statue of Clark, Lewis, York, and their female Indian interpreter, Sacagawea, now sits on the bluffs at Case Park overlooking the rivers and the Downtown Airport. Lewis and Clark climbed the bluffs on their return trip in 1806 and noted they appeared "to have a Commanding Situation for a fort. . . . [F]rom the top of the hill you have a perfect command of the river." Ambrose, *Undaunted Courage*, 392.

3. "Index to the Jackson County, Missouri, 1870 Census," viii.

4. Young and Young, *Your Kansas City and Mine*, 8.

5. The thirteen counties along the Missouri River from Jackson and Clay Counties into central Missouri had been a stronghold for slaveholders since the 1820s. Some of the slaves in this region were involved in small-scale production of cotton and tobacco, but many were involved in the production of hemp, which was used for cordage for sailing vessels. See R. Douglas Hurt, *Agriculture and Slavery in Missouri's Little Dixie*.

Other African Americans would join the country's westward advance in the years after the Civil War and settle in the Kansas City area. Included in this group of ambitious men and women was James Dallas Bowser, who arrived in Kansas City from Ohio in 1868. Bowser was just twenty-two when he, his parents, and a younger brother arrived in the Kansas City area.[6] In an essay written fifty years later, Bowser described his first impressions of Kansas City:

> I came to Kansas City, lured here by the growing accounts of the chances of a fortune to be made. . . . Being asleep when we reached Independence, Mo. (by train), we awoke to find ourselves at the Grand Avenue depot at Kansas City near midnight. Setting out to go up town we discovered that most of the would-be streets climbed some hill and led to nowhere in particular. At the time, there was one excuse for a hotel, the Gillis House at the foot of Main Street. The Coates Hotel was unfinished and roofless[,] having been occupied as a fort during Price's raid and was known as Fort Union. A war-time trench encircled the slope near the Auditorium Theatre. Main Street was the only paved thoroughfare[;] Delaware Street was a winding ravine, at the bottom of which just north of the junction stood an old flour mill. There were less than 10,000 people in the city. . . . The West Bottoms was a forest of giant sycamores, a winding wagon road along the river leading to Old Wyandotte. Indians were frequently in the market square. The white-tented wagons of the argonauts of the plains were busy loading their wares for their journey to the Great Southwest.[7]

Bowser was born in North Carolina, but shortly after his birth his mother fled with him to Ohio. His father, Henry Bowser, became one of the first black teachers around Chillicothe, Ohio. After arriving in Kansas City, James Dallas Bowser taught at the Penn School for black children in Westport for a year before taking over at the Lincoln School in the Kansas City school district. James Dallas Bowser later served twelve years (1868–1879) as principal at Lincoln School. He served as a railway postal clerk in the 1880s before returning to teaching. He was principal at Attucks School in the first decade of the twentieth century and also edited one of Kansas City's first black newspapers, the *Gate City Press*. A staunch member of the Republican Party, Bowser held a number of patronage positions in the federal government and through a series of real-estate investments gained a fortune valued at seventy-five

6. "Ninth Census of Population, 1870."
7. Bowser, "Reminiscences," *Kansas City Sun*, January 6, 1923.

thousand dollars in 1906. Bowser was considered Kansas City's leading black intellectual; he continued to write for various black newspapers throughout his life. His poem "Take Up the Black Man's Burden," a black man's response to Rudyard Kipling's poem "The White Man's Burden," was written sometime before 1899 and was printed and reprinted in black journals as far afield as Washington, DC, and Salt Lake City, Utah.[8] He was one of the city's most ardent supporters of the National Association for the Advancement of Colored People and an active member in the Inter-Racial Committee of Twelve, a group of blacks and whites organized by the all-white Citizens' League in 1920. Bowser's home in the 1920s, at 2400 The Paseo, was considered one of the finest in Kansas City's black community.[9] His poem is as follows:

Take up the Black Man's burden—
"Send forth the best ye breed."
To judge with righteous judgment
The Black Man's worth and need
To set down naught with malice
In hate or prejudice
To tell the truth about him
To paint him as he is.

Take up the Black Man's burden
Ye of the bold and strong
And might makes right as only
It does no weak race wrong;
When yours—his chances equal,
Give him the fairest test
Then "Hands off" be your motto
And he will do the rest.

Take up the Black Man's burden
Don't curse him in advance
He can not lift a White Man's load

8. Historian Jim Zwick ("'The White Man's Burden' and Its Critics") includes Bowser's poem among fifty responses to Kipling's poem, which appeared in the February 1899 issue of *McClure's*. Kipling's poem, though it matched a glorification of European imperialism with an accounting of the costs involved, would be adopted by imperialists in the United States and used to justify imperialism as a noble cause.

9. *Rising Son*, September 6, 1906; *Kansas City Sun*, January 6, 1923; Schirmer, *City Divided*, 117–20. The other black members of the committee, chosen by the NAACP and the Colored Civic League, were ministers William Alphin and Samuel W. Bacote, teacher R. T. Coles, and businessmen John Love and A. Frank Neal.

Without a White Man's chance
Shut out from mill and workshop
From counting-room and store
By caste and labor unions
You close industry's door.

Take up the Black Man's burden
Don't crush him with his load
Nor heap it up in courses
By scoff and jeers bestowed
The haughty Anglo-Saxon
was savage and untaught
A thousand years of freedom
A wondrous change has wrought.

Take up the Black Man's burden
Black men of every clime
What though your cross be heavy
Your sun but darkly shine
Stoop with a freedman's ardor
Lift high a freedman's hand
Stand with a freedman's firmness
March with a freedman's tread.[10]

Another African American drawn to Kansas City in the 1860s was James Milton Turner, a former slave from the St. Louis area. Turner became the first black teacher—at the original Lincoln School at Ninth and Charlotte Streets—in Kansas City. Turner served as teacher and principal at Lincoln School for a year (1868) before beginning a political and legal career that would make him one of the most visible black men in the state into the twentieth century.[11]

Bowser and Turner were atypical of the black men and women drawn to the two Kansas Cities in the mid-nineteenth century. Other African Americans found the Missouri side to be hospitable—although it had its limits. Missouri's former status as a slaveholding state shaped many

10. *Colored American* (Washington, DC), April 8, 1899; *Kansas City Sun*, January 6, 1923.

11. See Gary Kremer's excellent biography, *James Milton Turner and the Promise of America: The Public Life of a Post-Civil War Black Leader.* Turner, the only African American to hold political office in the state of Missouri during Reconstruction, was active as a spokesman and organizer of the Missouri Equal Rights League, which among other things campaigned for black male suffrage in the 1860s (before the Fifteenth Amendment to the U.S. Constitution was ratified). He later became a lawyer and was instrumental in helping former black slaves and their descendants regain their status as members of the Five Civilized Tribes.

of the interactions between black and white in Kansas City. As a result, many African Americans found their job choices limited. Even the packinghouses, which apparently opened their doors to black workers from their establishment, limited the types of jobs African Americans could hold. Adequate housing also proved difficult to obtain. The first African Americans in postwar Kansas City joined whites in settling along the Missouri River and followed the city's growth upward (from the riverbanks into what is now downtown) and outward (east along the riverbanks). Inferences from the 1870 manuscript returns are just those—inferences—but black and white are intermingled to a significant degree in the handwritten pages of the Kansas City census. Some boardinghouses, bordellos, and even the Gillis Hotel listed both black and white residents, although it is impossible to tell with any degree of certainty where in each establishment African Americans resided.

African Americans continued to migrate to the Kansas City area through the 1870s. One emigrant, a former slave from Tennessee, was one of thousands from Tennessee and Kentucky who journeyed to Kansas City during this period. Clayton Holbert, who eventually settled in Ottawa, recalled his less-than-spectacular first impressions of Kansas City in an oral history collected sixty years later: "We came in 1877 to Kansas City, October 1. . . . Then there was nothing but little huts in the bottoms. The Santa Fe depot didn't amount to anything. The Armours' Packing house was even smaller than that. There was a swinging bridge over the river."[12]

Kansas City's African American community would be bolstered in the spring of 1879 by the arrival of a group of immigrants from Louisiana and Mississippi. These "Exodusters," through printed handbills and word of mouth, had heard that there was fertile land to be had in Kansas. The Sunflower State, they had heard, was free of segregation and discrimination (it was, after all, the home of the martyr John Brown). For a brief moment, Kansas was the "Promised Land." Between six and ten thousand African Americans left the Deep South in March and April of that year. Most would at least make it into Wyandotte County; others would settle in Topeka or head toward Pap Singleton's colonies in southeastern Kansas or around Nicodemus in northwestern Kansas. A portion of the Exodusters fell short of their goal and chose to remain in Kansas City on the Missouri side. Aided by B. F. Watson, pastor of what was to become Allen Chapel African Methodist Episcopal Church,

12. Holbert, "Ex Slave Story: Ottawa, Kansas," interview conducted by Leta Gray, in *The American Slave: A Composite Autobiography,* edited by George P. Rawick, 1–7.

and other black residents, some of these immigrants quickly integrated into Kansas City's black community. A year later, at the time of the 1880 census, remnants of the migration were still to be found in three enclaves: along the Missouri River in the East Bottoms, in the West Bottoms, and on the southern edge of the city on the Kansas City Exposition Grounds. Some Exodusters may have turned around and headed back to the Deep South. At least one—a young black woman—returned to the South after a year in Kansas City, but she brought her family back to the area several years later.[13]

By that time, Kansas City, Missouri, was beginning to shed its image as a frontier community. The opening of the Hannibal Bridge, supplemented by the completion of the Armour-Swift-Burlington Bridge in 1909, helped transform the city. A small nucleus of businessmen in Kansas City had begun to look to establish links with the markets of the Southwest. The bridges linked Kansas City's downtown and the stockyards and packinghouses in the West Bottoms with the thriving metropolis of Chicago. In addition to becoming the southwestern locus for beef and pork production, Kansas City had become instrumental in the grain trade; much of the Kansas wheat moved through Kansas City on its way eastward.[14] Kansas City, now the crossroads of the country, saw its population mushroom. Its 1870 population of 32,254 was almost eight times that of 1860. The growth would continue into the 1880s. The grid of the city's streets was already laid out, and patterns of settlement become easier to ascertain. Kansas City's overall population continued to grow, as did its black population. By 1880, Kansas City claimed 55,785 residents, including almost 8,000 African Americans. The percentage of African Americans in the total population was the highest it would be until 1960, when white flight into the city's Missouri suburbs and across the state line into Johnson County, Kansas, contributed to a drastic change in the complexion of Kansas City.

By 1880, African American families could be found in almost every area of Kansas City, Missouri. A few blocks were all-white, but in the 1880 census, at least 90 African Americans were counted in each census enumeration district between the state line on the west and Woodland Avenue on the east, and between the Missouri River on the north and Twenty-third Street on the south. By far, the largest congregation of African Americans had formed around downtown, particularly on

13. B. Jones, "Oral Family History," paper in author's possession.

14. Missouri State Highway Department, *Missouri: The WPA Guide to the "Show Me" State*, 247–48.

Table 1.1.
Kansas City, Missouri's Black Population, 1860–2000

Year	Total	Black	Percentage
1860	4,413	190	4.3
1870	32,254	3,770	11.7
1880	55,785	7,914	14.2
1890	132,716	13,700	10.3
1900	163,752	17,567	10.7
1910	248,381	23,556	9.5
1920	324,410	30,893	9.5
1930	399,746	38,574	9.6
1940	399,178	41,568	10.4
1950	456,622	55,682	12.2
1960	475,539	83,746	17.6
1970	507,087	111,559	22.0
1980	448,159	122,336	27.3
1990	435,146	128,768	29.6
2000	441,545	137,870	31.2

Source: U.S. Census Bureau of Statistics

its eastern edge in the area that came to be called Church Hill. The area held the Lincoln School and was named for its two most prominent edifices: Allen Chapel AME and Second Baptist Churches, which sat on opposite corners at the intersection of Charlotte and Tenth Streets. In a rectangularly shaped area from Eighth to Twelfth and Locust to Forest, African American teachers and ministers lived adjacent to packinghouse laborers, barbers, and domestics.

African Americans composed almost one-third of the total population in the area between Main and Woodland from Ninth to Eleventh Streets.[15] Many of them lived within small one- and two-story wood-framed homes, in households that often contained extended or augmented families. Extended families would seldom include three generations; often, the household would contain an adult couple, an adult brother or sister, and perhaps a juvenile nephew or niece. Some households included lodgers; according to Dwayne Martin's study, 70 percent of nonnuclear families opened their doors to male and female roomers. The percentage of African Americans residing in a block increased dramatically the closer one got to the intersection of Tenth and Charlotte.

15. According to the 1880 census, 1,056 African Americans resided in these enumeration districts. That was just 13 percent of the city's total black population.

In the blocks in the immediate vicinity and in the blocks directly east, African Americans made up more than 90 percent of the population. No one block, however, contained nothing but African American families.[16]

Charlotte Street was the hub of black residences in the Church Hill area, particularly between Ninth and Eleventh Streets. Two white families lived on the northern edge of this stretch (one was a thirty-five-year-old cigar maker from Prussia and his wife and five children, the other a common laborer from Indiana and his wife); two other white families (a twenty-five-year-old clerk also from Prussia and his wife and another laborer and his family) and three single men lived between Tenth and Eleventh Streets. The rest of the residences listed in the 1880 census contained African American families. As Dwayne Martin has demonstrated in his statistical analysis, "The Hidden Community," most of the families contained two parents. Although many of the adult men were listed as common laborers, other occupations were represented. William A. Strong, a twenty-seven-year-old single male, and Samuel Woods, a forty-seven-year-old father of five, were bricklayers. Peter Jones, a twenty-seven-year-old single man from Virginia, and George H. Damon were stonemasons. Woods's twenty-year-old son, George, was a hotel waiter, as was twenty-five-year-old Robert Simpson. Among the residents at 1025 Charlotte were two barbers, Edward Gibbs and Pope Doane. Thirty-year-old Jackson King was a hod carrier, while forty-one-year-old Lafayette Walker drove an express wagon. Anderson Smith, a thirty-year-old husband and father, was a blacksmith. How long Smith had been in the area is unknown; he was born in Tennessee, but his wife and daughter were born in Missouri. At 1011 Charlotte, Margaret Jones and her sister, Gracy Harris, resided along with their families. Margaret's twenty-five-year-old son, Henry, was a preacher. Gracy's twenty-two-year-old son, James Silas, was a teacher at the Lincoln School; he would become one of black Kansas City's most respected citizens in the years before World War I.

Margaret Jones and Gracy Harris were unlike many of the adult women in this two-block span of Charlotte; they worked outside the home as laundresses. During Reconstruction and the years immediately following, many married African American women, particularly in urban areas, chose not to take employment outside the home. Whether they were attempting to emulate white standards of domesticity (a

16. Martin, "The Hidden Community: The Black Community of Kansas City, Missouri, during the 1870s and 1880s," 19–46; U.S. Department of Commerce, Bureau of the Census, Tenth Census of the United States (1880).

nineteenth-century invention) or to protect themselves from the threat of sexual assault, African American women, with the consent of their husbands, elected to remain in the home. With employment opportunities limited for African American women, even in urban areas, the choice to remain at home was logically simple (if not financially difficult). As stated above, for those women who, because of family or economic circumstances, were forced to find employment, there were few options. Some, particularly younger women, could work as servants in the homes of white upper- and middle-class families. Older women often preferred to work as washerwomen. As historians Jacqueline Jones and Tera W. Hunter have pointed out, laundry work was some of the most tedious and backbreaking work African American women could perform (as will be discussed in Chapter Three).[17]

If a black woman was fortunate, she could find work making and repairing women's clothes and furnishings. Lizzie Hawkins, a sixty-year-old African American woman apparently living alone on Charlotte Street, listed her occupation as seamstress, as did Julia Ross, a thirty-five-year-old black woman living with her mother and her son (among others) in that two-block span of Charlotte Street.[18] Among the more prominent seamstresses in 1880s Kansas City was Alphia Smith Miner, the daughter of a slave who left Leavenworth after the Civil War and moved to Kansas City. Using her expertise in dressmaking and her obvious business acumen, Miner developed a network of friends and neighbors to assist her. When she opened her shop in the West Bottoms in the 1870s, she had as many as four helpers and eight sewing machines.[19]

To the east of Charlotte Street, African American families could be found on each of the next six north-south streets. Troost Avenue, the dividing line between black and white in the second half of the twentieth century, was just another thoroughfare in 1880, with black and white families intermixed from Eighth Street to beyond Twelfth Street. There was little extraordinary about the residents of this four-block span, either. The white residents included a number of artisans (at least two carpenters, a house painter, and a jeweler) and what would later be considered white-collar workers (a grocery-store clerk, a druggist, a railroad conductor, and a bookkeeper). The African American residents in these blocks were primarily working class, though the Robertson

17. See Jones, *Labor of Love, Labor of Sorrow: Black Women, Work and the Family, from Slavery to the Present;* and Hunter, *To 'Joy My Freedom: Southern Black Women's Lives and Labors after the Civil War.*

18. U.S. Department of Commerce, Bureau of the Census, Tenth Census.

19. Young and Young, *Your Kansas City and Mine,* 103.

family was one exception. Father Henry was listed as a preacher, while the nineteen-year-old son, David, was listed as a schoolteacher. The Montgomery brothers were another exception. W. Montgomery (the first name is illegible in the 1880 census) was a porter in a hotel; James, the older brother, was a railroad porter. Several semiskilled occupations are listed for the black male residents of Troost. William Cranby was a bricklayer who shared a household with (among others) Henry Jamison, a twenty-nine-year-old stonecutter. Abner Phillips, a twenty-three-year-old from Kentucky, and William Clark, a twenty-seven-year-old from North Carolina, were carpenters. Phillips and Clark shared a household with four other single males. Two barbers were listed, including William Hanston, a thirty-six-year-old from Pennsylvania. Hanston's household included his wife, his eighty-seven-year-old great-grandmother, and his grandmother, who was working as a servant. In fact, these blocks on Troost are exceptional in the number of females working as servants.

Three noteworthy examples: Two families living on Troost each had two daughters living at home working as servants, presumably to supplement the income of their working-class fathers; the women's ages ranged from sixteen to twenty-one. One family of six rented out rooms to three female lodgers aged seventeen, nineteen, and twenty-one; all three worked as servants. Work as a servant could not have been difficult to find. At least one white family living on Forest, a block away, had a live-in domestic, and middle- and upper-class white families to the west of Church Hill also employed servants.

One more example from the census of the Church Hill area may be instructive. In the 1000 block of Harrison Street (two blocks east of Charlotte), black and white families intermingled. Isaac Smith, a hack driver, and his wife rented out space to Nellie Banks, one of the few female African American teachers listed in the census. Nearby lived Fred Knickerbocker, a wealthy white businessman. Listed with the Knickerbocker family was an eighteen-year-old black female servant. Clearly, neither racial nor class lines had been linked with geographical boundaries.

Church Hill was the hub of the African American community in the 1880s and 1890s, but as mentioned above, black residents were scattered throughout the city. In the West Bottoms, African American and Irish workers competed for living space and employment, but unlike in other communities, the competition appeared to be friendly. Black and Irish intermingled freely, and in some cases intermarried. In the 1894 strike against packinghouse operators, African American, Irish, and native-born white workers bonded to protest low wages and poor working conditions.

A significant proportion of the African Americans in the West Bottoms appear to have been single males under the age of forty-five; if they were married, they did not have families with them. There were, however, enough African American children in the West Bottoms for the opening of a second school for African Americans in the 1880s. The stockyards and railroads were the primary employers, but work was also to be found in public works and in the hotels and saloons around the Union Depot. Farther south, a stone quarry attracted a racially mixed workforce as well, with some of the workers—both black and white—living on the premises or nearby.

By 1910, Kansas City's black population had increased to more than twenty-three thousand. African Americans were still spread throughout the city, though the growth of industrial activity in the West Bottoms had driven most of the residents—black, Irish, and native white—into other portions of the city. But the largest concentration of African Americans had shifted eastward from Church Hill to the area east of Troost Avenue. Although the figures are open to dispute, it is safe to say that at least eight out of ten African Americans in Kansas City in 1910 lived between Troost and Woodland Avenue north of Thirty-first Street down to Independence Avenue. According to sociologist Asa Martin, between eight hundred and one thousand African Americans in Kansas City owned real estate about this time.[20]

The growth of black settlement east of Troost can be traced to a housing boom in the late 1880s. The market for these homes collapsed shortly after they were constructed, and home owners were sought, regardless of color. Fortune J. Weaver's Afro-American Realty and Investment Company put the entire 2500 block of Tracy up for sale "to highly-respected Negroes." For a down payment of five hundred to three thousand dollars, buyers could move into bungalows selling for between four thousand and seventy-five hundred dollars. Despite the actions of Weaver and "highly respected Negroes," African Americans remained in the minority in most neighborhoods in the Vine Street corridor. In 1900, these neighborhoods were still three-quarters white. At the same time, African American business districts began to develop in two locations east of Troost: around Twenty-third and Forest and around Eighteenth Street and Vine (which would become the hub of black businesses through the first six decades of the twentieth century). At the same time, more than a dozen churches relocated into the Vine Street

20. Martin, *Our Negro Population*, 30. According to Martin, these individuals owned property valued between ten thousand and one hundred thousand dollars.

corridor, and the Lincoln School moved to Nineteenth Street and Tracy. Weaver's Afro-American Realty was the first major real estate and financial firm for Kansas City's black residents. In addition to providing real estate and investment services for Kansas City's African Americans, the company also provided employment opportunities for black artisans. A study of African American workers in St. Louis before World War I compared the situation in Missouri's two major cities, and St. Louis came up wanting. According to the investigator, Kansas City supported twice as many black artisans as its eastern rival because of Weaver's firm. "The company contracts with private parties and real estate companies to do repairing, overhauling, cleaning, remodeling of buildings and houses at a reasonable rate. Most of the business comes from the whites." Weaver's company helped increase the number of skilled African American workers in Kansas City before 1914.[21]

By 1910, African American home owners were well entrenched on several thoroughfares east of Troost. Asa Martin's investigations determined that there were 104 black homeowners on Highland Avenue between Twelfth and Twenty-seventh Streets, 12 on Woodland Avenue between Twelfth and Fourteenth Streets, 27 on Woodland between Twenty-fourth and Twenty-seventh Streets, 37 on Flora between Twenty-third and Twenty-fifth Streets, 13 on Vine Street between Twelfth and Fourteenth Streets, 35 on Michigan Avenue between Twenty-fourth and Twenty-sixth Streets, 18 on Cottage Street between Flora and Woodland, and 7 on Howard Street between Vine and Woodland. African American working-class families had also begun to move back into the East Bottoms. In areas commonly known as Belvidere Hollow (roughly Fifth Street just west of the Paseo Bridge) and Hicks Hollow (north of Independence Avenue and just east of the Paseo Bridge), a number of landlords had installed substandard housing to be rented cheaply.[22]

Despite the physical expansion of African American settlement late in the nineteenth century, the Church Hill area remained the locus of black cultural and spiritual development. One factor was the presence of the Lincoln School. Lincoln, the first school for African Americans in Kansas City, opened in 1867, in space rented from the Second Congregational Church at Tenth and McGee Streets. The first teacher was Mrs. M. J. Copeland, who taught one week before her husband took over

21. William August Crossland, *Industrial Conditions among Negroes in St. Louis*, 65–66, quoted in Lorenzo J. Greene and Carter G. Woodson, *The Negro Wage Earner*, 173.

22. Martin, *Our Negro Population*, 23–24, 34–36; Sally Lamb Schirmer, "Landscape of Denial: Space, Status and Gender in the Construction of Racial Perspectives among White Kansas Citians, 1900–1958."

the responsibility. James Milton Turner came to Kansas City a year later and served a year before being replaced by James Dallas Bowser, who was hired as teacher and principal at a salary of sixty dollars a month. By that time, the school had moved into space at Ninth and Charlotte on land donated by Kansas City real-estate man Kersey Coates. By 1878, enrollment in the school had grown to 477 children, and more space was needed. The new building was built three blocks away, at Eleventh and Campbell.

The Lincoln School went through a succession of principals over the next five years, but easily the most flamboyant and most controversial of them was David Victor Adolphus Nero, who was appointed in 1881. The early details of Nero's life are sketchy, but apparently he was educated in Canada before moving to St. Louis in 1877. He spent three years as a teacher and principal in St. Louis before accepting a job as a teacher at the Lincoln School in Kansas City. In 1881, he replaced A. J. Agee as principal and settled in with his wife, Mary, at a home near the Lincoln School on Campbell.[23]

Less than nine months after taking over at Lincoln, Nero presented the Kansas City Board of Education with a detailed four-year curriculum for a black high school and requested the board's endorsement of the program. The board authorized the addition of a few high school courses at Lincoln in 1882, but presumably in retaliation, the board transferred Nero and his wife to the Sumner School in the West Bottoms. Nero continued to be an outspoken proponent of a full-fledged high school curriculum at Lincoln. He advocated both "general courses" and "classical courses," including Latin and Greek, English literature, algebra, chemistry, and geometry.

Nero continued his push for a full high school curriculum for Lincoln, even while working at Sumner. But after three years at Sumner, Nero resigned and headed to Europe.[24] Five years after Nero proposed his high school plan, the Board of Education acquiesced. In 1887, the first

23. Most details of Nero's life, including his tenure at Lincoln, are taken from Melton A. McLaurin, "Divine Convictions: The Tale of an African American Trickster in Victorian Britain." Nero, a tall, dark-skinned individual with a full moustache, at times claimed to be an African prince sold into slavery who had escaped to Canada. At other times, he claimed to be a native of British Guiana.

24. Nero's time in Europe, according to McLaurin, was spent fleecing British and Scottish investors. He solicited money ostensibly for the purpose of establishing Christian missions in Africa. Very little of the money Nero collected, if any, ever went to that purpose. In addition, he was involved in several romantic entanglements that led to further scandal. He returned to Kansas City twice, before eventually being arrested and convicted of fraud in December 1886.

Lincoln High School was built on the northwest corner of Nineteenth and Tracy Streets with G. N. Grisham as principal. The curriculum was much as Nero had proposed. For his advocacy of the high school curriculum, Nero was honored years later: a street in the bowels of the West Bottoms, near Sumner School, was named for him. By the end of the twentieth century, the street had been vacated and covered by the area's industrial development.

The Lincoln and Sumner Schools drew a cadre of dedicated African American teachers. Among the teachers at the Lincoln School before 1900 were three mainstays of black education in Kansas City: G. N. Grisham, Richard T. Coles, and W. W. Yates.

G. N. Grisham's background is sketchy, but by 1890 he had taken over as principal at the Lincoln School. He was active—at least briefly—in politics, joining with R. T. Coles and Paul Gaston to form a short-lived black political party late in the nineteenth century. In 1897, Grisham was invited to join the American Negro Academy (ANA), a society of African American scholars and educators that included W. E. B. Du Bois, the country's preeminent black scholar; Bishop Alexander Crummell of the African Methodist Episcopal Church; and Kelly Miller, a philosopher and dean at all-black Howard University in Washington, DC. The scholars in the American Negro Academy had joined Du Bois in denouncing Washington's acceptance of menial labor for African American workers. They believed there was a place for the black scholar, and Grisham delivered an eloquent address on that very subject at a meeting of the academy on December 28, 1897, in Washington, DC. Grisham's remarks were published three months later in Washington's black weekly, the *Colored American*. In his address, Grisham argued for a particular role for black scholars, a role that later generations would call that of the "public intellectual."[25]

Booker T. Washington would contend over the next two decades that there was little place in American society, particularly in southern society, for an educated black man. Grisham begged to differ. "The Negro graduate is here," he stated. "If any one questions whether the

25. Grisham, "The Negro Scholar," *Colored American* (Washington, DC), March 16, 1898, reprinted in Philip S. Foner and Robert James Branham, eds., *Lift Every Voice: African American Oratory, 1787–1900*, 857–61. Grisham considered leaving the ANA in 1906 and finally left the organization in 1908, citing the distance between Kansas City and the East Coast, where most of the group's members lived and where most of the meetings were held. The ANA ceased operations after its December meeting of 1928. See Alfred A. Moss, *The American Negro Academy: Voice of the Talented Tenth*, 117, 301.

Negro scholar has yet been discovered we will not debate the question of fact." Grisham recognized the unique status that he and his fellow academy members held; he warned them not to be swayed to overconfidence because of their lofty status within an oftentimes depressed community. "'He is a smart man for a Negro,'" Grisham warned, "is a compliment that has stunted the growth of many a smart person." He also emphasized caution for future scholars; he urged them to choose a particular field of inquiry and to become its master. "The medieval scholar undertook to know and discuss all questions of culture. The modern scholar is content to be ignorant of much. The young aspirant for fame often feels conscious of enormous powers of acquisition, but he will not have far before discovering the evil of sacrificing depth to extent of research."

The crux of Grisham's argument, however, was the demand that African American scholars be cognizant of the conditions within their community and become an active force for change. His comments are worth noting in depth:

> There was a time when the scholar stood aloof from the practical world, as if he formed no part of it. Scholarship cannot create and breathe an atmosphere all its own. It is commendable to search for truth as the thing best worth knowing, but not much is justified in directing his energies altogether without reference to the needs of the great world in which he lives. . . . There is a charge today that the better-favored Negro is disposed to desert his kind and dwell apart from the masses, but even in his own interest the Negro scholar must do something for his race. He can and should offer defense against unjust criticism and wrong. He should in his exalted personality, furnish a standard for budding aspiration, and his superior intelligence and keen foresight should offer guidance over the thousands of moral, social and political difficulties that throng the dark and devious pathway of the people. The race has a right to look to him for helpful suggestions, for kindly, sympathetic criticism, for a clear outline of policy and for the inspiration which can come alone from those whose lofty reaches of thought enable them to contemplate the depths from the standpoint of the heights. This is no mean or narrow task, for it can be best performed only by those who clearly recognize the fact that the Negro scholar must form the connection between his race and civilization. In him they breathe its spirit, think its thought, grapple with its difficulties, and aid in the solution of its problems.[26]

26. Grisham, "The Negro Scholar," 860.

Grisham's opposition to Washington drew the displeasure of the "wizard of Tuskegee." On at least two occasions, Washington took note of Grisham's public statements concerning the place of industrial education in black schools, but there is no evidence that Washington, who proved to be a vindictive and ruthless individual when crossed, ever interfered in Grisham's career. Grisham remained principal at Lincoln until 1915 (the year of Washington's death) and remained active in the African American community until his own death in 1930.[27]

Richard T. Coles had a lengthy and noteworthy career in the Kansas City schools. He was born in 1860 in Pittsburgh, Pennsylvania. His father, Nathaniel N. Coles, was a former slave who had fled to Pennsylvania from Virginia. Once in Pittsburgh, Nathaniel Coles took up the trade of shoemaker. There he married, and he and his wife, Mary Ann, had nine children. Mary Ann Coles had been educated in the public schools and colleges of Pennsylvania, and she passed her love of education on to her children. Of her nine offspring, four became teachers, including Richard. Richard attended elementary school in Pittsburgh, but in the early or mid-1870s, the family moved to Poland, Ohio, where Richard finished high school. Nathaniel Coles apparently became active in the Republican Party at this time; he later held a patronage position in the federal government during the Grant administration.

The Coles family moved again, this time to Farmville, Virginia, and Richard enrolled in Hampton Institute. Hampton Institute was one of the first of the schools established for freedmen and -women after the Civil War, and it would eventually be recognized for its curriculum. While offering a "classical education," Hampton also had a strong manual arts curriculum, in which young black men and women were taught practical skills for survival in post-Reconstruction America. The school's most famous alumnus was Booker T. Washington, who built on Hampton's manual arts model in establishing his school in Tuskegee, Alabama. Washington would be the leading voice in black America advocating manual arts training for African Americans. One of his classmates at Hampton was Richard T. Coles, who graduated with honors in 1879.

After graduation, Coles came to Kansas City and settled in the Church Hill area, and that fall he was hired as a teacher at the Sumner School. Coles spent two years at Sumner, and in 1881 he was assigned to teach at Lincoln School. Because of his background, Coles was a vigorous supporter of manual education, and in 1886 he started his own school, the Pleasant Green School, in the East Bottoms. Four years later, the

27. *Kansas City Call*, September 19, 1930.

school became a part of the Kansas City School District and was renamed the Garrison School, and Coles began to lobby the Board of Education to allow instruction in the manual arts. Board members were reluctant at first, saying they did not believe that manual training was a part of public education. Coles persevered, however, and in a magazine article written years later, he said, "After much persuasion I was able to convince the superintendent of [manual education's] values. The superintendent then gave me permission to get a few tools together, and to begin a small scale experimental setting in manual training courses that I might prove the claimed values."[28]

Coles's first class met in September 1893 at the Garrison School. It met one hour a day after regular school hours in a basement room of the school at Fifth and Troost. Like his good friend James Dallas Bowser, Coles also edited a weekly newspaper, the *Kansas City Dispatch,* and he served with Bowser on the Inter-Racial Committee of Twelve organized in 1920.[29]

Less is known about W. W. Yates, who served on the Lincoln School faculty before his appointment as principal at the Wendell Phillips School late in the 1880s. Yates returned to the Lincoln School as principal in 1896, remaining in that position for the next fourteen years, until his death in 1910. He was an active voice within the early African American community. He would join forces with G. N. Grisham, James Crews, and others in the founding of the black YMCA. He likely was a member of a black men's social club, the Attucks Club, and may have joined his friend Richard T. Coles in the operation of the *Kansas City Dispatch.* We also know that Yates married one of the more remarkable women in black Kansas City, Josephine Silone Yates, a leader in the African American women's club movement. A teacher and orator, she led the Kansas City Colored Women's League as well as the National Association of Colored Women (NACW).

Josephine Silone was born in 1859 in Mattituck, New York, to a well-respected family. Her mother started Josephine's education at an early age, and as a result, she had already mastered the fundamentals of reading, writing, and mathematics by the time she entered school. Although she was the only black student in the school, Josephine became a favorite of her teachers because of her "eagerness and readiness to learn." By the age of nine, she was studying physiology, physics, and

28. The quote and facts of Coles's life are taken from an undated obituary, likely from the *Kansas City Call,* in 1930, in Elvis Gibson, *Kansas City: Mecca of the New Negro.*

29. The *Kansas City Dispatch* was published for four years, 1886–1889.

advanced mathematics. She already was a voracious reader and an accomplished writer. According to one biographer, one of Josephine's stories was sent by her teacher to a New York newspaper. Although the manuscript was rejected, the accompanying letter of encouragement served only to increase Josephine Silone's ambitions.[30] When she was eleven, her uncle, the Reverend J. B. Reeve, invited her to live with him in Philadelphia so that she could attend the Institution for Colored Youth under the instruction of Fannie Jackson-Coppin. The institute, the most acclaimed educational institution for African Americans in the East, offered instruction in the classics as well as normal-school training. Although Josephine remained at the school just a year, it is likely that she gained her first exposure to Latin, Greek, and German under Jackson-Coppin's tutelage. And it is said that Jackson-Coppin maintained an interest in Josephine's subsequent career, often referring to her "as a brilliant example of what a girl can do."[31]

Josephine was later sent to live with an aunt in Newport, Rhode Island, where she swiftly completed the grammar school and high school curricula. She delivered the valedictory address upon graduation in 1877 and became the first African American graduate of Newport's Rogers High School. She then entered the Rhode Island State Normal School, where she graduated with honors in 1879 and posted the highest score in the city's history on the teachers examination.

In 1881, Josephine Silone joined the faculty of Lincoln Institute in Jefferson City, Missouri. She began her career at Lincoln, an all-black school, as head of the Chemistry Department but soon was given responsibility for all of the natural sciences. She remained at Lincoln Institute until 1889, when she resigned, moved to Kansas City, and married W. W. Yates.[32] Married women were forbidden to teach in many communities at the end of the nineteenth century, and Josephine Yates likely needed an outlet for her intellectual skills. As did many married middle-class women of the time—both black and white—she found sustenance in the women's club movement.

Many of these clubs began as social, art, or literary organizations, in which women gathered to pursue a common interest. But by the late nineteenth century, many of these clubs had extended their focus to issues that directly or indirectly affected women and their homes: temperance, suffrage, recreational spaces for children, and the establishment

30. Monroe A. Majors, *Noted Negro Women: Their Triumphs and Activities*, 44–48.

31. Hallie Q. Brown, *Homespun Heroines and Other Women of Distinction*, 178–80; Majors, *Noted Negro Women*, 45.

32. Majors, *Noted Negro Women*, 47.

of kindergartens. But for African American women, these issues were often seen as secondary to the more immediate concerns of social justice and "racial uplift." Many African American women in the club movement added their voices to the appeals of black men for racial equality. They also saw as their responsibility the assistance of the less fortunate. Because of their different agendas and the discrimination practiced by most white women's clubs at the time, African American women began to form separate organizations in the 1890s. It was in this climate that Josephine Silone Yates, her friend Anna Jones, and two other women established the Kansas City Colored Women's League in 1893.[33]

Josephine Yates, who was living at 3116 East Nineteenth Street, was clearly the driving force behind the Kansas City club. She was the organization's first president and became responsible for the "Kansas City Letter," a regular report on the club's activities sent to *Woman's Era*, the most recognized of the national publications generated by the black women club's movement. The Kansas City league began its work in one rented room in April 1893. By May, the league had settled into new quarters: four rented rooms at 1027 Charlotte, in the heart of the Church Hill area. The new quarters were "tastily furnished" through the efforts of the women of the league and members of the Attucks Club, an organization of African American gentlemen who represented the "intellectual bone and sinew" of Kansas City's black community.[34]

Yates and the women's league had ambitious plans. They hoped to raise at least five hundred dollars to purchase land for an industrial arts school, but there is no record that any such plan came to fruition. Sewing classes for young and old apparently were the extent of the industrial work offered by the league. But even these Wednesday and Saturday afternoon classes had multiple purposes. In addition to training girls and women in the art of making dresses, aprons, and undergarments, the sewing department was responsible for making overgarments for the needy in winter and for making garments that could be sold to cover the league's expenses.[35]

33. Dorothy Salem, *To Better Our World: Black Women in Organized Reform, 1890–1920*, in *Black Women in United States History*, edited by Darlene Clark Hine, vol. 14. The literature on the African American women's club movement has burgeoned since the 1980s. In addition to broad overviews of the club movement, historians have targeted clubs and their agendas in specific cities.

34. *Woman's Era*, March 24, 1894, 2–3; April 1894; January 1896; November 1894, 2; May 1895, 10–12.

35. *Woman's Era*, March 1894, 2–3.

Much of the league's work was charitable in nature. Although the league's mission was to improve the condition of African American women in Kansas City, its first work was to finance the return trip of an invalid boy to his home in the South. The league also assisted young female newcomers to the city with temporary lodging, helped an orphan find "a good home," and committed itself to providing decent clothing for the school-age children of a blind woman. The league's activities also included a junior league for girls at least fourteen years old and mothers' meetings, where practical talks were offered on child rearing, housekeeping, and homemaking.[36]

The league, however, was not blind to political events in the outside world. In June 1893, an African American woman was sentenced to be hanged in Kansas City. The league investigated the case and concluded that justice for the woman and "above all to the womanhood of our race" demanded that the sentence be commuted. A petition and fund-raising drive followed the investigation, and Yates was a member of the delegation that presented the petition asking the governor to commute the woman's sentence. The governor commuted the sentence to fifty years, "although the death had already been set over the unfortunate woman."[37]

Yates also was a frequent contributor to African American magazines of the era. In the pages of *Woman's Era, Voice of the Negro,* and others, she espoused the virtues of racial uplift, endorsed the work-first philosophy of Booker T. Washington, and challenged black Americans to stand strong against the power of racial oppression.

By 1895, Josephine Yates had stepped down as president of the Kansas City Colored Women's League. She remained the league's corresponding secretary, and Anna Jones took over as president. We know less about Jones, but through a careful reading of the sources, we can piece together the life of a woman who was equally influential in Kansas City's black community as well as nationally. She was born in Canada about 1860. Her father likely was an escaped slave from North Carolina who had used the Underground Railroad to escape across the border. Canada was a frequent destination for escaped slaves, who feared stopping in the North because of the possibility of their return to bondage under the Fugitive Slave Act. Jones's mother was born in New Jersey. Where Jones was educated is unknown, and when she moved to Kansas

36. Ibid.
37. Ibid.

City is unknown. We do know that by 1910, she had gained a teaching position at Lincoln, and in 1911 she became the first African American woman in Kansas City appointed as principal when she took over the Douglass School on the West Side. By this time, she had purchased a home at 2444 Montgall, a block that contained a number of African American teachers. By 1916, Anna Jones had joined the faculty at Lincoln High School, where she remained for the next three years before her retirement. At the same time, she was active in the Young Women's Christian Association movement; as chairman of the board of managers she led the fund-raising campaign for the establishment of the initial YWCA facility at Nineteenth and The Paseo. She was also active in the Missouri Association of Colored Women's Clubs, serving as the organization's president from 1903 to 1906, and in 1904 she was appointed supervisor of the NACW's Literature Department.[38]

The Kansas City Colored Women's League was one of the first clubs affiliated with the Washington-based Colored Women's League, and Anna Jones was chosen to represent the national organization in the talks that led to a merger with the Boston-based National Federation of African American Women. The two groups of African American women came together as the National Association of Colored Women, and Josephine Yates, who likely had also attended the meetings, was elected fourth vice president of the new NACW. In 1901, Yates succeeded Mary Church Terrell of Washington, DC, as president and served with distinction until 1906. After stepping down as president, Yates remained active in both the women's club movement and racial-uplift work (although she would not see the distinction between the two). In 1907, Yates was elected president of the Missouri Association of Colored Women's Clubs at its convention in Sedalia. She served as president through 1910. She was also among the women to address the annual conventions of the National Afro-American League, an early civil rights organization, and in 1910, she was a member of the Committee of One Hundred, the founding body for the National Association for the Advancement of Colored People.[39]

38. Elizabeth Lindsay Davis, *Lifting as They Climb*, 43, 167, 345–46; Young and Young, *Your Kansas City and Mine*, 20; "Kansas City School Board Minutes, July 18, 1919," Arthur Benson Papers, box 306, folder IR2, IR3; U.S. Department of Commerce, Bureau of the Census, Thirteenth Census of the United States (1910); *Kansas City Sun*, April 12, 1919. Anna Jones is not an uncommon name, and no record of Anna H. Jones appears in the 1880 or 1900 census for Kansas City. After leaving teaching, Jones moved to California in 1920.

39. Davis, *Lifting as They Climb*, 345–46.

In 1910, W. W. Yates died, and Josephine Yates was forced to return to teaching to support herself. She died suddenly in 1912. Their daughter, also named Josephine, became a teacher and an activist in the community as well. Their son, Blyden, became a pharmacist in Chicago.[40]

Josephine Yates and Anna H. Jones were joined by another black female activist in Kansas City, Ida M. Becks, in assisting black women in establishing a Young Women's Christian Association facility for African Americans on the Kansas side. Jones, at the time a teacher at Lincoln High School, and Becks, who was working with the Florence Crittenton Rescue Home in Topeka, were among the featured speakers at a mass rally in March 1911. And although Josephine Yates, who by this time had returned to teaching, was not listed as either a speaker for the meeting or on the provisional fund-raising committee, it is obvious that she provided some support for the effort. In 1919, the YWCA in Kansas City, Kansas, was named in her honor.[41]

As indicated above, Yates was a talented writer and orator. In 1895, she was one of five women representing women's clubs from the state of Missouri at the Congress of Colored Women at the Atlanta Exposition in December. Her address, "How Best to Raise the Moral Status of the Race," drew praise from Booker T. Washington. W. E. B. Du Bois also took note of her speaking ability. A year previously, she delivered the paper "Modern Education as Influenced by the Reformation" to the Greenwood Club, a group of some of the most prominent white men in Kansas City brought together by superintendent of schools James Mickleborough Greenwood. At the NACW convention in 1899, Yates delivered an address titled "Social Necessity of an Equal Moral Standard for Men and Women." She also was an established essayist and poet. Writing under the pseudonym R. K. Potter, she published a number of short stories and poems. She continued to write for *Woman's Era* as well as for several other African American publications, including *Voice of the Negro* and *Ringwood's Journal,* the first periodical published specifically for African American women. In 1895, Yates penned an essay on the virtues of industrial education for *Woman's Era,* and almost a decade later, she wrote "The Equipment of the Teacher" for *Voice of the Negro.* Although Yates's discussion in the latter essay was applicable to teachers of any race, her conclusion was directed straight at African American educators. They faced a "critical period" in the education of the race,

40. Ibid., 167.
41. Greenbaum, *Afro-American Community,* 59–61.

and those who did not uphold their responsibility would be labeled a "traitor" to the race. "He will not fail to receive," she wrote, "the just malediction of a long-suffering race."[42]

Anna Jones also contributed to *Voice of the Negro* and possibly other publications. In 1905, she submitted an article to *Voice of the Negro* summing up the educational achievements of African American women in the United States. In the article, which ran in two parts, Jones pointed to Fannie Jackson-Coppin, to the educated women involved in the racial-uplift and charitable activities of the club movement, and to the female principals in several cities across the nation. She also noted the number of African American women to graduate from various colleges, including ten from Kansas State University in Manhattan. In her conclusion, Jones argued: "The moral and social regeneration of a race is the work of centuries. But what has been done by one of that race shows the race capacity. To the impartial observer, the fact is established that there is no inherent inferiority, which education will not remove. What education, discipline, training have done for other races and have already done for ours, they will continue to do, as surely as harvest follows seed-time."[43]

The lines of community repeatedly stretched across city and state boundaries for Anna Jones and Josephine Yates. They saw their work as stretching across the boundaries of the two Kansas Cities and into their hinterlands. They were joined in their efforts by one more remarkable woman, Kathryn Johnson. Although a teacher for part of her life, Johnson could not match the intellectual abilities of Jones or Yates. She showed, however, an ability to function as an organizer and strategist at the grassroots level and possessed a tenacity that more than made up for any slight intellectual shortcomings. Kathryn Johnson was born in 1878 in Ohio, where she grew up and attended public schools. After attending Wilberforce University in 1897–1898, she began teaching in the Ohio and Indiana public school systems. She accepted a teaching position in North Carolina in 1904 before becoming the dean of women at Shorter College in Little Rock, Arkansas, in 1906. By 1910, Johnson had moved to Kansas City, Kansas, where she became involved in "race work." As noted earlier, she was among the women who came together and organized the Young Women's Christian Association facility for

42. A. Theodore Brown and Lyle W. Dorsett, *K.C.: A History of Kansas City, Missouri*, 85–87; *Woman's Era*, November 1894, 15–16; May 1895, 10–12; Yates, "The Equipment of the Teacher"; Davis, *Lifting as They Climb*, 46, 167.

43. Jones, "A Century's Progress for the American Colored Woman" and "The American Colored Woman," 694.

Kansas-side African Americans. She also was a charter member of the NAACP, and for the first half of the 1910s, Johnson made a living by making small commissions on branch memberships and subscriptions to *Crisis,* the official publication of the NAACP. Johnson was, according to Mary White Ovington, the NAACP's first "fieldworker."[44] Beginning in 1913, Johnson expanded her work; she traveled throughout the South and the West, educating African Americans on the work of the NAACP and helping to establish NAACP branches. Early in 1916, she was publicly recognized by the national office for her work, but six months later she left the NAACP.

Johnson then took up YWCA work; she was one of three black women who worked for the association in France during World War I. After the war's end, she traveled as a sales representative for Associated Publishers and the Association for the Study of Negro Life and History; she made her living on the commission of sales of works by and about African Americans. Although Johnson no longer worked *for* the NAACP, she was still willing to work *with* the organization. In May 1921, Johnson and four other men and women were arrested and convicted for distributing leaflets opposing the Ku Klux Klan in front of a New York theater showing *The Birth of a Nation.* Six months later, the convictions were overturned, and Kathryn Johnson and the other pickets were released from jail. Johnson's release merited front-page headlines in the *Kansas City Sun,* which noted the opinion of the appellate judge that affirmed the rights of citizens to protest publicly against a movement (in this case the Ku Klux Klan) they believed to be "subversive" of their rights as citizens.[45] Johnson remained an activist and an outspoken advocate for the rights of African Americans for the next three decades. She died in 1955.

Josephine Yates, Anna Jones, and Kathryn Johnson worked to change the material conditions of African Americans in the two Kansas Cities and throughout the nation. Through the written word, their speeches, and their ground-level organizing, they offered African Americans a different, progressive view of American society in the first decades of the twentieth century. Each, in her own way, would see the fruits of her labor. They could all look around the city and see examples of black men and women who had accomplished success despite the limitations placed on them by American society. Even in the 1890s, a period that historian Rayford Logan calls the "nadir" of race relations in the

44. Ovington, "The National Association for the Advancement of Colored People," 115.
45. *Kansas City Sun,* November 12, 1921.

United States, black men and women in particular professions in Kansas City could gain a measure of prosperity and sense of achievement.[46] Four such men, three members of the clergy and a doctor, deserve mention for their roles in guiding the development of Kansas City's African American community.

Samuel William Bacote came to Kansas City in 1895 to the pastorate of Second Baptist Church at Tenth and Charlotte.[47] Bacote, then just twenty-nine years of age, led the expansion of the church into a place of prominence in black Kansas City. He was born in 1866 in South Carolina to two former slaves. Samuel's mother died when he was three, and he was raised by his grandmother and his father, Dembo, a literate man who served as a deputy sheriff for Darlington County, South Carolina, for a number of years. At age seventeen, Samuel entered Benedict College, an all-black college in South Carolina. In three years, he completed the course work in the school's Normal Department, and in 1888 he received his teaching certificate. Bacote spent a year as a principal before entering a Virginia seminary. In 1892, he took his first assignment as a pastor, at Second Baptist Church in Marion, Alabama. In 1895, he came to Kansas City.

While serving as pastor at Second Baptist, Bacote began taking classes at Kansas City University in Kansas City, Kansas.[48] He received his bachelor's degree in 1898 and in 1901 gained his master's degree. Bacote was the only African American student at Kansas City University at the time and was the first to earn a degree from the school. In 1906, he was awarded the doctor of divinity degree by Kansas City University.

Through his work with the National Baptist Convention, Bacote became a correspondent of black educator Booker T. Washington. Little is known about the depth of their relationship, but after a Brownsville, Texas, incident in 1906, Bacote wrote to Washington seeking advice. The incident involved three African American companies of the Twenty-fifth Regiment; white citizens claimed that the black soldiers had fired upon anyone and anything during one hot night in August. After a brief investigation, President Theodore Roosevelt dismissed the entire battalion without honor and disqualified its members for service in

46. Logan, *The Negro in American Life and Thought: The Nadir, 1877–1901*, 52.

47. Most of the details of Bacote's early life come from the introduction in his collection of black biographies, *Who's Who among the Colored Baptists of the United States*, 8–11. The introduction was written by E. Arlington Williams, pastor of First Baptist Church, Muskogee, Oklahoma.

48. Kansas City University, which opened in 1895, should not be confused with the University of Kansas City, which opened in 1938 in Kansas City, Missouri, and later became the University of Missouri–Kansas City.

either the military or the civil service. Black Americans, as well as some whites, were outraged by the summary judgment. Protests were lodged in the black press and in Congress, and prominent African Americans were asked to lead the charge against Roosevelt's decision. Washington's advice to Bacote was to remain neutral in the controversy, an approach that Bacote apparently followed.[49]

When Bacote took over Kansas City's Second Baptist Church, the church had more than four thousand dollars in outstanding debt. Bacote led a fund-raising drive that eliminated the debt, and he then helped raise more than fourteen thousand dollars to construct a new church edifice. By World War I, Second Baptist's distinct structure, valued at more than one hundred thousand dollars in 1910, was one of the most recognizable landmarks in black Kansas City.[50]

During this time, Bacote married Lucy Bledsoe of Topeka, Kansas, and became involved in the National Baptist Convention, the organization of African American Baptists. In 1901, he was elected the organization's statistician and edited the *National Baptist Year Book*. Bacote's biographer credits him for simplifying and organizing the yearbook into a more useful format.[51] The focus for Samuel and Lucy Bacote, however, remained Second Baptist Church and the development of the African American community in Kansas City. Lucy Bacote, who had studied at music conservatories in Boston and Kansas City, organized the Second Baptist choir. Under the Bacotes' leadership, the church attracted a number of prominent African Americans, and before World War I the church on the hill at Tenth and Charlotte was the scene for many of the vital discussions affecting black Kansas City. Bacote served as pastor at Second Baptist for fifty-one years, easily the longest tenure of any African American clergyman in Kansas City. He remained an active force in the community well into the twentieth century, serving with James Dallas Bowser and R. T. Coles, for example, on the Inter-Racial Committee of Twelve.

49. Bacote to Washington, April 28, 1908, Booker T. Washington Papers, 1908, 3:513; May 16, 1908, ibid., 537–38. Senator Joseph B. Foraker of Ohio led the fight for the Brownsville soldiers, calling upon Roosevelt to convene a full and impartial hearing. In 1909, a special court of inquiry reinstated the soldiers' eligibility for future service, but for many African Americans, the discharge of the Brownsville battalion was another sign of the hostility facing black men and women in this country. In 1972, an act of Congress rescinded all of the dishonorable discharges. See Ann J. Lane, *The Brownsville Affair: National Crisis and Black Reaction;* and John Hope Franklin and Alfred A. Moss Jr., *From Slavery to Freedom: A History of African Americans,* 314–15.

50. Bacote, *Who's Who,* 8–9; A. Martin, *Our Negro Population,* 181.

51. Bacote, *Who's Who,* 10.

Bacote was not the only voice of black Baptists in Kansas City nor necessarily its strongest. His pastorate at Second Baptist allowed him a certain stature, but Reverends T. H. Ewing (Vine Street) and James Wesley Hurse (St. Stephens) gained prominence in the African American community for their outspoken views on economic development. As did Bacote, both men led their churches into the interwar period, but they gained recognition in the years of growth for Kansas City's African American community.

T. H. Ewing came to Kansas City in 1887, joining the city's rapid expansion and transformation from a frontier outpost to western metropolis. Vine Street was a small, struggling church when he arrived, but Ewing quickly asserted himself as a voice for change. His first target was the poor economic standing of his parishioners. In 1887, according to Asa Martin, just three of Ewing's parishioners owned real property.[52] Ewing preached that the acquisition of property was the key to earthly salvation. To acquire property required saving, and he urged his parishioners to put aside at least ten cents a day (out of weekly incomes that might be as low as six dollars). Ewing outlined a number of ways African Americans could save: they should walk to work rather than paying five cents one way for a ride on the streetcar, they should buy their groceries in bulk and always pay cash, and they should refrain from buying on credit. He told the members of the Vine Street congregation to live and dress according to their means and to avoid frivolous spending. They were, of course, to stay away from saloons and movie theaters. By the early 1890s, Ewing was urging his parishioners to open a banking account and start looking to purchase a home. He cajoled them if he met them on the street, asking if they were sticking with his savings plan.

Ewing organized an economic club for Vine Street members with a strict set of guidelines designed to get African Americans into their own homes as quickly as possible. Starting in 1904, he also promoted three financial clubs at Vine Street—one for men and two for women—in which the members pooled their resources and invested in real estate. In 1912, when Asa Martin conducted his study, all three clubs owned rental property in the African American community. By the same time, Vine Street had grown into one of the three largest black Baptist churches in Kansas City. It had six hundred members, Martin reported, and one hundred owned their own homes.[53] Ewing also practiced what he preached; by the time of his death in 1930 at age seventy-four, he

52. Martin, *Our Negro Population*, 38–39.
53. Ibid.

owned farms in Oklahoma and Kansas and other property in Kansas City; South Park, Kansas (just north of Merriam); and Leavenworth, where he and his family resided. When in Kansas City, Ewing lived in rooms at the back of his church.[54]

James Wesley Hurse led the formation of St. Stephen's Baptist Church in the early 1900s. He was born July 10, 1866, to two former slaves in Collierville, Tennessee. Hurse, who had little formal education, moved to Memphis, Tennessee, when he was nineteen and found work first at a cotton gin and then as a roustabout on a steamboat on the Mississippi River. He worked as a roustabout for more than seven years but became increasingly dissatisfied with the discrimination and racism he faced in Memphis and chose to move to Kansas City in the fall of 1896. Hurse, who had been "called" to the ministry at age fifteen, had been ordained as a minister in 1891. Before being called to the pastorate at St. Stephen's, Hurse worked as a laborer for city street crews.[55]

Hurse, a small, powerfully built man with an imposing round face, was considered one of the community's most powerful orators, and by the end of World War I, his congregation stood at more than eight hundred members. Like Ewing, he challenged his parishioners to become more financially minded. He also, according to oral traditions in the African American community, was one of the first ministers to encourage his parishioners to become more racially conscious, particularly in where they chose to spend their money. He encouraged them to patronize black-owned businesses, and in one unforgettable moment in 1915, he refused to deliver a funeral service for a parishioner because the family had chosen a white undertaker—there were at least three African American undertaking firms in the city at the time. Hurse also was an active supporter of the National Baptist Convention of America, the second-largest organization of black Baptists in the country. He served a three-year term as president of the convention, from 1930 to 1933. Hurse also made a brief but unsuccessful foray into the political arena; in 1924, he became the first African American nominated for alderman by either major party in Kansas City. Although he lost the election, Hurse remained active in Kansas City's African American community until his death in 1935.[56] The following is one of Hurse's sermons reprinted in the *Kansas City Sun:*

54. *Kansas City Call*, June 13, 1930.

55. Herman Kinsler, *The Biography of Kansas City's Negro Business and Professional Men and the Trip South.*

56. For a fuller description of Hurse's brief political fling, see Chapter Four. See also C. Eric Lincoln and Lawrence H. Mamiya, *The Black Church in the African American Experience*, 34–35.

Sermon by James Wesley Hurse
Pastor, St. Stephen's Baptist Church
November 20, 1921

Subject:—The honest judgment of God to man.
Text:—Psalms 7–8: "The Lord shall judge the people. Judge me Oh Lord according to my righteousness and according to mine integrity that is in me."

The minister began by explaining the application of the text and said that "he who wants to be judged fairly and impartially by the Lord must make sure that his integrity measures up to the Lord's requirements." "God alone is a proper Judge. In this land and in our Courts we have Judges who hear the evidence; ofttimes this evidence may not be true, but the Judges of the Courts must render decision and make his findings from the evidence presented before him." "But this Judge of ours, this righteous and Holy Judge who sees all we do, hears all we say and has his Scribes constantly writing down the time, needs no jurors nor attorneys, nor witnesses: for the Holy Bible declares that he is the Judge of all things: His name is Alpha and Omega the beginning and the end; and as in Psalms 41:12 He says: 'And as for me thou upholdeth me in my integrity and setteth me before thy face forever.' So God has today and always will have the power to condemn even without calling them to judgment.

"What is integrity? Integrity is the sublimest thing in nature, the moral grandeur of a righteous, conscientious soul. Buckminster says: That it is honesty and uprightness, rectitude and probity, unimpeachable honesty and candor and a strict performance of those obligations which the laws of the State cannot reach which are sometimes called imperfect but which come direct from the omnipotent hand of God himself.

"I want to talk to you for a little while of moral integrity and of racial obligations. You may not like it; it may be strong medicine for some but God in Heaven knows it's true. If you will only believe it, you can do anything any other race can do: I saw where in Chicago sometime ago a Negro physician sewed up a heart that had been pierced by a bully's knife and I saw in Detroit where a man's neck had been broken and by a system known to the Medical fraternity, this Negro Doctor patched him up so that he lived for many years with a broken neck. Our Negro women in the kitchen, or in the cotton-field work as faithfully and as incomplainingly as any other women and yet get less encouragement than any women on earth because there are many Negroes, I regret to say it,—but nevertheless it's true—who would treat the worst and most disreputable white women better than he would the purest Negro woman on earth. Say amen.

"But brethren, sisters, if you live right, I declare that God will take care of you and if you believe in right and justice you will stand up for our women and for right because our mothers were women and God is right.

"No race has progressed in so short a time as have we and yet no race has fought and back-bit and slandered each other as has our race. Some of you sneer at your less-fortunate neighbor and say ugly things about them but do any of you think you're so good that no one talks about you? I overheard a Negro say, 'I like Elder Hurse and I like to hear him preach but my God Chil dat darkey married too soon.'[57] Suppose he did, he didn't get in your way nor did he interfere with your family ties nor bring discredit upon the womanhood of the race. And let me tell you Mr. Negro that when you hear talking about me or someone else, and you join in the gossip, remember that somewhere somebody is talking about you and washing your dirty linen until it would make your ears tingle.

"But if you do right, they can do you no harm and always remember that if you do right, they'll talk about you and if you do wrong, they'll talk about you and the only thing to do is to put your hand in God's hand and put your trust in Him, and then go triumphantly marching on.

"I want you to join with me in singing, 'Where He leads me I will follow,' and as you sing it, remember that our God is a just God and that He will judge us by our integrity: but wait, do you mean what you say? Do you mean when trouble comes, when debts pile up, when friends forsake you, when sorrow overwhelms you, when sickness and poverty comes that you can continue to sing that good old song? Let me tell you children that every night before I retire and every morning when I arise, I say, 'Thank you Jesus for the preservation of my body and the comforts which I enjoy.'

"And finally brethren I want to say that I want the good will of everybody; I may not die in the bed with friends and nurses around me. I may die in a railroad collision, upon the battlefield or on the street, but I want you to know that I've got my marching orders and I shall continue to press forward until I hear my God say, 'Well done.'

"How many of you have marching orders? How many of you have died to die no more? And brethren when my feet shall come down to the Jordan, when my eyes are glazed and set, when my knees get cold and the Doctor says he can do no more I am going to

57. A reference to Hurse's marriage in 1921 to Lula Mae Butler of Indianapolis four months after the death of his wife, Leona, who succumbed after a long illness.

> sing, 'March down, march down to Judgment in that morning' and with Jesus Christ, the prophets, the saints, and the loved ones who have gone on before we shall rise triumphant through the Integrity given to us by God the Father, God the Son and God the Holy Ghost."[58]

T. C. Unthank was one of the most recognized physicians in black Kansas City prior to the war. Through his dedication and relentless lobbying, Unthank is credited with the establishment of three medical facilities for African Americans in the two Kansas Cities. Thomas C. Unthank was born in 1866 in Greensboro, North Carolina. He enrolled at the Howard University School of Medicine in 1894, and after graduation in 1898, he moved to Kansas City. Shortly after arriving in Kansas City, Unthank worked with black doctors on the Kansas side in establishing a private hospital for African Americans in Kansas City, Kansas. The Douglass Hospital, named for Reverend Calvin Douglass of Western University, opened in 1898. The Douglass Hospital drew patients from both sides of the state line and as a result quickly suffered from overcrowding. In 1902, Unthank helped establish a private hospital—the John Lange Hospital—on the Missouri side for African Americans. The hospital was named for the business manager of popular musical performer Blind Boone. Lange, who lived in an ostentatious home at 912 Park Avenue in Kansas City, had a net worth of a quarter of a million dollars. He used his fortune to sustain black schools and churches in Columbia, Missouri, and he made a sizable donation to start the John Lange Hospital in a twenty-six-room building at 1227 Michigan.[59] With Lange's death in 1916, the hospital lost most of its financial support, and it closed by 1920. The Douglass Hospital, however, remained a cornerstone of the black community in Kansas City, Kansas, until it closed in 1978.

The John Lange Hospital, the Douglass Hospital, and Perry's Sanitarium, operated by Dr. John E. Perry, proved inadequate to handle the number of black patients in the area. African Americans on the Missouri side, in particular, were leery of attempting to obtain treatment at the city hospital, where segregated facilities and neglect of black patients were commonplace. The flood of 1903 demonstrated just how inadequate were the facilities available to people of color. African American

58. *Kansas City Sun*, November 26, 1921.

59. Jack A. Batterson, *Blind Boone: Missouri's Ragtime Pioneer*, 40; Gibson, *Mecca of the New Negro*, 10.

and Hispanic victims of the flood, which washed through the West Bottoms, were taken to an improvised setup at Convention Hall. Black and Mexican patients were rudely treated and among the last to receive treatment. Unthank, incensed by the treatment minority patients received, began pressuring city officials to provide a separate hospital for African Americans.

If there was dissent within Kansas City's African American community in regards to Unthank's proposal, no record has survived. It should be noted that among African American elites in many cities, controversy arose over the creation of segregated public facilities, such as hospitals and YMCAs. Some argued for a practical approach—segregated institutions were better than none at all. Others argued that the acceptance of separate facilities strengthened the bastions of racism and discrimination. Each side had its adherents, but in most communities, compromise reigned. Segregated public facilities provided essential services and were acceptable for the present, but the fight for integrated institutions would continue. In Kansas City, compromise prevailed as well: African American patients would be admitted at the Old City Hospital. The hospital eventually became known as General Hospital No. 2, and Unthank would be one of its first superintendents.

Thomas C. Unthank, James Wesley Hurse, Samuel Bacote, Josephine Yates, Richard T. Coles, T. H. Ewing, and others helped shape Kansas City's African American community before World War I. The world in which they lived was sharply marked by the issue of race, and a growing sense of racial consciousness helped drive each of these individuals. American society had become more hostile to people of color by the turn of the century. The strange career of Jim Crow, as historian C. Vann Woodward puts it, hovered over African American communities throughout the South, Midwest, West, and even North. For many African Americans, the promise held out by the passage of the Thirteenth, Fourteenth, and Fifteenth Amendments in the years after the Civil War had been overwhelmed by the vicious realities of economic, political, and educational discrimination. Violence had greeted demands for equality of opportunity. Historian Rayford Logan would call it the nadir of African American life in this country, yet, in communities such as Kansas City, Missouri, in the fifty years between the end of the Civil War and the outbreak of a general European war, African Americans constructed a vibrant world. The promises of emancipation were not forgotten; they were just deferred.

By 1920, the U.S. Census counted 30,893 African Americans within Kansas City, Missouri, or 9.5 percent of the city's total population.

Another 14,405 were listed in Wyandotte County. Another 4,000 to 5,000 were scattered throughout the rest of the Kansas City area, including Independence and parts of Clay and Platte Counties in Missouri. The area's 50,000 black residents were linked by this time by educational, economic, and social ties. African Americans on the Kansas side drew the support of their Missouri counterparts for the development of institutions in Wyandotte County. In their quest for educational opportunities for their children, African American parents in outlying regions counted on the assistance of their urban relatives and friends. African Americans on the Kansas side, for their part, contributed to a number of Twin City organizations in the first decades of the twentieth century. For African Americans in Kansas City and the surrounding areas, state and city boundaries were not allowed to disrupt the bonds of family, friends, or race. This is the world in which John X. Brown and his wife lived. This is the world we shall begin to explore.

The Inconsistencies of Jim Crow

The racial obstacles facing African Americans in Kansas City have been frequently documented. Black customers were not allowed to try on clothes in most downtown stores. Seating in most of the major theaters downtown was on a segregated basis, as it was on most occasions at Convention Hall and later Municipal Auditorium. Although they were not subjected to segregated seating on public transportation, African American patrons were frequently abused by drivers and white passengers alike. Police brutality against black bodies was not an uncommon occurrence. Black children were not allowed to be educated with white children, nor were black teachers allowed in classrooms with white pupils. Medical care was routinely segregated as well. Attempts by African Americans to expand the area of residential settlement, at least in the Troost-Benton corridor, were met by violence. Many African Americans, as a result, could find only substandard housing stock. They found their job options limited, and the wage rates depressed, even before 1929. The major unions rejected African American workers. Kansas City's African Americans, particularly those of northern origins, could find plenty to chafe against.

It is worth noting, however, that Kansas City was both northern and western enough to allow some gaps in the city's racially based strictures. African Americans routinely used the major facilities downtown and on the East Side: Convention Hall, Municipal Auditorium, Lyric Hall,

Muehlebach Park, and the Labor Temple, for example. Black voters were not routinely disfranchised, but blatant fraud did occur. The city possessed a thriving black professional class, and black workers held semiskilled positions in a smattering of industries (primarily the packinghouses and related industries). On a limited number of occasions (the Inter-Racial Commission, for example), blacks and whites theoretically sat as equals. The black hod-carriers union was recognized by labor leaders, and the major unions in the meatpacking industry organized both black and white labor. Many African Americans, particularly those of southern origin, found opportunity awaited them in Kansas City. For most African Americans, then, Kansas City represented two worlds, in which opportunities for advancement coexisted with sometimes strict limitations. Growing up and living black in Kansas City then meant finding the best possible balance within the two. Nowhere was that more evident than in the world of work.

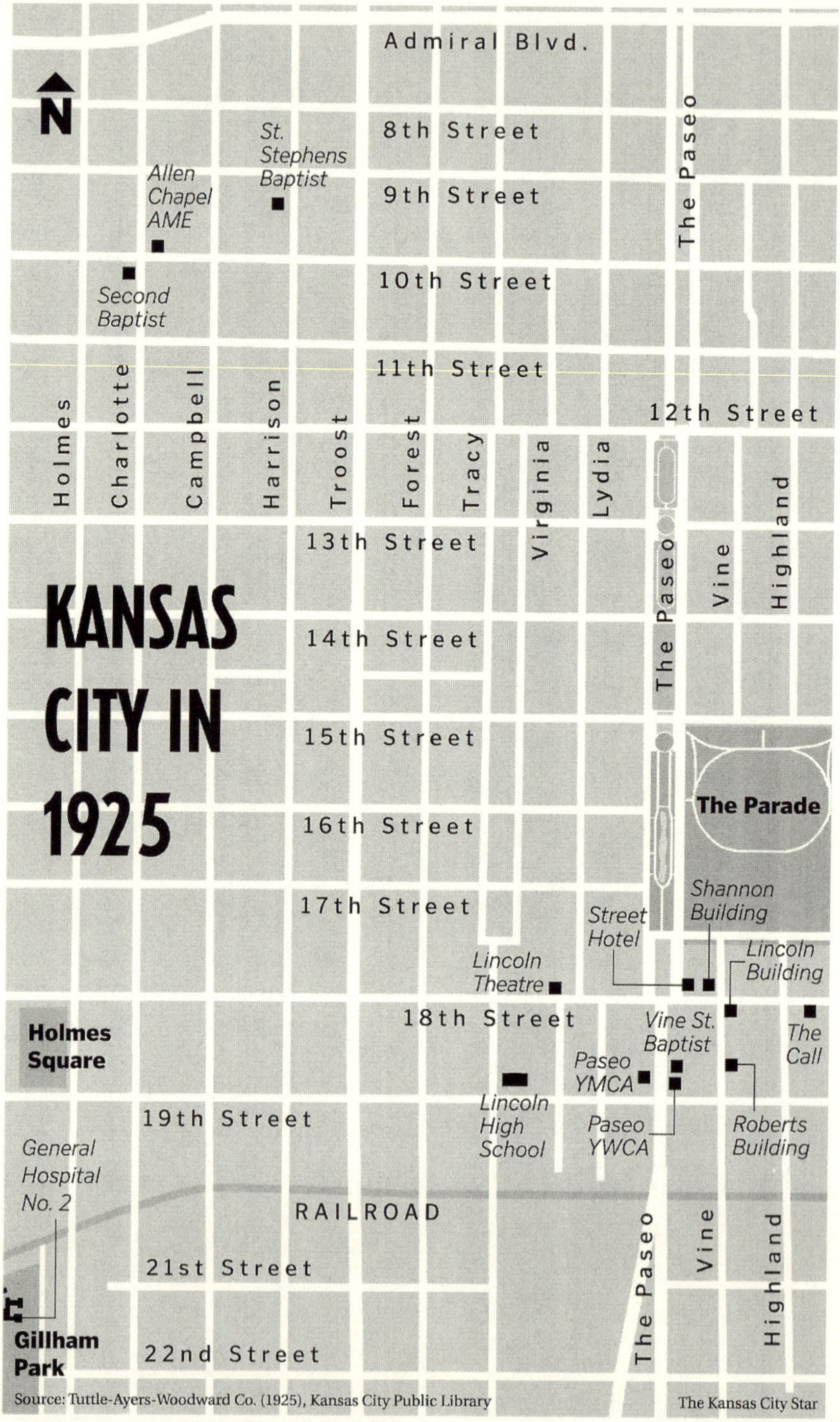
KANSAS CITY IN 1925
N
Admiral Blvd.
8th Street
9th Street
10th Street
11th Street
12th Street
13th Street
14th Street
15th Street
16th Street
17th Street
18th Street
19th Street
RAILROAD
21st Street
22nd Street
Holmes
Charlotte
Campbell
Harrison
Troost
Forest
Tracy
Virginia
Lydia
The Paseo
Vine
Highland
St. Stephens Baptist
Allen Chapel AME
Second Baptist
The Parade
Shannon Building
Street Hotel
Lincoln Building
Lincoln Theatre
Vine St. Baptist
The Call
Paseo YMCA
Lincoln High School
Paseo YWCA
Roberts Building
Holmes Square
General Hospital No. 2
Gillham Park
Source: Tuttle-Ayers-Woodward Co. (1925), Kansas City Public Library
The Kansas City Star

Two

The World of Work

Ditches and picks. Births and funerals. Stretching a dollar the length of ten. A job, no job; three children and a wife to feed; bread thirteen cents a loaf. For pleasure, church—where he was too tired to go sometimes. Tobacco that he had to consider twice before he bought. "I ain't lived hard! I ain't lived hard!" he said suddenly. "I have worked harder than I should, that's all."

—PETER JACKSON, THE PROTAGONIST IN MARITA BONNER'S "DRAB RAMBLES: THE FIRST PORTRAIT" (1927)

PETER JACKSON IS A fictional character, but his status, as portrayed with bitter irony by Marita Bonner, describes the working conditions for many African American men in Kansas City and other urban areas in the 1920s. Jackson is a day laborer for the city, a denizen of Chicago's Frye Street. He is a relatively young man, with an old man's heart; his body, after years of toil, is breaking down. When the doctor at the free clinic (the only kind of medical help men like Jackson could afford) suggests that the deterioration of Jackson's heart is because of hard living, Jackson responds angrily: "I ain't lived hard! I have worked harder than I should, that's all." It was a common refrain for African American men and women in the twentieth century, even in cities like Chicago and Kansas City that had a growing black professional class. Work—hard work, in many cases—was one of the primary conditions of African

American life. In every community, the black working class dwarfed the small professional class. By using the manuscript census for 1920 itself, as well as newspaper accounts, Urban League studies and charts, and the few surviving recollections of African Americans, we can at least partially reconstruct the texture, connections, and conditions of black working-class life. The broad numbers of the census statistics conceal a range of work experiences for African Americans. There are still blank spaces in the mosaic we are attempting to build, but a close examination of the census helps fill in the picture.

Two different pictures of working conditions in black Kansas City emerge from two different yet similar sources. Frayser T. Lane, executive secretary of the Kansas City Urban League (KCUL) in the early 1920s, painted a positive portrait of black employment in 1926, in the midst of what were boom times for the U.S. economy in general. In response to a general request from the organization's national office in late 1925 or early 1926, Lane noted the presence of black workers "in the majority of places where the services of any number of persons is needed." Although African Americans held no "unusual positions in industry," Lane noted, jobs that paid well were constantly filled. "This includes such work as moulders, shipping clerks, bakers and high class domestics and janitors." Lane noted some bricklayers and carpenters, most of whom were excluded from the unions representing their craft, also made "good money."[1] Fourteen years later, a study of the industrial status of black workers, conducted by the Kansas City Urban League under the direction of another executive secretary, Thomas B. Webster, painted a different—and much bleaker—picture of black work in the previous two decades. It, of course, was colored by the crash of 1929 and the subsequent Depression.[2]

In its introduction, the study noted the conditions and limits facing black workers in the city in 1930—one year after the stock-market crash and the onset of the Great Depression. At that time, the study pointed out, two-thirds of all African Americans in Kansas City were gainfully employed. They were spread out over a variety of occupations: for

1. *Opportunity* 4:2 (February 1926); 4:3 (March 1926): 94. The Kansas City summary appears in the March issue.

2. Kansas City Urban League, *The Negro Worker of Kansas City: A Study of Trade Union and Organized Labor Relations* (Kansas City: Urban League of Kansas City, 1939), Missouri State Archives, Local Records Preservation Program, Kansas City Urban League, microfilm, four reels, box KCULP, folder 2. Documents from this series hereafter are designation KCULP with appropriate box and folder numbers.

the 155 occupations listed for male workers in the 1930 statistical summary of the census, African Americans were engaged in 139 of them; for female workers, 41 of the 59 occupations listed were open to black wage earners.

The statistics, however, hide several disturbing elements: In 43 of the occupations listed for men (or more than one-third that listed black workers), fewer than 10 African Americans were engaged. For female workers, a similar percentage holds true: fewer than a dozen black women were engaged in 16 of the 41 open to their race in Kansas City. The Urban League study also noted that almost two-thirds of all black workers were congregated in two categories: 30.8 percent of the 14,167 employed men in 1930 were engaged in the manufacturing and mechanical industries (which included packinghouse work); 34.3 percent were involved in domestic and personal service.[3]

The Urban League study did not address occupations for black women, but the census summary shows a familiar pattern: African American females relied on domestic and personal service jobs. Of the 9,681 black girls and women over the age of ten counted in the 1930 census, 80 percent were servants, hairdressers, boardinghouse operators, laundresses, laundry workers, or waitresses.

The main obstacle to black employment in some categories of work, the Urban League study concluded, was discrimination by trade and craft unions, particularly those affiliated with the American Federation of Labor (AFL). Most unions in the AFL, the study noted, forbade black members, whether by the unions' constitutional provisions, gentlemen's agreements, or tradition. Some unions admitted black workers, but only in segregated locals. Chief among these were the Musicians' Union, the Organization of Hotel and Restaurant Employees, the Journeymen Barbers group, and the Laundry Workers Union. Yet in Kansas City, some unions had opened their doors to full participation of African American workers. The Building Trades, Hod Carriers, Iron Workers, Rock Quarrymen, and Truck Drivers Unions all admitted black workers, and African Americans found employment as helpers to bricklayers, carpenters, cement finishers, electricians, painters, plasterers, plumbers, stonemasons, and tile setters.[4]

The list of organized occupations that still excluded African Americans was long. Among them were unions representing asbestos workers,

3. Ibid., 8.
4. Ibid., 8–11.

boilermakers, carpet layers, elevator constructors, glaziers, hoisting engineers, insulators, lathers, marble setters, roofers, sheet metal workers, sign writers, and steamfitters.

Without union membership, work was difficult, if not impossible, to find.[5] "Many of the employers are reluctant to hire Negroes except as a last resort and in the least desirable jobs," the 1940 Urban League study said.

> Some persons object to seeing Negroes in dignified employment, and by passing these objections on to employers make the employer even more unwilling to employ Negro labor.
>
> Many white workers object to working in company with Negroes, or object to Negroes having any kind of skilled employment. Carrying their objections into trade unions, these prejudiced workers make it impossible for Negroes to be admitted to unions.
>
> Finally, because of the employers [*sic*] unwillingness to give Negroes experience and because of trade unions [*sic*] refusal to admit them to apprenticeship training, as well as the limited trades training opportunity in the schools, Negroes are frequently unable to acquire training and skill that will qualify them for jobs which do appear.[6]

In 1929, the study noted, just 30 percent of the 1,235 businesses in Kansas City employed African Americans, and in those companies almost half the black workers were identified as porters. The survey noted that the average wage for those workers was $21.50 a week. For white workers, the average wage was roughly double that amount. In the years around 1920, when the going wages were little different, the U.S. Bureau of Labor Statistics had determined that—in order to obtain the bare minimums in housing, food, and clothing—a family of five needed a salary twice that of the Kansas City average for black workers.

Other sources support the findings of the Urban League survey. For example, one Kansas City department store, which had paid its employees $22.50 weekly during the war, fired 470 men and women (both white and black) in 1921 and rehired only those willing to take a pay cut to $15 a week. When Chevrolet opened its Kansas City plant in 1929, editor Chester A. Franklin of the *Kansas City Call* pointed out that African Americans were hired only in janitorial positions at $15 a week. Rather than pay the "living wage of the automobile industry," Franklin

5. Ibid., 11.
6. Ibid., 13.

noted, the automaker was content with paying its African American employees "Kansas City's less-than-$20-a-week customary" for black men and women.[7]

Kansas City was not unique. Economist Abram L. Harris, in a survey conducted in 1926 during his stint as the executive secretary of the Minneapolis branch of the Urban League, found that few black male–headed families in that Minnesota city approached the Bureau of Labor Statistics' minimum standard of living either. The median annual income of a sample of more than 200 African American families in Minneapolis was about $1,172.60, or a little more than half of the minimum standard of living.[8]

Beyond the numbers, the vagaries of black employment became clear in anecdotes compiled by the Kansas City Urban League. A Kansas City steel company displaced 18 black workers on the night shift with white workers from another section of the plant. The black workers protested, and an investigation revealed that the white workers had refused during the summer months to work on the open hearth. The 18 black workers had done that job during the hottest part of the year. Once the weather cooled, the white workers were prepared to take over. Ultimately, the firm's president intervened, and one of the black workers was promoted to foreman with the authority to rehire the rest of the laid-off crew.[9]

When it organized a lumber mill in the 1930s, the Carpenters Union refused to accept a black man who had worked at the mill since 1911. Instead, he joined the Truck Drivers Union. This special arrangement existed until the carpenters elected a new union representative, who gave the African American's job to a white worker. After the Urban League intervened, the black employee returned to his job under the previous arrangement; the Carpenters Union still refused his membership.[10]

A black male glassworker, employed by a Kansas City firm for more than thirty years, was released along with several white workers when business slumped. The firm eventually rehired all of the workers—except the black man. An African American woman, working in a clothing mill for $6 a week, lost her job when she decided she could not afford to pay union dues.

7. *Kansas City Sun*, January 22, 1921; *Kansas City Call*, January 18, 1929.

8. In 1920, Minneapolis claimed ten thousand African American residents, about one-third as many as Kansas City, Missouri. According to one observer, part of the growth in Minneapolis's black population after World War I was due to the overflow from Kansas City.

9. KCULP, *Negro Worker*, 24.

10. Ibid., 25.

Black inspectors hired by the federal government to oversee the stockyards and packinghouses found themselves assigned to only those departments that employed African Americans. For the most part, those were the jobs on the killing floor. Regardless of experience, qualifications, or length of service, African American inspectors remained confined to the "most disagreeable" part of the industry.[11]

Labor unions organized under the auspices of the AFL's rival, the upstart Congress of Industrial Organizations (CIO), were more open to black participation. Even then, relatively few African Americans in Kansas City were admitted to union membership. Among Kansas City's steel plants, 140 African Americans workers at four plants belonged to the union; the remaining six plants had no black employees. The Kansas City locals of the Amalgamated Clothing Workers had just 30 or 35 members, and the three locals of the United Retail and Wholesale Employees had just 6 black members—all employed by Montgomery Ward. The most successful union organizing by CIO-affiliated locals came in the industry that supported the largest concentration of African American workers: the packinghouses. More than one-fourth of the union members in that industry were African Americans, and at the three largest firms, 3 out of 10 employees were African Americans.[12]

Kansas City's long history with livestock handling began even before the Civil War, according to historian Daniel Serda. Several slaughterhouses were established to cater to local retail traffic and to supply travelers on overland routes to the West. When the war began, all the slaughtering houses closed, and it was not until 1868 that the industry returned to Kansas City to stay. That year, Edward Pattison and J. W. L. Slavens opened a slaughtering plant capable of handling four hundred cattle or fifteen hundred hogs a day. Two years later, the Chicago packing firm of Plankinton & Armours opened a plant on the Missouri side of the West Bottoms. In 1871, the same company opened a new plant just west of the state line in Kansas. Over the next two decades, other meat packers joined the Armour operation in the West Bottoms: Fowler Brothers in 1881 and Swift and Company in 1888.

In 1892, Armour built a new plant at Central Avenue and James Street on the Kansas side of the West Bottoms. By 1908, the plant covered ninety acres of floor space from the state line west to James Street and north of Central Avenue. It had become one of the largest slaughterhouses in the world and employed workers in a myriad of tasks:

11. Ibid.
12. Ibid., 20–21. For a breakdown of union membership by plant, see table 2.1.

"butchers of every degree and branch known to the industry; painters; blacksmiths; wagon makers; car builders; horse shoers; carpenters; tinsmiths; galvanizers; box makers; coopers; can makers; electricians; draftsmen; mechanical engineers; boilermakers; lithographic printers; ice makers; chemists; firemen and many others. Each is a department to itself."[13]

By the end of the 1930s, the two Kansas Cities contained eleven packinghouses, including those of the "Big Four"—Armour, Swift, Cudahy, and Wilson—that required the services of seven trunk railroad lines.[14] The stockyards and packinghouses also offered the most opportunities for African American laborers in the 1920s. According to census statistics, about one in eight black male workers in Kansas City, Missouri, was employed in the stockyards and packinghouses. As works of fiction, contemporary studies, and more recent scholarship have demonstrated, the business of reducing cattle and hogs to slices of beef and pork for the dinner tables of eastern and midwestern elites was brutal, degrading, bloody, strenuous, and often dangerous work. When the Armour Brothers opened their plant in the West Bottoms in the 1870s, black and Irish men were employed in limited numbers to perform the unskilled labor in the plant; native-born whites were more likely to be offered the skilled and semiskilled positions. By the last two decades of the nineteenth century, eastern European immigrants began to compete with African Americans in the packinghouse workforce. Many of the new immigrants settled in enclaves on the Kansas side in the Armourdale area; unlike in Chicago, for instance, African Americans and eastern European immigrants did not immediately compete for housing space or stock.

Some African Americans were first introduced to the packinghouses as strikebreakers. Historian Sherry Lamb Schirmer notes that in 1904, for instance, meat packers brought in black workers from Kansas City and elsewhere to break up a strike by the Amalgamated Meat Cutters. In this case, however, African Americans were well represented on both sides of the strike. In fact, Schirmer points out that the first two decades of the twentieth century saw a constant increase in the number of African Americans in the packinghouses. In 1917, for instance, they represented almost 20 percent of the total workforce. Thus, when black and white women walked away from their jobs in the Cudahy cannery in 1917, it precipitated a "wildcat strike of momentous proportions" in Kansas

13. *Kansas City Journal-Post*, October 16, 1904.
14. Kansas Department of Education, *The WPA Guide to 1930s Kansas*, 210.

City's packinghouses. The Cudahy workers were joined by thousands of employees—many of them African American men and women—of the other meat packers. Within a week, workers in related industries (soap factories) had joined the strike. A crisis was averted, Schirmer says, when a federal mediator negotiated a settlement with increased pay and job security for the striking workers.[15]

The 1917 strike's effectiveness was aided by the changes in the packinghouse workforce. The increase of African Americans in the packinghouses and related industries noted by Schirmer can be attributed to two factors. The first was the outbreak of war in Europe in August 1914; the turmoil slowed the flood of eastern Europeans into this country to a trickle. In Chicago, Detroit, and other industrial cities of the North, employers turned to African Americans from the Deep South to fill the void. This Great Migration, as it came to be called, brought tens of thousands of African Americans into cities in the East and the upper Midwest for the first time, forever changing the geographical, economic, and political landscapes of a dozen urban areas.[16]

Evidence supporting the impact of the Great Migration on the Kansas City area is inconclusive. Both Kansas City, Missouri, and Kansas City, Kansas, saw significant increases in their African American populations between 1910 and 1920, but the percentage growth is virtually identical to the percentage growth in the black communities for the previous decade. And although the black population in Kansas City, Missouri, grew by one-third from 1910 to 1920, the growth pales in comparison with that experienced by cities farther north and east.[17]

The other significant factor affecting the presence of African Americans in the packinghouse workforce was a change in the nature of the work. In the nineteenth century, skilled butchers—by precisely carving the carcass into its various meat products—determined the pace of the work in the packinghouses; meat products could be moved only as fast as the butchers desired. By the 1920s, however, the butchers had been more or less replaced; the packinghouses had become vast disassembly lines, in which unskilled workers performed one or two motions as the animal carcasses raced past them. The gang boss or

15. Schirmer, *City Divided*, 59–61.

16. Scholars in the past two decades have begun to assess the impact of the migration on northern and midwestern communities. For example, see Carole Marks, *Farewell, We're Good and Gone: The Great Black Migration;* and Joe William Trotter Jr., ed., *The Great Migration in Historical Perspective: New Dimensions of Race, Class and Gender.*

17. U.S. Department of Commerce, Bureau of the Census, Thirteenth Census, Fourteenth Census.

foreman, with the interests of the company often foremost in his mind, determined the pace of the work. More workers were required, but they could be paid less than their skilled predecessors. Skill was no longer necessary, and race or country of origin did not disqualify one from employment. Few descriptions have survived of the work experience in Kansas City's meat-processing industry, although it can be reasonably assumed that the nature of the work was the same as it was in Chicago or Omaha or other centers of the industry. Work for most employees was physically demanding, dirty, bloody, and potentially hazardous. Melvin Tolson, a graduate of Kansas City's Lincoln High School, described his work experiences in the packinghouses in 1918 in the summer before he went off to Fisk University in Tennessee. In his recollection, written as one of his popular "Caviar and Cabbage" columns for the *Washington Tribune*, Tolson describes the arduous conditions, physical demands, and interracial camaraderie of the packinghouse. Also evident was the working-class enthusiasm that drove much of Tolson's writing as an adult:

> I hated the packing house world. I intended to escape through my college training. The men called me The Kid. They admired my toughness. The Boss boasted about me. He said The Company liked men like me. I usually ate my supper at midnight. You see, I was so tired when I got home that I went to sleep.
>
> The Boss promoted me. I became a loader of refrigerator cars. I could heave a quarter-beef to a hook. I got time-and-a-half for overtime. I was coming up in The Company. Sometimes, when there was a rush, bosses from the Big Office in long white coats came down to the docks. I was the lightest loader and the fastest. Later, I would overhear the bosses cursing the bigger and older hands. I saw the reason for that ten years later. . . .
>
> We worked under miserable conditions. Men stood in water all day. They were always scared of losing their jobs. Most of them bowed under debts. We had the eight-hour day, but we were killing as many hogs in eight hours as we'd killed in ten. This was the SPEED UP. The men grumbled, cursed.
>
> I was on The Tub. Five men set the pace for ten thousand workers in the packing house. First, there was the huge German downstairs who stuck the hogs as they passed on a long chain. In five minutes, he was covered with blood. He drank blood—and said nothing to anybody. Everybody feared him. Some said he'd cut a man's throat as soon as a hog's.
>
> Second, there was the Negro dropper. He stood above The Tub and dropped hogs from a turntable into tons of boiling water. He

> sang blues as he set the killing pace. One day I tried to do his job. A mammoth hog, in its death agony, almost hurled me into the Tub.
>
> Third, there was Old Man Jeff. Old-timers said he was slipping, yet he could souse hogs faster than a cat can lick its paw. Fourth, there was the little Mexican who hooked the hogs to the dehairing machine.[18] His hands were faster than Joe Louis' punches. Fifth, there was the big black man who split the hogs. With one mighty blow, he could half a 600-pounder. Stripped to the waist, his huge muscles worked like big ebony snakes.
>
> These five men who set the killing pace received big wages.[19]

In Kansas City, Africans Americans, native whites, and foreign-born whites each composed about one-third of the ten thousand men recorded as packinghouse or stockyard employees in the two Kansas Cities. Not surprisingly, however, race and occupational status were linked within the world of the packinghouse. Foreign-born and African American males were overrepresented in the unskilled and low-skilled jobs within the plants. Almost twenty-eight hundred black men (almost equally split between Kansas City, Missouri, and Kansas City, Kansas, residents) were listed in this category, accounting for more than 40 percent of the unskilled labor in the plant. Foreign-born whites made up just more than one-third of the unskilled workers employed. Native-born whites, not surprisingly, dominated the skilled positions: forty-two African Americans and seventy-nine foreign-born whites were counted among the almost seven hundred foremen, skilled butchers, and managers listed by the census. Semiskilled positions, however, were open to both African Americans and eastern Europeans. More than eight hundred black men and nine hundred foreign-born men filled these positions, representing almost two-thirds of the total.

The packinghouses drew unskilled workers from various parts of the black community. L. J. Blaso, a thirty year old from Texas, lived at

18. Workers of Mexican descent provided one of the quandaries for census workers in the 1920s. The census did not count Hispanic individuals as a separate category, and census takers apparently used their discretion in plugging those individuals into U.S. society's racial categories. The result, in Kansas City, is that some Hispanics living on the West Side were counted as black. Thus, we have repeated references to "black" individuals born in Mexico with parents of Mexican nativity.

19. Robert M. Farnsworth, ed., *Caviar and Cabbage: Selected Columns by Melvin B. Tolson from the "Washington Tribune," 1937–1944*, 246. After eventually graduating from Lincoln College in Pennsylvania, Tolson went on to teach at all-black colleges in Texas and Oklahoma. While teaching at Langston College, Tolson was elected six times as mayor of Langston, Oklahoma, as well as receiving acclaim for his poetry and prose. His 1939 work *Dark Symphony* won the National Book Award prize for poetry. Later in his life, he was recognized as the poet laureate of the African nation of Liberia.

Eleventh and Lydia Streets. James Giles, forty-four, lived at Twenty-sixth and Highland. Chester White, a twenty-three-year-old Mississippi native, lived with his twenty-two-year-old wife, Bessie, a native of Louisiana, at Tenth and Harrison.

Many of the workers tended to be young, single, and renters. Jeff Crosby, a thirty-one-year-old single male from Mississippi, rented a room at Sixteenth and Central. Two packinghouse employees, thirty-year-old George Hughes from Texas and twenty-nine-year-old John Fortson from Tennessee, rented rooms in the 1200 block of Woodland. James Whitney and R. Wilson made the trek from their households in the 1300 block of The Paseo. Three laborers—eighteen-year-old Robert Wright, possibly a recent migrant from Texas; twenty-four-year-old Eddie Edwards, who grew up in Kansas; and thirty-six-year-old John Harris of Mississippi—rented rooms around Fourteenth and Euclid. A black man living on West Prospect on Kansas City's West Side, thirty-year-old Adolph Holder, a packinghouse laborer, found a job in the packinghouses for his seventeen-year-old brother-in-law, David Miles.

One of the illuminating examples of the black working-class experience in the Kansas City area is that of forty-five-year-old Anthony Hoskin of 1710 East Thirteenth Street. Hoskin, a semiliterate laborer, was born in Tennessee in 1884 or 1885, but his family apparently made its home in Arkansas. Hoskin's wife, Katie, was born in Arkansas, as were both of their children, ten-year-old son Clarence and nine-year-old son William. When the family arrived in Kansas City, Anthony found work with the packinghouses, and Katie began taking in laundry. The household also included sixty-two-year-old Mary Jones, who is listed in the census as Anthony's mother but apparently was his mother-in-law, and nineteen-year-old Lonnie Williams, who is listed as Anthony's grandson. Lonnie Williams was also employed in the packinghouses as a laborer. Nearby lived Frank Moore, a forty-six-year-old immigrant from Arkansas, and his wife. Frank Moore also worked in the packinghouses.

The manuscript census leaves three questions unanswered: Did Anthony Hoskin and Frank Moore bring their families north as part of the Great Migration, or did they arrive in Kansas City before World War I? Did they know each other in Arkansas, or did they coincidentally land in the same block of Thirteenth Street? Did they find work at the same meatpacking facility, or were they working apart?

Historians studying the Great Migration have shown how networks of migration developed in the South, with extended families, neighborhoods, and, on occasion, entire church congregations deserting the South and moving north. Scholars of the black experience in northern cities have also demonstrated how networks of family and friends often determined residential patterns and employment opportunities. The fact that the youngest of the two children listed as living with Hoskin was born in Arkansas in 1910 or 1911 suggests that the family likely was a recent addition to Kansas City's African American community, but definitive answers to these questions remain elusive.

The sheer size of the packinghouse operations provided work opportunities for African Americans of various skills and of various ages. Tim Jackson, the thirty-seven-year-old nephew of Lena Bradley, was trained as a butcher, as were Perry Crowder, thirty-nine, of the 2600 block of Highland; Biddell Enyart, a twenty-six-year-old native of Missouri who lived with his mother in the 1800 block of Terrace; and Henry Sutton, a twenty-eight-year-old single man from Arkansas who rented a room in the 1300 block of Lydia. Ester Davis, a twenty-two-year-old man born in Missouri, worked as a carpenter. Jackson and Davis both lived in the 1100 block of Vine Street. Men unable to keep pace with the work of the killing floor might find other employment opportunities in the industry. Sixty-five-year-old B. Merritt, of the 1000 block of Harrison, worked at a packinghouse as an elevator operator. The example of W. J. Jackson, who retired from the packinghouses in 1921, also is illustrative. Jackson, a native of Spring Hill, Alabama, came to Kansas City in 1893. Then just twenty-one years old, he began working in the packinghouses for fifteen cents an hour. He was soon transferred to work in the meat coolers before receiving a promotion to janitor in the company office. Finally, he took over the company's employee restaurant, where he served until his retirement. Jackson recalled a frightening moment as a packinghouse worker. He said he narrowly escaped the flood of 1903, which inundated much of the West Bottoms, by traversing the chute by which cattle were led into the packinghouse.[20]

Many African Americans preferred to live on the West Side, near the packinghouses. The West Side district of Kansas City extends from the state line east to Summit Street. Although the smells from the West Bottoms could be overpowering, living in the area from the state line east to Summit Street made walking to work practicable.[21] For example,

20. Office of Housing and Community Development, *The Spirit of Freedom: A Profile of the History of Blacks in Kansas City, Missouri,* 11; *Kansas City Sun,* September 17, 1921.

21. Walking out of the West Bottoms could be as hazardous as working in the packinghouses, though. At least one worker was killed walking home from his job with one of the meat packers, and Oliver Watts, a Texan, employed at the Peet Brothers soap-making factory near the stockyards, was killed by a passing car as he walked along one of the viaducts. Watts lived near Seventeenth Street and Vine on Kansas City's East Side. U.S. Department of Commerce, Bureau of the Census, Fourteenth Census; *Hoyes City Directory* (1920).

four residences in the 2000 block of Belleview Street, two blocks west of Summit, contained five packinghouse employees, including two African Americans employed as butchers, Andrew Wooten and John Work.

The home at 1738 Madison contained eight adults; all six of the men were employed in the packinghouses. Amanda Basy, who lived in the 1700 block of West Prospect on the West Side, worked as a waitress in the packinghouses; one of her four tenants was a packinghouse laborer.

One of the more fortunate African Americans in the packinghouses was John Price, who lived with his wife and three daughters at 1722 Belleview. Price, a forty-seven-year-old native of Missouri, had gained the status of foreman. Nearby in the 1800 block of Terrace, Oscar Gilham was employed as a packinghouse laborer, as were his sons Dewey, twenty-one, and Sam, fourteen.

The packinghouses also employed a few women, most of them foreign born or African American. Amanda Basy worked as a waitress, presumably in the packinghouse lunchroom, but most of the women likely were employed in arduous and demeaning work. According to a U.S. Department of Labor study conducted at the end of the war, African American women were employed in all capacities of the packinghouse operation except for the butchering and inspecting of meat. They trimmed, sorted, and graded different portions of the carcasses; they prepared and cured the meats, and were involved in all portions of tanning of the hides. One of the less pleasant duties of female packinghouse workers was the task of cleaning and separating the viscera.[22] Thirty-four-year-old Lillie Jenison of 1812 Summit lists her occupation in the 1920 census as bone cleaner at a packinghouse (husband Ira was employed as a tank filler at the packinghouse). It was one of the few positions on the killing floor that did not require speed and strength. Thus, this tedious and demeaning job fell primarily to female workers.

Meatpacking workers faced the potential of serious bodily injury while dealing with living creatures weighing several hundred pounds or more. Workers also risked being scalded by the boiling water or losing a limb in the jaws of the machinery. One misstep could be fatal. William Porter, twenty-four and married, was killed when he was drawn into the machinery in the bone house of the Morris and Company plant.[23]

Wages in the packinghouses did not compensate for the physical dangers. At the end of World War I, unskilled laborers (about two-thirds

22. U.S. Department of Labor, *The Negro and Work during the World War and Reconstruction*, 126; Greene and Woodson, *The Negro Wage Earner*, 272–73.

23. *Kansas City Sun*, January 14, 1922. Porter lived on the Kansas side, just west of the packinghouse district.

of the employees) in the city's meat-processing industry were making 45¢ an hour or $3.60 for an eight-hour day.[24]

The wage rate had increased during the war, and packinghouse operators looked in the first years of the 1920s to cut wages. Owners were offering a reduced wage of 37¢ an hour ($3.00 a day), a pay cut that laborers—both black and white—found unacceptable. On December 5, 1921, more than six hundred members of the Amalgamated Meat Cutters and Butcher Workmen walked out of the plant. One of the key organizers of the walkout was an African American minister, G. W. Reed of 2736 Highland.[25]

Reed, who had toured the Midwest in the years after the war preaching the virtues of an eight-hour day and the value of collective strength, apparently was instrumental in organizing African American workers in the Kansas City plants. Reed's work did not escape the attention of the meatpacking owners, either. He was targeted by police, and in late January or early February 1922, Reed was arrested and charged with carrying concealed weapons. His arrest and trial were anticlimactic; on February 1, the strike ended and laborers returned to the packinghouses—at the lower wage.[26]

Packinghouse workers held a unique place within the occupational hierarchy of black Kansas City before World War II. Although to an outside middle-class observer such as the Urban League author the work performed in the packinghouses was demeaning, it is important to remember that for many African Americans in Kansas City, the wages paid by Armour, Wilson, and others were a step toward a better future. By saving and with careful planning, a packinghouse worker could find the wherewithal to improve his or her personal lot. The case of John X. Brown, mentioned in Chapter One, is just one example. Professionals such as doctors, lawyers, teachers, and clergy, as well as members of several service occupations such as barbers and railroad porters, might hold pride of place among black wage earners, but the development of Kansas City's African American community rested in large part on the work of those laboring on the killing floor.

Railroad porters held a special but conflicted role within African American communities in the 1920s and 1930s. Their job often required

24. *Labor Herald*, January 6, 1922.
25. Ibid.; *Kansas City Sun*, July 2, 1921.
26. *Kansas City Sun*, February 4, 1922; *Labor Herald*, February 3, 1922.

them to live down to racial stereotypes of the time, yet they were held in esteem by many segments of the black community because of their job's fringe benefits and relatively high wages. Within the railroads' work culture, their ritualized jobs were menial and degrading. The performance of their duties—and their wages and tips—often relied on flattering, subservient, and even obsequious behavior. Porters were often asked to conduct themselves in ways that met the lowest expectations of and lived up to the racial stereotypes held by the railroads' white passengers. Porters were treated like personal servants, and they held no identity of their own. To white passengers, all black porters were simply "George."

Yet within the black community, many veteran porters adopted a professional demeanor, consistently demonstrating the pride they took in their work inside and outside the Pullman cars. They traveled and saw parts of the country that their friends at home could experience only vicariously; for example, James T. Steele, a railroad porter based in Los Angeles, recalled that he visited 48 states and 155 principal cities while employed by the Pullman Company from 1936 to 1960. Within the African American communities, the porters and railroad waiters constituted a kind of "aristocracy of [black] labor."[27]

When summer came and railroad transportation increased, many young black males took temporary jobs as Pullman porters to finance their college education. Harlem Renaissance poet Claude McKay and future NAACP leader Roy Wilkins were just two notable African Americans to temporarily hold railroad service jobs.[28]

The confluence of changes in the transportation industry along with whites' perceptions of African Americans opened the doors for black participation in railroad service. Before and for several years after the Civil War, railroad passenger accommodations were primitive, and few railroads offered eating or sleeping arrangements aboard trains. To obtain meals, railroad passengers either had to race off the car and grab a hasty meal at a stop or had to buy food from vendors who came aboard. This began to change during the 1870s and 1880s when George Mortimer Pullman helped popularize dining-car service on the nation's

27. Beth Tompkins Bates, *Pullman Porters and the Rise of Protest Politics in Black America, 1925–1945*, 20, 23–25.

28. Eric Arnesen, *Brotherhoods of Color: Black Railroad Workers and the Struggle for Equality*, 24. See also William B. Thomas and Kevin J. Moran, "The Illusions of Aristocracy: Intra-racial Divisions in a Racist Labour Market, 1910–1930"; and David D. Perata, *Those Pullman Blues: An Oral History of the African American Railroad Attendant*, 69.

railroads. Dining and sleeping spaces were separated, and the dining car—complete with kitchen, pantry, wine cellar, removable tables, and African American porters and waiters—became a fixture in the railroad industry.

Pullman then introduced the railroad car for which he would become famous: the Pullman sleeper. Instead of sleeping in their seats or on hard benches, passengers willing to pay extra could sleep on one of two pullout berths in separate compartments in each car. Pullman sought, in the sleeping car, to emulate the conveniences of fine hotels. His sleeping cars offered plush accommodations as well as high-quality personal service. The railroad porter was asked and expected to fulfill most of his customers' wishes. By the beginning of the twentieth century, most Pullman car porters were African American men, and their work fell into four categories.[29]

The busboy and the café–food service attendant had similar responsibilities, working in food preparation, waiting on tables, and resetting them. The attendant might also be asked to double on sleeping-car berths that combined sleeping compartments with a buffet section. The sleeping-car porter was responsible solely for the sleeping car. He made up the compartments while the train sat in the rail yard, he greeted passengers, and he helped them get settled. He was responsible for monitoring the car's air-conditioning and heating systems, for cleaning rooms, and for making up beds. He was also expected to shine shoes, press suits, mail letters, and send telegrams. After 1920, he was expected to provide entertainment for the passengers. Porters with the most experience and expertise were handpicked to serve as private-car porters. They worked on special cars and assignments, serving presidents, celebrities, and dignitaries.

Kansas City claimed 465 railroad porters in its 1920 population, and almost 9 out of 10 of them were African American.[30] Many of them were veterans with the Pullman Company. Cicero Smith of 1320 Michigan worked as a Pullman porter for more than thirty years before he died in 1920. Frank Duncan had more than twenty years of experience before his death in 1923.[31] Other porters were just getting started. Paul Smith, the nineteen-year-old son of plumber Lewis Smith, likely was just learning the trade in 1920. Porters lived throughout Kansas City's black communities, but because of the nature of their occupation,

29. Arnesen, *Brotherhoods of Color*, 24–26.
30. U.S. Department of Commerce, Bureau of the Census, Fourteenth Census, table 2.
31. *Kansas City Sun*, December 20, 1919; December 23, 1923.

few sought permanent homes. Augustus Allen was an exception; he and his wife, Julia, owned their home at 2648 Highland. Their son and daughter-in-law shared the residence. Other porters found more temporary arrangements. J. B. Taylor, a forty-five-year-old porter from Louisiana, and his wife rented rooms at 2608 Highland. Clarence Ewing, the twenty-eight-year-old stepson of Henry Brooks, lived with the family on West Prospect. J. W. Peach, a forty-nine-year-old Pullman porter, rented a room from John Gaskings and his family on East Eleventh Street. Ira Booker and his wife rented a home in the 2400 block of Highland. D. A. Campbell and his wife rented a room(s) from William McKnight, a waiter, and his wife on Woodland Avenue. Charles Brice, a sixty-three-year-old veteran porter, and his wife rented a small home in the 1300 block of Vine. Leon Hill, thirty-four, from Texas, and his wife rented a home in the 1000 block of Virginia; they shared the dwelling with at least two other families. Keneth Mason, a thirty-two-year-old Kansan employed by the Pullman Company, was one of four roomers listed as living with Dave and Alice Buckner in one of the third-floor units of a residence in the 1300 block of Euclid. In the same residence, forty-one-year-old porter James McCall was one of six residents of a first-floor unit.

One of Kansas City's most well-known porters was also one of its most successful residents. George Fowler, who owned a two-story frame residence at 2203 Flora Avenue, had worked for the Pullman Company for seven years—most of it on the Santa Fe Railroad run between Kansas City and Wichita, Kansas. Before joining the railroad, he owned and operated businesses at Twenty-third, Terrace, and Vine and built apartment buildings at 907 and 909 East Eighteenth Street. He also owned other property in Kansas City as well as in Kansas City, Kansas. But the lure of travel or the access to prominent and wealthy people may have drawn Fowler—as it did other African Americans—to the job of porter.[32]

The porters, like most of the occupational groups in Kansas City's black communities, supported a variety of churches and fraternal organizations. Cicero Smith was a member of the Second Baptist Church. When the porters organized their annual memorial service in 1923, they had their pick of black churches to use; Vine Street Baptist was eventually selected.[33]

32. Ibid., March 12, 1921. Fowler's wife, Laura, was held up at gunpoint by two burglars. They reportedly made off with more than five thousand dollars worth of jewelry and cash taken from the Fowlers' safe.

33. Ibid., April 24, 1920; May 19, 1923.

Kansas City's role as a railroad hub undoubtedly was a factor in the size of its Pullman porter population. It also meant that the industry spawned some related enterprises. Most notable was a laundry operated by the Pullman Company at Twenty-fifth Street and Southwest Boulevard. The laundry employed at least sixty-five African American men and women.[34]

The biggest concerns for the Pullman porters were working conditions and wages. In 1925, Pullman porters were paid $67.50 a month; the rest of their wages was generated by tips. To receive his full monthly salary, a porter had to put in four hundred hours on the job to make the eleven thousand miles of travel required by the company. As early as 1919, porters in Kansas City were asked to form the second local of the Railway Men's International Benevolent Industrial Association, an independent Chicago-based black labor federation organized by former porter Robert Mays. The Chicago group attempted to bring all black railroad employees—not just porters—together in one big union, but the effort disintegrated by 1924 when met by the Pullman Company's counterattack. The company used spies, fired union activists, and created a company union, the Pullman Porters Benefit Association (PPBA) to drive a wedge between its employees and any labor organization.[35]

None of the porter labor organizations succeeded against the might of the Pullman Company until the Brotherhood of Sleeping Car Porters (BSCP) was finally recognized by the company in 1935 as the porters' official representative.[36] The ten-year battle between the BSCP and the Pullman Company reached into Kansas City's African American communities. In 1929, the company conducted three weeks of closed meetings in Chicago with representatives of its union, the PPBA. The company union asked that porters' wages be raised to $100 a month (still short of the BSCP's demand of a $155 monthly salary). The company responded by offering a raise of $5 a month, and in June 1929 Pullman officials announced that the company union's representatives had "accepted" the offer.

Ashley L. Totten, assistant general organizer of the BSCP, had been sent to Kansas City to organize the porters, but he returned to Chicago to monitor the "talks" between the company and its union. "The company

34. Ibid., December 23, 1922; May 5, 19, 1923.

35. Ibid., December 20, 1919; Arnesen, *Brotherhoods of Color,* 54–62, 119.

36. For the full story of the lengthy battle between the Pullman Company and the Brotherhood of Sleeping Car Porters, see Arnesen, *Brotherhoods of Color,* 42–150; and Jervis Anderson, *A. Philip Randolph: A Biographical Portrait.*

employed its bullying, browbeating method of intimidation, and its agents among the porters told the men they would receive a substantial increase at the conference. . . . Instead they got an increase of five dollars a month, or slightly less than 17 cents a day," Totten reported. "This conference ought to prove to any doubters that the company union, organized and controlled by the Pullman company, can never truly represent the porters and maids."[37]

Pullman porters who advocated an independent union also became targets of violent reprisals. In April 1930, J. H. Wilkins, a porter from Kansas City, was either pulled or lured away from his coach on the Kansas City–Florida special. His body was found several hundred yards away from the tracks in Locust Grove, Oklahoma. Although Pullman and railway officials conducted an investigation, no arrests had been made nor had any suspects been identified six weeks later. A mass meeting at Vine Street Baptist Church, under the auspices of the BSCP, started a campaign for an independent investigation. New York attorney Frank P. Walsh, a labor activist in Kansas City early in the twentieth century, was retained to head the investigation.[38]

Totten's success as a union organizer had also made him a marked man in Kansas City. From the BSCP office in the Lincoln Building, Totten fought against company pressure to bring black porters into his union. On April 13, 1929, as he walked along Tracy Avenue, Totten was struck from behind. Lying on the ground, bleeding and stunned, Totten received another blow across the face. The assailant, who was scared off by a crowd drawn by the screams of Totten's companion, was later identified as a cook who worked for Ellis Burton, a prominent figure in Kansas City's criminal world.[39]

The railroads also offered employment to African Americans in the rail yards and along the rail lines. More than 2,500 men from Kansas City were employed by the railroads as laborers; almost one-fourth of them were African Americans. John Frazier, thirty-four, and O. Willis, forty-three, both lived in the 900 block of Charlotte in 1920. The railroads, at least during the First World War, also offered employment opportunities to African American women. The women filled unskilled

37. *Kansas City Call*, June 7, 1929.

38. Ibid., May 16, 1930. Arnesen (*Brotherhoods of Color*) notes that acts of violence against pro-BSCP porters were not uncommon, although the Wilkins case is an extreme example.

39. *Kansas City Call*, April 19, June 7, 1929. Totten, as well as *Call* publisher Chester A. Franklin, believed Burton was the "middle man" in the attack. The source of the money that was allegedly given Totten's assailant was never determined.

positions in the railroad yards and roundhouses; the Santa Fe employed African American women as roundhouse laborers in Kansas City as well as Emporia, Kansas.[40]

Kansas City's African American communities contained a significant population of janitors and domestic workers. The 1920 census lists 822 African American males working as janitors in Kansas City, or more than half of the 1,461 recorded by the census. If employment in the packinghouses was inevitably dirty, and in Pullman cars sometimes demeaning, working as a janitor or domestic could be both. It also was low paying.

Yet, for some African American men, working as a janitor was a strategy toward obtaining security for themselves and their families. The job offered steady wages through the 1920s and 1930s as well as often providing much-needed living space for black men and their families. A number of apartment buildings throughout Kansas City employed African American janitors, with a room in the building apparently part of the benefits of the job. The space undoubtedly was the least desirable in the building, but as living space for African Americans became scarce, many families likely welcomed the opportunity for a place they did not have to share with other individuals or families.

Most of these live-in janitors found housing on the fringes or completely outside the major African American communities in Kansas City. Charles Smallwood, fifty, was the janitor for an apartment building in the 3200 block of Gilham Road. He shared the janitorial duties with his thirty-two-year-old son, Willie. Forty-three-year-old Bruton Andrews and his wife were janitor and housekeeper for rooms in the 3200 block of Van Trump Court (near Linwood Boulevard and Cherry Street). William Walker, a thirty-five-year-old Missouri native, was employed as the janitor at 3806 Walnut. He and his wife, Ethel, lived on the premises. Jefferson Walker (no relation) was a sixty-year-old janitor for a building in the 3600 block of Forest. He lived there with his wife, Maggie, fifty. Henry Smith, sixty-eight, lived with his wife, Elizabeth, fifty, in a rear apartment in the 1600 block of Broadway. Henry was the janitor for the building. Tom Andrews, a twenty-eight-year-old from South Carolina, was the janitor for a building in the 1800 block of Jefferson. His wife, Irene, a twenty-eight-year-old native of Texas, was the building's maid. Ray Jeffers, a twenty-eight-year-old African American male from Iowa,

40. Arnesen, *Brotherhoods of Color*, 46.

was the janitor for apartments on West Thirteenth Street. The census records indicate that Jeffers was married, but no spouse is listed.

Although the census does not indicate how many African American women were employed as janitors, it is obvious that on occasion wives or single women took over janitorial responsibilities completely. Marie Brown, thirty-three, was the janitor for apartments in the 400 block of West Thirty-fourth. She lived there with her husband, Carson, a laborer for the Kansas City Bolt and Nut Company.

By the time of the 1930 census (a few months after the October 1929 stock-market crash and the onset of the Great Depression), the number of male janitors counted in Kansas City, Missouri, had increased by 50 percent (to 2,374). African Americans accounted for almost two-thirds of that increase; there were 1,429 black janitors counted in the census, or 607 more than a decade earlier. Kansas City's Urban League office, whose mission was to increase employment opportunities for African Americans, responded to this increase by taking a page out of Booker T. Washington's philosophy: if black Kansas Citians were going to be janitors, they should be the best janitors possible. In 1932, the Urban League office instituted the Janitor Training School.

The philosophy behind the course was best expressed in an unsigned and undated news clipping contained in an Urban League scrapbook, written around the time the first class was to graduate. The anonymous author argued that the graduates of the course, by increasing their knowledge and skill levels, had also increased their opportunities for better wages. Yet financial rewards were not to be the only incentive; a firm belief in the Protestant work ethic contained its own benefits. "Every step toward more skill among Negro workers is a gain," the article stated. "If there was no higher wage to be hoped for, still it would be a gain, because in doing his job the best way the worker gets satisfaction out of life."[41]

The workers who advanced through the janitor school also were performing a vital service for the race. "Improving our industrial standing is an essential worth our best thinking and effort," the article said. Implicit in the brief article's conclusion was an understanding of the perceptions of black workers held by many white Americans of the time. By excelling at that chosen occupation, African American janitors, it

41. KCULP, "More Skilled Workers," box 3, undated item in "Scrapbook." The clipping appears to be from the *Kansas City Call,* and the opinions expressed are consistent with those of the *Call*'s publisher, Chester A. Franklin.

was hoped, could help dispel many of the stereotypical opinions held by the outside society. "By all means," the article concluded, "let the janitor school go on until in this city there will be janitors who are known to be as good as any, with records behind them to prove it."[42]

The first class of men began meeting on November 1, 1932. More than 170 janitors were enrolled in the first year of classes, and on an average night, 115 were in attendance. For eight straight Tuesdays, the janitors met at the Urban League offices at 1905 Vine Street for a series of lectures delivered by professionals from various Kansas City industries. The lecturers were authorities in the practical aspects of the janitorial trade; they discussed heating systems, engineering, fuel consumption, architecture, and sanitation. One stirring talk was on the "importance of the fuse." The social aspects of the job were also addressed. Topics covered also included employee-employer relations and race relations.[43] On January 10, 1933, the first class of 61 janitors graduated. Commencement ceremonies were held in front of a packed house at the Paseo YMCA gymnasium. Chester A. Franklin, editor and publisher of the *Kansas City Call,* was the featured speaker.[44]

Several larger questions remain to be asked. What drove 61 men to give up one night a week to learn the practical skills needed to perform a low-paying, dirty job (albeit one of the few options for many black men during the Depression)? According to one press account, most of the men were "janitors of experience" and came highly recommended. Did their employers require their attendance, or were they there of their own free will? Did the men see the course as a route to a better life? And what kind of an impact did the course have on their lives?[45]

Using city directories, an attempt was made to identify each of the 61 graduates and provide some tentative answers to the questions above.[46] Six of the graduates were listed as janitors in 1932, before they

42. Ibid.

43. *Kansas City Call,* January 6, 1933.

44. KCULP, "Minutes, 20 December 1932," Urban League Minutes, Board of Directors, box M1, vol. 1, 1932; *Kansas City Call,* January 13, 1933.

45. KCULP, "Industry Shows Growing Interest in Janitors' School of Efficiency" (1934), box N1, file 2.

46. Attempts were made to track participants in the janitor school in each of three years: in 1932 (before they enrolled in the janitor school); in 1933, after their graduation; and in 1938, five years after the commencement exercises but before the outbreak of World War II altered the job market. City directories have limits, however, particularly when dealing with the congested housing conditions of black Kansas City in the 1930s. The directories, when dealing with single-family structures converted into multifamily dwellings, list just one head of household and possibly a spouse. Also complicating the identification process was the 1930s convention of using initials rather than full first and middle names. When multiple possibilities existed for a match, all were discarded. The directories also did

started the class. Three possibilities exist: they enrolled in the janitor school at the request of their employers, they wanted to gain additional skills to secure their job in an unstable job market, or they sought skills that might allow them to improve their job status. Four of the 6 were listed as janitors in the 1933 directory. Gus Goff, a janitor at the Meyer Building in 1932, was listed as a laborer in 1933, as was William N. Milton.[47] Just 2 of these 6 were listed as janitors for all three years sampled: Moses Allen, custodian at the Urban League offices, and George Faulkner. One of the 4 graduates mentioned in both 1932 and 1933—Clarence Peniston—was not listed in the city directory for 1938. The last of the 4, Daniel C. Houston, however, had moved up in the world: he had lived in the janitor's basement apartment in a building on Linwood Terrace in 1932 and 1933, but by 1938 he had moved into a home at 1008 Virginia and was working as a meat cutter.

Some of the graduates apparently took advantage of the janitor school (and possibly the Urban League's employment services) and quickly secured employment to display their skills. Eight more graduates were listed as janitors in 1933, but how secure those positions were is open to challenge. Five of the 8 could not be identified in the 1938 directory, and another was listed as a laborer. Of the 8, Eugene Hatcher and Vernon Scott were the only graduates still working as janitors five years later. Surprisingly, however, at least 6 of the graduates tapped into their knowledge and gained janitorial jobs (and often the basement apartment that went with it) by 1938. Among them were Manuel (sometimes Emanuel) Vanzant, who had worked as a cook and laborer before becoming the janitor at the Broadfair Apartments on Broadway; Carter Perry, a laborer in 1932 who lived and presumably worked in apartments on The Paseo; Grant Mason, who lived in the janitor's basement apartment at 1214 Garfield; and Matthew Williams, janitor at 4114–16 The Paseo (he too lived in the basement apartment).

Just 20 of the 61 graduates were listed as janitors in the three years sampled, but among the other 29 graduates identified were several

---

not always list an occupation for each head of household, and the accuracy of the occupations listed can be suspect, particularly among those on the bottom rungs of the economic ladder. Despite those obstacles, I identified all but twelve of the graduates in at least one of the three years (see Appendix B for a list of the graduates). The most positive identifications made for any one year was 38 in 1933, the year after graduation. Just 24 matches could be made with any certainty in 1932, and a little more than half (31) of the graduates could be found five years later. Just 16 of the graduates could be identified for all three years selected, but the number is sufficient to allow us to draw some tentative conclusions about the motivations of the men attending the class.

47. Goff was listed as an elevator operator in 1938; Milton was not listed.

intriguing stories. LeRoy Grant, who lived on the West Side, was identified as a pastor in 1938, and one of the graduates may have worked as a Pullman porter before entering the janitor school in 1932. But possibly the most successful of the graduates were the Rose brothers, Robert R. and James B. Neither of the brothers could be identified in the 1932 city directory, but both are listed as laborers in 1933 when they and their spouses shared a dwelling in the 2400 block of East Twenty-third Street. Five years later, the Rose brothers were working as butchers and had moved into homes in the 2300 block of Olive. Robert and his wife, Louella, were listed as owning their home at 2325 Olive. James Rose and his wife, Jessie, were listed as living at 2323 Olive. Whether James and Jessie had purchased their home was not listed.

The first janitor school, it is apparent, attracted a wide spectrum of men with various degrees of skill and ambition. As in any setting, those with the proper motivation and ambition will benefit from any learning experience. The Rose brothers are a prime example of that fact.

Urban League officials apparently believed the school was beneficial; in the fall of 1933, a new group of janitors started a twelve-week course, in which 28 experts in a variety of fields addressed the men. More than 100 men enrolled in the course, but when graduation was held January 18, 1934, just 40 men received diplomas.[48]

By 1935, when the fourth set of sessions was held, the janitor school curriculum was pretty much set. The classes started with a mass meeting at Bethel AME Church, followed three days later by a meeting at the Urban League offices, where janitorial equipment was on exhibit and demonstrated. Then came twelve weekly sessions on such maintenance esoterica as "rug cleaning," "lubricating oils," and "combustion." The students also took field trips to the Power and Light Company, the Kansas City Water Works, and the Sears and Roebuck store at Fifteenth and Cleveland.[49]

What happened to the janitor school? In October 1936, the Urban League reported that 36 men on average were attending classes each week. In that year, the janitors were offered a special class in box refrig-

48. *Topeka Plaindealer,* January 12, 1934; *Kansas City American,* January 19, 1934; KCULP, "Scrapbook," box KCULP3, file 1.

49. KCULP, "Building Supervision and Management" (circa 1930), box KCULP3, file 1, ii; KCULP, "1935 Janitor Training School," box PPE1, file 1; KCULP, *Pilot* 11:9 (September 30, 1937). The janitor school caught the attention of the black press as well as mainstream media. The *Kansas City Call, Kansas City American, Topeka Plaindealer,* and *Pittsburgh Press* (all black weeklies) carried regular items on the progress of the school. The mainstream *Kansas City Star* and *Kansas City Journal-Post* both carried short news items on the start of the second session in 1933.

eration taught by the building-maintenance instructor from the R. T. Coles High School. The school was offered for a fifth year in 1937 and again in 1938. Surviving Urban League records from the period do not indicate whether the school was offered after that time. It is apparent, however, that the janitor school served a need within Kansas City's labor market; throughout the Depression, janitors' jobs were among the most frequently filled by the KCUL's employment services. Nevertheless, the janitors' training likely still did not qualify them for a living wage. In August 1933, an industrial code submitted to the federal government under the Wagner Act sought to limit the number of hours for Kansas City's janitors, house men, window cleaners, and maids to forty-eight per week. It also sought a pay raise for the 2,700 men and women in those occupations to the less-than-princely sum of fifty dollars a month.[50]

Most African American women employed in Kansas City in the years after World War I worked in domestic or personal service. Of the more than 6,400 African American working women in 1920, almost 88 percent (5,629) were employed in service occupations. The five largest categories for black women's work fell under the general heading of domestic and personal service. In other words, the 247 African American women employed in Kansas City as actors, music teachers, charity and welfare workers, teachers, trained nurses, and other professional occupations stood as a minority within a minority. They represented just 4 percent of the African American working women counted by the census and just 1.6 percent of all African American females.

Historians Jacqueline Jones, Elizabeth Clark Lewis, and Tera W. Hunter, among others, have addressed the work and working conditions of African American women in domestic and personal service.[51] If given a choice, they note, most of these African American women opted for taking in laundry. In Kansas City—as in Atlanta; Washington, DC; and elsewhere in the country—by bringing laundry work into the home African American women gained a measure of control over the pace and conditions of their work; it also allowed them some degree of flexibility in dealing with the needs of family while at the same time providing much-needed income. Lula Hill, thirty-one, of the 1000 block of Virginia, did laundry work to supplement the income of her husband, a Pullman porter. Eva Whitney, a twenty-nine-year-old native of Tennessee,

50. KCULP, *Pilot* 11:8 (August 31, 1937), box KCULP1, file 18; *Kansas City Call*, August 11, 1933; KCULP, "Monthly Report, October 1936," box M1, vol. 1.

51. See Jones, *Labor of Love, Labor of Sorrow;* Clark-Lewis, *Living In, Living Out: African American Domestics in Washington, D.C., 1910–1940;* and Hunter, *To 'Joy My Freedom.*

provided a second income in the household she shared with her husband, a packinghouse worker, and their fourteen-year-old daughter.

For some women, their income as laundresses was essential for survival. Wanda Johnson, a thirty-five-year-old widow living on Tenth Street, washed laundry to support herself, her fifteen-year-old daughter, and her eleven-year-old son. Her fifty-nine-year-old uncle contributed to the household income as a coal peddler, but Johnson's income undoubtedly sustained the family. Mattie Woods, a thirty-year-old widow living in the 1400 block of Main, took in laundry as the sole support of herself and her four children. Often, laundresses shared the same residence and undoubtedly some of the work. Mary Hall, fifty-four, who lived in the 1000 block of Campbell, took in laundry, as did one of her lodgers, a fifty-seven-year-old widow.[52]

Commercial laundries also employed African American women in substantial numbers. More than half of the laundry employees counted in the 1920 census were black women. The laundry employees tended to be younger women. Perhaps they were believed to be more capable of handling the physical rigors of the work, or perhaps they had not yet developed the ties within the community to generate in-home laundry work. John Walls's seventeen-year-old granddaughter, one of ten members of the extended family living on East Tenth Street, had left school and was employed at a laundry. Sophia Law, a seventeen-year-old bride from Texas, worked in a laundry; her husband was a janitor. Arma Harvey, nineteen, found work in a laundry while living in a boardinghouse on Broadway; her twenty-three-year-old husband was a truck driver.

Opportunities for laundry work, however, were limited. Many more African American women found that domestic work, as a maid or housekeeper, was the only option available. The start of World War I, which restricted the flow of European immigrants into the United States, increased opportunities for domestic work for African Americans. In Kansas City, that meant that almost half of the black women employed in 1920 worked as maids or domestic workers. African Americans also accounted for three-fifths of all women employed as servants at the time.

These black women ranged widely in age, marital status, and place of origin. Some worked in hotels or large boardinghouses; others were employed by private families. Some lived on the premises; others re-

52. Hall's other two "lodgers" were minors, a twelve-year-old girl from Louisiana and a ten-year-old boy from Arkansas. Whether they were related to Hall or to her other lodger is not reflected in the census.

Table 2.1.
The Top Ten Occupations of African American Women Workers in Kansas City, 1920

Occupation	Number
Servants	2,855
Laundresses[A]	1,569
Laundry operatives	509
Boardinghouse keepers	177
Housekeepers	140
Seamstresses	116
Waitresses	109
Hairdressers[B]	108
Laborers[C]	87
Teachers	86

[A]Not in laundry
[B]Includes manicurists
[C]Working in unspecified manufacturing and mechanical fields

turned home daily to their own loved ones. The mother of George J., mentioned below, found work as the family maid for the Fitts family, owner of the Fitts Dry Goods Store on Eighth Street. Charlie Parker's mother, Addie, worked as a cleaning woman at Western Union and for private families in the 1930s. Unfortunately, no real description exists of the working experiences of women in domestic work in Kansas City. Pay was poor. The South Side Employment Agency advertised in 1919 that it had positions open for chambermaids, general housework, laundry work, and daily cleaning and dusting. Laundry work and dusting and cleaning, though contracted on a daily basis, offered the best pay: $2.50 a day (or $12.50 if a woman found work five days a week). Chambermaids were to be paid $6.00 to $10.00 a week; general housework paid $7.00 to $12.00 a week.[53]

Although some skills were taught in the public schools, many young women wishing to enter domestic service availed themselves of the training of the School for Maids, run by Viola J. Williams. Williams's husband, W. H. Williams, was principal at the Bruce School at Fourteenth and Jackson. From 1908, Viola Williams offered training in domestic skills to African American girls and women. Historian Victoria W. Wolcott

53. Georgette Stanley Page, *George: A Divided Soul . . . and a Divided City, 1913–1992*, 41; Gary Giddins, *Celebrating Bird: The Triumph of Charlie Parker*; *Kansas City Sun*, February 1, 1919.

has noted the ubiquitous nature of schools such as Williams's. Wolcott sees the programs as concrete examples of a "female uplift" ideology that linked female respectability and racial empowerment and exalted household labor, thrift, and modesty of dress as its key components.[54]

From her home in the 1300 block of Jackson, Williams trained her pupils to be efficient homemakers, not only for the benefit of potential employers but for themselves as well. Seventy-five students were enrolled in the school in 1920. They studied sewing (plain sewing, children's clothes, embroidery, mending, and millinery) and cooking (bread, pies, muffins, salads, and vegetables). Additionally, they studied chores such as cleaning kitchens, sinks, stoves, pantries, and bathrooms and washing dishes. The students, some of whom were high school dropouts, worked half the day and tested their skills in the real world at pay ranging from $1.50 to $2.00 a day.[55]

When the fall session in 1933 began, Williams explained to sixty-five new students how the school enabled women to help themselves. "It is a wonderful investment," she argued, "when you find out just what you want and that the world is made of two kinds of people, those who want to succeed and wish for it and those who want to succeed and wade right into the work." Williams urged the women to be self-confident. "One can be as big or as small as your mind will make you; boost your work and you will make enough to enjoy every moment of your life."[56]

In 1934, perhaps buoyed by the success of the Janitor Training School, the Urban League organized a Maids Training School. Its goal was to increase the efficiency of maids by training them in the use of "modern electrical appliances." The nine-week course covered the proper utilization of irons, coffeemakers, toasters, waffle irons, and other small appliances as well as heavy appliances such as refrigerators and electric ranges.[57]

Many African Americans were employed as live-in servants. The area bounded by Main, Gilham, Thirty-fourth, and Thirty-eighth contained a significant number of wealthy white families, all of whom apparently employed at least one African American servant. The ser-

54. Wolcott, *Remaking Respectability: African American Women in Interwar Detroit*, 18–21.

55. Young and Young, *Your Kansas City and Mine*, 156; *Kansas City Sun*, October 9, 1920; May 27, 1922. Young and Young note that the school was still operating in 1949.

56. KCULP, "V. J. Williams School for Maids Opened, Sept. 5," unattributed newspaper clipping, box N1, file 2.

57. KCULP, "Maids Training School," box PPE1, file 1.

vants ranged in age from ten to seventy. Robert Carl, born in Georgia around 1850, was employed as a house man for a lawyer and his family living on Main Street; nearby, forty-seven-year-old Georgia Stephens worked as a maid for a prominent insurance executive. A prominent banker living on Armour Boulevard employed three African Americans, apparently unrelated: a forty-year-old chauffeur, a fifty-two-year-old cook, and a fourteen-year-old maid. Some families were fortunate to find employment together. Twenty-eight-year-old Charles Cox and his twenty-six-year-old wife, Hazel, worked as chauffeur and maid for a mortgage company salesman living on The Paseo. Daniel Pennington, a forty-seven-year-old chauffeur, worked for a lawyer's family living on Thirty-sixth Street; his wife, Inez, thirty-two, was employed as the cook, and the couple's twelve-year-old daughter also lived on the premises. Undoubtedly, she assisted her mother in performing her duties.[58]

The example of fourteen-year-old packinghouse worker Sam Gilham illustrates another aspect of the black working-class experience in the 1920s. It was not uncommon for African American youths, particularly males, to end their formal education in their early teens. For example, according to census records, Sam Gilham's sisters—Leona, fifteen, and Beatrice, twelve—were both still enrolled in school. His brother Bob, eleven, was listed as not attending. School attendance was not mandatory after sixth grade, and many African American families needed the income generated by their sons. George J., a twelve-year-old newcomer to Kansas City in 1926, was told by his mother and uncle one day that he had to find work or not to return home.[59]

After receiving the ultimatum from his uncle and mother, George recalled years later, he walked "along Eighteenth Street from Troost to Brooklyn, stopping at every store front" and inquiring about work opportunities. He found many businesses were not willing to hire a young African American. But at last, he encountered a white coal-and-ice dealer who offered young George J. a job. The coal-and-ice dealer, known to the community as "Irish Bill," kept his horse and wagon in a garage at Fifteenth and Brooklyn. It also apparently was Irish Bill's home. For fifty cents a day, George J. began working with Irish Bill, caring for his horse and wagon and ultimately carrying loads of one hundred pounds of coal or twenty-five pounds of ice to homes and

58. According to census records, residents of the 3500 block of Main Street included a lawyer, an oil company owner, a doctor, and an insurance broker.

59. Page, *George*, 42.

apartments throughout the Eighteenth and Vine district. An icehouse sat at Twenty-fourth and Vine, and the coal-supply house was at Nineteenth and Campbell, within the heart of the African American community. George J. worked for Irish Bill for a year or two, before finding other employment.[60]

After attending Lincoln High School for a year, George J. left school and went to work as a clerk in the Garfield Grocery Store at 2021 East Twelfth Street. The owner was Harry Esrig, one of several Russian Jewish immigrants who operated stores in the Eighteenth and Vine district during the 1920s. "He was a generous man," George recalled, "always kind to me. . . . He even called my mother 'Mrs.' rather than by her first name as servants were normally addressed. He knew the importance of treating a Negro person with respect." Later, George became a fountain clerk and delivery boy at the Prospect Pharmacy at Thirty-fifth and Prospect. The pharmacy was run by J. J. Flynn, a white physician. All of the patrons of the pharmacy were white, a fact that required some adjustment for both new employee and customer: "I wore a tan coat and tie every day. At first I was hesitant in serving the whites, as hesitant as they were in being served by me, a black boy. After all, this was something new. Was I safe? Did I carry germs? Dr. Flynn's faith and trust in me eventually carried over to his customers."[61]

George's employment at the Prospect Pharmacy ended with the Depression; Flynn was forced to sell the drugstore. Employment opportunities for uneducated African American youths were slim, but through his mother's employer, George found part-time work doing yard work for white families living around William Rockhill Nelson's home. His salary was seventy-five cents a day.[62]

Like Peter Jackson, Marita Bonner's fictional character, many African American men in Kansas City between 1900 and 1939 were consigned to the bottom of the labor heap. They were laborers—unskilled, ill-paid, with little or no opportunity to advance. They did the hauling, the digging, the cleaning that other workers could not or would not perform. They worked for the city and county governments, as well as private industry. Excluding packinghouse workers, the 1920 census counted 3,953 African Americans working as common laborers in Kansas City, about one-third of all black males employed at the time.

60. Ibid., 42, 44.
61. Ibid., 44, 46.
62. Ibid., 49.

A decade later, at the start of the Great Depression, the number of African American laborers enumerated by the census actually diminished, to 3,610 and just one-quarter of the black male workforce.

A significant portion of African American workers remained at the bottom of the job ladder. For example, the number of janitors counted in the 1930 census increased by more than 600 over the 1920 figure. Outside of the packinghouses, the ordinary laborer often found employment to be inconsistent. Although no evidence has survived to document how much or how little work was available to the average unskilled laborer in Kansas City, students of other African American communities have demonstrated that unskilled laborers were often limited to two or three days' work a week, even before the onset of the Depression. For the majority of black workers in Kansas City from 1920 to 1939, work was dirty, physically demanding, and demeaning and often paid little. Yet this work was the foundation for Kansas City's African American communities and sustained them during even the hardest economic times. The average black laborer doubtlessly worked harder than he should, but without his or her efforts, black Kansas City would not have prospered. The average black worker provided the base on which many of black Kansas City's institutions stood and from which the region's privileged class drew.

Three

Professionals, Businesspeople, and Others

I am a part of all that I have seen and heard
and done, and had done to me.

—JOHN HOPE, PRESIDENT OF ATLANTA UNIVERSITY,
IN A SPEECH IN KANSAS CITY, MISSOURI, 1923

IN 1919, EDUCATOR J. Silas Harris penned an essay for the *Washington Tribune* in which he described the "distinguished leaders of the race" in Kansas City.[1] Harris identified individuals who had excelled in business, medicine, education, law, and public speaking. His essay, of course, reenforced the class distinctions that some of these distinguished leaders wished to draw. Not all African Americans in Kansas City looked up to or followed these leaders of the race, but it is safe to say that many black Kansas Citians held them up as examples of what was possible.

Historians have variously described this group as "aristocrats of color," "black elites," and the "emerging black middle class." Darlene Clark Hine has proposed using the term *black professional class,* but if rigorously defined, that includes only those groups—like lawyers, doctors, and dentists—that had established professional standards. It would exclude individuals among Harris's "distinguished leaders" such as educators, businessmen and -women, and newspaper editors. Thus, for the purpose of this study, which strives to see the world of black Kansas Citians as they perceived it in the 1920s and '30s, we will adopt Harris's less precise, less scientific viewpoint.[2]

1. Originally published in the *Washington Tribune,* and reprinted in the *Kansas City Sun,* July 5, 1919.
2. Hine, "Black Professionals and Race Consciousness," 1281.

The "distinguished" African Americans that Harris identified were the self-appointed leaders of black Kansas City. They were the nucleus for the leadership of various institutions in the community. Connected through various political, social, and religious organizations and activities, they attempted to guide black Kansas City through the Jim Crow era. Their influence, well out of proportion to their small numerical number, was felt throughout the interwar period. Some of these distinguished individuals—including Chester Franklin of the *Kansas City Call* and educator Hugh O. Cook—would be mainstays of post–World War Kansas City. The others, through their activism and persistence, helped set the stage for the end of segregation.

Religious Leadership

All that the people of my race ask is that we be treated as any other Americans, and it doesn't take any special laws to do that. We have a good Constitution and all we ask is that it be enforced.

—THE REVEREND D. A. HOLMES, PASEO BAPTIST CHURCH, 1948

The dominant occupation—at least numerically—for the African American professional class in Kansas City in the 1920s was as a member of the clergy. Seventy-nine African American males were so identified in the 1920 census. In many communities, religious life was one of the few areas in which African American males could assert themselves as individuals. Since the end of the Civil War, ambitious and intelligent black men had found their calling within one of the two dominant religious denominations: the Baptist Church or the African Methodist Episcopal faith. Because of the segregated nature of religious bodies in that seventy-year span, the religious arena had become one of the few in which African American men could develop and practice leadership skills. As Eric Foner has argued, many of these men became clergy because they were leaders, not leaders because they were clergy. That was true in Kansas City, though no member of the clergy would dominate the scene as did, for example, Adam Clayton Powell Sr. in New York City.

Samuel Bacote (Second Baptist), James Hurse (St. Stephen's) and T. H. Ewing (Vine Street) remained influential ministers in 1920, but they would be joined a year later by D. A. Holmes, who would take over at Vine Street Baptist in 1921 after Ewing followed a faction that left Vine Street and started Park Avenue Baptist. Daniel Arthur Holmes was born in Macon, Missouri, on September 22, 1876. His father, a former slave, was a minister and plasterer. When Daniel was three years old, his father died, leaving Daniel and his fourteen siblings to the care of their mother. By the age of seventeen, Daniel had begun working in the coal mines of north-central Missouri; he also earned money as a cobbler, working in his own shop. By the same time, Daniel had also decided he wanted to be a preacher.

Holmes entered Western Baptist College, an all-black school that sat on twelve acres about three-fourths of a mile from Macon.[3] Holmes received his bachelor's degree from Western Baptist and subsequently a bachelor of theology degree from Des Moines College in Iowa. With the help of supporters in Illinois, Holmes received his bachelor of divinity degree in 1906 from Morgan Park University (now incorporated into the University of Chicago Divinity School). After serving congregations in Fayette and Springfield, Missouri, Holmes in 1914 moved to Metropolitan Baptist Church in Kansas City, Kansas.[4]

After Holmes was called to Vine Street Baptist, one of his first tasks was to lead a fund-raising drive for expansion of the church. The $165,000 goal was reached, and the decision was made to build a new structure at Twenty-fifth and The Paseo. Holmes and his congregation moved into the new structure late in the decade, and the church was renamed Paseo Baptist.[5] Holmes was soon regarded as one of the most outspoken and courageous of the black preachers. When school authorities organized a "Loyalty Parade" of the city's children in 1922, it was announced that African American children would be placed at the rear of the parade. Holmes, assisted by E. C. Bunch, a prominent physician, and principal Hugh O. Cook of Lincoln, organized a protest. Fliers were distributed, a mass meeting was held, and Holmes and other ministers

3. Western Baptist Bible College was founded in 1889 by the Baptist General Association of Missouri. Its first location was at the Second Baptist Church in Independence, Missouri. It bore the distinction of being the first Christian school for African Americans west of the Mississippi. The school moved back into the Kansas City area in 1920, and by the middle of the decade had moved near its current location of 2119 Tracy.

4. Two stories collected by Young and Young (*Your Kansas City and Mine,* 152) attest to Holmes's courage. Shortly after leaving Fayette for Springfield, Holmes was called and asked to preside at a funeral service for one of his former parishioners, who had been lynched. None of the local preachers apparently would have anything to do with the funeral, but Holmes returned to Fayette and without incident preached a sermon challenging local officials to protect black citizens. Years later, while serving as pastor at Metropolitan Baptist in Kansas City, Kansas, Holmes was appointed a major in the Kansas National Guard. When city officials failed to take any action when homes of black residents along North Fifth Street were dynamited, Holmes assembled his company of 250 men as protection for the black home owners. The idea of more than 200 armed black men patrolling the city quickly spurred local officials to take action.

5. Jacqueline Sharp, "Daniel Arthur Holmes, D.D.," paper in possession of author; Olive Hoggins, *Centenary History of Kansas City Churches,* in *Mecca of the New Negro,* by Gibson, 153–54; *Western Messenger,* October 4, 1918.

built their sermons around the injustice of the parade as planned. School authorities finally relented, and the parade went off with the schools marching in alphabetical order. "And thank God," the *Kansas City Sun* saluted in a May editorial, "...they kept two thousand Negro youth from being humiliated and degraded." Holmes also led the vocal protests against the use of excessive force by Kansas City police officers. Even when the offending officer was an African American, Holmes stood firm on his principles. "He has no business on the force, and I don't want him there," Holmes was quoted as saying. Holmes was an outspoken critic of the Pendergast machine, calling it dishonest government that bribed black voters for support. "When this city was in the hands of corrupt leaders," one admirer said, "Dr. Holmes rose in his pulpit and on street corners to preach against those who were dipping into the city treasury. His mighty effort took forth until the citizens of Kansas City joined Dr. Holmes in sweeping this city clean." Holmes also championed the cause of African American teachers, demanding that they receive the same salaries as white teachers.[6] The school at 3007 Benton was named in Holmes's honor.

Educational Leadership: Teaching the Race

I regard teaching as sacred a work as the ministry.

—JOHN ROBERT E. LEE, PRINCIPAL OF LINCOLN HIGH SCHOOL (1915–1921)

In 1920, Kansas City had almost 130 African American teachers. All taught in the city's twelve black schools. Exactly two-thirds of the teachers (86 of 129) were women, although few female teachers had obtained the public status accorded to Josephine Yates or Anna Jones

6. *Kansas City Sun*, May 6, 1922; *Kansas City Times*, January 24, 1955; *Kansas City Times*, June 12, 1945. Holmes remained at Paseo Baptist for forty-six years. In that time, he was a fixture on the various boards of directors of black-run institutions in Kansas City. He served on the board of directors, along with Samuel Bacote, for Western Baptist College and in 1955–1956 served as president of the school. He was a frequent speaker at Lincoln High School's Sunday Extension Programs. He was the first black minister elected to lead the General Ministerial Alliance of Kansas City and served on the city's Recreation Committee. Holmes was one of the founders of the Carver Neighborhood Center. An ardent Republican, Holmes was asked by the Citizens Association, an interracial Republican group, to run for city council in 1955, but he refused. Seven years earlier, at a gathering of black Republicans, he chastised President Harry Truman for his limited civil rights program. "It was just a bait held out for the Negro vote," Holmes said. "How can they hope to catch us with that bait when for sixteen long years, when they controlled both the houses of Congress, and did nothing." *Kansas City Times*, July 17, 1948. In 1955, the Benton school was renamed D. A. Holmes School in his honor. Holmes died October 24, 1972, in Lincoln, Nebraska.

in the previous twenty years. Part of the explanation lies in the gender conventions of the times: by mandate or by tradition, most school districts demanded that female teachers remained unmarried; matrimony was grounds for immediate dismissal. Even for Bessie J., a teacher at Lincoln High School, to live with her former brother-in-law and his three-year-old son in the 2600 block of Highland might have challenged the prevailing standards concerning propriety. The women employed as teachers were of all ages; a sample of one block of Montgall shows 6 female teachers ranging in age from twenty-three to forty-five. They might be young single women, divorced, or widowed. It is possible that the older teachers living on Montgall were either of the latter two, but all 6 were listed in the census as having never married. Bessie J., mentioned above, was a divorcée.

Finding lodging was a difficult matter for female teachers, regardless of age or previous marital status. Teachers' salaries were notoriously low, and in Kansas City, as in most places in the country, African American educators' salaries were lower than those of white teachers in comparable situations. In searching for housing, female teachers also had to be conscious of where they resided. Most female teachers sought lodging with relatives or in "respectable" households. Hattie Sprague was fortunate; she could live with her sister and brother-in-law, Fredericka and John Perry. Others had to turn to strangers, though it is reasonable to assume that the female teachers on Montgall were guided there. Arthur Patterson, a teacher, and his family resided at 2449 Montgall. It is possible he guided other teachers to families with suitable spaces to rent. The Newsom sisters from Colorado found lodging at 2440 Montgall, while Slater Logan, a packinghouse butcher living at 2434 Montgall, rented rooms to forty-three-year-old Caroline B. and twenty-three-year-old Ethel W. Among the six residents of the Arthur Patterson household was another teacher. Complicating the teachers' search for lodging was the fact that all may have been relative newcomers to the Kansas City area. None of the six female teachers on Montgall in the 1920s was born in Missouri or Kansas. Three were born in Colorado; Indiana, New York, and Georgia were the home states of the others.

Although female teachers outnumbered male teachers two to one, African American men held most, if not all, positions of status within the black schools. Only black men were listed as principals, although it was not uncommon for veteran female teachers to be listed in charge at some of the elementary schools. By 1920, James Dallas Bowser and G. N. Grisham had left teaching, but Richard T. Coles remained the principal at Garrison School. A new generation of black educators had emerged, however.

John Robert E. Lee was one of the most visible individuals in black Kansas City right after World War I. In addition to his status as principal at Lincoln High School (1915–1921), Lee was an active member of St. Stephen's Baptist Church, a member of the board of directors for Wheatley-Provident Hospital, the Paseo YMCA, and the Kansas City chapter of the Urban League. Editor Nelson Crews repeatedly referred to Lee as the "dynamic principal" of Lincoln.[7]

Lee was born in Texas in 1864 in the final months of the Civil War. He grew up in Texas and received his bachelor's degree from Bishop College in Marshall, Texas, in 1889. His first teaching job was at Booker T. Washington's Tuskegee Institute, where he taught mathematics. Within a year of his appointment, however, Lee was at odds with Washington—not over the philosophy of the school but over the workload handed to him as a teacher and supervisor. In a letter dated January 3, 1900, Lee asked Washington why he was being asked to teach eight classes daily (six during the day and two night classes). Lee also was being asked to supervise the other mathematics teachers and help advise and guide them in the latest advances in mathematical theory and instruction. Lee, while assuring Washington that he was not afraid of hard work, said he believed it to be impossible for even an *extraordinary* teacher to adequately teach eight classes in one day. "I have given the work of *teaching* the most earnest study for more than ten years[,] and I am convinced that every institution in the land that professes to do really first-class work, has found it necessary to have each teacher make special preparations for every class he or she is to teach. *The lower* the *class the more careful the preparation.*" Lee then went on to argue that the school's reputation required a more diligent teacher than would be possible under such a heavy teaching load. "I regard teaching as sacred a work as the ministry and should be as *conscientiously* done as *true ministerial work*. . . . I came here to work," Lee assured Washington, "to do the *best* work not the *poorest*."[8]

Washington's response, if there was one, is not included among his edited papers, but Lee remained at Tuskegee until 1904, when, with

7. Details of Lee's early life are drawn from Leedell W. Neyland and John W. Riley, *History of Florida A&M University* (as cited in the Washington Papers, 5:399); and Kinsler, *Trip South*, 5.

8. Lee to Washington, January 3, 1900, Washington Papers, 5:397–99 (emphasis in original).

master's degree in hand, he joined the staff of Benedict College in Columbia, South Carolina. His absence from Tuskegee was a short one. In 1906, he returned as director of the institute's Academic Department. In 1904, Lee also helped organize the National Association of Teachers in Colored Schools and served as the organization's first president for five years. During his second stint at Tuskegee, he also was a promoter of the Alabama State Teachers' Association, and under his direction, the association grew from one hundred members to more than seven hundred.[9]

Lee spent more than a decade at the Tuskegee Institute in Alabama. In 1915, he was appointed the new principal of Lincoln High School, replacing G. N. Grisham. Lee, his wife, Ardella, and their children made a home in the 2100 block of East Twenty-fourth Street, on the eastern fringe of black settlement at the time. Lee quickly asserted himself, and by the end of the decade he was firmly entrenched among Kansas City's black professionals. He was considered a man of high energy and high principles, one who stood up for those things he believed were right.

Lee, as shown by his letter to Washington twenty years previous, believed in delivering a high-quality education to African American students. In a 1919 meeting of all of the school district's teachers (black and white), he received "vigorous and prolonged applause" for his forceful appeal for equal treatment of students, regardless of race, in the classroom. Although some of his ideas were apparently met with initial opposition, Lee and Lincoln became an even larger source of pride within Kansas City's African American community.[10]

During his tenure at Lincoln, Lee also maintained his connections with educators in the South. In the summer of 1919, he went on a whirlwind speaking tour where he addressed more than one thousand African American teachers. First it was to Tuskegee to address the six hundred teachers attending summer classes there. Then it was on to Miles Memorial College, where he delivered a series of lectures over a three-day span to more than three hundred teachers, and finally it was to the State Agricultural and Mechanical College in Huntsville, Alabama (now Alabama State University), where he lectured to more than two hundred. Then fifty-four years old, Lee returned to Kansas City for a

9. Neyland and Riley, *Florida A&M University; Kansas City Sun*, July 2, 1921. Historians Woodson and Wesley (*Negro in Our History*, 546) also noted Lee's work with local interracial committees that worked behind the scenes to reshape public opinion in the South.

10. *Kansas City Sun*, March 22, 1919.

two-day stop before he joined a group of men harvesting wheat in Kansas (from what was then the nation's largest crop).[11]

By that time, Lee was already serving on the boards of Wheatley-Provident and the Paseo YMCA. He had also spearheaded a Liberty Loan campaign in the black community during World War I, and he had been associated with other war drives. Lee continued his activism after the war. He was director of the Negro Campaign Drive during the 1920 Community Chest Campaign and was credited with raising more than ten thousand dollars that year. He was also elected chairman of the board of directors of Kansas City's Urban League chapter.[12]

By 1921, Lincoln's student population had more than doubled (from 315 to 750), though that likely was more a function of continued black migration into Kansas City and the closing of black high schools in the surrounding area than of Lee's charisma. Nevertheless, when he decided that year to resign his post at Lincoln and accept a position as extension secretary for the National Urban League, African Americans on both sides of the state line were stunned. Lee was obligated to make a round of speaking appearances, and shortly before he and his family moved away, a ceremony was held in his honor at St. Stephen's Baptist Church. Among the speakers that night were James Dallas Bowser; Joe E. Herriford, principal at W. W. Yates Elementary; I. F. Bradley of Kansas City, Kansas; John E. Perry; Nelson C. Crews; and the Reverend John Wesley Hurse, pastor at St. Stephen's.[13]

The man chosen to succeed Lee as principal at Lincoln, Hugh O. Cook, had also been an active member of Kansas City's African American communities. Cook was born in Washington, DC, and by the turn of the century had arrived in Kansas City, where he began teaching. In 1916, shortly after Lee's arrival, Cook was appointed vice principal at Lincoln. Upon Lee's departure, the board of education members unanimously voted to promote Cook, who had already displayed an aptitude for service and community development. Around 1910, Cook and W. W.

11. Ibid., July 12, 1919.

12. *Western Messenger*, January 23, 1920; *Kansas City Sun*, July 2, October 29, 1921; Neyland and Riley, *Florida A&M University*.

13. *Kansas City Sun*, October 29, 1921. Lee remained with the Urban League for almost three years before being appointed president of all-black Florida A&M College in Tallahassee. Lee remained at the school until 1944, and during his twenty-year tenure, he led a successful reorganization of the school and attracted contributions from a number of white philanthropists, including the Rosenwald Fund and the Carnegie Fund. For Lee's contributions to Florida A&M, see Neyland and Riley, *Florida A&M University*. For the role of northern white philanthropy in the direction and survival of black higher education in the South, see James D. Anderson, *The Education of Blacks in the South, 1860–1935*.

Yates became two of the leading proponents for the construction of a Young Men's Christian Association building for African Americans. When the United States entered the war in Europe, Cook joined the Army YMCA. As the organization's representative, he was attached to the 371st Infantry Regiment (an all-black unit), where he was responsible for supplying soldiers with some of the small comforts of home: tobacco, hot chocolate, and so on. During the Champaign offensive of the fall of 1918, Cook was gassed while tending to the wounded. For his action he was recommended for the Distinguished Service Cross.[14]

Cook returned to Kansas City as a war hero. His return to the city in February 1919 was a cause for celebration. Cook was met at the station by his wife and several close friends before motoring to the Paseo YMCA, where a veritable Who's Who in black Kansas City joined him for a banquet.[15] Cook quickly resumed his duties as vice principal and his career as an activist within the black community. He and his wife, Myrtle Foster Cook, joined the Urban League in 1922.[16] Two years earlier, Cook was elected vice president of the National Council of Negro Teachers. In 1926, he joined T. B. Watkins in establishing a cooperative credit union, the People's Finance Corporation.[17] Cook also was an outspoken critic of racial segregation and discrimination. As mentioned above, he was one of the first African Americans to protest an attempt by organizers to segregate black students at the end of the line in the mayor's annual parade of schoolchildren. Cook's influence was also recognized within the greater Kansas City community. When the Reverend L. M. Birkhead, a white minister, compiled a list of individuals who had made distinct contributions to Kansas City's culture, Cook was one of three African Americans chosen. He was cited as a "modest example" who set up "standards of moral and intellectual ideals which have had an inspiring influence on his fellow citizens." Cook remained principal at Lincoln until 1944, when he retired and he and his wife moved to Los Angeles. Hugh Cook died in 1949.[18]

14. Young and Young, *Your Kansas City and Mine*, 14; *Western Messenger*, February 28, 1919; *Kansas City Sun*, March 8, 1919.

15. Among the guests were Dr. and Mrs. John Perry, Mr. and Mrs. Nelson Crews, Dr. and Mrs. T. C. Unthank, Mr. and Mrs. L'Amasa Knox, and Lincoln music teacher N. Clark Smith and his wife.

16. Myrtle Foster Cook was an activist in her own right. See Chapter Five.

17. *Kansas City Sun*, November 20, 1920; June 17, 1922; Young and Young, *Your Kansas City and Mine*, 29, 104, 145. The People's Finance Corporation emulated a similarly named institution in St. Louis. Unlike the St. Louis corporation, Kansas City's People's Finance Corporation survived the Depression and lived to see its twenty-fifth anniversary.

18. Young and Young, *Your Kansas City and Mine;* KCULP, "In a Tribute to Culture," undated newspaper clipping, box N1, file 1.

Medical Leadership: Protecting the Race

Thomas C. Unthank was the most recognized African American doctor in either of the two Kansas Cities, but members of the African American community also recognized and supported the efforts of physicians such as D. Madison Miller, Thomas B. Jones, John E. Perry, and Howard B. Smith. The careers of Miller, Perry, and Smith transcended their medical practices, however; each was involved in the establishment and operation of key institutions within the African American community.

John Edward Perry was born April 2, 1870, in Clarksville, Texas, to Anderson and Louise Perry. Because the local school for African Americans was open only three months out of the year, John Perry did not begin his education until the age of nine. At age fifteen, however, he entered Bishop College in Marshall, Texas, and over the next six years, with the help of the meager savings of his parents, Perry worked his way to a bachelor's degree. Perry began by milking a neighbor's cow to pay his monthly laundry bill of one dollar. He then taught summer school for African Americans in a rural community outside of Marshall. In 1891, he graduated with honors from Bishop. By that time, he had become enthralled with the idea of practicing medicine. With the help of businessmen from Clarksville, Perry entered Meharry Medical School in Nashville, Tennessee.[19]

Perry graduated from Meharry in 1895 and a month later opened his practice in Mexico, Missouri. Six months later, he moved his practice to nearby Columbia, where over the next eight years he would treat both African American and white patients. After a stint as an army lieutenant during the Spanish-American War, Perry moved to Kansas City and opened his practice. At the time, African American physicians had no hospital facilities on the Missouri side in which they were allowed to work. Perry persevered, however, and in 1910 he opened his own private hospital, Perry's Sanitarium. The two-story facility at 1214 Vine Street, with room for twenty beds, both followed and was contrary to prevailing trends in the medical profession. In the fifty years after the Civil War, hospitals had evolved from benevolent institutions for the treatment of lower-class patients into medical workshops, where skilled practitioners honed and perfected their craft. Perry opened his

19. See Kinsler, *Trip South*. Meharry Medical School and Howard University Medical School in Washington, DC, trained at least nine out of ten African American physicians in the first half of the twentieth century.

sanitarium in part to give black physicians on the Missouri side a place to practice, yet the increasing professionalization of the medical field had made it more difficult for small proprietary hospitals such as Perry's to survive.[20]

To keep his facility running, Perry agreed in 1913 to allow members of the New Movement Association, a group of African American elites, to take over the hospital's operation. Its name was changed to Provident Hospital. At the same time, another group of African Americans in the Phyllis Wheatley club had begun to raise funds to build a black-owned and -operated hospital in Kansas City. After a year of negotiations, the New Movement Association and the Phyllis Wheatley group agreed to merge efforts. The facility was renamed again, this time as Wheatley-Provident Hospital. In 1917, Nelson Crews, Chester Franklin, Fred Dabney, and Eva M. Fox led a campaign to raise twenty-five thousand dollars to purchase and equip a permanent home for Wheatley-Provident. The committee appealed to racial pride and the city's lackluster attitude toward medical care for African Americans. "Don't you think we deserve better treatment than that?" the committee asked in an advertisement promoting the fund-raising campaign. "BLACK MEN. LET US DO OUR DUTY." The group had already arranged to obtain a large stone building, with twenty rooms, at 1826 Forest; the building had previously housed a Catholic school, but by the end of the World War, it sat squarely in what was emerging as the heart of Kansas City's largest African American community. Throughout the interwar period, Wheatley-Provident remained a vital and beloved institution among Kansas City's African Americans. Fund-raisers for the hospital were an annual event; although a blizzard hindered the turnout in 1919, for example, more than twenty-five hundred dollars was raised. Eventually, a benefit fashion show organized by Minnie Crosthwaite became the biggest financial supporter for the hospital.[21]

John Perry remained director of the facility throughout the changes in name and location. He also joined T. C. Unthank among the four African American physicians on the staff at the Old City Hospital. Like Unthank, Perry was a tireless worker for other institutions within the African

20. For a discussion of the evolution of American hospitals in general and African American hospitals in particular, see Vanessa Northington Gamble, *Making a Place for Ourselves: The Black Hospital Movement, 1920–1945.*

21. *Kansas City Sun,* December 1, 1917, in *Mecca of the New Negro,* by Gibson, 92 (emphasis in original); *Western Messenger,* January 3, 1919. Wheatley-Provident remained a fixture in Kansas City's African American community until it closed in 1972.

American community, serving at various times on the board of the directors of a number of facilities. In 1921, he was a unanimous choice as president-elect of the National Medical Society, the black counterpart of the all-white American Medical Association. Perry remained at Wheatley-Provident until 1935, when he was appointed director emeritus. By 1920, Perry and, his wife, Fredericka, had bought a home at 2451 Montgall, amid all of the black teachers. Perhaps not coincidentally, one of Perry's next-door neighbors, Arthur Patterson, was born in Texas; Perry would be involved in at least one attempt to organize a club of Texas migrants in Kansas City.[22]

D. Madison Miller was born September 30, 1884, in Georgia. He received his bachelor's degree from Central City College before obtaining a medical degree from Meharry. He attended the Rush Medical School at the University of Chicago for a year before opening his practice in 1911. In 1917, he moved to Kansas City, where he quickly established one of the largest and most lucrative practices among black doctors. In 1930, Miller succeeded Howard Smith as superintendent of General Hospital No. 2. By 1920, Miller and his wife, Clara, had purchased a home at 2642 Highland. Like most of the residents on that block, the Millers did not find it necessary to provide space in their home for lodgers. Among the Millers' neighbors were Augustus Allen, a Pullman porter, and Nelson and Marguerite Crews.[23]

Howard Smith was born in Baltimore, Maryland, in about 1880. He received a bachelor's degree from Lincoln University in Pennsylvania and received his medical training at the University of Pennsylvania. He began his practice in Philadelphia and then moved to Chicago before coming to Kansas City in 1911. In 1920, Smith served as superintendent of the Jackson County home for elderly black men and women. He also served on the steering committee for the Miles Bulger Industrial Home for Negro Youth. Smith was appointed superintendent of General Hospital No. 2 in 1926 and served four years before being replaced by D. Madison Miller. Smith and his wife, Anna, lived at 2329 Tracy. Although Smith enjoyed a substantial position among Kansas City's black elites, he was apparently not able to make ends meet on the income from his medical practice and his county post. Smith and his wife

22. Young and Young, *Your Kansas City and Mine; Kansas City Sun,* September 3, 1921; Gamble, *Making a Place;* U.S. Department of Commerce, Bureau of the Census, Fourteenth Census. Perry left Kansas City in the 1950s and returned to Texas, where he died in 1956.

23. Kinsler, *Trip South;* Office of Housing and Community Development, *Spirit of Freedom,* 44; U.S. Department of Commerce, Bureau of the Census, Fourteenth Census.

rented out room to two families in their home; neither family appeared to be related to the Smiths.[24]

Kansas City possessed a small cadre of lawyers. L. Amasa Knox was the most prominent, but two other men—Charles H. Calloway and William C. Hueston—were well known in the African American community. Calloway was born in Cleveland, Tennessee, around 1880 and grew up in Nashville. He graduated from Fisk University in Nashville before receiving his law degree from the University of Minnesota in 1904. A year later, he moved to Kansas City and set up his law practice. Calloway and his wife, Cora, joined Allen Chapel AME Church, and he became involved with many of the institutions in Kansas City's African American communities. By 1913, Calloway had joined those groups attempting to establish a private hospital for African Americans on the Missouri side, and when Wheatley-Provident Hospital was established, he was a member of the board of directors. Calloway served on Wheatley-Provident's board into the 1930s, and he also served as the board's attorney. Shortly after the formation of a Kansas City branch, Calloway joined the NAACP, and he served as president of the local chapter during the 1920s and 1930s. He also served on the board of directors of the Kansas City Urban League.[25]

Calloway, whose squared jaw and rugged shoulders gave him the solid look of a movie lawyer, was also noted for his success in the legal profession. In 1926, he was elected to a two-year term as president of the National Bar Association (the African American equivalent of the American Bar Association). In 1941, Calloway became the first African American lawyer appointed to the staff of the city counselor's office, where he served until his death in 1944.[26]

Calloway's partner, William C. Hueston, was an up-and-comer in his own right. Hueston was born in Kentucky around 1880. Although little is known about his background, Hueston lived in Washington, DC, at some point before coming west. He graduated from the University of Kansas, where he received high marks as an orator and debater.[27] By

24. Kinsler, *Trip South*, 7; *Kansas City Sun*, August 13, 1921; U.S. Department of Commerce, Bureau of the Census, Fourteenth Census; Office of Housing and Community Development, *Spirit of Freedom*, 44.

25. KCULP, *Pilot* 11:6 (March 1937), box KCULP1, file 15; *Kansas City Call*, undated article.

26. *Kansas City Call*, undated article; Young and Young, *Your Kansas City and Mine*, 162.

27. Hueston's wife, Jessie, was born in Washington, DC, as was their oldest daughter, Margaret. U.S. Department of Commerce, Bureau of the Census, Fourteenth Census; *Kansas City Sun*, April 3, 1920.

the early 1910s, Hueston and his family were living in Kansas City. Like his partner, Hueston was an active Republican and an active supporter of institutions within the African American community. He served as president of the Civic League (a group of Progressive-minded African Americans), served on the board of directors at Wheatley-Provident Hospital, was a member of the Elks, was one of the key organizers for the parade of the all-black Ninety-second Regiment through Kansas City in 1919, and supported, at least in principle, the activities of the National Negro Constitutional Conservation League of America (NNCCLA, discussed in Chapter Four). Hueston's activism within the Republican Party led to his consideration as a candidate for city alderman in 1918 and gained him a spot on the party's credentials committee for its convention in 1920. Early in the 1920s, Hueston began splitting his time between Kansas City and Gary, Indiana, where he became involved in real estate. By 1930, Hueston had moved permanently to Gary, where he held a judgeship.[28]

Newspaper Leadership: All for the Race

Kansas City's African American communities were bolstered in the early 1920s by the presence of two progressive-minded newspaper editors—Nelson Crews of the *Kansas City Sun* and Chester A. Franklin of the *Kansas City Call*. The two men were of two different generations—Crews was about fifty-three when the thirty-nine-year-old Franklin published his first edition of the *Call*—and Franklin could not match Crews's skill in oration, politics, or shameless self-promotion. Crews and Franklin, however, shared a number of qualities aside from their passion for newspaper work. They both were staunch Republicans, though Franklin would live long enough to at least be tempted by Democracy as practiced by Franklin D. Roosevelt and Harry Truman. Both believed fervently in the potential of Kansas City, and both were what would be called "race men."

Both demonstrated a pride in being black and a strong sense of pride in Kansas City's African American population. Both worked tirelessly to promote the institutions that sustained the black communities; their names show up repeatedly for functions with Wheatley-Provident

28. A. Martin, *Our Negro Population*, 36; *Kansas City Sun*, March 8, 1919; *Western Messenger*, January 23, 1920; *Kansas City Sun*, May 1, 1920; March 26, April 30, 1921; March 25, 1922; *Kansas City Call*, September 20, 1929.

Hospital, the black YMCA and YWCA, the NAACP, the Urban League, and Lincoln High School. Both sought to promote a Kansas City that allowed African Americans to live up to their potential.

Nelson Caesar Crews was born in Howard County, Missouri, just northwest of Columbia in the central part of the state. It is impossible to state the date of his birth with any certainty, but most documents point to a birth toward the end of or right after the Civil War. As Hazel Rowley notes in her examination of Mississippi's records in her search for relatives of twentieth-century black author Richard Wright, manuscript census returns from the 1870s and 1880s are "wildly inconsistent." There are no surviving records of the Crews family before 1900. Of his background and that of his brother James, we have the conflicting evidence of his obituary and census records (which also tell conflicting stories). Nelson Crews, according to his obituary, had two sisters and three brothers who survived him. According to the same source, he grew up in Chillicothe, about seventy miles northeast of Kansas City, but little else about his early life or his education has survived.[29]

Crews and his wife, Tillie, moved to Kansas City in 1889 where he quickly became involved with some of the city's most prominent black men. Crews and James Dallas Bowser, for example, began a friendship that lasted until their deaths in the 1920s. Crews also quickly became involved in politics, where he gained a reputation as an articulate and forceful speaker. His speaking ability and influence within the black community led to a series of political appointments before World War I. He served two years as assistant superintendent of streets, four terms as clerk of the police court, one term as deputy city clerk, and one term as a special agent of the Department of Agriculture during the Taft administration.[30]

29. Rowley, *Richard Wright: His Life and Work*, 3–4; *Kansas City Sun*, April 28, 1923; *Kansas City Call*, April 27, 1923. Another of Crews's brothers, the Reverend P. C. Crews, was the presiding elder for the Hannibal District of the AME Church and a member of the board of trustees at Western University in Quindaro. The final brother, Smith Crews, lived in St. Joseph, Missouri, in the 1920s. *Kansas City Sun*, May 15, 1920; *Kansas City Sun*, June 4, 1921. What year Nelson Crews was born is unclear. His obituary listed his date of birth as October 15, 1866. Yet the 1900 manuscript census, the first in which he could definitively be located, lists his birthday as October 15, 1864. To further complicate matters, the 1910 census lists Crews's age as forty-four (consistent with an 1866 birth date), but the 1920 census lists his age as forty-eight. No mention of the Crews family could be found in the Missouri censuses for 1870 or 1880, and as historians of the period and genealogists know, the 1890 manuscript census was destroyed by fire.

30. See Kinsler, *Trip South*. Crews's appointment with the Department of Agriculture was reported as being one year by Kinsler but for four years in his *Kansas City Sun* obituary. According to census documents, Crews was employed as clerk of the police court in 1900. The Crews family lived in the East Bottoms at 608 East Sixth at that time.

Throughout his career, Crews maintained a vigorous speaking schedule. He appeared throughout central and northwestern Missouri, addressing audiences large and small. His topics usually revolved around one central issue: the attainment of political equality for African Americans. In March 1919, five months after the armistice in Europe, Crews appeared at St. James AME Church, where he delivered a stirring talk. "In eloquent words," the *Kansas City Sun*'s unbiased account read, Crews "urged that the race strike now with all of its might for its civil liberty." When LeRoy Bundy (one of the black men convicted of murder for allegedly instigating the East St. Louis, Illinois, race riots in 1919) appeared at a mass rally at Eighteenth Street and Michigan to raise money for an appeal, Crews was one of the speakers to address the five thousand African Americans in attendance.[31] Three of Crews's addresses, however, stand out and are worth noting.

In 1903, the Missouri state legislature again addressed the idea of segregated facilities on railroads operating in the state. Rural Democrats, who had pursued a number of antiblack initiatives since overturning Reconstruction in the 1870s, advocated Jim Crow arrangements for railroad travel in the state. According to Herman Kinsler, Crews's speech to the legislature helped galvanize state Republicans, who teamed with urban Democrats to defeat the bill.[32] Sixteen years later, Crews addressed an assembly at all-black Sumner High School in Kansas City, Kansas. Hostilities in Europe had ended just four months earlier, and African American intellectuals were demanding that the just-concluded war for democracy overseas be considered a prelude to a successful fight for the rights of African Americans at home. In his speech to the students, Crews invoked traditional American ideals and American heroes, mingled with particularly African American themes and concerns.

Crews began his February address by noting the great Americans who had been born in that month.[33] The first three names Crews mentioned would have been instantly recognizable to any American—George Washington, Benjamin Franklin, and Abraham Lincoln. The last three were well known to Crews and the students: Sumner history instructor Greene B. Buster, drama instructor J. P. King, and assistant principal J. J.

31. *Kansas City Sun*, March 8, July 12, 1919.

32. Kinsler, *Trip South*, 8; Lorenzo J. Greene, Gary R. Kremer, and Antonio F. Holland, *Missouri's Black Heritage*, 112. Crews led a six-man delegation from Kansas City to the state capitol. Among the contingent were teacher J. Silas Harris and Lewis Woods, publisher of the *Rising Sun*. James Milton Turner, a former Kansas City teacher who by then had become an influential lawyer in St. Louis, also addressed the legislature. *Kansas City Rising Sun*, February 6, 1903; *Kansas City Rising Sun*, February 13, 1903.

33. *Western Messenger*, February 28, 1919.

Lewis. Two of the names were important figures in African American history and culture: Richard Allen, founder of the African Methodist Episcopal Church, and Emmett Scott, former top lieutenant of black educator Booker T. Washington who had served as assistant secretary of war during the World War. Crews argued that each of these gentlemen was worthy of study and emulation. That was not, however, the crux of Crews's message, which unfolded in two parts.

First, he encouraged the students to believe in the ideals professed by American society. The Constitution, he contended (echoing the words of many prominent African Americans of the time), did not need to be changed to provide black citizens with their rights; it need only be "honestly and justly enforced." His second message was a warning and a demand. In words strikingly similar to those used by W. E. B. Du Bois two months later in an editorial in *Crisis,* Crews put the nation on notice that black soldiers returning from Europe came home with one thought in their minds: "We heard the call of the country; we answered; we left our homes and those we loved; while gone we learned this: We've been fighting for Democracy, and we have come home to enjoy the same."[34]

In August of that year, Crews again was the featured speaker at an emancipation celebration in Maryville, Missouri. In his nineteenth appearance in Maryville, Crews challenged the underlying perceptions that seemed to drive racial violence. The summer had seen race riots in the urban South, the Midwest, and the Great Plains, in which rampaging whites had attacked black individuals, homes, and institutions.[35] Crews was obviously disturbed by the violence, and he asked why the "whole race must answer for the wrongs of one of us." Black Americans, he argued, wanted nothing more than a fair deal, something that appeared to be lacking that summer.[36]

Sometime before World War I, Crews purchased the *Kansas City Sun* from Lewis Woods. Crews treated the *Sun* as though it were a small-town newspaper. No happening in the African American community was so small it could not receive a mention in Crews's paper. No one was

34. Ibid. In the May edition of *Crisis* magazine, Du Bois published what biographer David Levering Lewis calls his second-most famous editorial, "Returning Soldiers." The final lines: "We return. We return from fighting. We return fighting. Make way for Democracy! We saved it in France, and by the Great Jehovah, we will save it in the United States of America, or know the reason why." *Crisis* 18 (May 1919): 13–14, in *W. E. B. Du Bois: Biography of a Race, 1868–1919,* by Lewis, 578.

35. There were about twenty-five race riots that summer. James Weldon Johnson would label it "The Red Summer."

36. *Kansas City Sun,* August 9, 1919.

too poor or too rich to be excluded. For example, when two prominent members of Kansas City's African American communities married in 1919, the *Sun* published the entire guest list attending the nuptials, along with the present for the newlyweds brought by each guest—on the front page. The club meetings, the social events, the comings and goings of members of the African American communities helped fill the *Sun*'s columns.

Crews, however, also saw the advancement of the race as a fundamental part of the *Sun*'s mission. Whether on the front page or in its editorials inside, the *Sun* strove to be an advocate for African Americans. As it became apparent that Lincoln High School had become outdated and inadequate, Crews ran the entire contents of a petition to the Kansas City Board of Education outlining the community's grievances concerning the condition of the school. When a group of Kansas City African Americans formed an organization to champion the cause of civil rights, Crews ran its platform in its entirety. And he did not show favoritism toward one school of thought or another: meetings of the local chapter of Marcus Garvey's United Negro Improvement Association, appearances by black scholar W. E. B. Du Bois, and meetings of the National Negro Business League (of which Crews was a member) received equal treatment in the *Sun*. Crews's goal, simply put, was to address those concerns "that tend to uplift and inspire the race." The paper's mission was consistent with Crews's personal philosophy. As much as any man or woman in the two Kansas Cities, Crews was involved with all of the significant issues facing black Kansas City. He sat on the board of directors for Wheatley-Provident and the YMCA, and he had strong ties to Western University. He joined Allen Chapel, the city's first and preeminent African Methodist Episcopal Church, shortly after his arrival in Kansas City. He was a member of several fraternal orders, and historian Janet Bruce notes Crews's participation in the meetings that led to the formation of the National Negro League and the creation of the legendary Kansas City Monarchs. At least one admirer labeled Crews "the Moses" of black Kansas City. "He has laid his life on the altar for his people," the letter to the *Sun* concluded.[37]

Crews also saw the *Sun* as a way to maintain connections between Kansas City and the smaller rural communities in its hinterlands. Each week's edition contained reports from the *Sun*'s "foreign correspondents": from Lathrop, Liberty, Excelsior Springs, and Plattsburg on the

37. Ibid., May 3, 1919; April 2, 1921; Bruce, *The Kansas City Monarchs: Champions of Black Baseball*, 149n.

north side of the Missouri River; from Springfield, Marshall, Louisiana, and Columbia, Missouri; from even smaller Missouri locales such as Blackburn, Fairville, Clarksville, Utica, Meadville, and Kissenger. The *Sun* even claimed a foreign correspondent in Lincoln, Nebraska, and when teacher Anna Jones retired in the early 1920s and moved westward she served briefly as the *Sun*'s "California correspondent."[38]

The *Sun*'s editorials reflected the concerns of African Americans in Kansas City and throughout the country. Crews lobbied for the commonplace—the establishment and support of black-owned businesses, the need to beautify parts of black Kansas City—to the extraordinary. His editorials sometimes reflected a combination of the need for racial uplift, affirmations of racial identity, as well as paternalistic views toward the less fortunate. For example, in a 1921 editorial, he reminded his readers that "by the process of association, they as individuals are constantly representing the entire race." Shabbily dressed black men and women, he argued, "can do more to arouse opposition to blacks than one hundred carefully refined properly dressed Negroes can overcome in a decade." His final comment: "If you go into a white place of business demanding service, see to it that your dress is beyond reproach; your linen immaculate; your voice modulated; your laughter signifying culture. Never mind about the white fellow who doesn't come up to that standard. HE BELONGS. YOU ARE AN ALIEN."[39]

On the other hand, when Kansas City voters approved a bond issue in 1921 for the construction and maintenance of buildings in the school system, Crews urged that African Americans remain vigilant, in case the monies were spent "as usual," "without due regard to the interests of our children." "Let the Negroes of Kansas City organize," Crews said, "to intelligently and firmly demand that their share of improvements materialize." And when U.S. troops occupied the black Caribbean republic of Haiti earlier that summer, Crews and the *Sun* joined the cries of black journalists and intellectuals denouncing the move.[40]

Although Crews would fairly cover the news of black Democrats, he stayed firmly in the Republican camp. He particularly chafed, however, at the violence that typically accompanied election day in Kansas City. Crews was particularly offended by physical assaults on African American women who attempted to vote in November 1920, the first national

38. *Kansas City Sun*, April 1, 1922.
39. Ibid., August 13, 1921 (emphasis in original).
40. Ibid., April 16, August 13, 1921.

election in which women were allowed to cast their ballots. Crews lashed out at the "criminal element" that had attacked women voters. Under huge headlines—"DEMOCRATIC CUSSEDNESS UNSURPASSED: Brutality of Their Negro Puppets without a Parallel in Human Depravity"—Crews outlined the case against Democratic stalwarts in a front-page editorial.

> The crucifixion of Christ upon Calvary has stood for nearly twenty centuries as the very acme of human *depravity,* only to be dethroned by Kansas City Negro Democrats at the recent election. For years white men have *intimidated, beaten* and even *murdered* inoffensive Negro men who sought to exercise their right of *franchise* at the ballot box, but the brutal acts of those white men were God-like in comparison with the treatment of our *best* and most refined women, at the polls, on last Tuesday by the so-called Negro Democrats of Kansas City. Their acts of *inhumanity* toward the women of their own *race* at the several voting places, is beyond description. To have witnessed the outbursts that greeted the poor old white-haired *mother,* the young *wife,* the innocent *sister* as they approached the polls would have frozen the blood in the veins of a man of iron. But, thank God, the "*day of vengeance*" has arrived. Mr. Governor, the presence of these Negroes in this community is not desired. They are protected criminals, a MENACE TO SOCIETY.[41]

Crews and his staff were not above playfully chastising other elements of the community—black or white—that deserved it. Willa Glenn, the *Sun*'s business manager, also authored a weekly column, "Betty and Sam's Little Corner." In her column, Glenn fired off one-line comments on whatever caught her eye. The foibles of white Kansas City, the challenges facing black Kansas City, the mischief of prominent African Americans—all were targets of Glenn's acerbic, but impersonal, comments. Each column began with the words THEY SAY, followed by a series of Glenn's comments. For example:

"That Negroes who never had jumped out of windows before jumped out of windows the other evening when the police descended on a well-known flat in this city."

"That a married woman fired a shot at another married woman about her husband. Well he ran too fast to shoot at him."

"That when a white man stood up in Kansas City and offered his seat on a trolley to a colored woman, everybody's jaws dropped wide. Sho' nuff."

41. Ibid., November 6, 1920 (emphasis in original).

"That white folks like to visit Negro cabarets even if the law doesn't permit it. They say they get more warmth and jazz than they do at their own."

"That it's another case of marriage in haste and repentance at leisure. Guess who."

"That you cannot build a reputation on the things you are going to do. You must do them. Amen."

"That just as a certain society lady was proudly declaring how promptly she paid her bills, a sheriff rang her doorbell and produced a summons for her to appear in court and show reason why she had burned up ten tons of anthracite coal of a coal company and did not pay for it. She fainted."

"That a certain young Miss whose feet come together and whose knees are about two feet apart is wondering how she can wear the narrow skirts to be in vogue this spring. Well, we don't know, either."[42]

Glenn, a graduate of Western University who had worked at the *Sun* since 1910, was not afraid to let "Betty and Sam" discuss racial politics, either. In fact, she seems to have been more militant and more assertive in some respects than was Crews. One column in 1920 notes "that a nigger-hater is not only an enemy to Democracy but a curse to himself," whereas another offered "that the order 'SHOOT TO KILL' is fine, just right, just the thing, PROVIDED the man you shoot is a Negro." Like Crews, Glenn believed firmly in the uplift and the advancement of the race. Whereas in one column she lamented the number of conservative African Americans in the two Kansas Cities, in another she complimented "Kansas City Negroes" for a "display of race consciousness and racial loyalty that should be inspiring to the race everywhere."[43]

In 1921, Nelson Crews's health began to falter. For the next two years, operation of the *Sun* was left up to Willa Glenn, though Crews still made occasional appearances at the newspaper offices and maintained a limited speaking schedule. But on April 24, 1923, Crews died at his home at 2624 Highland Avenue. His death brought forth tributes from all over the country: J. Silas Harris, who was then employed by the federal government in Washington, DC, sent his condolences, as

42. Ibid., February 14, December 4, 1920; March 6, March 27, 1921; May 6, 1922.

43. Ibid., July 3, 1920; March 6, May 14, 1921 (emphasis in original); May 6, 1922. Glenn started at the *Sun* for a five-dollar weekly salary. Because "Betty and Sam's Little Corner" was picked up by other black newspapers, Glenn's income was two hundred dollars a month in 1919. She married C. Lloyd Peebles, an intern at the Old City Hospital, in 1919.

did friends in New York, St. Louis, Denver, Chicago, and Omaha as well as acquaintances from communities throughout Missouri.[44]

After Crews's death, a group of sixteen investors purchased the *Sun* and attempted to keep it operating. The group included some of the most prominent and prosperous names in black Kansas City: Fred Dabney, Samuel R. Hopkins, Theron B. Watkins, Reuben Street, L. Amasa Knox, the Reverend D. A. Holmes, and the Reverend James Wesley Hurse, among others. The group, however, lacked any journalistic experience. It also soon proved that a group with sixteen leaders actually had none, and by the end of 1925, the *Sun*'s almost thirty years of operation came to a close.

Fortunately, black Kansas City had another strong newspaper already in operation by the time of the *Sun*'s demise: Chester A. Franklin's *Kansas City Call.*

Chester Arthur Franklin was born June 7, 1880, in Denison, Texas. In 1887, his parents decided to join the migration north to the promised land of Kansas; their original goal was the all-black community of Nicodemus, in northwestern Kansas. On the way, the Franklins changed their minds and opted for Omaha, Nebraska. There, Chester's father, George, first operated a barbershop before he began a career as a newspaper publisher. In 1891, the first copy of the *Omaha Enterprise,* a black weekly, appeared. Chester Franklin recalled years later that his father started the newspaper to give his son experience in his chosen profession.[45]

Chester finished high school in Omaha and attended the University of Nebraska at Lincoln for two years before his father's health began to fail. Chester took over the operation of the newspaper, assisted by his mother, Clara, and was forced to leave the university. In 1898, the family moved to Denver, Colorado, hoping the drier, colder climate might help George Franklin's health. The Franklin family bought the *Colorado Statesman* and renamed it the *Star,* but meanwhile, George Franklin's health continued to decline. His death in 1901 left Chester and Clara with the responsibility for running the *Star,* which they did for the next twelve years. In that span, the *Star* became the leading voice for African Americans in Colorado. It was only at the *Star*'s insistence, for example, that white-collar jobs within state government were opened up to African Americans before World War I.[46]

44. Ibid., May 5, 1923.

45. Young and Young, *Your Kansas City and Mine,* 12–13; Thomas D. Wilson, "Chester A. Franklin and Harry S. Truman: An African-American Conservative and the 'Conversion' of the Future President," 49.

46. Young and Young, *Your Kansas City and Mine,* 13.

Table 3.1.
Kansas City, Missouri's Black Newspapers

Newspaper	Years published	Editor (where known)
Colored Messenger	1900–1902	
Dispatch	1886–1889	R. T. Coles
Freedman's Record	1886	
Free Press	1800	H. H. Johnson
Gate City Press	1880–1889	J. Dallas Bowser
Independent	1879–1883	
Kansas City American	1928–1943	Felix Payne
Kansas City Call	1919–present	Chester Franklin
Kansas City Sun	1914–1925	Nelson Crews*
Kansas-Missouri Enterprise	1881–1884	
Liberator	1901–1910	
Messenger	1894–1900	
National Mirror	1885–1918	
New Missouri	1894–1900	
Observer	1896–1901	
Record Searchlight	1908–1927	
Rising Son	1896–1914	Lewis Woods*
Searchlight	1901–1910	
Signal	1908–1927	
Sun	1800–1881	
Western Argus	1891–1892	
Western Messenger	1908–1920	Rev. James Goins

*There is some confusion as to the tenure of the *Rising Son* (or *Sun*) and the *Kansas City Sun*. Nelson Crews, publisher of the *Kansas City Sun*, included the life of Lewis Woods's *Rising Son* as part of his paper's history. According to city directories, Crews served as editor of Woods's paper early in the 1910s before purchasing the paper from Woods in 1914 and moving it to new offices on Eighteenth Street. Woods remained as the paper's business manager through World War I.

Source: Elvis Gibson, *Kansas City: Mecca of the New Negro*, 23, undated clipping likely from the *Kansas City Call*.

Seeking a larger market, Chester Franklin moved to Kansas City in 1913, intent on starting another newspaper. The outbreak of World War I delayed Franklin's plans, but in the interim he opened a printing business at 1408 Main Street and established himself as one of the community's leading citizens. On May 6, 1919, he published the first edition of the *Kansas City Call* from his new offices at 1311 East Eighteenth Street. That first edition was a four-page sheet, and Franklin printed just two thousand copies, but it marked the beginning of a long and venerable run in Kansas City.[47] Getting the newspaper started was no easy task. The local printers' union, with its all-white membership, would not allow any of its members to assist Franklin. Subscriptions were raised by word of mouth. Despite these obstacles, Chester and Clara Franklin made the *Call* a viable enterprise. In 1922, the *Call* moved into new offices at 1713–15–17 East Eighteenth Street, which remained its home into the twenty-first century. With Clara Franklin going door-to-door selling subscriptions, the *Call* soon had one of the largest circulation bases of any black weekly in the country. By 1940, the *Call* sold twenty thousand papers a week, a not-so-negligible total in a metropolitan area with just seventy thousand African Americans.[48]

Like Crews, Franklin saw one of the roles of his journalistic enterprise was to promote the African American community. The *Call*, like the *Sun*, became a powerful advocate for the concerns of black Kansas City. His philosophy was a mixture of fervent Republicanism with a strong dose of personal responsibility and black economic self-help. In 1922, he wrote:

> Our business used to center around 12th Street in what is near down-town territory now. We did not buy and we were shoved back. We moved to Eighteenth and again as renters we have been dispossessed. If we do not see tomorrow with all its wondrous growth we are not worth-while citizens. We must be builders of greatness if we would share it. Let us buy homes and then investment property too. Too many dollars are going into the froth of life. Too much social furbelows, too little savings accounts. Too many empty honors, too little hardy businesses. Too much common labor, too little craftsmen. Our grip on the industries of our section cannot be strong if we are content with anything less than a man's share of responsibility. Kansas City does not owe us a living nearly as much as we owe it a real benefit from our living here.[49]

Franklin, in the first years of the *Call*, was more conservative than many of his readers. Yet, like Crews, he was much in demand as a speaker. Shortly after his arrival in Kansas City, for example, Franklin addressed the congregation at Second Baptist on "worth-while life purposes."[50] He and Crews, in particular, disagreed on some issues, but

47. Ibid.; Wilson, "Franklin and Truman," 49–50.
48. Young and Young, *Your Kansas City and Mine*, 130–31.
49. *Kansas City Call*, February 4, 1922, as quoted in Wilson, "Franklin and Truman," 51.
50. *Western Messenger*, January 10, 1919.

even Crews had to compliment Franklin for his stand against an article published in the *Kansas City Star* in 1922.

Crews in an editorial took an opportunity "to compliment the Editor of the *Kansas City Call*" for his "courageous and unanswerable defense of our race from the scurrilous and unwarranted attack that appeared recently in the columns of *The Kansas City Star.* His article had the right ring and brought back to our minds the militant and forceful Franklin of the *Denver Star.* After all, the Negro Journals and Journalists may disagree on minor things, yet on those things affecting the rights, liberties and solidarity of the race, they stand as one."[51]

Franklin remained a conservative throughout his long tenure with the *Call,* particularly in matters economic. In 1930, as the weight of the Depression was beginning to be felt, Franklin reiterated his stance on free-market capitalism and matters of economic self-help:

> Opportunity is on every hand, but somehow our minds work in a groove and we stay on our treadmill and starve rather than attempt anything new. For instance here in Kansas City where some 60,000 of us live, we are a great big city in itself. We specialize in restaurants, and other businesses where small capital will enable us to go. But there we stop, like a lot of sheep halted at a stream a foot wide. It ought to be equally obvious that we could supply the food to be cooked. Capital for stores is a bigger problem, but we do not attempt to supply ourselves even with the vegetables. The sight of men and women of other races making their daily round of Negro neighborhoods with the product of truck gardens, is enough to make one despair of a people who bewail their lack of employment but refuse to grasp such evident opportunity.[52]

That did not mean that Franklin adhered to a rigid, individualistic stance. In an address to the annual meeting of the Kansas City Urban League in 1937, he argued that black joblessness was not completely a societal issue. "The problem of the unemployed mass of Negroes," Franklin said, "is equally the problem of employed Negroes who produce, and it is for all to carry on the struggle together. Organized, persistent effort is the only solution. We must fight with our heads and not with our tempers."[53]

51. *Kansas City Sun,* January 21, 1922.

52. *Kansas City Call,* September 19, 1930. Franklin also was an ardent supporter of the National Negro Business League, started by Booker T. Washington earlier in the century.

53. KCULP, "Minutes, Annual Meeting, February 11, 1937," box M1, vol. 2.

In other areas, the *Call* had become more moderate by 1930, in part because of two changes in Franklin's life. In 1925, he married Ada Crogman, the daughter of William H. Crogman, longtime president of all-black Atlanta University. Presumably, Chester and Ada met for the first time when she traveled from New York to Kansas City to produce her race pageant, *Milestones,* a festival of African American history and accomplishments, complete with music. By that time, Franklin had also hired Roy Wilkins, a journalism graduate from the University of Minnesota, as a beginning reporter. Wilkins, an active member of the NAACP, soon won a following with his "Talking It Over" column.[54]

Wilkins believed he had much to learn from Franklin, but he was not afraid to voice his displeasure with some of his boss's editorial decisions. In deciding what would go on the *Call*'s front page, Franklin followed many of his contemporaries in the newspaper world and looked for the most sensational item. Scandals, sex, and murder, in this view, deserved the largest headlines possible, and Franklin obliged. Wilkins said years later that he was dismayed by some of the headlines that Franklin ran: "WIFE MURDERED IN COLD BLOOD: HUSBAND SAYS HE COULDN'T STAND HER 'ARGUMENTS'" and "GIRL'S THROAT CUT IN FIGHT OVER MEN."[55]

With the help of Ada Crogman, Wilkins persuaded Franklin to give equal attention to political news and items that affirmed the African American community. Franklin relented, somewhat. News vital to the African American community worked its way onto the front page—next to the blaring headlines about the latest sensational murder.

By 1928, the *Call*'s staff had grown to twenty-one employees. Its circulation continued to grow, and in 1928, Franklin purchased a thirty-two-page Goss Straight Line printing press, described by Wilkins as "a wonder of steel and ink drums 19 feet long, 5 feet 6 inches wide and 13 feet high that could print and fold 24,000 papers an hour."

With the installation of the Goss press, which was completed in 1929 just after the *Call*'s tenth anniversary, the *Call* had the second-best printing facility of any black newspaper in the country—behind only the *Chicago Defender.* To help defray the costs of the new press, the same year the *Call* produced a "Progress Edition" of fifty-six pages, which for years stood as the largest single issue published by a black weekly. In addition, with the help of a collection system devised by Clara Franklin,

54. Young and Young, *Your Kansas City and Mine,* 131; Chester A. Franklin Collection, box BA4.FRA12, BA4.FRA16; Willard B. Gatewood, *Aristocrats of Color: The Black Elite, 1880–1920,* 92, 270.

55. Wilkins, *Standing Fast: The Autobiography of Roy Wilkins,* 58.

the *Call* became the first black newspaper to have its circulation certified by the Audit Bureau of Circulations.[56]

Throughout the 1920s and 1930s, Franklin, Wilkins, and the *Call* stood out as champions for Kansas City's African American communities. For one of their first victories, Franklin and paper are credited with forcing the court system to end the long-standing tradition of banning African Americans from serving on juries. Through its editorials and front-page coverage, the *Call* also fought for the right of African Americans to purchase and reside in homes wherever they could afford them. It lobbied vigorously for employment opportunities for black residents. In 1930, Roy Wilkins organized a boycott of a local bakery that, despite the black community's strong patronage, refused to hire African Americans as truck drivers. After a few brief weeks, the bakery relented, and soon black men were driving its trucks.[57]

One of Franklin's most unrelenting crusades, however, was against black-on-black crime. It was not a new phenomenon, even in the 1920s. W. E. B. Du Bois had noted the prevalence of intraracial violence in the Seventh Ward of Philadelphia in the last decade of the nineteenth century. The problem, as Du Bois saw it, was created by poverty, poor education, crowded living conditions, and a growing sense of despair in a society that treated most black men and women as nonpersons or as less than human.[58] Hoping to address the problem in Kansas City, Franklin began in 1926 to run a front-page box, complete with an illustration of the gallows, with the number of African Americans killed by African Americans for the year. His motives for decrying black-on-black crime were both moral and practical. In an editorial in 1929, Franklin asserted that behind the continuation of black crime loomed the threat of race riot. "When indignation at some crime stirs this community," Franklin wrote, "the mob will not be choosy in whom it attacks. 'Race' will leap into the foreground, and Kansas City will have its race riot—all because Negro murders are treated as matters of small moment." Franklin then argued for the vigorous prosecution of acts of violence against African Americans or the community would face the consequences. Franklin had adopted a similar tone in an editorial earlier in the year, after an all-white jury acquitted a black defendant accused of murdering another African American man. "Murder is murder," Frank-

56. Young and Young, *Your Kansas City and Mine,* 130–31; Wilkins, *Standing Fast,* 81.

57. Young and Young, *Your Kansas City and Mine,* 130; Wilkins, *Standing Fast,* 99.

58. Du Bois, *The Philadelphia Negro: A Social Study,* 282–86. See also Roger Lane, *Roots of Violence in Black Philadelphia, 1869–1900* and *William Dorsey's Philadelphia and Ours.*

lin wrote. "That verdict amounted to saying the killing of Negroes by Negroes is no crime."[59]

By 1931, Wilkins was making twenty-six hundred dollars a year as the *Call*'s columnist, and the paper's circulation had topped twenty thousand a week. The paper published editions in communities across the Southwest, and had subscribers in a dozen states. The bulk of its circulation, however, was in Missouri, with about five thousand subscribers in rural parts of the state. It appeared the newspaper had put together a winning team, but in February 1931, officials with the NAACP again approached Wilkins about taking a post as the organization's assistant secretary. After much deliberation and reaching a compromise on salary (thirty-three hundred dollars a year plus ten dollars to cover the cost of Wilkins's train ticket to New York for an interview), Wilkins accepted the post. It was the beginning of a long and illustrious career with the NAACP for Wilkins. In 1949, when the organization's head, Walter White, took a leave of absence for health reasons, Wilkins was appointed acting executive secretary. Six years later, after White died from a heart attack, Wilkins was hired as the NAACP's executive secretary, a position he held until 1977.[60]

To replace Wilkins as news editor, Franklin appointed Lucile Bluford, the twenty-year-old daughter of a Kansas City schoolteacher. Bluford had worked for the *Call* on a part-time basis as a teenager, and was familiar with the staff and Franklin's goals. The *Call* continued on the same course under Bluford; its pages continued to mix themes of racial uplift, self-help, and sensational crimes. Franklin had become more moderate in his use of the latter, however, and by the end of the 1930s, the *Call* had adopted a more activist stance. In 1939, Franklin encouraged Bluford, who had a bachelor's degree from the University of Kansas, to apply to the graduate program at the University of Missouri's School of Journalism. The school had not accepted African American students before, but in the wake of Lloyd Gaines's successful suit against the university and its law school, Bluford thought there would be no obstacle to her enrolling. School officials, however, said they would not enroll Bluford until the Gaines case had been completely settled. Bluford filed suit, but the state and the university refused to budge. In 1941, to remain in compliance with the U.S. Supreme Court ruling in the Gaines case, the State of Missouri established a school of journalism at all-black Lincoln

59. *Kansas City Call*, January 4, March 22, 1929; November 14, 1930.
60. Wilkins, *Standing Fast*, 203, 220, 341.

University. The state spent sixty-five thousand dollars that first year for the "school's" three students.[61]

Chester Franklin entered semiretirement in 1948, leaving the operation of the *Call* to his wife, Ada, and Lucile Bluford. When Chester Franklin died in 1955, Ada Franklin became publisher and Bluford was appointed editor. The two women carried on the *Call*'s activist tradition, and after Ada's death, Bluford was left to maintain the paper. She remained the most visible member of the *Call* until her death in 2003.

The *Call* remained a Republican paper throughout Chester Franklin's lifetime, though his enthusiasm for the Party of Lincoln may have waned from time to time.[62] He remained critical, however, of the political machinations and the crime and violence associated with Tom Pendergast's Democratic machine. Whether Pendergast or his associates considered Franklin and the *Call* as any type of a threat is open to debate, but in 1928, one of Pendergast's black associates, Felix Payne, with the help of Dr. William J. Thompkins, started the *Kansas City American.* Payne was well known in the black community as a gambler connected with an illegal club on Twelfth Street. At the same time, he was known as a smart and generous businessman who gave freely of his time and money to causes affecting African Americans.[63]

According to an obituary published by his rival, the *Kansas City Call,* Felix Payne was born November 14, 1884, in Marshall, Missouri. He grew up in Marshall, but early in the twentieth century he moved to Kansas City where he met and married Emma C. Collins. He also quickly became involved with community issues. In 1909, he was co-owner of a black baseball team, the Kansas City Giants. In 1913, he was one of the charter members of the Paseo YMCA, and in the 1920s, he served on the board of directors of the Wheatley-Provident Hospital. By 1919, Payne was an active voice among the city's black Democrats. His most significant contribution came in 1919, the year after the World War ended. City leaders chose to erect a monument to the men who had died in the war and to the principles of freedom and liberty for which

61. "Lucile Bluford Deposition," Benson Papers, box 102; Bluford to Franklin, July 7, 1950, Franklin Collection, box BA4.FRA13; Greene, Kremer, and Holland, *Missouri's Black Heritage,* 155–56; Richard Klugler, *Simple Justice: The History of "Brown v. Board of Education" and Black America's Struggle for Equality,* 202–4.

62. See Wilson, "Franklin and Truman."

63. Historians have begun to take note of the role underworld figures played in the development of African American communities. See, for example, St. Clair Drake and Horace R. Cayton, *Black Metropolis: A Study of Negro Life in a Northern City;* and Robert E. Weems Jr., *Black Business in the Black Metropolis: The Chicago Metropolitan Assurance Company, 1925–1985.*

they had fought. A citywide fund-raising drive began, and Payne's team, with a boost from bandleader Bennie Moten, collected the biggest donation. In 1920, a site south of Union Station was chosen for the monument, and on Armistice Day (November 11), 1926, Liberty Memorial was dedicated by President Calvin Coolidge.[64]

In the mid-1920s, Payne entered a partnership with Thompkins for the establishment of a black Democratic weekly as a challenge to the blatant Republicanism of Franklin and the *Kansas City Call.* Payne apparently provided the financial wherewithal, leaving the day-to-day operation of the paper to Thompkins, who had served twice as superintendent of Old City Hospital (General Hospital No. 2). Thompkins had been born in Jefferson City in 1884, and after earning his medical degree, he moved to Kansas City in 1906. His political connections and medical expertise allowed Thompkins to attain a modest fortune, some of which he poured into real estate (he financed the construction of the Thompkins Building at Eighteenth Street and The Paseo) and some of which he put into the newspaper. The *American* supported Democratic candidates at both the statewide and the national levels. Its influence (with a big help from the Pendergast operation) put Kansas City's African Americans in the Franklin Delano Roosevelt camp long before most other urban areas.[65]

The *American* survived through the worst of the Depression, but it could not survive the dismantling of the Pendergast machine. Thompkins, as reward for his political work within the African American communities, was appointed recorder of deeds by President Franklin Roosevelt in 1934 and moved to Washington, DC, where he lived out the last ten years of his life. In 1939, Tom Pendergast pleaded guilty to tax-evasion charges. He served fifteen months in prison but died shortly after his release. Without Pendergast's protection, the rest of the machine fell apart. The *Kansas City American* ceased publication in 1941.[66]

Until sometime in 2001, two photos hung in the main lobby of Kansas City's main post office. One showed the city's postal employees in 1895 standing in front of the new postal building. A score or so of

64. *Kansas City Call,* date unknown; *Kansas City Sun,* October 4, 1919; Rick Montgomery and Shirl Kasper, *Kansas City: An American Story,* 204–5.

65. In 1932, black voters in Kansas City supported Roosevelt by a margin of almost three to one. Ten years earlier, they had supported Republican candidates by almost an identical margin.

66. *Kansas City Call,* date unknown; Montgomery and Kasper, *Kansas City,* 204–5. Felix Payne and his wife celebrated their fiftieth wedding anniversary in 1961 at a special celebration at the Beau Brummels Club, of which Felix was a charter member.

men—all white—stand at crisp attention. In the background, hand wrapped around one of the pillars, stands one sole black man—James H. Crews, the city's first black postal worker. The next year, in 1896, a similar photo was taken. In this one, James Crews, mustachioed with heavy sideburns, sits prominently among all of the uniformed postal workers, along with two or three other black postal carriers. The photos again illustrate the vagaries of racial segregation in Kansas City. At a time when African Americans were being pushed more and more out of the picture across the country, Kansas City's postal workers were inviting black men in.

Like his brother Nelson, James Crews was born in Howard County, Missouri, sometime before or during the Civil War.[67] He may have been the oldest of the four Crews brothers to reach adulthood. He moved to Kansas City in 1877, when he was just seventeen or eighteen. Nothing can be said with any certainty as to how young James earned his living before the 1890s or how he met his wife, Florence, a native of Washington, DC.[68] We can say that by 1900, James was working for the post office and that he and Florence and their four sons were the only black family living in the 2400 block of Wabash (one block west of Prospect). By 1910, at least one other black family had joined the Crewses, but by 1920, James Crews had remarried and moved to 2735 Vine Street, about two blocks away from his brother's home. Like his brother Nelson, James Crews was involved with a number of institutions and causes in Kansas City's African American communities. He was instrumental in the founding of the Paseo YMCA, was a staunch member of the Masons, belonged to the Kansas City Urban League, and was an active member of the NAACP in the early 1920s. In 1921, James Crews was one of the city's five delegates to the NAACP's national convention in Detroit, and he reported back, through brother Nelson's *Sun,* on the proceedings. In September of the following year, James Crews, at age sixty-two, survived an emergency appendectomy; his condition was serious enough that his youngest son, Blanton Crews, rushed from San Francisco to be with his father. At the same time, Nelson Crews was stricken with the illness that would take his life the next

67. Young and Young, *Your Kansas City and Mine,* 176. Young and Young and the 1900 census list James Crews's birth date as 1859. The 1910 census, however, lists his age as forty-seven, but ten years later, the census reports his age as sixty, consistent with an 1859 or 1860 birth date.

68. The 1910 census lists Florence as a mulatto and the two sons still living at home as such as well.

year. James Crews would outlive his younger brother by more than two decades; he died in 1946, and a postal station later was named in his honor.[69]

African Americans continued to work as carriers for the postal service through the interwar period. Few, however, worked as clerks. One exception was James Silas Harris, a former teacher and a former clerk for a U.S. Senate committee who worked in the COD and insurance division at the Gateway Station across from Union Station.[70]

Business in the Black Community

When it is considered that Blacks started out without capital or independent business experience and faced severe racial discrimination . . . the record of black ownership by the early twentieth century was remarkable.

—ECONOMIC HISTORIAN GILBERT C. FITE

By the beginning of World War I, African Americans in the United States had accumulated more than seven hundred million dollars in wealth. Much of this wealth can be attributed to the rise in urban areas of a substantial black entrepreneurial class; in 1913, more than forty thousand black businesses existed. Many of them were "mom-and-pop" operations, with few if any black employees. Yet within many communities, these small operations became community landmarks. Through perseverance, hard work, and occasionally a little luck, black businesses in cities such as Kansas City overcame their limited capitalization and gained a modicum of success.[71]

Perhaps the two most recognized black entrepreneurs in Kansas City in the 1920s and 1930s were Homer B. Roberts and Reuben Street. Roberts, a war veteran, became one of the first African American car salesmen in the country; he also was a partner in several other businesses around Kansas City. Street went from managing a café to owning a hotel that became one of the symbols of the Eighteenth and Vine district.

69. Ibid., 16; *Kansas City Sun*, June 25, July 2, 9, 1921; June 17, September 30, 1922; Young and Young, *Your Kansas City and Mine*, 176.

70. *Kansas City Call*, September 18, 1925.

71. See U.S. Department of Commerce, Bureau of the Census, *The Social and Economic Status of the Black Population in the United States: An Historical View, 1790–1978.*

Roberts came to the Kansas City area around the beginning of the twentieth century.[72] He was born in 1885 in Ash Grove, Missouri, a rural community northwest of Springfield. Sometime in the next ten years, Roberts's father, Francis M. Roberts, moved the family to Wellington, Kansas, and it is there that Homer Roberts grew up. After attending Tuskegee Institute briefly, Roberts enrolled in the fall of 1906 in the newly established "subfreshman" program at Kansas State University; he became one of the first African Americans admitted to the university. At either Tuskegee or Kansas State, Roberts gained a passion for electrical engineering. His engineering skills also fed into his interest in a "new contraption—the automobile."

Roberts enlisted in the army in 1917 after recruiting thirty other soldiers and was assigned to the Signal Corps. In April 1918, he was commissioned a first lieutenant with the 325th Field Signal Battalion, the only signal unit of African Americans at the front lines, and sent to France; Roberts was the first African American commissioned in the Signal Corps. He served eight months in Europe, where he participated in some of the heaviest battles of the war. By the time the armistice was signed, Roberts had been recommended for promotion to captain.[73] Between 1907 and 1917, he is believed to have worked intermittently in the automobile business, although the nature of his activities cannot be determined. We do know, however, that his career as an entrepreneur was interrupted by the entrance of the United States into the First World War. Roberts returned to Kansas City in 1919 as a war hero, but without any definite plans. As he began to ponder his future, Roberts became known throughout the African American communities as an expert on automobiles. Black men and women interested in buying cars often consulted with Roberts on the strengths and weaknesses of various models. This, combined with the reluctance of white automobile dealers in Kansas City to deal directly with African Americans, suggested a career option for Roberts.

Roberts, by then thirty-three years old, began contacting automobile dealers in the Kansas City area with a simple proposition. He would serve as a broker for the various dealerships within the African American community. In exchange for a commission on each sale, he would contact potential black buyers, help them choose a car, and arrange for the sale, financing, and delivery of each vehicle. Over the course of the

72. B. S. Restuccia, E. Edward Gibson, and Geraldlyn Sanders, *An Extraordinary Man: Homer B. Roberts, 1885–1952*, 5–7.

73. Ibid., 5–7; *Kansas City Sun*, March 29, 1919. The *Sun* account was a reprint of an article from the *Kansas City Post*, March 25, 1919.

next three years, Roberts brokered the sales of new and used automobiles to African Americans on both sides of the state line. He aggressively advertised his services, primarily through ads in the *Kansas City Sun* and later through the *Kansas City Call*. In addition to acting as the middleman for the sale of automobiles, Roberts offered to help buyers arrange financing and insurance. His business grew rapidly, and by the end of 1919 he had hired two salesmen—Robert L. Sweeney and Chauncey Davis—to join him in his office at 1509 East Eighteenth Street. Sweeney and Davis were among the first African Americans in the country hired as automobile salesmen.[74]

In 1921, with his business booming, Roberts decided to take the next step. He realized that he needed room to showcase and service the automobiles and trucks that he sold. On May 7, 1921, the Roberts Company moved into a rented space at 1516 East Nineteenth Street. The new space, though larger than the company's previous site, still allowed room for just one vehicle on display. And within a year, Roberts began to contemplate changing his status: He no longer wanted to be just a broker. He aimed to become a car dealer, receiving automobiles straight from the manufacturer for sale.[75]

His first priority was to obtain a suitable site. With the help of Samuel Hopkins (owner of Square Deal Realty), Roberts obtained a site in the middle of the 1800 block on Vine. Construction on the facility, which was built from the ground up, began in early 1923, and in late July, more than three thousand African Americans attended the opening of the Roberts Company Motor Mart. The building at 1826–28–30 Vine Street contained approximately 9,400 square feet of space with a showroom of 1,750 square feet (enough space to adequately display three vehicles). The facility would also contain a garage large enough to handle sixty cars and offer the latest in accessories. The site offered a filling station as well as space for body work, painting, and repairs. In December 1923, Roberts purchased the building from John Sears for seventy thousand dollars, and the site was christened the Roberts Building. By that time, Roberts likely had established a relationship with the Hupp Motor Company, makers of the Hupmobile. Rusty Restuccia, on the basis of his experience in the automobile industry and an analysis of the Roberts Company advertisements between 1922 and 1928, concludes that Roberts by that time had become a franchised distributor for Hupmobile, making him one of the first black men, if not the first, to become

74. Restuccia, Gibson, and Sanders, *Extraordinary Man*, 11–13.
75. Ibid., 25–35.

a dealer for one of the major manufacturers. During that time, Roberts also established business relationships with Oldsmobile and two other manufacturers.[76]

By the end of 1928, Roberts acquired two new partners: Kenneth Campbell, the husband of Sarah Rector, Kansas City's first black female millionaire; and Thomas J. "Piney" Brown, club owner, gambler, and associate of Felix Payne.[77] Early the next year, Roberts and Campbell moved to Chicago and opened a showroom for the Roberts-Campbell Motor Company, leaving Brown to manage the Kansas City showroom. By the end of 1929, Roberts had closed the Kansas City operation, and a chapter in the history of black business in Kansas City had ended. For most of the decade, Homer Roberts had maintained a presence around Eighteenth and Vine. The Roberts Building, one of the first black-owned retail and commercial complexes in the country, would stand as a monument to Homer Roberts's initiative and business acumen.[78]

The most well known of Kansas City's early business owners were Henry Perry, the city's first barbecue king, and Reuben and Ella Street, owners of a restaurant and hotel. Perry came to Kansas City in 1907, believing that there was a market for his specially prepared beef sandwiches. Operating first from a stand along Banks Alley on the west side of downtown, Perry developed a booming business, catering to the palates of both black and white Kansas Citians. Perry's reputation soon spread beyond the boundaries of the metropolitan area, and by 1920, his restaurant at Nineteenth and Vine was one of the destination points within the African American community. By 1930, despite the onset of the Depression, Perry was operating stands throughout the city and was known as Kansas City's "barbecue king." He also became known for his philanthropy. By 1921, Perry had established a tradition: for four hours on one day of each year, with the help of some of his patrons, Perry gave free barbecue sandwiches to the elderly, the young, and those too poor to afford to buy a meal. In 1929, Perry distributed 150 pounds of meat and countless loaves of bread at his annual giveaway. Even in 1930, when he was pondering whether to sell his business and move west, Perry felt obliged to offer one last free meal. On

76. Ibid., 39, 47, 59–61.

77. Eddie Barefield, a veteran of the Bennie Moten, Count Basie, and Duke Ellington orchestras, alleged that Brown ran the numbers racket on the East Side of Kansas City. Nathan W. Pearson, *Goin' to Kansas City,* 98. Brown was eulogized by jazz singer Joe Turner in his classic "Piney Brown Blues." Restuccia, Gibson, and Sanders, without an intimate knowledge of the Kansas City scene in the 1920s and 1930s, do not speculate on the nature of the relationship between Brown and Roberts.

78. Restuccia, Gibson, and Sanders, *Extraordinary Man,* 61.

June 21, he gave away free barbecue and five hundred gallons of lemonade to children under the age of eight. Perry eventually elected to remain in Kansas City. A 1939 issue of the *Negro Business Review* contains an advertisement for "HENRY PERRY: *The Barbecue King*" at Nineteenth and Highland.[79]

Reuben and Ella Street owned the most recognized hotel catering to African Americans in Kansas City. The Street Hotel, at 1510 East Eighteenth Street, played host to dignitaries and the masses alike. Reuben and Ella Street moved to Kansas City from Oklahoma shortly after their marriage in 1900. The Streets' first business was a restaurant between Forest and Tracy on Eighteenth Street. By World War I, they were operating a restaurant in the 2400 block of Vine. In 1917, they moved their business to Eighteenth Street, and by 1920 they took over the entire building and began operating their hotel. It became the favorite stop for musicians, athletes, and other celebrities as well as catering to a contingent of permanent guests. The pool hall on the first floor was the Monarchs' unofficial headquarters, and the Blue Room offered some of the finest of Kansas City's jazz artists (for a time, the Bennie Moten Orchestra was the house band). The Streets continued to operate the hotel through the interwar period.[80]

Kansas City, unlike many urban areas, offered employment to African American men in public service. Kansas City, for instance, employed eight of the eleven black men listed as police officers in the state of Missouri in the 1920 census statistics. One of the six black police detectives listed in the census was from Kansas City, as was one of the two firemen.[81] Black public servants tended to work in segregated circumstances. Fire Company no. 11 originally was housed at 1812 Vine Street before moving to Nineteenth and Vine in 1931. Both locations were in the heart of the emerging African American community on the East Side. Black police officers were often assigned to districts within these same communities, though editor Nelson Crews applauded the ability of black officers to apprehend criminals whether they were black or white.[82]

79. *Kansas City Sun*, June 25, July 2, 1921; *Kansas City Call*, May 10, 1929; June 13, 1930; Negro Chamber of Commerce, *Negro Business Review of Kansas City, Missouri*, September 22, 1939, in *Mecca of the New Negro*, by Gibson, 240.

80. Undated news clipping in Gibson, *Mecca of the New Negro*, 211.

81. U.S. Department of Commerce, Bureau of the Census, Fourteenth Census, "Selected Occupations: Tables One and Two."

82. *Kansas City Sun*, January 29, 1921.

Kansas City employed African American policemen throughout most of the twentieth century.[83] With apparently very little fanfare, the city hired Lafayette Tillman, a longtime Kansas City resident and veteran of the Spanish-American War, sometime around 1900.[84] Tillman was born March 15, 1858, in Evansville, Indiana. He was educated in the Evansville public schools before entering Oberlin College of Ohio, one of the nation's only mixed-race coed institutions of higher learning. At Oberlin, Tillman developed a passion for music and began a career as a vocalist. Over the next two decades, he sang with several touring vocal groups and as a soloist. Tillman also began working as a barber, and in 1885, shortly after marrying Amy Dods of St. Louis, he opened a shop in Wellington, Kansas. Four years later, he and his family moved to Kansas City, Missouri, and eventually Tillman opened his own shop at Twelfth and Grand Streets. He became involved in the developing African American community, joining Allen Chapel AME and participating in its choir.

The first step by the United States onto the world stage as an imperialist power (the Spanish-American War) altered Tillman's life. In July 1898, he enlisted in the United States Army and was enrolled at the rank of sergeant. By September, he had been promoted to first lieutenant, and in late December, Tillman and the Forty-ninth Infantry Regiment set sail for the Philippines, which had been "acquired" by the United States from Spain as part of the spoils of war. The natives of the Philippines objected to their new colonial masters as much as they had the old Spanish conquerors, and from 1899 to 1902, U.S. troops, including Tillman and other African Americans, were used to crush a native insurrection.[85]

The skills Tillman learned in the military were recognized when he returned to Kansas City early in the 1900s, as shortly after his return he was hired as a police patrolman. Little information about Tillman's police career has survived. By 1904, he and his family had moved into a home at Seventeenth and Lydia. Lafayette Tillman would remain at

83. The first African American on the Kansas City police force was William F. Davis, who was hired in 1874 and served fifteen years.

84. The details of Tillman's life are taken from an undated, unpaginated typescript held in the Archival Collections of the Kansas City Museum, box C14 (hereafter referred to as "Lafayette A. Tillman"). The museum's collections guide describes Tillman as the city's second black police officer; Sherry Lamb Schirmer and Richard D. McKinzie refer to Tillman as the first in *At the River's Bend: An Illustrated History of Kansas City, Independence and Jackson County.*

85. For the role of African Americans in putting down the insurrection in the Philippines, see Willard B. Gatewood, *Black Americans and the White Man's Burden, 1898–1903.*

that address until his death in 1914. A son, L. M. Tillman, would become a key member of the medical staff at Wheatley-Provident Hospital, and use the homestead as his office. His two daughters would become teachers, one in Kansas City and the other in Tipton, Missouri.[86]

Tillman's career as a patrolman would set the stage for the employment of other African American patrolmen. Some would, as mentioned above, reach the rank of detective. The most well known and efficient of Kansas City's black policemen after Tillman was Cornelius "Tug" Carter. Carter was born around 1875 and raised in Lawrence, Kansas, and before joining the police force had worked for the Rock Island Railroad. Carter was assigned primarily to African American communities but also worked a beat in the downtown districts. In 1919, he was credited with the arrest of a couple wanted in connection with a string of robberies of Chinese-operated businesses in the River Market area. In January 1921, Carter was responsible for apprehending two thieves who had taken more than seven thousand dollars' worth of jewelry. Later that year, he was commended for breaking up "the silk shirt degenerates, frequenters of gambling dens, policy shops and boot legging joints" who had begun to congregate around the businesses on Twelfth Street. In recognition of his services, black businessmen awarded Carter a medal in 1919, and in 1930, when he became the first black sergeant in the Kansas City police department, a gala banquet organized by African American citizens was held in his honor. Carter shared a home at 2124 Woodland with his sister and his brother and sister-in-law in 1920, but in 1922, he and his new wife purchased a five-room cottage at 2204 Garfield for forty-five hundred dollars.[87]

Carter was one of the two black patrolmen who survived a change in the city administration. New police commissioners dismissed all of the black officers except for Carter and John W. Hughes but then added two full-time African American officers and awarded probationary status to sixteen black officers. As a result, by the early 1920s, African Americans in Kansas City could see more than twenty of their peers wearing police uniforms.[88]

One other black police officer deserves mention, but more for his political work and his tragic end than for his exploits on the job. J. J.

86. "Lafayette A. Tillman," box C14.

87. U.S. Department of Commerce, Bureau of the Census, Fourteenth Census; *Kansas City Sun*, November 15, 1919; January 29, December 17, 1921; November 4, 1922; *Kansas City Call*, August 30, 1929.

88. *Kansas City Sun*, February 26, 1921. Among those dismissed were officers Bush Wells and Walter Howard, who were lauded by the *Sun* in 1920 for their efficient work.

Mattjoy was one of the main links between the city's white Democrats and the African American communities. In September 1919, a gathering of fifty or sixty African American Democrats unanimously selected Mattjoy as their representative. Although Mattjoy had only been in the city three years, he undoubtedly was well known in Democratic circles by this time as he had the support of Casimir Welch, a ward boss and crony of Tom Pendergast.[89] A month later, Mattjoy survived an attempt by a separate faction of black Democrats to wrest control from him. Although his opponents included some of the more prominent men in black Kansas City (Felix Payne, Homer Roberts, and doctors L. V. Tillman and E. B. Ramsey), Mattjoy maintained control. In 1920, he was selected as a Democratic committeeman and as the only black delegate from the city for the state Democratic convention.[90]

Mattjoy's reign as Democratic spokesman for the African American communities ended in 1920. Mattjoy, who was employed as a juvenile officer, had a violent confrontation with the owner of an Eighteenth Street soft drink establishment. The confrontation spilled onto the street, and gunshots were exchanged. Mattjoy, struck twice, retreated into the hallway of Fire Station no. 11 on Vine Street, where he died.[91]

Although Kansas City offered more employment options for intelligent and ambitious African American men than some of its southern counterparts, it could not always support all of them. The case of Hezekiah Walden is suggestive. In 1910, Walden, a forty-three-year-old native of Virginia, was working as a teacher at Lincoln High School. Whether he was terminated or chose to leave teaching, by 1911 he was working as a waiter to support his wife, Mary, and three children. He then began selling life insurance to African American customers for Standard Life Insurance Company of Atlanta, one of the nation's largest black insurance companies. Whether Walden was unable to make a go at selling life insurance is unknown, but in 1915 he accepted an appointment with Kansas City's Board of Public Welfare. Undoubtedly, one of his assignments was to gather information for that agency in Kansas City's various African American communities. He is listed in the city directory as one of the agency's employees for the next two years, but

89. Despite their political differences, Nelson Crews, an ardent Republican, often portrayed Mattjoy in favorable terms. "As a race man, he can not be excelled, being for his people first, last and always." *Kansas City Sun*, September 27, 1919; Montgomery and Kasper, *Kansas City*, 212.

90. *Kansas City Sun*, October 4, 1919; February 7, April 24, 1920.

91. Ibid., August 14, 1920.

after 1917 there is no record of Walden in Kansas City. He is not listed in the city directory for the next three years, nor is he or his family listed in the 1920 census for Missouri.

For a variety of reasons, insurance companies such as Standard Life could cover only a fraction of the African American market. In their stead stood a uniquely African American venture: the fraternal burial insurance company. Members of the "company" paid a monthly assessment, and at the time of a member's death, the company paid the burial expenses. In Kansas City, the most successful of these fraternal entities was the American Woodman's Fraternal Life Insurance Company. For as little as seventy-five cents a month (nine dollars a year), an individual could join American Woodman's, attend the monthly meetings, and rest assured that family members no longer faced the prospect of having to raise funds for an unexpected funeral. Through the efforts of its Kansas City representatives—supreme clerks W. A. Campbell and Nathaniel Spencer Adkins—the American Woodman's company drew the support early in the interwar period of many of black Kansas City's most prominent men and women. Among the members of Camp Five in the early 1920s were educators John R. E. Lee and Henly Cox, doctors John Perry and D. Madison Miller, lawyers Charles Calloway and William C. Hueston, editors Nelson Crews and Chester Franklin, realtor Fortune J. Weaver, Mrs. Eva Fox, Mrs. Jean McCampbell, and, surprisingly, undertakers R. V. Adkins, Theron B. Watkins, and H. B. Moore.[92]

The American Woodman's company was founded in 1900 and by the end of the First World War was well established in Kansas City under Campbell's direction. With Campbell's sudden death in 1919, Adkins, a native Texan who had come to Kansas City sometime before the war, was appointed supreme clerk and supervisor for Camp Five. Adkins and the American Woodman's company were among the first tenants of the new Lincoln office building on Eighteenth Street. Adkins was instrumental in the expansion of the Kansas City Negro Business League. During his three-year term as the organization's president, it expanded its membership from 17 to 138 members. He and his family settled in the 1300 block of Michigan Avenue, and Adkins also owned property in the area between Thirteenth and Fourteenth Streets on Highland, Michigan, and Euclid. In his role with the American Woodman's company and later as president of the Community League, Adkins eagerly counseled African Americans on financial matters. He was especially noted for the advice he gave to young couples just starting out. He was

92. Ibid., January 1, 1921.

a talented speaker and was called to address a variety of topics. In 1919, for example, he addressed the black and white employees of the Armour packinghouse on the "value and appreciation of service."[93]

Kansas City's black professional class was relatively small, but as recent immigrant James Silas Harris argued, the city attracted a number of talented black men and women in the 1920s and 1930s. From these ranks came the directors of public institutions; the organizers of political, social, and economic endeavors; and the religious and lay leaders of the black churches. Some of these professionals were home grown (or at least natives of the city's hinterlands); others were attracted from as far away as Alabama, Texas, and Colorado. The African American community's biggest loss, however, was that it could not sustain all of the talented professionals that came its way in the interwar period. Kansas City's loss would be other communities' gain.

93. Ibid., March 22, 1919; *Kansas City Call*, May 22, 1925.

Four

Institutions of Uplift

The American Negro, child of the culture that crushes him, wants to be free in a way that white men are free; for him to wish otherwise would be unnatural, unthinkable. Negroes, with but minor exceptions, still believe in the hope of economic rewards; they believe in justice, liberty, the integrity of the individual. In the heart of industrial America is a surviving remnant, perchance a saving remnant of a passion for freedom.

—RICHARD WRIGHT, 1945

AFRICAN AMERICAN AUTHOR Richard Wright understood the values that resonated with black Americans. They had internalized American ideals of freedom, justice, faith, and hope; these values would influence the ways African Americans would attempt to manipulate the concept of "race" in the twentieth century. Nowhere was that more apparent than in Kansas City. In a variety of organizations, using a wide spectrum of tactics, members of Kansas City's African American communities contributed to the nationwide quest for black freedom and equality. The cause drew business and professional elites and the packinghouse worker, the articulate and the barely literate. As the struggle continued over the boundaries between white/black and freedom/restriction, African Americans in Kansas City developed a number of strategies to promote their ideas of justice and humanity. Some of these strategies were adopted from the national arena; others appear to be unique to the Kansas City area.

The National Association for the Advancement of Colored People was the most well known of the national organizations fighting for equal rights for African Americans. At least two Kansas City–area women—Josephine Silone Yates and Kathryn Johnson—were among the representatives to the discussions that led to the organization's founding in 1910. Unlike the Kansas City branch of the Urban League, which maintained and retained a bountiful collection of committee minutes, pamphlets, newspaper clippings, and sociological surveys, the Kansas City chapter of the NAACP left little such documentation. Historian Sherry Lamb Schirmer, drawing on the history of black Kansas City started by Clifford Naysmith in the 1960s, notes that the city had an active NAACP chapter by 1914. The chapter was led by teacher Woody Jacobs and counted among its active members Charles Stark, an advertising copywriter and a frequent contributor to the *Kansas City Sun* and *Kansas City Call* in the 1920s, and Hugh O. Cook, vice principal of Lincoln High School.[1]

It is obvious, however, that by the early 1920s, the chapter had attracted the interests of black Kansas City. In 1921, the Kansas City chapter sent five official representatives to the NAACP's national convention in Detroit. Two women activists, Myrtle Foster Cook and Ida M. Becks, were among the delegates as were mail carrier James H. Crews, theater owner John Love, and a J. Moten. Veteran teacher and activist James Dallas Bowser also attended on his own.[2] By 1923, the Kansas City chapter was meeting monthly at the Urban League's Community Center, and a 1923 report on committee assignments included a veritable Who's Who: Ida M. Becks, who had led the drive to bring the Urban League to Kansas City; Lincoln teacher David N. Crosthwaite, whose wife, Minnie, would emerge as a leader of the black women's club movement in the city; Frayser T. Lane, executive secretary of the Urban League; Myrtle Foster Cook, who was also active with the Urban League and the YWCA; attorneys L. Amasa Knox and Charles H. Calloway; doctors T. C. Unthank and J. E. Dibble; minister D. A. Holmes; mail carrier James Crews; and firefighter Edward Simpson.[3] The chapter's visibility, no doubt, was boosted earlier that year when the two Kansas Cities played host to the NAACP's annual convention. Although one of the convention sessions was held on the Kansas side (at the First Methodist Church in downtown Kansas City, Kansas), two other sessions

1. Schirmer, "Landscape of Denial," 160, 170.
2. *Kansas City Sun*, June 25, 1921.
3. *Kansas City Call*, November 30, 1923.

were held in downtown Kansas City, Missouri. One session met at Second Baptist Church; the final Sunday session was held in the Convention Hall after a massive "silent" parade through the heart of black Kansas City. During the convention, black scientist George Washington Carver received the NAACP's Springarn Medal in a ceremony that drew more than ten thousand black residents of the two states to the city's Convention Hall.[4]

The energy and vitality provided by the NAACP convention and the silent parade undoubtedly invigorated the local chapter. Through the work of the Reverend D. A. Holmes, lawyer Charles H. Calloway, and others, the NAACP maintained a strong presence in Kansas City into the 1930s. When an African American man was lynched in nearby Excelsior Springs in 1925, John L. Love, president of the Kansas City branch of the NAACP, filed a protest with the governor's office. And although the author of *The Spirit of Freedom* described the local chapter as "moribund" by 1939, Nathan Young, writing a decade later, noted the presence of an active NAACP chapter in Kansas City. According to Young, the Kansas City chapter took the lead in police brutality cases and unjust prosecutions based on race, while at the same time supporting the national office's campaigns against lynching, disfranchisement, and peonage.[5]

Kansas City's chapter of the Urban League owed its existence to the lack of recreational opportunities for young black men in the city and the perseverance of Ida M. Becks. The national organization was founded in 1910, but the Urban League did not have a Kansas City presence until after World War I. From 1919, the Kansas City branch, its staff, and its interracial board followed its mission of promoting improved race relations and improved material conditions for African Americans in Kansas City through employment, recreational, and housing services.[6]

Desiring to offer wholesome recreational activities for African American soldiers from Camp Funston (near Manhattan, Kansas), a group of black Kansas Citians led by Becks organized and established a community center on the second floor of the Shannon Building at 1518

4. Ibid., August 31, 1923.

5. Office of Housing and Community Development, *Spirit of Freedom*, 8; *Kansas City Times*, August 8, 1925; Young and Young, *Your Kansas City and Mine*, 51.

6. The Kansas City Urban League counts its annual meetings from its origins in 1919, although the "official" founding date often is given as June 26, 1920. See KCULP, "1952 Annual Report," box KCULP2, file 15.

East Eighteenth Street (the northwest corner of Eighteenth and Vine Streets). The center opened in July 1919 under the auspices of the War Camp Community Service Club. The center originally offered lodging, employment assistance, and recreational activities for black servicemen and veterans. Early in 1920, with the war over, operation of the community center was assumed by the Vine Street Community Service group (among the group's officers were Becks and James Dallas Bowser), and the facility was opened up to the black community as a whole. At the same time, negotiations began with the National Urban League (with Dr. John E. Perry leading the Kansas City representatives), and on June 26, 1920, the Community Service Urban League office opened in Kansas City at the community center on Eighteenth Street.[7]

An interracial board of directors was established, and with a substantial donation from white businessman William Volker, the office began operations. The goal of the league was to increase the participation of African Americans in every phase of community life, thereby improving living conditions for black Kansas Citians. Lincoln principal John R. E. Lee was chosen president of the board of directors, and Dr. John E. Perry served as secretary. The board included Ida M. Becks, J. J. Allen, James Dallas Bowser, doctors T. C. Unthank and D. Madison Miller, and lawyers L. Amasa Knox, William C. Hueston, and Charles Calloway. The board also drew from a group of white reformers who sought to restructure Kansas City's government. Nat Spencer, secretary and guiding hand of the Citizens' League, served as the KCUL board's treasurer, and Burris Jenkins, editor of the daily *Kansas City Post,* was a board member.[8] One of the board's first chores was to hire an executive secretary who would be responsible for the day-to-day operation of the league. With the help of T. Arnold Hill of the National Urban League's staff, the Kansas City board chose Frayser T. Lane of Chicago as its first executive secretary. Lane was a graduate of Morehouse College in Atlanta and had done course work at the University of Chicago. For four years

7. Young and Young, *Your Kansas City and Mine,* 139; *Kansas City Sun,* July 26, 1919; KCULP, "Minutes, Twenty-Fifth Anniversary Committee," December 20, 1942, box CM1, vol. 1.

8. Schirmer, *City Divided,* 116; Young and Young, *Your Kansas City and Mine.* The Citizens' League was organized in March 1917 and aimed to promote honest and efficient government by reforms in the electoral process and in the structure of city government. Spencer, who owned a medium-size business, also served for two decades as secretary for the Society for the Suppression of Commercialized Vice. Jenkins, upon assuming editorship of the *Post,* endeared himself to many in the African American community by declaring that henceforth the paper would capitalize the word "Negro." Jenkins's announcement was in direct contradiction with the editorial policies of Kansas City's other dailies, all of which insisted on using "negro" despite repeated pleas by black Kansas Citians.

Lane had worked with the black YMCA in Chicago before joining the staff of the Chicago Urban League.[9]

Lane enthusiastically jumped into his duties in Kansas City, and by January of the next year, he and the staff were offering a variety of services and programs for Kansas City's African American communities. The large room on the second floor of the center was used as a gymnasium for both girls' and boys' activities. In the first month of 1920, more than 2,500 African Americans used the community center. Some came to meetings of the various social and literary groups that used the center; others came to avail themselves of the recreational and employment opportunities. That same month, almost 100 African Americans came to the league offices seeking jobs. Ten of the job applicants found permanent work; another 13 were offered temporary work. The league office also handled 46 "special cases" in that month. A smaller community center run by the league at 941 Bell Street in the West Bottoms drew another 500 African Americans in January 1921. The month of February brought almost another 2,500 visitors to the main community center, including 48 groups who held 108 different meetings at the center. Girls from Lincoln High, as well as from the Wendell Phillips and Cherry Street Schools, used the gymnasium regularly, as did boys from the Douglass school. By February, the center had also organized a boys basketball team to represent it. The center began organizing a class of volunteer social workers to assist the league in its various undertakings. By May 1921, Lane said the center was averaging 850 visitors a week, and 40 to 50 groups were meeting there each month. The executive secretary also said that, in the six months since his arrival, 244 applications for employment had been taken by the league's staff; unfortunately, that had led to just 45 jobs filled.[10]

One of the first targets of league activities was single young men, many of them recent immigrants who had "sacrificed everything" in their desire to obtain higher wages than those available in rural areas. The community center staff at first worked to get these "roaming and adventurous youths" or "floaters" into gainful employment and reconnected with family and friends. One young man, ashamed because he had been unable to find work, had stopped corresponding with his family until the Urban League staff intervened. By the next year, the problem was straining the resources of the community center. Black

9. *Kansas City Sun*, November 6, 1920.
10. Ibid., February 5, February 12, March 5, May 21, 1921.

men unable to find lodging elsewhere in the African American communities during the winter of 1921–1922 began sleeping in the community center wherever they could find room—on chairs, on floors, in hallways. Some had been brought to the center after approaching the police station and asking to be sheltered there for a night. The league began searching for a suitable dwelling to use as a settlement house for men, but neither a home nor the funding to support it was obtained. A year later, as the problem intensified, Lane again set out to establish a shelter for homeless men, turning to the city's charitable organizations for assistance. Again, the KCUL's efforts apparently were futile.[11]

Frayser T. Lane remained busy, speaking to various constituencies within the African American communities about the work the Urban League was doing. He appeared before Parent-Teacher Association groups at the black schools, at an assembly at Lincoln High School, at Baptist Young Peoples Union meetings in the churches, at Sunday schools, and in community meetings. He could point with pride to the integral role the Urban League and the community center had accepted within Kansas City. Lane pointed out in one talk that the community center had provided a home for baseball teams, drill teams, and civic meetings, as well being the starting point for a cleanup campaign, an NAACP membership drive, and various charitable organizations. The center also remained a popular site for social entertainments.[12]

A year after Lane's arrival, the number of people in and out of the community center had increased threefold. In one month, the KCUL reported that 14,000 individuals—job seekers, members of various social and fraternal organizations, homeless men seeking shelter, and participants in various social and educational functions—had passed through the center's doors. Although the figure seems exaggerated, it should be noted the center was open twenty-four hours a day, seven days a week. Whether the attendance figure was inflated should not overshadow the fact that by 1922, the Urban League's community center was one of the cornerstones of the Eighteenth and Vine area.[13]

In 1931, the Urban League office moved to 1905 Vine Street. In 1936, the building was purchased by the West, Anderson, Jones funeral home, and the KCUL moved into new quarters. Its choice was a three-story

11. Ibid., April 2, 1921; March 4, 1922. With the Urban League's help, the young man wrote a letter to his mother, and her reply was used to advertise the league's effectiveness. *Kansas City Sun*, December 30, 1922. No references to any homeless shelter operated by the KCUL can be found in any of the existing Urban League records or newspaper accounts.

12. Ibid., May 14, 1921.

13. Ibid., December 17, 1921.

home at 1408 The Paseo. The residence contained ten rooms, two porches, a large kitchen, a two-car garage, and ample yard space. The first floor of the renovated structure was used for the general offices and conference room. The second floor contained the employment services and Industrial Relations Department. The third floor was given over to the Urban League's Little Theatre, under the direction of Lincoln teacher J. O. Morrison.[14]

Urban League Programs

The community center on Eighteenth Street consumed a great deal of the Urban League's resources, but through it the KCUL offered a variety of social services to the African American community. In the early 1920s, the KCUL recognized the need for outreach to the primarily working-class African Americans living in the West Bottoms and on the West Side. A community center was established at 941 Bell Street in the West Bottoms, and by May 1921 the center was organizing recreational activities for children; offering educational talks to adults on industrial efficiency, civic pride, and racial cooperation; and providing Friday night frolics for adults, in which movies, music, and board games were offered. E. J. Unthank, son of Dr. Thomas C. Unthank, served as the center's resident social worker.[15]

A free nursery school under the auspices of the Works Progress Administration (a 1935 New Deal program that offered work to the unemployed on a variety of projects) opened at the Urban League offices at 1408 The Paseo. The staff included trained nurses, and doctors and dentists made periodic visits.[16]

Each summer during the interwar period, the KCUL broadened the range of its program offerings for children. A picnic was held each August for African American children over the age of five. In 1937, for example, more than six hundred children attended the picnic in Swope Park. Starting in 1936, in conjunction with the Paseo YWCA, the KCUL sponsored a summer camp for girls near Pleasant Hill, Missouri. Although it was not as elaborate an affair as the camp sponsored by the Detroit Urban League in the 1930s, the KCUL's camp annually served between fifty and one hundred girls ages eight to eighteen. The camp,

14. *Kansas City Call*, September 11, 1936, in KCULP, box N1, file 2.

15. *Kansas City Sun*, May 14, July 30, December 17, 1921.

16. "Urban League WPA Nursery School Opens," undated news clipping, KCULP, box N1, file 2.

dubbed Camp Three Trees in 1937, sat on a wooded area near Allendale Lake. Under the leadership of Elsie Mountain of the YWCA, the campers undertook nature studies, studied astronomy and Native American lore, swam, hiked, and fished. The girls lived in tents equipped with wooden floors and slept on new army cots.[17]

Big Sisters Program

The Kansas City Urban League organized a Big Sisters program in 1928, but it took four years for the program to get off the ground. In 1932, a group of women led by Fredericka Perry (wife of Dr. John Edward Perry) came together to operate a shelter home at 2426 Brooklyn. The group was able to offer temporary shelters to girls placed in the program by the county court.[18]

Garrison Field House

In 1914, the city opened a recreational facility in the East Bottoms for the use of African Americans. The Garrison Field House, near the Garrison school, served as a meeting place for African Americans and as a cornerstone of the black community. In 1935, possibly because of the financial strains created by the Great Depression, the city pondered closing the facility but, at the organization's request, turned over operation of the facility to the Kansas City Urban League in October of that year. According to an Urban League report, visitors to the field house were most appreciative of the change in operators. Under the direction of Tina Blanchard, the field house offered activities for junior and senior boys and girls, among which were handcraft and athletic programs. Activities at the field house also included an indoor carnival, a Christmas play by the blind club, and a children's Christmas party. The blind club was reported to be the most consistent patron of the field house.[19]

17. "Summer Camp for Girls to Open July 5," undated news clipping [1937]; "Fifty Girls to Leave for Camp Monday," undated news clipping [1937]; "600 Children Enjoy Picnic," undated news clipping [1937]; all in KCULP, box N1, file 2. "Girls Camp Period Ends," *Kansas City Call*, undated clipping [1937], in KCULP, box N1, file 2. "Girls Camp is Situated on Lakefront," *Kansas City Call*, July 11, 1936, KCULP, box N1, file 2.

18. "Big Sisters Organization for Women," KCULP, box PPC1, file 2, 1932 report; "Minutes, February 15, 1932," box PPC1, file 2.

19. KCULP, "Monthly Report, October 1936," Urban League Minutes, Board of Directors, box M1, Volume 1; "Neighborhood Department, November 1939," Urban League Minutes,

Through activities at the four sites—the Urban League offices, the Community Center at Eighteenth and Vine, the Garrison Field House, and its smaller mission in the West Bottoms—the Kansas City Urban League reached a substantial portion of the city's African American communities. In the first decade of its existence, the KCUL helped fill recreational, employment, and social needs of black Kansas City. The economic devastation wrought by the Great Depression would be another test for the KCUL, one that it was well equipped to handle (see Chapter Eight).

The "Y" Movement

[They say] that what Lincoln and Roosevelt did for us was good, but what we do for ourselves should be infinitely better.

—"BETTY AND SAM," *KANSAS CITY SUN*, JANUARY 18, 1919

African American life in Kansas City was bolstered by the presence of both Young Men's Christian Association and Young Women's Christian Association facilities near the intersection of Nineteenth Street and The Paseo. The facilities, although segregated from their inception, provided recreational and entertainment opportunities for young black men and women. They also served as two of the primary sites for meetings of the various African American organizations in Kansas City.

The Paseo YMCA grew out of the concerns of Edward Ross, who believed that the Christian principles underlying the YMCA movement had much to offer to Kansas City's African American communities. Around 1900, Ross, a clerk at a wholesale drug company in the West Bottoms, joined forces with several other like-minded men, including postal worker James H. Crews and Aaron J. Starnes, a teacher at the Garrison school.[20] This small group began meeting regularly at the home of Lucinda Day on Lydia Street and attempted to interest others in the "Y" program.[21] By 1903, the Colored Young Men's Christian Association of Kansas City had opened a room at 912 East Twelfth Street and

---

Board of Directors, box M1, Volume 2; "Urban League in New Home September 8," *Kansas City Call*, July 11, 1936, box N1, file 2.

20. Young and Young (*Your Kansas City and Mine*, 16) cite 1907 as the beginning of the YMCA movement in black Kansas City, but articles in Lewis Woods's *Rising Son* (February 13, 1903) indicate the Y club already had begun offering activities as early as 1903.

21. Young and Young (*Your Kansas City and Mine*) place Day's home on Twelfth Street, but the city directory for 1903 indicates Day, who apparently worked as a domestic, was living at 1411 Lydia with two other adults.

was offering activities. G. J. Starnes, a male relative of Aaron Starnes, was listed as the YMCA's secretary. Its program at this time consisted of a Sunday meeting for men, a night school, monthly practical talks, and a reading room, which was open for three hours nightly. The group by this time hoped to add public baths, a gymnasium, and an employment bureau.[22] The Y program and the group's ambition soon outgrew the room on Twelfth Street, and by the end of the decade, the group, which had added teachers W. W. Yates and H. O. Cook, obtained a small facility at 1417 East Eighteenth Street.[23] It soon became apparent that the facility on Eighteenth Street also was inadequate for the community's needs, and a fund-raising campaign was launched early in the 1910s. The goal of ten thousand dollars was reached, and three small buildings on The Paseo were soon obtained for the YMCA program. These, too, proved inadequate, and in 1913, a campaign for a larger facility on the same site began. Eastern philanthropist Julius Rosenwald, a firm believer in the YMCA program, had offered twenty-five thousand dollars to any community that raised seventy-five thousand dollars for a YMCA facility. Kansas City's central governing body for the YMCA program agreed to raise fifty thousand dollars if the African American community raised the rest. Behind the efforts of Felix Payne, T. B. Watkins, and others, the last twenty-five thousand dollars was quickly raised, and in 1914, the new Paseo YMCA at 1824 Paseo opened.[24]

By the end of the World War, Frank A. Harris had taken over as the YMCA's executive secretary. Harris was born in southeastern Kansas in 1883. In 1908, he moved to Kansas City and began working as a printer. Four years later, he joined the YMCA staff, and in 1917, he was appointed executive secretary. From his arrival in Kansas City, Harris was involved with the major organizations and institutions in black Kansas City. He served on the board of directors at Wheatley-Provident Hospital until he was replaced in 1922 by G. A. Gregg.[25]

Under Harris and Gregg, the YMCA became one of the focal points of the African American community. It was seen by *Kansas City Sun* editor Nelson Crews as "the largest single enterprise" in Kansas City's African American community. Although the YMCA's employment service was quickly supplanted by that of the Urban League, the structure

22. *Rising Son*, February 13, 1903; *Polk City Directory*, 1903.

23. Young and Young, *Your Kansas City and Mine*, 16; *Kansas City Sun*, December 13, 1919.

24. Young and Young, *Your Kansas City and Mine.*

25. Kinsler, *Trip South*, 23–24, in Gibson, *Mecca of the New Negro*, 56–57. Harris and his wife, Florence, lived at 1627 Park.

was home and haven for many. Its meeting rooms served as hosts for a variety of organizations: the board of directors at Wheatley-Provident, the members of the Texas Club, and the pastors involved in the Ministerial Alliance. Its gymnasium was used for basketball and volleyball games involving high school boys and girls and college teams from Western and Lincoln Universities and a team of African American students from the University of Kansas. Its spacious lobby was the setting for graduation ceremonies, public rallies, and even musical performances. In 1920, the Kansas Conservatory of Music held a grand recital at the Paseo YMCA; tickets were twenty-five cents each. When Bishop William Tecumseh Vernon, former president of Western University in Kansas City, Kansas, returned to Kansas City after a two-year stint as a missionary in Africa, the lobby held an overflow crowd for his brief but spellbinding talk. Under the guidance of physical secretary Earl W. Beck, a range of athletic activities was made available. For example, in August 1922, Beck led nineteen of the boy members on an all-night hike in Swope Park. Edward Ross joined the staff in 1920 and was placed in charge of the institution's religious work. The YMCA's cafeteria offered "home-like" meals at a reasonable price seven days a week, although it served only breakfast and dinner on Sundays. In the 1920s and '30s, however, one of the YMCA's most significant functions was as a refuge for the down-and-out among the city's African American populations.[26]

Early in the 1920s, as African Americans moved into the two Kansas Cities in greater numbers, the Paseo YMCA saw an increase in the number of men seeking shelter. Its forty-five dormitory rooms and ninety beds were consistently filled. This increase was exacerbated by the policies and practices of local law enforcement agencies. African American men arrested for vagrancy were passed on to the YMCA to find shelter in its dormitory rooms. If arrested a second time for vagrancy, however, black men were sent to the Municipal Corrections facility at Leeds. This forced many young men into turning the YMCA's temporary shelter into a long-term residence. In addition, Kansas City police officers often turned elderly black men and women over to YMCA officials, requesting that the YMCA be responsible for placing them in the county's Old Folks Home. Although executive secretary Frank Harris noted that the YMCA's resources were inadequate to meet the demand, few were

26. *Kansas City Sun* for dates of March 6, 20, December 4, 1920; September 10, December 24, 1921; January 7, August 12, December 9, 1922. See also *Western Messenger*, January 23, 1920.

turned away. Young men, in particular newcomers to the city, found a welcoming hand at the Paseo YMCA. In 1922, a young migrant from California took ill and entered the Old City Hospital. When asked if there was anyone in Kansas City to be contacted, the young man responded with the only name he knew: a member of the Paseo YMCA's staff. After the migrant's death, members of the YMCA staff constituted the funeral party.[27]

Young men who took shelter at the YMCA, as they would with many of the institutions driven by a Progressive mentality, were also offered spiritual and intellectual guidance. Prominent ministers such as D. A. Holmes as well as experts in a variety of fields offered lectures on a regular basis. Lincoln teacher W. B. Williams, for example, described his experiences during his thirty-year stint in the United States Army. Other topic titles included "Choice," "Remaking Men," "Father and Son," and (the physical side of) "Love Making."[28]

The 1913 campaign to raise funds for the construction of the Paseo facility did not end the African American community's commitment to the YMCA. Less than eight years after the facility's opening, executive secretary Frank Harris asked the community to raise five thousand dollars for replacement and upkeep of equipment. Furniture and carpeting needed to be cleaned and repaired, the woodwork required painting, and mechanical systems needed to be checked and updated. A campaign in the summer of 1921, led by teacher G. N. Grisham, quickly raised the necessary funds.[29] A year later, G. A. Gregg asked for another fund-raising drive to purchase much-needed equipment for the building. Among the items desired, Gregg noted, were a heater for the swimming pool (the lack thereof had forced the closing of the pool in the winter), more games for both the men's and boys' game rooms, laundry equipment, and a curtain to divide the gymnasium, allowing its use for two or more purposes at the same time. Again, the community responded.[30] For the next two decades, Kansas City's African Americans demonstrated their support for the YMCA and its programs. Its membership during this time ranged between five and eight hundred boys and men. A three-dollar fee provided a year's membership (it was one dollar for youths).[31] The following is a typical schedule of events by Earl W. Beck, the physical secretary:

27. *Kansas City Sun*, December 24, 1921; August 12, 1922.
28. Ibid., May 14, November 19, December 3, 1921; August 12, 1922.
29. Ibid., June 25, 1921.
30. Ibid.
31. Ibid., December 24, 1921; *Kansas City Call*, September 26, 1930.

Paseo YMCA Fall schedule, starting Monday, September 19th	
Monday	
Business and Professional men's volleyball	1–2:30 p.m.
Tuesday	
Senior Class gym	8–9:15 p.m.
Wednesday	
Business and Professional men's volleyball	1–2:30 p.m.
Adult Scouts gym	7–8 p.m.
Thursday	
Scout Class gym	7–8 p.m.
Senior Class gym	8–9:15 p.m.
Friday	
Business and Professional men's volleyball	1–2:30 p.m.
Football boys meeting	7 p.m. Tuesdays[32]

The Paseo YWCA

For the future happiness of Our Girls and Young Women.

—YWCA ADVERTISEMENT, *KANSAS CITY SUN*, MARCH 20, 1920

The Paseo YWCA grew out of the activities of the Kansas City Colored Women's League in the first decade of the twentieth century. By 1913, the league had acquired a two-story frame house at 1625 Cottage Avenue (now Twenty-second Terrace) as a women's shelter. Jean McCampbell, the president of the league, contacted the general secretary of the Kansas City YWCA concerning the possibility of opening a separate branch for African American women and girls. Two years later, an investigative committee led by Anna Jones confirmed the interest in, need for, and feasibility of a separate YWCA for the black community, and in 1916, Ida M. Becks was appointed to organize clubs within the churches as a foundation for the YWCA work. Becks was soon serving as the black YWCA's "general manager," and by late 1918, a home for "friendless girls" was established at 2228 Michigan (near Becks's home). Its purpose was to prevent black girls and women from falling "into

32. *Kansas City Sun*, September 10, 1921.

the hands of those that only degrade and commercialize vice and drunkenness and everything that tears down humanity." By the beginning of 1919, thirteen clubs had been formed, representing an active membership of more than a thousand men and women. In February of that year, a black branch of the Kansas City YWCA, with headquarters in the Paseo YMCA, was chartered. The first girls-reserves activities began in June, and in November, the Blue Triangle League, as it was then known, purchased a small brick building at the southeast corner of Nineteenth Street and The Paseo for its activities. At this point, the organization changed its name to the Paseo YWCA.[33]

Support for the Gate City YWCA, as it was first sometimes known, came from practically every segment of Kansas City's African American communities. This support was demonstrated by the range of organizations that came together for a benefit concert in January 1919 at the Convention Hall. The concert featured a seventy-five-piece violin orchestra and a chorus of one thousand. The supporting cast, as it were, were members of a general committee composed of representatives of every black school, church, and major organization in the two Kansas Cities and surrounding area. Like the Emancipation Day celebration described in Chapter One, the benefit concert tapped the resources of African Americans in western Missouri and northeastern Kansas.[34] Lincoln music teacher N. Clark Smith was director of the program committee, but a significant portion of that committee came from outside the two Kansas Cities. African Americans from Marshall, St. Joseph, and Independence in Missouri and from Lawrence and Leavenworth in Kansas also assisted in the development of the program. The general committee, of which the program committee was just one part, also contained representatives of forty-six women's clubs (from the Book Lovers club to the Inter-City Dames), a half-dozen or so men's clubs and organizations, the twenty-six black schools in the two Kansas Cities (including Western University), thirty-eight churches from both sides of the state line, the Kansas City Medical Society (black doctors), the National Negro Business League, the two NAACP branches, as well as various businesses, marching bands, and political groups. All in all, more than 150 individuals (aside from the performers) contributed their time and energy to making the concert a success.[35]

33. Young and Young, *Your Kansas City and Mine*, 20; *Western Messenger*, December 6, 1918.

34. *Kansas City Sun*, January 4, February 15, 1919.

35. Ibid., January 4, 1919.

Ticket prices for the benefit: 50¢ for a seat on the arena floor or arena balcony and 25¢ for a seat in the upper balcony. Boxes of ten seats were available for $7.50. More than three thousand spectators overcame erratic streetcar service and fears of large gatherings (both brought on by a flu epidemic that ravaged the United States in the winter of 1918–1919) to witness the concert and show their support for the YWCA. Total receipts for the concert were more than $700, but expenses (including rent for the Convention Hall and Clarence White's fee of $150) left a little less than $100 to go to the YWCA fund. Yet the concert helped raise visibility of the YWCA program on the Missouri side, and Nelson Crews could announce that more than one thousand paid memberships had been obtained by that time.[36]

The new YWCA began operating from space in the men's facility on The Paseo, with Jennie McCampbell as its office secretary and Estella F. Lovett in charge of organizing girls' programs. A management committee was established, with some of the more prominent women in Kansas City as its members. Among them were Anna Jones, Jean McCampbell, Myrtle Foster Cook, Ida M. Becks, Ardella Lee (wife of Lincoln principal John R. E. Lee), Clara Miller (wife of physician D. M. Miller), and Josephine Yates (the daughter of nineteenth-century activist Josephine Silone Yates). Almost immediately, the YWCA began offering programs under the banner of the Blue Triangle League. In March, Jean McCampbell and YWCA workers found housing for five young women who had recently migrated to the city. By July, YWCA workers had established a routine for the girls-reserves programs. Early that summer, they began organizing hikes for the various classes (the seventh-grade girls from W. W. Yates Elementary hiked from the YMCA to Penn Valley Park and back; the class from the Douglass school trekked to the Rosedale community on the Kansas side). In November 1919, a small brick building on the southeast corner of Nineteenth and The Paseo (1501 East Nineteenth Street) was purchased.[37] The black women's clubs and sororities volunteered to provide furnishings for the structure. Its second floor was to be used as a dormitory and the first floor for offices. The name of the group was then changed to the Paseo Branch YWCA, and in 1920, Mabel Bickford was hired as its first executive secretary.[38]

36. Ibid., February 15, 1919. The Yates YWCA for African American women and girls in Kansas City, Kansas, had opened a decade earlier (see Chapter One).

37. Kansas City businessman William Volker donated $1,000 toward the purchase of the building. Ibid., December 6, 1919.

38. Young and Young, *Your Kansas City and Mine,* 20. See also *Kansas City Sun,* March 29, July 5, December 27, 1919; January 17, 1920.

The Paseo YWCA opened in March, with a musical program provided by Clyde Glass and members of the girls reserves. The opening of the YWCA was a triumphant moment for the women involved in its creation. Myrtle Foster Cook, writing for the *Western Messenger*, described the facility thusly:

> The Center is well located on this beautiful boulevard, in easy walking distance of a great portion of our people, and with car service, and easily accessible for the girls of four of the largest schools. The interior space has been remodeled, refreshed with soft-toned paints and papering, and furnished very attractively.
>
> The large assembly room with its deep window seat, piano and easy chairs is suitable not only for Vespers and large gatherings but for girls classes and club meetings. The Rest Room on the sunny west side will be a boon to weary womanhood. The offices of the secretaries are equipped for real service and the chief, Miss Mabel Bickford, has already won the hearts of the Association members and friends.
>
> The Girls Reserve Pageant was the first of the formal opening exercises, and was a delightful presentation of the ideals of American girlhood accompanied by a chorus of sweet little white robed misses, who sang like young angels. . . .
>
> The second floor contains the secretary's room furnished by Sorosis Club, the girls' room furnished by the Woman's [*sic*] League, house-mother's room, bath room, dining room, furnished by Harmony Art Club and the kitchen. The dining room and kitchen are for the use of the girls' clubs.[39]

By March 1920, almost two hundred girls were already enrolled in the YWCA's programs, and the recreational committee was making plans for a summer camp. Mrs. T. C. Brown, formerly instructor of nurses at the Old City Hospital who would soon become one of Kansas City's two black female physicians, was enlisted to instruct the high school girls' class. In May, a series of social education conferences held at the black schools reached more than nineteen hundred women and girls, and the center purchased equipment for recreational activities ranging from table games to volleyball. At the same time, the administration of the facility and its programs was strengthened by the designation of new standing committees led by four of the more prominent women in black Kansas City. Pearl Dabney headed the membership committee;

39. Myrtle Foster Cook, "Kansas City Notes," *Western Messenger*, March 26, 1920.

Pinkie Osborne, wife of the Ebenezer AME pastor, took charge of finances; Mrs. Thomas Jones directed the education committee; and Eva L. Fox was placed in charge of publicity. Mary Goins, wife of Baptist minister John Goins and an important voice among black Baptist women in the state, led the religious work, and Katherine Washington directed recreation.[40]

With the establishment of the standing committees and the earlier interest expressed by women like Ida Becks and Myrtle Foster Cook, the Paseo YWCA was on its way to becoming a fixture in the heart of black Kansas City. Black women took control of the facility and made it responsive to their needs. It is worth our while to look at the lives of five of the women instrumental in its creation.

Ida M. Bowman Becks, a graduate of Lincoln Institute in Jefferson City, had worked for racial uplift in the African American communities of Wichita, Kansas, and Dayton, Ohio, before marrying H. W. Becks and moving to Kansas City in 1908. She was born March 28, 1880, in Armstrong, Missouri, in Howard County.[41] Her father, Milton Bowman, died when she was eleven years old, leaving her mother with the care of Ida and seven siblings. After finishing the courses at the public grammar school, Ida moved to Carrollton, Missouri, before enrolling at Lincoln Institute. To finance her education, Ida Bowman worked as a domestic for a private family—for the sum of one dollar per week. In 1899, Ida—one of just nine women to receive degrees that year—graduated from Lincoln as the class valedictorian.

Ida Bowman spent a year in Wichita after graduation before moving to Cleveland, Ohio, where she elected to dedicate her life to the work of racial uplift. She moved to Dayton, where she became secretary of that city's Colored Women's League. In Dayton, she met her future husband, H. W. Becks, and they were married in 1907. The next year, the couple moved to Kansas City, and H. W. Becks obtained an appointment with the postal service. After marriage, Ida Becks continued her work for the race. For two years, she was field representative for the Florence Crittenton Home in Topeka, Kansas. She also served as a field representative for the National Training School, operated by Nannie Helen Burroughs in Washington, DC. As we have seen, she was instrumental in the development of the Yates YWCA in Kansas City, Kansas. Her work

40. *Kansas City Sun*, March 6, April 3, 1920; *Western Messenger*, April 6, 1920; *Kansas City Sun*, May 15, June 5, 1920.

41. Information on Ida Becks's life before 1913 is found in Bacote, *Who's Who*, 108–10.

led to the formation of Kansas City's Urban League branch. She was an ardent supporter of women's suffrage, and by 1920, she was an important figure within state and national Baptist organizations, within Missouri's black women's club movement, and in the African American communities on both sides of the state line. Like many black women activists of the time, Ida Becks refused to bow to the twin oppressions of gender and race. "She is a fearless advocate of women's suffrage," Samuel Bacote wrote in 1913, seven years before the passage of the Nineteenth Amendment, "and is an uncompromising defender of the Afro-American race."[42]

Becks also was a trained public speaker and a much-sought-after orator. In a community filled with the likes of Nelson Crews, William C. Hueston, D. A. Holmes, Chester Franklin, and others, Becks had as many speaking engagements as any African American orator in the region. At a memorial service for Theodore Roosevelt in 1919 at Second Baptist Church, Becks spoke of the former president's views on woman suffrage. Later that year, she gave a talk titled "Purity" at a meeting of black Baptist women at Central Baptist Church, and she led a debate at Ebenezer AME Church on woman suffrage. In 1920, she joined Chester Franklin and three other speakers for a talk in front of the Budding Genius Literary Club of St. James AME Zion Church.[43]

Becks was not afraid to challenge anyone—black or white—who stood against what she believed was right. Tapping into a wellspring of black religious language and morality, she argued vociferously for improvements in African American life. When some in the African American communities, for example, argued against the passage of a school bond issue in 1921, Becks came out in favor of it, saying the monies were needed to relieve congestion in African American schools, particularly Lincoln High School. In a somewhat rambling political advertisement in the *Kansas City Sun,* she wrote:

> If a few disgruntled politicians have any axes to grind, it should not be at the expense of our children who are in need and are helpless and unaware of what is going on. Leave politics out of the matter and think of a cause that is just. . . . It has been said, "The Negro woman in politics would be a failure." Let us make this statement false. Let us not be like tape wrapped around the finger of the one in the fight that got whipped. . . . Let us have a mind of our own and

42. Ibid., 109.

43. *Western Messenger,* January 24, March 21, 1919; *Kansas City Sun,* March 1, 1919; April 17, 1920.

> use it, make it do your own thinking, asking God for divine leadership, unselfish, untarnished and unbiased.
>
> Take a stand for the right, and stand anyhow, stand for the right if you must stand alone. Remember that God and one is a majority. We have come to help purify, not to pollute. We have come to throw light on, we have walked in darkness long enough. We have come asking for justice, liberty and equal rights as American Citizens, and we accept no compromise, but we want to be able and intelligent enough to distinguish men with principles, who dare to do the right; from those that deceive and stoop to accomplish their personal interests. We should not insult real men when their cause has been thoroughly vindicated.[44]

Becks and her husband also were members and leaders of Second Baptist Church. Becks was a Red Cross fund-raiser in 1919, and she served on the board of directors of Wheatley-Provident Hospital in the early 1920s. She was one of five delegates from Kansas City to the 1921 NAACP convention in Detroit, and in 1921, the Negro Women's National Republican League appointed Becks to organize a chapter in Kansas City. The Kansas City chapter drew about forty members, and Becks was elected chairman of the group. Ida Becks and her husband resided at 2227 Michigan until around World War II, when they moved into the 3000 block of Walrond. They remained active in the Baptist Church through the war years.[45]

Like Ida M. Becks, Myrtle Foster Cook was an accomplished speaker and activist for a number of causes. Myrtle Foster was born sometime around 1872 in Amherstburg, Ontario, in Canada, but before she began school her parents moved to Monroe, Michigan, and became U.S. citizens.[46] In Monroe, Myrtle was educated. Two pictures emerge of young Myrtle at this point. A biographer described her as "a very timid young woman." Yet, while still living in Michigan, she became an active church worker, filling in as Sunday school teacher, treasurer, and church organist

44. Becks, "Why We Should Vote for the School Bonds," *Kansas City Sun*, April 2, 1921. Becks's support for the school bond issue proved naive. School board officials had declared that no new high schools, for either black or white students, would be built if the bond issue passed. But shortly after the measure passed, plans for Paseo High School were announced. According to most accounts, black voters strongly supported the bond issue.

45. *Kansas City Sun*, November 22, 1919; *Western Messenger*, January 23, 1920; *Kansas City Sun*, February 5, June 25, 1921.

46. The information on Myrtle Foster Cook's early life is taken from Davis, *Lifting as They Climb*, 200–202. Davis does not include a date of birth for Myrtle Foster but in the 1920 census her age is listed as forty-eight.

and on occasion *stepping into the pulpit* as leader of various programs and services. This same timid young woman, after accepting a job as the principal of a normal school in Kentucky supported by a Baptist district association, drove a buggy forty miles to confront the elders of the association and to demand back salary owed her.

Myrtle Foster then accepted a teaching position at a black high school in Frankfort, Kentucky, and there she met Louis G. Dodd, a doctor. The couple moved to the new state of Oklahoma, and Louis Dodd set up his medical practice in Muskogee. Myrtle Todd was recruited to teach, first at a government school for African American children of members of the Five Civilized Tribes and then into an all-black high school. In Muskogee, she became involved with the black women's club movement. The Dorcas Club, which she founded, was organized to raise money for a black hospital (which was built after she left Muskogee). Todd was a charter member of the Oklahoma Federation of Colored Women's Clubs and was responsible for drafting the organization's constitution. She also became involved in the arts and was responsible for bringing black celebrities such as actor Richard B. Harrison and educator Kelly B. Miller for speaking engagements in the state.

By the outbreak of World War I, Myrtle Foster Todd was a widow, and her life's path took a turn along the same line followed by countless African Americans in Oklahoma and the lower Great Plains in the early twentieth century: she was bound for Kansas City. A teaching position opened at Lincoln High School, and Todd became head of the school's English Department. Once at Lincoln, she became involved with the Kansas City Colored Women's League activities and the state federation of black women's clubs. Also at Lincoln, she met Hugh O. Cook, at the time in charge of the school's Math Department. After four years of teaching, she and Cook were married, and she resigned her position at Lincoln to take care of her new family (Hugh Cook had two young sons and a foster daughter in college).

Her duties as wife and mother could not totally occupy Myrtle Foster Cook's time. She became a volunteer for practically every cause in the African American community, particularly those that affected black women. In addition to her support for the YWCA, Cook was active in the NAACP's Kansas City branch and with the Kansas City Federation of Colored Charities. Through her work with the Women's League and the Colored Children's Association, she helped launch the Jackson County Home for Negro Boys. She also was an active Republican, as well as in the NACW, where she served as program chairman for six national conventions and as a member of the organization's board of control.

She would also be instrumental in the operation of the People's Finance Corporation (founded by her husband and Theron B. Watkins) as well as secretary-treasurer of the Home Seekers' Savings and Loan Association, a home-buying cooperative.

Though able to match Ida M. Becks in the diversity of her interests and in her contributions as an activist, Myrtle Foster Cook could not match Becks's speaking ability. Cook was more comfortable with the written word than the spoken. She edited the national notes for the NACW, and for at least two years after World War I, Cook, an active Baptist, provided a column on Kansas City news for the *Western Messenger,* a weekly newspaper for and about black Baptists on the western side of the state.[47] Cook's opinion was actively sought on matters affecting the African American communities. In 1921, she was among 150 black men and women (and apparently the only woman from Kansas City) called to Jefferson City to discuss the state of black education in Missouri.[48] In the mid-1920s, she served a term on the Missouri Negro Industrial Committee, although her voice was likely muted by the more conservative members who dominated the panel. In the 1930s, she served on the executive board of the Paseo Housewives League. Myrtle Foster Cook remained active in Kansas City until the final years of World War II, when she and Hugh O. Cook moved to Los Angeles.[49]

Little information has survived on three other women behind the establishment and early operation of the Paseo YWCA—Pearl Dabney, Pinkie Osborne, and Eva Fox. Pearl Dabney, a native of Bucklin, Missouri, and a graduate of Lincoln Institute, was active in the black women's club movement, and for two years (1919–1920) served as president of the State Federation of Colored Women's Clubs. She was also active in Republican politics and in 1921 served as a committee chair for the Kansas City chapter of the Negro Women's National Republican League. In 1929, she led the leading team of fund-raisers in the annual Colored Charities drive. But Pearl Dabney and her husband, Fred (a dealer in tea and coffee), were better known for their involvement with the Prince Hall Grand Lodge, an organization of black Masons. Pearl Dabney headed the women's auxiliary, the Order of the Eastern Star, for three years.[50]

47. Ibid., 202. For example, see the *Western Messenger,* March 12, 1920.

48. *Kansas City Sun,* February 5, 1921; *Opportunity,* 3:6 (June 1925): 191.

49. Young and Young, *Your Kansas City and Mine,* 104, 145; "Paseo Housewives League," *Kansas City American,* September 28, 1933, KCULP, box N1, file 2.

50. Davis, *Lifting as They Climb,* 346; *Kansas City Sun,* February 12, 1921; *Kansas City Call,* March 1, 1996. The Dabneys lived at 2432 Montgall for most of their lives in Kansas City. Fred Dabney died in 1949 at age sixty-seven; Pearl Dabney died in 1972.

Pinkie Osborne, wife of Ebenezer AME pastor William T. Osborne, was a native of Missouri who was known for her ability as a musical and stage director. In 1920, her production of *Under the Shadow of a Crime* drew more than seventeen hundred spectators to the Auditorium Theater.[51] Little else about her background is known.

Eva M. Fox also served on the board of directors at Wheatley-Provident Hospital in the 1920s and was a member of the Inter-City Dames as well as the Matrons Round Table Club, but like Pinkie Osborne, little else about her life is known.[52]

The dramatic increase in programs, an increase in the number of transient women who used the facility, and the inability of the center to collect all of the funds pledged a year earlier created a quick financial strain on the YWCA. In May, center officials noted that a payment of $500 due on the purchase of the YWCA site was due in June, and that the facility still needed another $175 for equipment. The funds were raised, but budgetary concerns hovered over the YWCA for much of its early life. The Beau Brummels, a men's social club, raised more than $300 through a benefit dance at the Labor Temple in 1921 and paid off the debt on the facility's piano, and a massive fund-raising drive in 1921 set $8,400 as its goal to cover the center's operating expenses.[53]

Despite its financial struggles, the YWCA continued to offer programs for the benefit of girls and women of all ages. One of its most ambitious ventures might have been a summer camp established in Edwardsville, Kansas, in western Wyandotte County. The camp was on land donated by Junious Groves, one of Kansas's most noted black entrepreneurs.[54] It sat about forty-five minutes from downtown Kansas City, Missouri, and only a half mile from the interurban car line.[55] The camp offered fresh air, "constantly flowing (spring) water," fresh vegetables, and milk from the Groves farm. There were large trees for shade yet enough open space for croquet and baseball. The camp was open

51. *Kansas City Sun*, February 28, 1920.

52. *Western Messenger*, January 23, 1920; *Kansas City Sun*, May 8, 1920; January 8, 1921.

53. *Kansas City Sun*, April 2, 23, May 14, 1921.

54. Junious Groves was known throughout the Kansas City area and most of the state of Kansas as the "Potato King." His farm on the western edge of present-day Kansas City, Kansas, was the most productive for growing potatoes in the state. His crops were of such a size that a railroad spur was built specifically to his property. On his property, Groves built a twenty-four-room brick and stone mansion. Booker T. Washington took special notice of Groves and held him up as an example for other African American farmers. Greenbaum, *Afro-American Community*, 78; *Kansas City Call*, February 7, 1930.

55. "To get there, take the Lawrence or Bonner Springs car which leaves 10th and Main every hour on the half hour. Get off at Bett's Creek also known as Grove's Centre [*sic*]. Walk north and follow signs. Car fare is 38 cents." *Kansas City Sun*, June 4, 1921.

to both girls ($3.50 per week) and young women ($5 per week). The camp was also open to both members and nonmembers of the YWCA; the only requirements were that the campers possess a good moral character and a belief in the work of the YWCA and that they be flexible enough to adhere to camp regulations. Because of space limitations the first year, just sixteen campers could be on the site at one time.[56]

How many girls and young women spent time at Camp Groves in 1921 is unknown, and it appears the YWCA turned its efforts toward bolstering its in-house programs. For the next few years, the YWCA's activities centered on improving the health and domestic skills of the women it encountered. In 1921, women could pay $1 and enroll in a fifteen-week class in embroidery, homemaking, or Spanish. In 1922, separate classes in sewing, cooking, and home furnishing were offered. Earl Beck, physical secretary for the men's association across The Paseo, volunteered at the YWCA as well and taught basketball and volleyball.[57] The most successful venture for the Paseo YWCA in the 1920s, however, might have been its organization of girls reserves in the schools. When a new girls-reserves corps was organized at W. W. Yates Elementary, it meant almost five hundred black girls in Kansas City were involved in the YWCA program. The girls reserves developed a series of seasonal activities and in 1922 began holding an annual picnic at Swope Park.[58]

Despite its ambitions, the Paseo YWCA never involved more than a fraction of the black girls and women in Kansas City's African American communities. Even supporters of the YWCA were obliged to admit that most of the six thousand females targeted by the organization's activities abstained from using the facility.[59] The direction and scope of the YWCA's program changed in 1928, however, with the appointment of Elsie Mountain as executive secretary. Mountain emphasized creating and securing employment opportunities for African American women. She encouraged African American women to be better prepared for job openings, and with this in mind, Mountain arranged for a series of lectures on the proper attire for female workers, punctuality, and dedication to the job, once obtained. She hoped to eliminate common complaints and stereotypes about black females in the workforce. Through her efforts, Nathan B. Young and William H. Young point out, more women were successfully placed in jobs than previously.

56. Ibid., June 4, 18, 1921.
57. Ibid., January 21, February 18, November 11, 1922.
58. Ibid., June 17, November 4, 1922.
59. Ibid., April 23, 1921.

Mountain also sought to develop domestic skills in those women not in the workforce. In 1932, the Board of Education agreed to partially fund a vocational program developed by Mountain at the Paseo YWCA. Classes were held during the winter months in beginning and advanced sewing, foods and table service, handcrafts, and mending.[60]

In addition to reenergizing many of the YWCA's other programs, Mountain also oversaw a change in the organization's physical space. Dormitory space was limited in the Paseo YWCA, and in October 1928, Mountain secured a two-story home at 2200 Brooklyn. At the same time, she arranged for the girls and young women to use the gymnasium at the men's facility across The Paseo. Mountain would serve the Paseo YWCA until her death in 1945. In 1948, the old Paseo YWCA was razed, and a new facility was constructed.[61]

Riot in Oklahoma

To darkest Tulsa
O Tulsa! Darkest Tulsa!

A deed performed by cruel, barbarous fiends,
Has shocked the universe. Not siege of Lucknow,
Nor bloody St. Bartholomew; no more savage in
Atrocity, and acts of utter heartlessness.
A nation hides its face in very shame;
A horror-stricken race looks on aghast.

O Tulsa! Darkest Tulsa!
Rise from the ashes of thy desolation:
This holocaust by fiendish demons kindled
This bonfire of thy pride of well-kept homes—
The envy of thy jealous, rival foes
Who hated thee for all thy toil and thrift,
Thy costly dwellings, shops and factories,
Be but an inspiration to rebuild
On lands and homesites thou hast owned, meanwhile,
Thy erstwhile church spires where to serve thy God
Mount skyward, till they pierce the blue ethereal,

60. Young and Young, *Your Kansas City and Mine*, 153; KCULP, "Y.W.C.A. Vocational Course Supported by School Board," *Kansas City American*, October 27, 1932, box N1, file 1.
61. Young and Young, *Your Kansas City and Mine*.

To mock the pagan horde that burned them down.
Let thy fair homes, thy lawns and things of grace
Show even greater charm, and style magnificent
Than ere the fiery blast had laid them low.

O Tulsa! Darkest Tulsa!
Let heartless brutes that burned thy homes
And maimed and massacred thy citizens,
Cold blooded beasts disguised in human shape
Mark well the might of thy unconquered soul,
Thy dauntless purpose, born to work and wait.
God is not mocked; nor dead; He'll vengeance take
On thy despoilers. In fire and flood,
In storm and quake He thunders his rebuke.
Then forward: Onward! Till thy humblest cot
Shall be again the pride of Tulsa's best.

—James Dallas Bowser, *Kansas City Sun,* October 1, 1921

In the spring of 1921, a race riot 250 miles away—in Tulsa, Oklahoma—drew the attention of Kansas City's African Americans.[62] The riot, in terms of loss of life and property the most devastating of any of the outbursts of racial violence between 1917 and 1929, seemed to strike African Americans in Kansas City particularly hard. For example, Kansas City's reigning black intellectual, James Dallas Bowser, was moved to put his feelings into verse. The riot was particularly felt, however, among those black Kansas Citians who either had lived in Oklahoma or had friends or relatives in the state. Although the number of migrants from Oklahoma to Kansas City would not match those from Tennessee, Kentucky, and the upper South, at least a few black Kansas Citians had Oklahoma roots. Physician C. P. Wallace and his wife, who lived at 2433 Tracy, had moved from Oklahoma to Kansas City just twelve months previously. Leon Hill, a mulatto from Texas, and his Oklahoma-born wife, Lula, lived at 1019 Virginia. Their twelve-year-old son, Thomas Nelson, had been born in Oklahoma. William Kellison, of the 900 block of Charlotte, also had been born in Texas, but his wife and five of their seven children were Oklahoma natives. John and Jane Willis of East Tenth Street had six of their grandchildren living with them; four were Oklahoma natives. Frank Lightener, an Alabama native living

62. The best account of the Tulsa race riot remains Scott Ellsworth, *Death in a Promised Land: The Tulsa Race Riot of 1921.*

in the 1300 block of Vine, had apparently met and married his wife in Arkansas, but their two youngest children were born in Oklahoma.

These examples were pulled in a brief, random survey of a few pages of the manuscript census. They help demonstrate why the events in Tulsa had such an emotional impact on the African American communities in Kansas City. Within days of the riot, relief committees were established by several black Kansas Citians. The *Kansas City Sun*, in its June 11 edition, ran a banner headline: "HAVE YOU HELPED THE RIOT SUFFERERS IN TULSA?" The *Sun* also published a list of the known dead and wounded from the African American community.[63] A committee set up by funeral parlor operator Theron B. Watkins raised more than four hundred dollars in a little less than ten days. By this time, a number of refugees from the riot had reached Kansas City, and Watkins's committee interviewed forty-three cases and provided meals, clothes, lodging, employment, and cash. Some were assisted in making contact with relatives, while rooms were found for others. In addition, donated clothing valued at three hundred dollars was shipped to Tulsa. More than three hundred of the dollars raised by Watkins's committee was sent south as well.[64] One of the problems for Watkins's committee—and for any who sought to alleviate the suffering of Tulsa's black community—was the appearance in the city of a few unscrupulous individuals seeking to take advantage of the situation. The Urban League and the *Kansas City Sun* cautioned Kansas City residents against responding to these fraudulent riot victims.[65]

One of the few surviving descriptions of the aftermath of the riot was written by G. Archibald Gregg, executive secretary of the black YMCA in Tulsa (which was destroyed during the riot). Gregg was not in Tulsa during the violence. In fact, he was in the Kansas City area to attend the graduations of two of his daughters, one from Western University in Quindaro. Gregg's account, published in the *Kansas City Sun* on July 2, 1921, and heretofore unnoticed by scholars, provides depth to the descriptions of black Tulsa before and after May 30, 1921 (see Appendix A).[66] Gregg's account, although rambling and at times marred by difficult syntax, is a testament to the grief experienced by African Americans in the region after the riot. It also is a poignant account of the hope and despair that marked African American life in the 1920s. "I left," Gregg says of his departure from Tulsa on May 26, "a happy,

63. *Kansas City Sun*, June 11, 1921.
64. Ibid.
65. Ibid., June 25, 1921.
66. Ibid., July 2, 1921. For Gregg's full account of the aftermath of the riot, see Appendix A.

hopeful, progressive people. I found a crushed, humiliated, discouraged humanity. I felt [left?] a praying people. I found them wondering if God is just."[67]

Gregg, a forty-seven-year-old Kansas native and a graduate of the University of Kansas, taught mathematics and psychology at Western University in the first two decades of the twentieth century while serving as the faculty adviser for the student YMCA program there. In early 1921, he entered the training program for YMCA secretaries and was appointed executive secretary of the newly established black YMCA in Tulsa. He had been in Tulsa just two months when the riot occurred. Driven possibly by a variety of motives—bitterness in the aftermath of the riot and the desire to return to his family—Gregg left Tulsa late that summer and replaced Frank A. Harris as the executive secretary of the Paseo YMCA.[68]

Service organizations such as the Urban League may have changed—in a limited way—the material condition of Kansas City's African American population, while protest organizations such as the NAACP may have offered an even more limited range of results. For most African Americans in Kansas City early in the twentieth century, political and social salvation was seen as most easily obtained through the political process. Much has been written about the Pendergast machine's control of Kansas City government in the 1920s and 1930s and the tactics of bribery, intimidation, and outright violence it used against the electorate. In many ways, the Pendergast forces made elections irrelevant, but African Americans in Kansas City nevertheless held on to the idea that transformations in the community could occur if they successfully placed a black candidate in city government. Although African Americans had held appointed positions within the state and federal bureaucracies in Kansas City, they had not by 1920 mustered sufficient voting power to put a black man on the city's board of aldermen.

The ratification of the Nineteenth Amendment (giving women the right to vote) and the concentration of African Americans in the Eighth Ward gave black political leaders reason to believe that in 1922 they could break the color line in city government. Black lawyer William C. Hueston had vied for the Republican spot on the ballot in 1918 but had been edged out by a white candidate. In 1922, black residents of the

67. Ibid.

68. Ibid., September 17, 1921; U.S. Department of Commerce, Bureau of the Census, Fourteenth Census.

ward began looking for another suitable candidate. In February, the *Kansas City Sun* published a list of the names being discussed in the shops, stores, and homes around Eighteenth and Vine, which was the center of the Eighth Ward.[69] All of the possibilities were men, of course, and all had strong ties to the area east of Troost. Few, if any, of the names would have been surprising to African Americans in the two Kansas Cities: doctors Thomas C. Unthank, M. H. Lambright, Theodore Smith (owner of the People's Drug Store), and E. C. Bunch (a member of the ward's Republican committee); teachers Joe E. Herriford and G. N. Grisham; and Nathaniel S. Adkins, supervisor of the American Woodman's Fraternal Insurance Company.[70] But in the days following the publication of the list, support began to coalesce around a name not among the *Sun*'s potential candidates: undertaker Theron B. Watkins. The campaign to get Watkins on the ballot and the subsequent election make a profound statement on the state of race relations in Kansas City in the period yet demonstrate that African Americans would also assertively challenge the constraints imposed on them.

Theron B. Watkins ("T. B." to many), like most of the prominent African Americans in the two Kansas Cities, was not native to the area.[71] He was born March 24, 1877, on a farm about thirty miles east of Indianapolis, near the farm community of Charlottesville. His father, John D. Watkins, died when Theron was five years old, and his mother, Martha Lyons Watkins, moved Theron, his brother, J. T., and two sisters a few miles south to Carthage, Indiana. Theron and the rest of the Watkins children attended the Carthage public schools, and Theron eventually graduated from high school with class honors. From Carthage, Theron followed a circuitous path to Kansas City. Watkins worked his way through Indiana State University in Terre Haute and received his degree in political economy. As did many young ambitious and intelligent black men of the period, Watkins worked first for the Pullman Company. Then he began working for a white undertaker, Raymond Johnson. From Johnson, Watkins received the motivation for opening his own funeral parlor. In 1908, Watkins graduated from the Cincinnati School of Embalming, and in 1909, he and J. T. moved to Kansas City. Within a few months they had opened Watkins Brothers Funeral Home

69. *Kansas City Sun*, February 11, 1922.

70. Ibid.

71. Details of Theron B. Watkins's early life are from an undated manuscript biography distributed by the Bruce T. Watkins Cultural Center and from a published obituary in the *Kansas City Call*.

at 1729 Lydia Avenue. By 1920, despite J. T. Watkins's death in 1917, Watkins Brothers was one of the most successful black businesses in the two Kansas Cities.

Theron Watkins quickly moved into leadership roles in the black community. Theron, who was described by one contemporary as a gifted orator, served on the original board of directors at Perry's Sanitarium and in 1913 was one of the leading fund-raisers for the establishment of the Paseo YMCA. He also sat on the steering committee of the Miles Bulger Industrial Home for Negro Boys in Jackson County and by 1921 was serving on the board of directors at Wheatley-Provident Hospital. He was one of the featured speakers at a fund-raising event for LeRoy Bundy of East St. Louis. Watkins's speaking ability, his business acumen, and his commitment to the Eighth Ward made him a perfect candidate in the eyes of many of his contemporaries. Even those individuals who had been mentioned as possible candidates for the Republican nomination rallied to support Watkins. E. C. Bunch, who, according to oral tradition in the black community, was used by white Republicans to split the African American vote and thus thwart Watkins's candidacy, came out publicly for Watkins in the latter stage of the campaign. Nevertheless, white Republicans, still a significant presence in the ward although outnumbered better than two to one, controlled the canvass enough to select a white candidate. Watkins's supporters were furious. Shortly after the Republican gathering, five hundred African Americans gathered at Highland Avenue Baptist Church, and Theron B. Watkins was elected by the gathering to run for alderman as an independent candidate.[72]

A campaign committee, led by E. C. Bunch, was appointed, and immediately petitions were drawn up to get Watkins's name on the April 4 ballot. Nelson Crews and Chester A. Franklin quickly threw the editorial weight of their respective papers behind the Watkins candidacy. Crews, in particular, was infuriated by the outcome of the Republican canvass. In no uncertain terms, he argued that a ward that was two-thirds black should have an African American representative. In Crews's mind, "justice and right" demanded support of Watkins by every "red-blooded self-respecting" black man and woman in the Eighth

72. "Theron B. Watkins biography," *Kansas City Sun*, March 4, 1922. Watkins was nominated by N. S. Adkins. Two other candidates—lawyer L. Amasa Knox and physician L. V. Miller—were nominated but quickly withdrew their names from consideration and threw their support to Watkins. The Watkins biography and the *Call* obituary both incorrectly say Watkins entered the 1922 election as the Republican candidate.

Ward. Watkins's campaign, at least for that one month in 1922, eliminated divisions of gender, geography, and status within the African American community. From the outset, he stated that if elected, he would represent more than the Eighth Ward; he would represent all of the forty thousand African Americans on the Missouri side. Watkins drew support from African Americans from all walks of life; even his competitors in the funeral industry rallied to his side. Early in April, the Undertakers' Association of the two Kansas Cities—including C. H. Countee, A. T. Moore, and Adkins Brothers Funeral Home—endorsed Watkins. Watkins's campaign was not limited to African American males. Nannie C. Bunch, wife of E. C. Bunch, and Eva Fox, both community activists in their own right, were among the speakers at Highland Baptist arguing for a black candidate to represent the Eighth Ward.[73]

Nelson Crews, meanwhile, continued his fervent support for Watkins. The issue became, in Crews's hands, twofold: Watkins's more-than-sufficient qualifications to represent the ward and the racial pride and self-image of Kansas City's African American communities. In an editorial three days before the election, Crews spelled out the situation:

> One of the most gratifying features of the municipal campaign now being waged in this city is the evident determination on the part of the masses of our people to study, reason and THINK out for themselves the best method by which to serve the race and the Republican party. It has been amply demonstrated that the time has long since passed when white men can label any collection or conglomeration the Republican ticket and win the support of thinking Negroes. Our people are now demanding that men shall be measured up four-square to the principle and policies of a square deal and fair treatment to all races that go to make up American citizenship or they cannot hope for the support of the THINKING NEGROES of this community.[74]

Watkins's campaign was spectacularly effective but ultimately unsuccessful. When returns from the election were posted, Watkins had received more than 2,000 votes. The Democratic candidate for mayor, Frank Cromwell, however, won in a landslide and carried the entire Democratic ticket into office. Watkins's losing margin—some 170 votes—was the smallest of any of the races. The Republican candidate from the Eighth Ward received just 800 votes.

73. Ibid., March 4, April 1, 1922.
74. Ibid., April 1, 1922 (emphasis in original).

Watkins's career of public service did not end that April day. He remained a supporter of many of the key institutions and causes in the African American communities of the two Kansas Cities. Before 1920, he invested with Reuben Street in the Street Hotel; sometime in 1924 or 1925 the partnership was dissolved. Watkins was instrumental in the founding, with H. O. Cook, of a cooperative credit union, the People's Finance Corporation, and he served as the cooperative's president for almost twenty years. In 1941, he was the only African American appointed to the newly organized Kansas City Housing Authority, and during World War II he served on the Selective Service Board. In 1944, Watkins unsuccessfully ran for the Missouri legislature. He also was an ardent supporter of issues affecting African American youth. As noted above, he was instrumental in the operation of the Miles Bulger Home. He also supported a number of African American students financially. In addition, Watkins was interested in athletics, and he was one of the founders of the Gateway Athletic Club for black youths. He died September 4, 1950, shortly before the new Watkins Brothers funeral parlor at Eighteenth and Benton Boulevard was completed.[75]

Watkins's campaign reflected the growing political strength of African Americans in the Eighth Ward and on the East Side. In 1924, therefore, it was not a question of *if* a black man would gain the Republican nomination for alderman, but *which one.* The two final candidates were real-estate broker Herman L. Kinsler and the successful nominee, the Reverend James Wesley Hurse. Hurse received endorsements from all of the key individuals and institutions within the black community, and African American voters outnumbered whites in the ward. Despite these advantages, Hurse lost a closely contested election. It would be the last time in the interwar period that either of the major parties ran an African American for a spot in city government. A new city charter, overwhelmingly approved by voters in 1925, streamlined city government and in the process diluted black voting strength. In place of a thirty-two-seat, two-tiered governing body, a nine-man city council would oversee the city. The new council districts were composed of three or four wards, and the black voters in the Eighth Ward again found

75. "Theron Watkins Biography"; Gibson, *Mecca of the New Negro,* 119 (unattributed newspaper clipping dated 1925). Watkins's legacy continued beyond the operation of the funeral home. A housing project in the East Bottoms was named in his honor. More important, one of his sons, Bruce Riley Watkins, emulated his father's activism and political ambitions. Bruce Watkins was one of the founders of the black political organization Freedom Incorporated. He also served on the city council and was the first black man to run (unsuccessfully) for mayor in Kansas City. The current Watkins Brothers location sits just east of the center built as a tribute to Bruce Watkins on Brush Creek Boulevard.

themselves outnumbered by whites in their council district. As a result, it would take almost another forty years before African Americans elected two black men—former principal Earl D. Thomas and Theron B. Watkins's son, Bruce Watkins—to the city council.[76]

African American voting strength in Kansas City, ironically, would be felt more on a statewide level than it would in city elections. The concentration of black voters bolstered lawyer L. Amasa Knox in his run for the state legislature. Knox's successful bid in 1928 made him just the second black man to sit in the Missouri House of Representatives and the first black man elected to represent Jackson County.[77] His election owed as much to the strength of black Republicanism as it did to the peculiar geography of the legislative district. The Fourth District, from which Knox was elected, wound serpentine through the city's East Side and included both the Eighteenth and Vine district and a portion of the Church Hill area.[78]

Knox was born four years after the end of the Civil War, in 1869, in Poplar Mount, Virginia. His father, Africanus, was a former slave who claimed pure African lineage. Africanus Knox was a blacksmith by trade, and as a youth, L. Amasa served as an apprentice in his father's shop. L. Amasa, however, was driven by a desire to learn, and he spent his spare time reading and studying. In 1889, he entered Virginia State College in Petersburg, and after five years he graduated. Knox taught school for a year before enrolling in the law school at Howard University in 1895. He received a bachelor of law degree in 1897. Knox contemplated a return to Howard for further education, but friends in Virginia persuaded him to return home and run for a seat in the Virginia House of Delegates.[79]

Knox, according to his obituary in 1949, had long been intrigued by politics. His father had been a county committeeman in the Republican Party, and L. Amasa had made connections with many of the African American political leaders in the state. Knox gained the Republican nomination, but Democrats in the state, through a combination of

76. Brown and Dorsett, *K.C.*, 150–53, 190, 266; *Kansas City Call*, March 14, 21, 28, 1924.

77. Greene, Kremer, and Holland (*Missouri's Black Heritage*, 170) mention Knox's election but do not include him in a list of Missouri's black legislators in the appendix.

78. The district was bound by Ninth Street on the north and Armour Boulevard on the south. Its eastern limits jogged from Park (three blocks east of Prospect) to Indiana (eleven blocks east). Its western boundaries were Campbell, Harrison (both just west of Troost) and Tracy (two blocks east of Troost). *Kansas City Call*, October 17, 1930.

79. Unattributed newspaper clipping dated August 12, 1949, in Gibson, *Mecca of the New Negro*, 197.

intimidation and bribery of black voters, secured the seat in the legislature. Beaten but not deterred, L. Amasa Knox returned to Howard and received his master's of law degree. In the spring of 1899, he headed west to Missouri, where he passed the bar examination.[80]

Knox spent the next five years in St. Louis and St. Joseph, Missouri, before moving to Kansas City around 1905. He soon became a fixture in the affairs of the African American community. He was one of the many organizers of the Wheatley-Provident Hospital and for many years served as the hospital's treasurer. He supported the Kansas City chapter of the NAACP in its early years and served on the board of directors of the Urban League branch. He joined Hugh O. Cook and Myrtle Foster Cook in the establishment of the People's Finance Corporation. Knox also was among Kansas City's representatives to the conference on black education held in Jefferson City in 1921, was an early supporter of the Paseo YMCA, and served on the steering committee for the Jackson County Home for Negro Boys. He was a Master Mason and for many years served as the legal adviser to the grand lodge, and, along with fellow lawyers Charles Calloway and William C. Hueston, Dr. Lon Tillman, and undertaker Theron B. Watkins, Knox was a leading member of Kansas City's Elks lodge. Knox and his wife, Clara, lived in the 1800 block of The Paseo, just two blocks from Vine.[81]

Knox also had been an active voice in black Republicanism, and in 1926, he made a strong run at the state legislature as the Republican candidate from the Fourth District. Walthall M. Moore of St. Louis had become the first black man to serve in the Missouri legislature with his successful bid in 1920. Moore had returned to the legislature in 1925, and Knox was attempting to join Moore and John A. Davis, another African American man from St. Louis, in widening the gap in the state legislature's color barrier. Emboldened by his strong showing in 1926, Knox chose to run again in 1928, and he edged Albert Morris by 903 votes.[82]

While in the legislature, Knox gained one notable success. He authored legislation that required the establishment of a school within any district containing eight school-age children. Previous state law had set the limit at fifteen children, and Knox's legislation mandated continued

80. Ibid.

81. Ibid.; Young and Young, *Your Kansas City and Mine*, 51, 139, 142; *Kansas City Sun*, February 5, April 9, August 13, 1921.

82. Greene, Kremer, and Holland, *Missouri's Black Heritage*, 242–43; Charles U. Becker, *State of Missouri Official Manual for Years Nineteen Twenty-nine and Nineteen Thirty* (Jefferson City: Botz-Hugh Stephens Press, 1930), 422.

state support of schools for black children in areas where African American populations were in decline. The change proved important during the Depression of the 1930s, when school districts in the state might have pondered closing all-black schools as an economy measure.[83]

Knox ran for reelection in 1930, but his bid apparently fell victim to the political shenanigans of the Pendergast machine. Knox's 1930 opponent, insurance man Gil P. Bourk, received 2,000 fewer votes than the Democratic challenger in 1928. Knox, however, was credited with almost *9,000 fewer votes* than he had received two years previously and was soundly trounced. Chester Franklin of the *Kansas City Call* was furious at the outcome and alleged that Pendergast associate Casimir J. Welch had rigged the election.[84]

After leaving the legislature, Knox returned to private legal practice. In 1944, he was appointed to the city counselor's office after the death of Charles Calloway. Knox served in the city attorney's office until his death in 1949.[85]

In 1922, black Kansas City opened its arms to a black Jamaican activist by the name of Marcus Josiah Garvey. At the time, Garvey was at the peak of his political prominence. He came to Kansas City preaching his particular version of black nationalism, pan-Africanism, anticolonialism, and black economic development. He found a receptive audience for his three talks, including one at St. Stephen's Church. By the early 1920s, a Kansas City branch of Garvey's Universal Negro Improvement Association had grown to about three hundred members and had established an office on East Eighteenth Street. In 1923, when Garvey returned to the Kansas City area, more than a thousand spectators crowded into the auditorium at Sumner High School to hear him speak. Although the UNIA drew the majority of its American membership from the black working class, its most prominent supporters in Kansas City were barber Rucker Smith and music dealer Winston Holmes. Smith, who had a shop in the 1400 block of Walnut, was a self-described expert on Liberia and organizer of the Liberian Investment Company and served as president and secretary of the Kansas City chapter in the early 1920s. Holmes's record store at 1704 East Eighteenth Street was one of the landmarks of the Eighteenth and Vine district. Smith and Holmes continued to build the Kansas City chapter in

83. Gibson, *Mecca of the New Negro.*

84. Becker, ibid., 281.

85. Young and Young, *Your Kansas City and Mine,* 162, 167; Gibson, *Mecca of the New Negro; Kansas City Call,* October 12, 1923.

the early 1920s, but the arrest and conviction of Garvey on federal charges ultimately sapped the movement's strength.

Garvey's supporters outnumbered those African Americans attracted to the American Communist Party in the 1930s. One prominent black Communist was Abner Perry, who was arrested and fined in 1933 for vagrancy (apparently for conversing with a white female Communist outside the Provident Association offices).[86]

The Battle for Equality

No fair mind will condemn the colored people for arraying themselves against those who are unwilling that they should have a fair chance to advance in all the occupations and educational opportunities of life.

—*NEW HAVEN (CT) TIMES-LEADER*, 1923

How African Americans arrayed themselves in the fight for racial equality followed no patterns of logic. In fact, organizational ties for various protest groups cut across all classes, professions, and social ranks in Kansas City's African American communities. For instance, the Reverend John Goins of Kansas City joined the National Race Congress, a short-lived civil rights organization that appears to have been a self-appointed body of ministers (possibly all of the black Baptist Church) who sought to articulate the needs and aspirations of African Americans on a national level. The congress met in Washington in October 1919 in the aftermath of the outbreak of racial violence of the previous summer. During its session, the National Race Congress drafted a memorial to be sent to the United States Congress. The memorial, apparently based on the "14 points" enumerated by American President Woodrow Wilson at the Paris Peace Conference, set forth what African Americans expected "after helping to win the war for democracy." The National Race Congress's agenda likely was also elaborated in an address to the American people, published in black newspapers throughout the country.[87] Seventeen men were appointed to a committee to draft the public appeal; at least fourteen members of the committee, including John Goins, were members of the clergy. The address drew heavily on black protest traditions dating back at least one hundred years. It demanded the fulfillment of American ideals and rights, as

86. *Kansas City Call*, February 3, 1933.
87. *Western Messenger*, November 14, 1919.

expressed in the Constitution, for *all* of the citizens of the United States. The public address, although couched in nonthreatening terms, also made specific demands concerning the conditions of African American life, both north and south. The address asserted that among other matters—the right for collective bargaining, equal appropriations for schools, the end of Jim Crow laws, and protection for black homes and bodies—were issues that must be confronted. And although asserting the need for full obedience of the law, the address also affirmed the right of African Americans to defend themselves: "When it becomes a matter of self-protection—a question of life existence—the man who does not rise up in his own defense is not worthy of citizenship in a republic like these United States." Again, drawing on the ideals expressed in the Declaration of Independence and the Constitution, the framers of the National Race Congress's public address sought to broaden the definition of *American citizen* to include people of color, while at the same time, President Woodrow Wilson was seeking to expand upon those ideals in a European context. The National Race Congress's address again tapped into those ideals in its final paragraph. Among the hopes and wishes of the members gathered in Washington that fall were "the promotion of righteousness and in the end, the dawn for a better day for all."[88]

At the same time the National Race Congress's brief burst on the national scene, another grassroots organization was seeking to make headway in Kansas City. Founded by two Kansas City black businessmen in 1919, the National Negro Constitutional Conservation League of America (NNCCLA) sought to recruit masses of African Americans—throughout Kansas City, the West, and ultimately the entire country—to support its demands for a complete fulfillment of black political rights. The following is the league's open invitation to join the cause:

> If you believe in the Divine Providence of the Powers of God; if you believe Justice, in the end, should triumph over Wrong; if you believe that the Negro has proven himself to be a tried, true and loyal citizen; if you believe that he should be given the preference over the incoming foreigner to earn a livelihood in this country; if you believe that the fingers of the Negro are worthy of marking the ballot after they have pulled the trigger in defense of it; if you believe that the chastity of Negro women should be protected the same as any other race of women; if you believe the Negro should have the same opportunities to receive the proper education; if

88. Ibid.

> you believe that he has the same right to live in peace and harmony wherever and in whatever home he is able to buy; if you believe that the Negro soldier, who is good enough to protect the Southern border of our country, is, at the same time, good enough to ride indiscriminately in trains in the same section; if you believe he should be permitted to enter into the different lines of legitimate business, industries and professions; if you believe that the Negro's rights should not be bought and sold from the political auction block by a few of our "hand-picked" "self-first" and self-appointed race leaders; if you believe that the sacrifice made by the Negroes in the great World War for Democracy should not be without proper results; if you believe that the Negro woman who is good enough to give her son to fight and die for her country is at the same time good enough to be protected by it; if you believe that the blood of these true, loyal and brave soldiers should not be shed in vain; if you believe that the Negro citizens of America should enjoy the security of life, liberty, property and the pursuit of happiness as ordained by the Constitution of the United States; if you believe that discrimination and prejudice, Jim-Crowism and disfranchisement, mob violence and injustice should be wiped out and eliminated from this great Nation of ours; if you are willing to assist us in bringing these great and just things to pass—then you should and ARE most cordially and most sincerely invited to become a member of our League.[89]

The founder and leading advocate of the NNCCLA was Clarence R. Groves, nephew of Kansas City, Kansas, entrepreneur Junious Groves. He was joined by Samuel Richard Hopkins, founder and president of Square Deal Realty and Oil Company. The league's aim, as stated in a January newspaper article, was "to see that the blood of our brave and noble soldiers who fought for World Democracy shall not have been shed in vain, by waging an unending and ceaseless fight to wipe out and eliminate discrimination and prejudice, Jim-Crowism and disfranchisement, mob violence and injustice from the United States of America FOREVER." To achieve these lofty aims, which presaged W. E. B. Du Bois's ringing rally cry ("We return. We return from fighting. We return fighting."), the league sought to craft a petition to the United States Congress demanding that the federal government enforce the provisions of the Fourteenth and Fifteenth Amendments of the Constitution. Clarence Groves and Samuel Hopkins hoped to obtain at least a million signatures and argued that "every true and race loving" African

89. *Kansas City Sun*, January 25, 1919.

American would demand a chance to place their signature on such a petition. The league, as did the NAACP and the Urban League, would seek the support of white Americans, but its target audience was the mass of black men and women in Kansas City and its environs.[90]

The league received support from across the spectrum of black Kansas City. If the supporters of the league found its objectives redundant to those of other civil rights organizations or its strategy unnecessarily ambitious, few expressed such sentiments in the heady atmosphere of the first few months of 1919.

By March, the league had a separate chapter among "prominent individuals" in Independence and had been endorsed in meetings of black ministers and black club women. W. H. Harrison, principal of Attucks School, was the first to sign the petition. By the time a draft of the petition was circulated in late February, the signatures already included those of Nelson C. Crews, Chester Franklin, and Felix Payne; lawyers William C. Hueston and Charles H. Calloway; physicians Thomas C. Unthank, John Edward Perry, and J. E. Dibble; T. B. Watkins; Fred and Pearl Dabney; teacher Henley L. Cox and his wife; as well as several members of the faculty at Western University in Kansas City, Kansas. Many of the signatories were members of the NAACP.

An elaborate and lengthy signature and membership campaign was planned for the first three weeks of March; from its offices at 1315 East Eighteenth Street, the league dispatched teams led by "generals" and "captains." Yet although the leaders of each team were some of the more recognized names in black Kansas City, it is fairly obvious that the league never caught on with the masses. Nelson Crews and his *Kansas City Sun* were some of the most ardent boosters of the league, but there is no mention of the league, its objectives, or its petition in the weekly newspaper's pages after March 15. The enthusiasm so apparent in January and February had been met with indifference in March. The league's short life span, however, is no reason to dismiss its objectives. The league represented a bold attempt by black Kansas Citians to articulate, on their own terms, their grievances concerning their status in twentieth-century U.S. society. The NAACP and the Urban League, each in its own patient way, would address many of these same grievances, but the NNCCLA was among the first black organizations to put those concerns out for all to see.[91]

90. *Kansas City Sun*, January 18, 1919 (emphasis in original). For example, Samuel R. Hopkins sought and received an endorsement of the league's principles from Burris Jenkins, editor and publisher of the *Kansas City Post*.

91. See *Kansas City Sun*, January 25, February 1, 8, 15, 22, March 1, 8, 15, 1919.

Even among black organizations ostensibly constructed for other purposes, issues of political equality and racial identity often dominated the agenda. In the summer of 1925, eighty black men and women from seventeen states—primarily in the South—gathered in Kansas City for what purported to be an educational forum. The agenda of the twenty-seventh annual meeting of the National Negro Educational Congress, however, journeyed far beyond the boundaries of pedagogical methods and challenges facing teachers in the interwar period. Instead, its program, shaped by James Silas Harris, the congress's president and a former Kansas City teacher, attempted to address the conditions facing African Americans in twentieth-century U.S. cities. Although press accounts tended to mute the radical content of the congress's program,[92] Harris and other members of the Kansas City delegation—including Ida M. Becks, lawyer L. Amasa Knox, and Dr. J. E. Dibble and his wife—intended to use the congress as a forum for a critique of American society and of black responses within that society. The first page of the official souvenir program contained an appeal not just to the delegates in attendance but to black America in general: "READ—ponder—act," the appeal, written by Harris, started.

> After passing through nearly two and a half centuries of SLAVERY, during which time they cleared the FORESTS, tilled the FIELDS, bridged the RIVERS, tunneled the MOUNTAINS, built the cities and heroically fought the battles of the REPUBLIC, the NEGRO is NOW, after more than half a century of FREEDOM, of EDUCATION, of unparalleled MORAL and MATERIAL growth, pleading at the Bar of PUBLIC OPINION for LIFE, for LIBERTY and for JUSTICE, A "PLEA" that we do not believe the AMERICAN PEOPLE will suffer to go UNHEARD. To find SOME way by which this can be accomplished is an EFFORT, RICH in POSSIBILITIES, worthy of the TIME and ENERGY devoted to the same. With this and only THIS object in view, The Negro National Educational Congress will meet in Kansas City, August 25–29, 1925.[93]

To achieve this worthy objective, the delegates devoted the final day of the congress to a series of topics relevant to African American life but well beyond the usual purview of educators. Among the addresses were "How Can We Make Negro Citizenship a Reality?" "Will the Future Progress of the American Negro Depend upon the Preservation of Their

92. The *Kansas City Star*, for example, ran a two-paragraph item on each day of the Congress under the headline "Negro Teachers Meet."

93. Gibson, *Mecca of the New Negro*, 81–84.

Race-Identity?" "May the Highest Possibilities of the Negro Be Reached in America?" "Have We Too Many Churches in the Large Cities?" and "Are We Given an Equal Opportunity in the Field of Industry with Other American Citizens?"

Although historian Sherry Lamb Schirmer has questioned J. Silas Harris's commitment to African Americans' quest for social equality, there is no doubt that he supported, if not authored, the radical message of the educational congress's agenda. The teachers sought a dramatic change in the American racial status quo. The teachers—like the members of mainstream organizations such as the Urban League and the NAACP, the followers of Marcus Garvey, and those willing to listen to and voice support for the egalitarian arguments of short-lived organizations such as the National Race Congress and the NNCCLA—recognized the limits that race placed on their lives. All of these organizations, regardless of ideological posturing, sought in their own ways to reshape the construct of race in meaningful ways. Some would be more successful than others; all contributed to the creation of a climate where change was possible, albeit slow. The ideals of these organizations would be repeated in countless forums across Kansas City and across the country over the years. It would take decades, but eventually society responded to the concerns of black Kansas Citians.

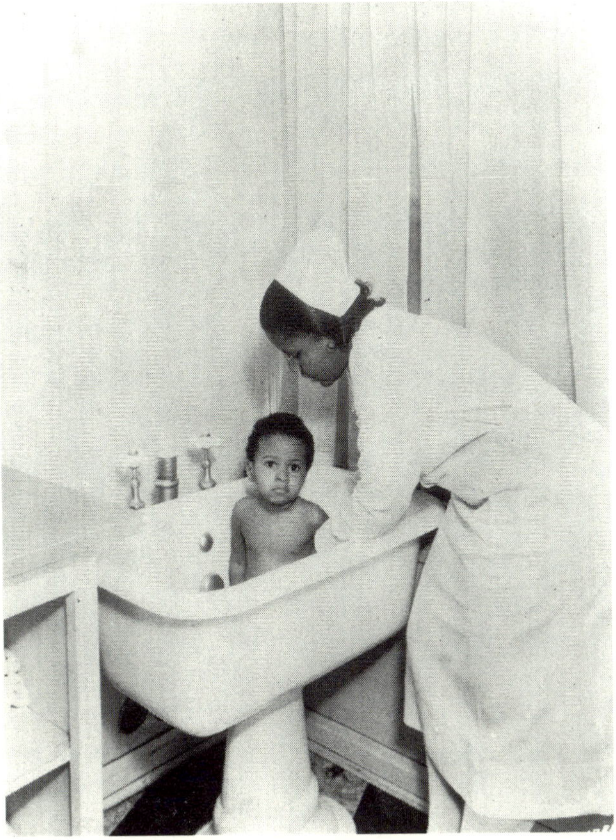

A nurse bathes a child at the Florence Crittenton Home for unwed mothers. Courtesy of Kansas City Public Library, Missouri Valley Room.

Although job opportunities for African Americans were limited, black workers were employed in the construction of the Fidelity National Bank Building in 1930. Courtesy of Kansas City Public Library, Missouri Valley Room.

The Kansas City Monarchs with team owner J. L. Wilkinson (*standing, far right*) in 1934. Courtesy of Kansas City Public Library, Missouri Valley Room.

African Americans who lived in the Belvidere section of Kansas City took advantage of a settlement house in the area. Courtesy of Kansas City Public Library, Missouri Valley Room.

African Americans living in the Church Hill area did not give up all of their rural traditions. This family worked a garden in a plot east of Troost. The view looks back to the west. Courtesy of Kansas City Public Library, Missouri Valley Room.

The Church Hill area extended several blocks south of Tenth and Charlotte Streets. An African American couple sits on a porch in the 1700 block of Charlotte. Courtesy of Kansas City Public Library, Missouri Valley Room.

Many African Americans in Kansas City lived in subpar housing. These homes sat in the 1700 block of Troost Avenue. Courtesy of Kansas City Public Library, Missouri Valley Room.

Western Baptist Bible College moved into its site at 2125 Tracy in 1934. Courtesy of Kansas City Public Library, Missouri Valley Room.

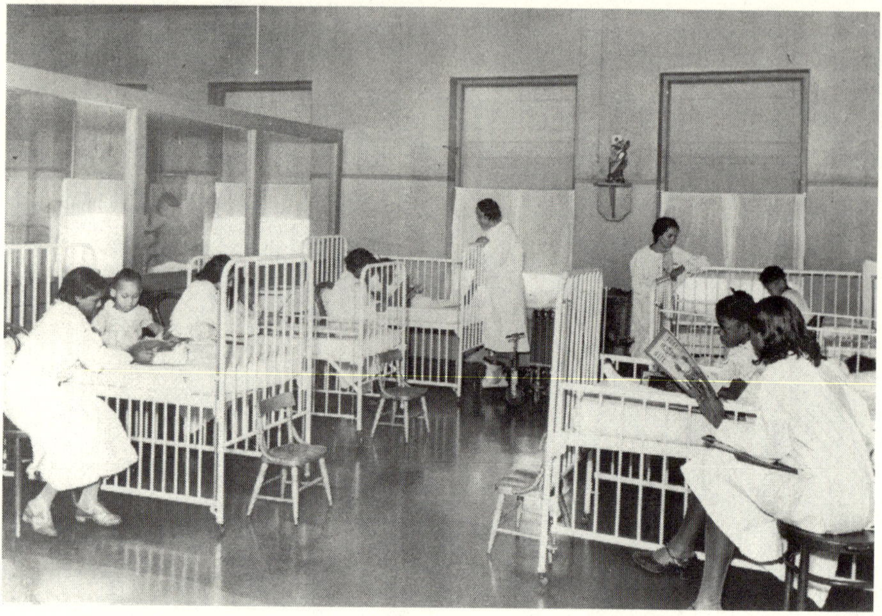

Nurses attend to children during the 1930s at the Wheatley-Provident Hospital at 1826 Forest. Wheatley-Provident was one of two hospitals that served African Americans in the interwar period. Courtesy of Kansas City Public Library, Missouri Valley Room.

Black employees of the Densmore Hotel in downtown Kansas City. Courtesy of Kansas City Public Library, Missouri Valley Room.

During the early years of the twentieth century, the Garrison Branch library in the East Bottoms served African American children. Courtesy of Kansas City Public Library, Missouri Valley Room.

African Americans who lived on the West Side would have used these terraced steps leading west from Twentieth Street and Belleview Avenue. A black child can be seen at lower right. Courtesy of Kansas City Public Library, Missouri Valley Room.

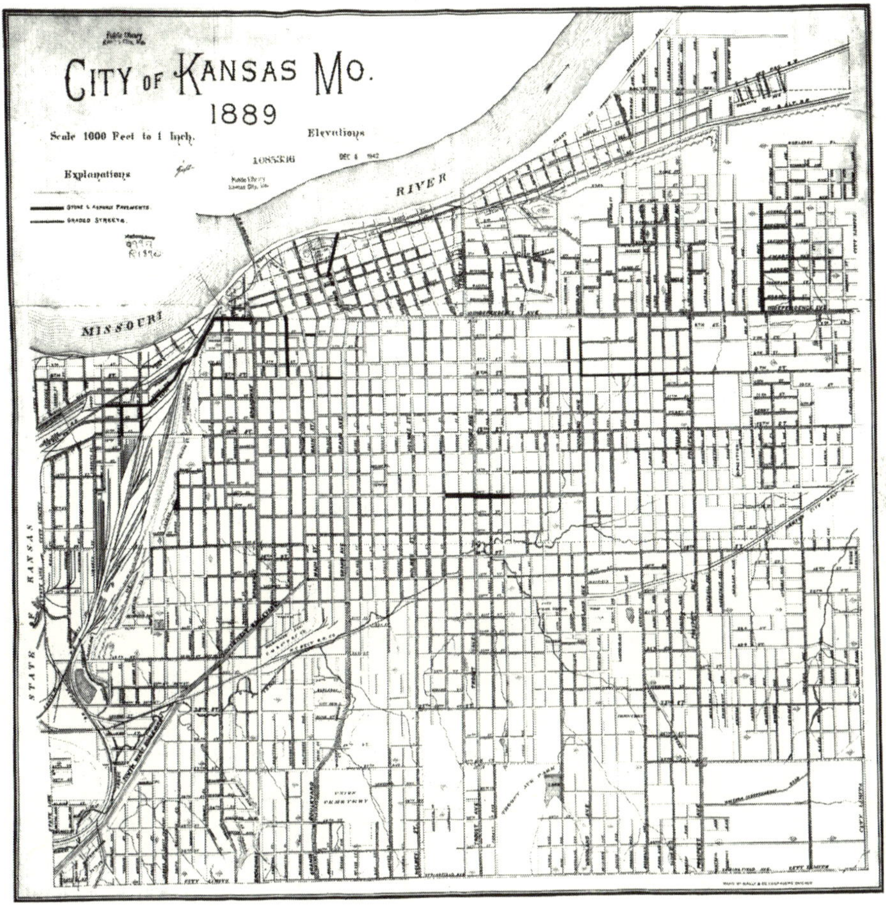

A map of Kansas City in 1889. Courtesy of Kansas City Public Library, Missouri Valley Room.

The Bennie Moten Orchestra, one of Kansas City's greatest contributions to jazz. Reprinted with permission of the *Kansas City Star*.

Theron B. Watkins, founder of Watkins Brothers Funeral Home, was one of the leading voices in black Kansas City during the interwar period. Courtesy the Bruce R. Watkins Cultural and Heritage Center.

Five

School, Church, and Health

Institutions of Salvation

SCHOOL OPENS TUESDAY: PARENTS PLEASE SEND YOUR CHILDREN TO SCHOOL.

—HEADLINE IN THE *KANSAS CITY SUN*, SEPTEMBER 4, 1920

IT WAS THE START of another school year, and more than 550 students—the school's largest enrollment up to that time—crowded into the Lincoln High School in the second week of September for the first day of classes. Before the learning process could begin, the students were joined in the auditorium by many of their parents and friends for an early morning assembly. The assembly, like the festival in the Convention Hall earlier that year, demonstrated those principles of community and racial pride that drove Kansas City's African Americans in the interwar period. The assembly also demonstrated how school life became one more vehicle for the transmission of important values and codes of conduct from one generation to the next. African American schools in Kansas City sought to instill in the students the American ideals of hard work, personal responsibility, and the value of an education. They also helped inculcate the dual mechanisms of resistance and acceptance while delineating for the students the limit of Jim Crow life. All of these complex, interrelated forces were at work during the assembly at Lincoln High School.

On the auditorium's stage that day, as the guests of principal John R. E. Lee, were many of the prominent men in black Kansas City: lawyer

William C. Hueston, Dr. D. Madison Miller, the Reverend William Thomas of Allen Chapel AME, Frank Harris of the Paseo YMCA, newspaper editors Nelson Crews and Chester Franklin, and retired Lincoln principal G. N. Grisham. Joining them that morning was former Lincoln student Doris Novel, a talented vocalist who was a student at the University of Kansas. Each was given an opportunity to address the students, and their remarks were dutifully recorded by Willa Glenn of the *Kansas City Sun.*[1]

Principal John R. E. Lee was the first of the speakers. In his remarks, he reminded the students—and their teachers—of the obligations they faced as representatives of black Kansas City. "I trust that you young men and young women," Lee said, "will appreciate the responsibility which is being daily forced upon you. It will be up to you teachers and students whether you are going to do your whole duty." Lawyer Hueston echoed Lee's remarks and bluntly laid out the challenge for the young men and women listening. "This high school," Hueston said, "represents our race in the contest that we are to have in this country and let it be understood that a contest is to come and you must decide for yourself whether or not this test is to be won by you." The contest, of course, would be one in which African Americans would continue their quest for political equality and the end of discrimination and segregation in American society. Hueston reminded the students that more than just the assembled guests and parents would be watching them. "You are not here to get an education for your own use," Hueston cautioned the students. "It is for something in which we all are interested and the question is whether or not you as representatives of the race of ours are going to measure up."[2]

Lee then asked Grisham, whose demeanor through the assembly was that of the proud parent of 550 children, to make a brief statement. After wryly noting that it once took him three hours to say what he could then say in three minutes, Grisham expressed the pleasure he took on that day "because it represents that a large number of our future generation is preparing for its life's work. I remember quite vividly the times when I expressed a desire to see the enrollment of Lincoln High School reach the mark of fifty but it more than reached my fondest expectations. . . . Young people, the manner of numbers is not the most important thing; it is how much good will come out of that number."

1. *Kansas City Sun,* September 13, 1919. Novel, a founding member of Kansas City's chapter of the black sorority Alpha Kappa Alpha, would be a featured performer at a number of musical events in Kansas City during the 1920s. See Young and Young, *Your Kansas City and Mine,* 64–65.

2. Ibid.

The students, however, provided some of the most illuminating comments of the assembly when they were asked by Principal Lee to discuss their summer vacations. Most of the students' responses reflect the tensions between work and education that faced American youth, particularly African American youth, in the interwar period. All, predictably, asserted that they were happy to be back in school, but many of the students had already been exposed to the world of work in serious capacities. William Love, for instance, spent his summer working for a box company and then at the Swift packinghouse. James Johnson worked at the Clay Manufacturing Company, and Alla May Nelson worked at a bag company. Many found their summer work experiences to be arduous. Alvin Starks worked painting ventilators and fire escapes at the twenty-six school buildings in the Kansas City district. He fondly referred to the fire escapes as "knee-breakers." Lillian Campbell started the summer working as a domestic for a private family, which she found "too hard," before finding easier work in a theater. At least one student took the difficult work at the Armour packing plant in stride. "It was pretty hard down there," Richard Carper said, "especially the kind of work I was doing, but I thought that I might as well get used to going up against hard things." Several of the students had spent the summer working in the various vocational departments at Lincoln. Victoria Simpson worked in the Millinery Department, George Smith worked in Auto Mechanics, and Harry Walker worked in the Printing Department. Student Cecil Newman offered the most interesting response. He spent the summer in the school's Carpentry Department. "We intended to build a gymnasium," Newman said, "but found there was a need for lunchroom tables and chairs. We made several of each and finding that there was need for an annex to Attucks school, went over and built that. If you want to see some good work, just inspect the annex to Attucks school."

Newman's pride in his work also was a reflection of the pride he and the other students shared for Lincoln High School. It was a sense of pride that linked a generation of African American youths through the interwar period. It was a pride reflected by the speakers on the stage that Tuesday morning. Editor Nelson Crews pointed out that, with the exception of Hueston and Reverend Thomas (both of whom had children enrolled at Lincoln), none of the invited speakers had any real connection to the high school. For once, Crews was wrong; the connection was the recognition of the place Lincoln High School and its students held in the Kansas City's African American communities and their hinterland.

Kansas City's Black Schools

What can I do tomorrow to improve upon the work of today?

—JOSEPHINE SILONE YATES, 1905

Education was a priority, if not the first priority, for African Americans in the years after the Civil War. Historian Eric Foner, among others, has demonstrated the value the former slaves put on the ability to read and to write; many figured that there must be something valuable in something that slave owners had fought to deny them all those many years. Historian James Anderson argues that for the former slaves, reading and writing were viewed as a "contradiction" to oppression. Freedmen and -women, with or without the cooperation of white authorities, organized schools within months of the end of the war in communities throughout the South. The pupils in these schools, held in churches, storefronts, or even the fields, were the very young to the very old. Some former slaves sought enough literacy to be able to sign their names; other wanted to be to read the Bible. Whatever the motivation, the quest for knowledge figured prominently in the plans of black men and women in the 1860s and 1870s.[3] Over the next five or six decades, black men and women stepped in to organize, construct, and lead schools of various levels. The first public school systems in the South—for white and black students—were organized during Reconstruction; the black graduates of these schools often became the teachers of the next generation of scholars. State-funded black schools were established throughout the Reconstruction South; all-black institutions such as Fisk University in Nashville, Atlanta University in Georgia, and Grambling University in Louisiana all have their roots in the years after the Civil War. In Missouri, Lincoln Institute (now Lincoln University) in Jefferson City was founded in the 1870s, and in Kansas, what began in Quindaro as a school for former slaves evolved into Western University.[4]

Prior to the Civil War, the state of Missouri prohibited the education of slaves and made no provisions for the education of the children of the state's small free black population. The postbellum era brought a new state constitution, and with it a provision for the education of all children, black or white. The first general assembly to meet under the new constitution then mandated that all townships, where necessary,

3. Foner, *Reconstruction: America's Unfinished Revolution, 1863–1877;* J. D. Anderson, *Education of Blacks,* 17.

4. J. D. Anderson, *Education of Blacks;* Greene, Kremer, and Holland, *Missouri's Black Heritage,* 98–100; Greenbaum, *Afro-American Community,* 55.

were to establish schools for African Americans. The assembly also prohibited the establishment of separate school districts or school governing bodies for black schools; policies regarding African American and white children were to be issued from the same school board in each township.[5]

By the 1920s, more than three thousand African Americans were enrolled in Lincoln High School and eight grade schools in Kansas City. The material conditions in many of the schools were substandard, and black parents and their children faced a series of obstacles produced by tensions between black educators and the all-white Board of Education, the constant closing or moving of schools, and the debates over the role of vocational training in the Kansas City school district. These tensions seldom erupted into direct confrontations. Instead, they lingered under the surface and informed many of the decisions made by school officials concerning African American youth in the years before World War II. It should be noted, however, that despite the schools' physical shortcomings, many graduates of the schools expressed fond memories of their experiences there. As in segregated schools around the country, black students in Kansas City benefited from the experiences of a number of talented educators. Because of the limited opportunities available at the college level for black teachers, black high schools attracted educators of the highest quality. That appeared to be the case in Kansas City.

In October 1867, the newly formed Kansas City Board of Education established schools for its 1,900 white and 250 African American students. As mentioned in Chapter One, the first school for African American children on the Missouri side was the Lincoln School in a building rented from the Second Congregational Church at what is now Tenth and McGee Streets. Mrs. M. J. Copeland was assigned teaching duties for that first year, 1867, but after one week she was replaced by her husband, who completed the school term. After James Milton Turner's short stint at the school in the spring of 1868, James Dallas Bowser was appointed principal for the fall term. At the same time, the Board of Education purchased a building on a low-lying lot at Ninth and Charlotte Streets. Under Bowser's direction, the school grew, and by 1878 almost five hundred students were enrolled at the Lincoln School. The Board of Education recognized the need for a larger school and, in 1878, opened a new facility at Eleventh and Campbell Streets. Under a succession of

5. See W. Sherman Savage, "The Legal Provisions for Negro Schools in Missouri from 1865 to 1890."

principals, Lincoln continued to grow. As noted above, at the prompting of principal David Victor Adolphus Nero and others, high school courses had been added to the Lincoln curriculum. In 1887, a high school annex was added to the Lincoln building, and in 1890, a separate high school for African American students was built at Nineteenth and Tracy with G. N. Grisham as its first principal. Grade school classes were still held at the Lincoln School site on Campbell. Noted teacher W. W. Yates took over as principal in 1896 and served until his death in 1910. Joe E. Herriford succeeded Yates as principal, and at his insistence, the Board of Education eliminated the confusion of two Lincoln Schools in the district by renaming the elementary school in honor of W. W. Yates.

By that time, the growth of African American communities in other parts of the city had prompted the Board of Education to establish other all-black schools. In 1870, the school board hired Anna Wilson to teach African American students living in the West Bottoms. Classes met in one room of the Benton school, at Fourteenth and Liberty Streets. The other classrooms were filled by white students, but apparently there was no interaction between the black and white students. After a decade, the school board opted to establish a separate school for the African American children and in 1880 purchased and remodeled a building at Santa Fe and Eighth Streets in the West Bottoms. The school by then had been named in honor of Charles Sumner, the noted Massachusetts abolitionist. Three years later, the Sumner School moved into a three-story building at Ninth and St. Louis. It would remain at that site until it was closed by the school board with apparently little fanfare or debate in 1921. Students were transported to the Garrison School, at Fourth and Troost in the East Bottoms, for a year before they were sent to the Douglass School at Twenty-fifth and Jarboe Streets in 1923. That situation lasted only a year as well. The students from the West Bottoms and West Side were then moved to the old Wendell Phillips School at Nineteenth and Cherry before they moved into the old Morse School at 2121 Charlotte Street. That school, which had formerly housed white students, was renamed Sumner Elementary in 1927.

The Wendell Phillips School, also named for a white abolitionist, opened in 1883 in a rented building at Nineteenth and Cherry with W. W. Yates as its first principal. The facility was originally known as the Cherry Street School. The next year, the school was renamed Wendell Phillips and over the next two years would move into a succession of rented spaces before the Board of Education built a new facility on Cherry between Nineteenth and Twentieth Streets in 1885. The Wendell Phillips School remained at that site until 1912, when the Board of

Education moved African American students into the Bryant School at Howard (now Twenty-fourth Terrace) and Vine Streets. The school, with an enrollment of almost five hundred African American youths, was renamed the Phillips School the same year. In 1932, students from Sumner Elementary were moved into Phillips as well.

Phillips Elementary, under principal Henley Cox, adopted a number of innovative teaching strategies. In 1921, Phillips began offering a special education program for students with learning disabilities. In this "Opportunity School," the students were offered academic classes as well as some basic vocational skills: rug weaving, cooking, and laundry.

The Douglass School was established in 1886 at Twenty-ninth Street and Broadway in an old house once used to store gunpowder. The school, taught by Alberta Brodie, was nicknamed the "Powder House School" and moved to a different site for each of the next three years before the Board of Education purchased a site at Twenty-seventh and Jarboe Streets on the West Side. The new Douglass School, named for African American orator Frederick Douglass, opened in 1891. It was the first school in the district named for an African American and boasted the district's first black female principal (Anna H. Jones in 1911).

In 1899, the Kansas City Board of Education added yet another all-black school after Westport Township was annexed by the city. The William Penn School dated to 1868, when African American children in the area were brought together and taught by the wife of Sam Ellis, a recently retired businessman. The first classes were taught in a rented building on Penn Street between Archibald and Westport. After several moves, the school settled into a building at 4237 Penn Street (now Pennsylvania Avenue) in 1869. There, on a site it shared with St. James Baptist Church, the Penn School remained until it was closed in 1955.

In the 1890s, two more schools for African Americans were opened: the Attucks School on Eighteenth Street and the Bruce School on Fifteenth Street. The Attucks School opened in 1893 at Eighteenth and Brooklyn, on the fringe of black settlement. In 1894, the school moved to 2108 East Eighteenth Street before moving into a new site at Nineteenth and Brooklyn in 1906. The Bruce School opened in 1898 near Myrtle and Fifteenth Streets. It was moved a block away a year later before being relocated into a one-room building at 1329 Jackson in 1900. Lincoln High students would construct an addition for the Bruce School in 1921, and it would remain at that site for almost fifty years.[6]

African American students also attended the Booker T. Washington

6. *Kansas City Sun*, September 3, 1921.

and Blue Valley Schools. Booker T. Washington opened in 1902 at Twenty-ninth and Norton before moving a year later to Thirtieth and Myrtle, where it remained for the next thirty-four years. In 1937, Booker T. Washington was closed, and its students transferred to Attucks School. In 1942, a new Booker T. Washington School opened at Twenty-fourth and Prospect, in the building that had once housed the Washington Irving School. The Blue Valley School opened in 1903 for children living near the city's eastern edge around Twelfth Street and the Amoco Steel plant. That school would close in 1928.

Improving Conditions in the Schools

It is an undisputed fact that there never was a time in the history of this city that schools devoted to Negro youth were in a more dilapidated, unkempt and insanitary condition than they are today.

—NELSON CREWS, 1921

By the end of the First World War, African American children were housed at eight elementary schools and one high school in Kansas City. By 1919, black residents like William H. Dawley were asking if the schools for African Americans in Kansas City were keeping pace with those for white children. Since many of the facilities for African Americans had been used by white students before being turned over to the education of black children, Dawley concluded the only response to the question was to answer in the negative.[7] Dawley's concerns would be echoed by Kansas City's African Americans over the next decade and a half. Two of the most articulate and comprehensive critiques of the conditions facing African American students came early in the interwar period. A memorial signed by every prominent organization within the African American communities was one of the first broadsides launched in the battle for a new Lincoln High. In excruciating detail, the memorial presented to the school board in March 1920 outlined the crowded conditions and lack of equipment that hindered the educational process at Lincoln High School.[8]

7. Ibid., December 27, 1919.

8. Ibid., March 20, 1920. The memorial was signed by the Parent-Teachers Association, the Kansas City branch of the NAACP, the City Federation of Colored Women's Clubs, the Kansas City Medical Society (black doctors), the Civic League, the Lincoln High Alumni Association, the Inter-City Lawyers Club, the Negro Business League, and the Inter-Denominational Ministerial Alliance.

Lincoln High School, the memorial noted, was serving more than twice the number of students for which it was built, and in the fifteen years since the facility was constructed, not an inch of space had been added. Among the grievances listed: the Physical Science Department lacked equipment and laboratory space; the kitchen in the Domestic Science Department was antiquated and inadequate—the gas lines to the stove leaked, requiring that all classes be held with the windows open; the domestic arts program was held in two small, dreary storefronts nearby; lockers in the building were shared by from two to five students; the school lacked a gymnasium, requiring girls physical education to be held in the school auditorium while the boys trained outside when weather permitted; six to eight classes daily were held on the stairs; seventeen teachers lacked desks; and the school lacked a library, a librarian, a study hall, and an art department. The lunchroom was so small that students spilled out into the hallways and adjoining classrooms. The memorial went beyond criticism; it also compared Lincoln High to the educational opportunities for African Americans in other municipalities, and by comparison, Kansas City came up wanting. The memorial challenged the school board to provide a modern high school for African Americans as well as a normal training school and a junior college. Needless to say, the school board took the memorial under advisement and upheld the status quo.

The decision a year later by the school board to seek voter approval for a bond issue for new school construction brought a new round of criticism from African Americans. No voice was more strident than that of *Kansas City Sun* editor Nelson C. Crews. In a series of editorials, Crews urged African American voters to reject the school bonds, unless the Board of Education offered guarantees that a portion of the bond money would be spent on improving black schools. "It is cowardly," Crews wrote in one editorial, "to cringe and whimper and beg for what properly, fairly belongs to you, and as taxpayers and citizens who pay their proportionate share of the taxation of this community according to their holdings, we have a right to DEMAND EQUAL FACILITIES that are accorded under the damning and humiliating segregational laws of this State to the white youth of this city." Crews asserted, in particular, that the "degrading and deplorable conditions" surrounding Lincoln High School made it impossible for black youth to receive the instruction "necessary to make them capable young men and women." And as would be argued thirty years later in the landmark *Brown v. Topeka Board of Education,* the segregated and unequal facilities established in Kansas City taught the white child to believe that he was superior to the black child. "And in the treatment accorded the Negro youth of this City, it would seem to an unbiased party that the School Board assiduously fosters this idea and belief."[9]

Crews's first editorial on the school bond issue, though filled with passion, lacked concrete details of the circumstances facing black youth in Kansas City. He rectified that situation in a spate of editorials before the bond election in April. In one editorial, Crews noted the shortcomings of three of the elementary schools. The Cherry Street School, he noted, had once been abandoned as unfit for use. Although some repair and renovation work had been done, Crews described the facility as "dark, unsanitary, miserably located and wholly un-modern." Yates Elementary, Crews said, "is about ready to collapse from old age," and the Bruce School consists of "a bevy of shacks with no sewage outlet nor anything else that is modern in the way of equipment."[10]

George J., who moved to Kansas City from Oakland, California, in the 1920s at the age of thirteen, recalled, years later, his experiences at the Attucks School at 1818 East Nineteenth Street. "The books were old and worn, the desks were shabby and in need of repair, and the kids were all poor and unruly."[11]

Crews's largest concern was the inadequacies of Lincoln High School. "GIVE US A HIGH SCHOOL," he demanded in a front-page headline in February. He feared, rightly, that if black Kansas City did not get a new high school from the 1921 bond issue that it might be a number of years before another opportunity presented itself. He urged the *Sun*'s readers, and the African American communities as a whole, to rally against the bond issue unless school board officials presented concrete plans for a new black high school.[12]

The need for a new Lincoln facility was obvious, Crews argued. As had the signatories to the 1920 memorial, Crews described Lincoln High School as "cramped, crowded and wholly lacking in modern school conveniences." Two weeks later, he maintained that no city north of the Mason-Dixon line had such deplorable conditions in its black schools.

9. "Negro Schools a Disgrace," ibid., February 5, 1921 (emphasis in original).

10. Ibid., February 19, March 5, 1921. The deplorable condition of the Bruce School, in particular, would anger parents, teachers and concerned citizens. In 1922, Mrs. C. W. Ferguson, an (unsuccessful) candidate for the Kansas City Board of Education on the Farmer-Workers Party ticket, complained of unsanitary conditions at a number of schools; she said she discovered a cesspool on the grounds of the Bruce School. School board officials said Ferguson was exaggerating, but Ferguson refused to withdraw her allegations. *Labor Herald,* March 17, 1922.

11. Page, *George,* 42.

12. *Kansas City Sun,* March 5, 1921.

In his final editorial before the election, Crews outlined in no uncertain terms the deplorable situation at Lincoln:

- The school, by then thirty years old, had been built for 250 pupils; its enrollment in 1921 was 750. As a result, some classes were held in stairways and exits, with the students sitting on folding chairs.
- The school lacked a library, a reading room, and a study hall. Its reference shelf consisted of one dilapidated set of encyclopedias.
- The school lacked a science laboratory, lockers, and storerooms.
- The school's Domestic Science Department had an inadequate kitchen, with its plumbing in disrepair, a played-out gas stove, and ragged linoleum covering part of the floor.
- The school lacked a gymnasium, even though students were required to take physical training daily. After their exercises, students did not have the use of a dressing room, a shower or even a bathtub.[13]

Crews was not alone in his criticisms of the physical conditions of the schools and of board of education officials. David N. Crosthwaite Jr., a recent graduate of Lincoln, wrote in support. Activist Myrtle Foster Cook, writing in this case as president of the Negro Women's Republican Club of Kansas City, and Jonathan B. Isaacs, pastor of Allen Chapel (Crews's church), wrote letters to the *Sun* thanking Crews for fearlessly taking a stand on the issue.[14] Fearful of a backlash by black voters, school board officials made vague promises to correct some of the conditions, particularly at Lincoln. With black opposition somewhat muted by the school board's promises, the bond issue passed. Crews, still bitter almost a year later, noted angrily that the board's promises had been more or less empty ones. The "splendid" additions to Lincoln High School, including "a spacious auditorium" that would meet the needs of African Americans for "years to come," had not been adequate to handle even a portion of the overflow of students at Lincoln. Meanwhile, Crews noted, two new schools were being built for white children, and plans called for construction of a new high school at Forty-eighth and Flora (Paseo High School) to start in the summer months. Black voters had been duped again, Crews exclaimed, at the expense of their children. "A NEW HIGH SCHOOL—Just go look at it," he concluded bitterly.[15]

13. "What Are You Going to Do about It?" ibid., March 19, 1921; "Defeat the School Bonds," ibid., March 26, 1921.
14. Ibid., February 12, 1921.
15. Ibid., March 4, 1922.

The debate over the bond issue did, however, solidify African American support of Lincoln High School and the other black schools. In April 1921, after the school bond issue passed, African Americans formed the Negro School Improvement Association. Dr. E. C. Bunch was president, and social worker Minnie Crosthwaite was elected secretary. The organization, although apparently short-lived, maintained some pressure on school board officials and acted as a monitor for the conditions of black education in the city. Its one notable success was the installation of a free lending library, open to any resident of the city, at Lincoln High School for the 1922–1923 school term.[16]

Crews's fear that it would be years before another opportunity would arise to substantially improve conditions at Lincoln proved valid. It would be fifteen years before the school board would erect the new Lincoln High School, at its present location at Twenty-first and Woodland.

Lincoln High also served as an important link between Kansas City's African American communities and their hinterlands in western Missouri and eastern Kansas. From 1904 through 1940, Lincoln drew on average about 13 percent of its student body from outside the boundaries of the Kansas City school district. Lucile Bluford, who attended Lincoln in the 1930s, remembers attending classes with black students from Independence, Liberty, and Excelsior Springs. As early as 1898, the Kansas City School Board accepted high school students from outside the district who paid the requisite tuition. Changing rural demographics and statewide educational policies and practices fed into the development of Lincoln as a regional high school. In 1889, the Missouri legislature gave sanction to rapidly prevailing practice by requiring the establishment of separate schools for African American children. By the 1920s, practicality mixed with prejudice had reduced black educational opportunities in many rural districts. State law by this time required the establishment of schools for black students in any locale with at least fifteen school-age children. But as Missouri's black population became increasingly urban, fewer rural districts felt compelled to establish or maintain black schools. As Nathaniel Bruce, state inspector of black schools, pointed out in 1923, 40 of Missouri's 108 counties each had between one and fourteen students. In addition, some rural districts simply could not afford to maintain separate school systems for black and white students and as a matter of course refused to establish black schools. Education for African Americans, particularly at the high school

16. Ibid., May 1, 1921; April 29, September 9, 1922.

level, increasingly fell on a select few institutions: for example, Sumner High School in St. Louis, the Bartlett School in north-central Missouri, and Lincoln High School in Kansas City.[17]

Lincoln High School also stood at the center of a network of interlinked African American schools and organizations. For example, in 1920, more than three thousand spectators attended an indoor track meet sponsored by Lincoln. Competitors were drawn from the Bartlett School; Sumner High School and Western University in Kansas City, Kansas; the Topeka Industrial School; George R. Smith College; the Olathe Athletic Club; and the Lawrence YMCA.[18]

Teaching Successes

Every child has certain inalienable rights, the right to be born and reared in rooms that have sunshine, fresh air, and space; the right to an education; the right to play and work under conditions that develop, not stunt, body and soul. The nation also has the right to demand these rights for every child of every complexion.

—MARY McDOWELL, SPEAKING IN KANSAS CITY, 1923

Despite lack of funding, crowded conditions, and the constraints of segregation, black schools in Kansas City produced a number of outstanding students. Roy Wilkins, for eight years a reporter and sometime columnist for the *Kansas City Call,* observed: "The black schools [in Kansas City] were much better than they had any right to be, partly because they were full of talented teachers who would have been teaching in college had they been white, and partly because Negro parents and children simply refused to be licked by segregation."[19]

Within the classrooms of Lincoln High School, for example, students could be taught music by N. Clark Smith and later by William Levi Dawson, dramatic and oratorical skills by J. Oliver Morrison, art by Aaron Douglas, and chemistry and science by Dr. David N. Crosthwaite.

17. "Lucile Bluford Deposition," July 19, 1983, Benson Papers, box 102; "Pupils Enrolled In and Dropped from Black High Schools in Kansas City, Mo., for Years 1904–1910; 1913–1917; 1922–30; and 1935–40," ibid., IR 2, IR 3, box 306; Greene, Kremer, and Holland, *Missouri's Black Heritage,* 107, 147. Records of the Kansas City, Missouri, school board reflect requests from the parents or guardians of black students from as far away as Fayette, Missouri, to attend Lincoln. Those who could not pay tuition were routinely turned away except in the most unusual of circumstances.

18. *Kansas City Sun,* May 1, 1920.

19. Wilkins, *Standing Fast,* 76.

Morrison and Smith were known most for their contributions to black Kansas City's artistic endeavors. Morrison, a native of Philipsburg, Pennsylvania, was educated at Howard University and the University of Chicago. He began his teaching career at the University of New Orleans before coming to Kansas City in 1918 and accepting a post as a teacher in the English and Dramatics Department at Lincoln High School. Early in the 1920s, he organized a community chorus, which performed at various functions in the African American communities. In 1923, for example, the chorus performed four gospel numbers for a gathering at Convention Hall of volunteers for the Allied Charities drive. In 1933, under the auspices of the Kansas City Urban League, he founded a little-theater group, the Morrison Players, in which young African American men and women were encouraged to develop their artistic and theatrical skills. In the spring of 1933, for example, the theater presented *The Thirteenth Chair,* a murder mystery, in front of a full house at the Lincoln High School auditorium. During the 1935 Christmas season, the Morrison Players presented three one-act plays at the Urban League offices. George Hurse, twenty-one-year-old son of the Reverend James Wesley Hurse, was a member of the cast of *The Grass Grows Red.* Morrison remained at Lincoln until his death in 1949, but the Morrison Players remained an active force in the African American community.[20]

Maj. N. Clark Smith, who lived at 2337 Tracy, was the first of a line of outstanding music instructors at Lincoln. Little is known about Smith's early life, but before coming to Kansas City he studied in Chicago and in Europe. He had also traveled extensively in Africa. Before taking over at Lincoln, Smith led the Music Department at Tuskegee Institute in Alabama. At Lincoln, he showcased his skills as a choral director, a band master, and a composer. During the second decade of the twentieth century, Smith organized a band of black professionals that toured Europe and brought Smith international acclaim. Upon his return to the United States, Smith enrolled in special summer classes in composition and voice at the University of Kansas. His work that summer drew praise from Harold L. Butler, dean of the university's Fine Arts Department. In a letter to Smith, Butler praised Smith for his "exceptional talent" and "unbounded enthusiasm and energy" and then called him "without doubt the most able student in music in the summer school." Butler closed by noting that two Lincoln graduates were

20. KCULP, box PPE1, file 1; "Urban League in New Home September 8," *Kansas City Call,* September 11, 1936, box N1, file 2; "Little Theater to Give 'The Thirteenth Chair,'" undated newspaper clipping, box N1, file 2; *Kansas City Call,* November 17, 1923; Young and Young, *Your Kansas City and Mine,* 94.

enrolled in the Music Department at Kansas and that they both displayed a measure of Smith's passion.[21]

Smith's goal as a musician and composer was to tap the folk music of black America and introduce it to a wider audience. Many of his compositions were based on spirituals, and his renditions of the spirituals themselves were lauded worldwide. Before leaving Tuskegee, Smith directed a concert for some of the institute's favored guests. The program included Smith's versions of "Swing Low, Sweet Chariot," "Bye and Bye," and "Couldn't Hear Nobody Pray." White philanthropists Andrew Carnegie and Julius Rosenwald, the honored guests, reputedly described the concert as the most delightful musical treat they had ever received. Smith also organized a glee club, named for black composer Samuel Coleridge-Taylor, which performed in Kansas City and around the region.[22]

Smith was a stern taskmaster, as demonstrated by this anecdote told by musician William Saunders, who played with the Bennie Moten Orchestra after graduating from Lincoln:

> One day Major Smith told the class that music was melody, harmony and rhythm. Being a kid, I paid no attention. The next week the first thing he said [was], "Saunders, stand up here and tell me what music is. . . . You don't know, do you?" He had a ruler and he said, "Put your head on the table. Music is melody." BOOM! "Harmony." BOOM! "Rhythm." BOOM! "Now go home and tell your Mammy I hit you." But I know what music is.[23]

As mentioned above, Smith's abilities received national and international acclaim. When Smith and pianist Clyde Glass, head of the Music Department at Western University in Quindaro, organized a concert at Drake University in November 1919, the *Des Moines Register* was effusive in its praise, even if some of its comments perpetuated the stereotypes of the time.[24] Among the highlights of the performance was an octet's rendition of "Steal Away," as arranged by Smith, and "Suwanee River." Smith also gave a brief lecture called "Elements of Negro Melody." Two years later, Smith was feted by some of his former Tuskegee students living in Chicago. More than five thousand

21. *Kansas City Sun*, November 22, 29, 1919; March 13, 1920: February 25, May 20, 1922.
22. Ibid., April 10, 1920; February 25, 1922.
23. Pearson, *Goin' to Kansas City*, 20–21.
24. "The whole program was given by Colored people and they again demonstrated the ability of their race along musical lines." The *Kansas City Sun* reprinted the article in its December 13 edition.

spectators—both black and white—turned out for a tribute to Smith and to his music.[25]

Smith's talents were too large to be contained by Kansas City for very long. In March 1922, Smith was approached by representatives of the George Pullman Company. The company, pioneers in the use of sleeping cars for railroad trips and employer of several thousand African American porters nationwide, planned to create two thousand singing quartets from among its porters, and Smith was asked to lead the training, for a lucrative salary. Smith could not refuse, and by September, the *Kansas City Sun* reported, Smith already had some demonstrated success. In a trial run from Chicago to New Orleans in April, each of the three crews had organized choruses. By September, choruses and accompanying bands had been organized among the crews in Philadelphia, Washington, and New York. The goal, historian Eric Arnesen notes, was to provide entertainment for the passengers but also to break up the tedium and monotony of the porters' work experience. In 1923, a quartet of Pullman porters performed to much acclaim at Kansas City's Union Station.[26]

Before leaving Kansas City and Lincoln, Smith had already touched a number of aspiring musicians. Smith and his equally talented successor, Alonzo Lewis, helped tutor such notables as Lamar Wright, cornetist with the Bennie Moten Orchestra; Walter Page, who later worked as a bassist with the Count Basie Orchestra; alto saxophonist Eli Logan; and bebop pioneer Charlie Parker.[27]

Also on the Lincoln music faculty in the 1920s was William Levi Dawson, who in 1930 would be credited with composing the first symphony by an African American using particularly African American themes.[28] Dawson was born in Aniston, Alabama, in 1899. After leaving school, he took a position as bandmaster at Tuskegee Institute in Alabama, and in 1922 he came to Kansas City and accepted a teaching position at Lincoln. Clarence Love, who led a succession of jazz bands through

25. *Kansas City Sun*, December 13, February 25, 1922.

26. Ibid., September 30, 1922; December 23, 1923. The singing program, Arnesen argues (*Brotherhoods of Color*, 87), also was part of the Pullman Company's attempt to manage black employees' growing discontent. Around the same time, the company began publishing an in-house magazine for its porters, promoted a limited stock ownership plan, and sponsored athletic and recreational activities, solely for the porters.

27. Office of Housing and Community Development, *Spirit of Freedom*, 68–69.

28. William Levi Dawson is not to be confused, as did two major surveys of African American history, with William L. Dawson, a native Georgian who represented Chicago in the U.S. Congress from 1942 to 1970.

the region, remembers Dawson as "one of the toughest music teachers in the country." While teaching at Lincoln, Dawson was enrolled in music courses in Topeka and at the Kansas City–Horner Conservatory, from which he graduated with honors. Dawson spent four years at Lincoln before returning to Tuskegee as director of music. By that time, he had apparently begun working on his first symphony, and in 1930 he handed the 537-page musical score to noted conductor Leopold Stokowski of the Philadelphia symphony orchestra. "I'm not trying to emulate Beethoven or Brahms, Franck or Ravel," Dawson said before the symphony's premiere. "I want the audience to say: 'Only a Negro could have written that.'" Throughout the interwar period, Dawson continued to compose and arrange music for classical audiences.[29]

Aaron Douglas, after spending two years teaching at Lincoln, would emerge as the most recognized visual artist during that outpouring of African American art and literature known as the Harlem Renaissance. Douglas, a native of Topeka, Kansas, started teaching at Lincoln in the fall of 1922. At the same time, he took a commercial art class, probably by correspondence. His biographer, Amy Helene Kirkschke, contends that correspondence courses were likely the only way a black man could study art in Kansas City at the time, yet it should be noted that around the same time, the Kansas City Art Institute played host to an exhibit of the work of noted African American painter Henry Ossawa Tanner. At the same time, Douglas began a serious study of his craft, reading widely on the historical and theoretical background of modern art.[30]

Douglas, Kirkschke says, apparently was not influenced by Tanner or any of the other African American painters and sculptors who had burst briefly onto the art scene in the previous seventy years. He would, Kirkschke maintains, "forge a new tradition depicting black subject matter."[31]

Shortly after the school year of 1925 ended, Douglas resigned from his teaching position at Lincoln to pursue his art career full-time. His original goal was to travel to Paris to study and work, but he stopped in Harlem in New York, and it is there he made his major contribution to

29. KCULP, "An All-Negro Symphony," undated news clipping, box N1, file 1; "Negro's Soul in Music," undated news clipping, box N1, file 1; Pearson, *Goin' to Kansas City,* 13, 20; Franklin, *From Slavery to Freedom,* 417; Harry A. Ploski and Earnest Kaiser, eds., *The Negro Almanac: The Black Experience in America,* 792.

30. Amy Helen Kirkschke, *Aaron Douglas: Art, Race and the Harlem Renaissance,* 9; *Kansas City Sun,* November 4, 1922. The *Sun* noted that the Tanner exhibit "must be a source of pride as well as surprise to many Colored people of this city."

31. Kirkschke, *Aaron Douglas,* 11.

the artistic world. One of Douglas's primary reasons for staying in Harlem, Kirkschke argues, was to find other artists who shared his developing racial consciousness. In Harlem, Douglas found other well-educated African Americans, as well as other men and women of color seeking to define and expand their artistic visions. Most of these artists were, like Douglas, seeking to express African American viewpoints and folkways through their paintings, sculptures, poetry, and prose. Shortly after his arrival in New York, Douglas submitted two drawings (and a bit of poetry) to *Opportunity*, the official journal of the National Urban League. Douglas's "Self-Portrait" and "The Black Runner" appeared in the September issue of that journal. Over the next five years, Douglas's angular drawings and stark renditions of African American life would adorn the covers of both *Opportunity* and *Crisis*, the NAACP's official journal. His most important work, a series of large-scale murals depicting "the story of the Negro's progress from central Africa to present day America," now adorn the walls of Fisk University in Tennessee.[32]

David N. Crosthwaite, a native of Tennessee, came to Kansas City in 1895 when he was offered a position teaching physiology and chemistry at Lincoln. He was born in 1856, the oldest son of a free black carpenter and his wife. Scott Crosthwaite died when David was nine years old, and for the next several years, David withdrew from school and was the sole provider for his mother and siblings. A teacher at Fisk University in Nashville recognized David's desire to learn and arranged for him to continue his education while still working. As a result, David finished the grade school program in the Nashville schools and in 1881 graduated from Fisk. After leaving the college, David Crosthwaite took over as teacher at Nashville's black grade school, and in 1884 he was appointed principal of Nashville's first black high school. While teaching in Nashville, Crosthwaite received his master's degree from Fisk and in 1891 completed the medical program at Fisk's Meharry Medical School. Although he was now qualified to practice medicine, Crosthwaite elected to continue teaching.[33]

While in Nashville, David Crosthwaite met another young teacher, Minnie L. Harris. In 1889 they were married in Nashville, and over the next five years they had three children: David Jr., Anne, and Paul.[34] In

32. Ibid., 110–14.

33. *Kansas City Call*, March 19, 1948.

34. All three of the Crosthwaite children graduated from Lincoln High School in Kansas City. David Jr. became a mechanical engineer, first for a firm in Iowa and then in Indiana. Paul became a dentist but died in 1919 in Chicago.

1895, David Crosthwaite was offered a position teaching physiology and chemistry at Lincoln High School, and the family moved west, where they became firmly entrenched in Kansas City's African American communities.

Crosthwaite became a member of several black fraternal orders, and, in addition to his teaching responsibilities, he tutored African American candidates for the civil service examination required for employment with the postal service. John Work, a Lincoln High School graduate who attended Harvard and taught at Fisk, credited Crosthwaite with much of his professional success. Minnie Crosthwaite, meanwhile, also went back to school and gained a degree in social work. She became Kansas City's first black social worker and through her work with various black women's groups and at Wheatley-Provident Hospital assisted hundreds of families in Kansas City's African American communities. Among her accomplishments was the establishment of a fashion show for the benefit of Wheatley-Provident; the show became one of the major social events in the African American community through the interwar period.[35]

The schools, like the churches, were instruments of community and racial formation in the 1920s and 1930s. The schools established links between various elements of the African American community and served as meeting places and forums for the exchange of ideas and concerns. Lincoln High School, for instance, was the site of a regular Sunday forum. Speakers ranged from newspaper editors Nelson Crews and Chester Franklin to ministers (such as D. A. Holmes) and educators (Professor G. A. Gregg of Western University, for example). The forums might deal with esoteric topics or serve as the starting points for discussions on issues facing the African American communities. And at least through the 1920s, when the advent of talking movies and commercial radio broadcasts made the forums seem quaint and outdated, they likely also served as a form of free entertainment for many African Americans in Kansas City.

One of the biggest challenges facing the faculties of the black elementary schools in the 1920s was the influx of recent migrants from the South who had little or no formal education. The teachers, Phillips principal Henley Cox wrote in 1928, "accept the responsibility of re-

35. Ibid., March 19, 1948. See also Wilkins, *Standing Fast;* and Jane Fifield Flynn, *Kansas City Women of Independent Minds.*

organizing their (students from the South) whole life process and so redirecting their habits, ideals, interests and activities that would become an actual asset to the community."[36]

In 1926, Nathaniel Bruce, former head of the Bartlett Agricultural and Industrial School and newly appointed state inspector of Negro schools, told the members of the all-white Moberly school board that "blacks must be trained to take pride in any work, . . . cooking, washing, ironing, scrubbing or driving nails. The Negro must be taught his place and how to work like his old parents." This comment by an African American educator brought out the full fury of *Kansas City Call* columnist Roy Wilkins:

> The harm is not in Mr. Bruce's belief that this kind of "practical" education . . . is good for Negroes, but in his unqualified recommendation of it as a general program for all Negroes to be placed in local school systems of the state INSTEAD OF HIGH BOOK LEARNING AND TRAINING. . . . We can't get along without the higher book learning and the man who says so is either playing to a "cracker" "hill billy" gallery for a mess of pottage or else he is woefully ignorant.[37]

After leaving Lincoln High School, a number of Kansas City's black youth chose to continue their educations. They took advantage of a number of opportunities: in 1921, the *Kansas City Sun* noted seventy-six African Americans who were preparing to start their college term, including the sons and daughters of principal Joe Herriford, Dr. T. C. Unthank, and the Reverend Samuel Bacote. Their destinations were remarkably disparate: of the seventy-six, just less than half were enrolled at the University of Kansas in Lawrence; they were following in the footsteps of Lincoln graduate James Scott, who in 1919 entered the university's chapter of Phi Beta Kappa, the national honor society. Other Lincoln graduates were headed to the teachers college in Emporia, Kansas, or the Conservatory of Music in Ithaca, New York. Just one of the seventy-six listed by the *Sun*, remarkably, was enrolled at Lincoln Institute in Jefferson City.[38]

36. Quoted in a *Kansas City Call* series on education in black Kansas City, September 2, 1994.

37. Ibid., June 11, 1926; Wilkins, *Standing Fast*, 74 (emphasis in original). For a full discussion of Nathaniel Bruce and his impact on African American education in Missouri, see Patrick J. Huber and Gary R. Kremer, "Nathaniel C. Bruce, Black Education and the 'Tuskegee of the Midwest.'"

38. *Kansas City Sun*, September 10, 1921.

Lincoln High School graduates, of course, became the foundation for Kansas City's African American communities. In addition, several of the school's graduates went on to illustrious careers elsewhere. For example, David Crosthwaite Jr., son of women's activist Minnie Crosthwaite and David Sr., became an electrical expert for an Iowa engineering firm in the 1920s. Another success story was that of Clarence Bacote, son of Second Baptist pastor Samuel Bacote and his wife, Lucy. Clarence was born in 1906, and after going through the Kansas City schools, he found his way to the University of Chicago, where, with the help of scholarships from the General Education Board, he completed his master's degree in history in August 1929. Upon completion of his master's work, he accepted a teaching position in the Graduate Studies Department at all-black Atlanta University. Like a few of the all-black schools in the South, it was a vehicle for the training of future "aristocrats of color." The school's faculty, however, strove to also make Atlanta University an excellent liberal arts college. For Clarence Bacote, his career at Atlanta then must have been equal parts fulfilling and frustrating. With just a master's in hand, he would have known that in 1930s America, a teaching position at a white university was impossible without a doctorate degree. And most doctoral programs were reluctant to accept African American candidates. Bacote persevered, however. As racial perceptions and the social climate changed after World War II, he returned to the University of Chicago and began work on his doctorate under noted historian Wesley Craven. With the help again of General Education Board funds, in 1955, Clarence Bacote completed his dissertation, "The Negro in Georgia Politics, 1880–1908," one of just a handful of completed doctoral studies at the time on the history of African Americans. He followed with scholarly articles in the *Journal of Negro History* in the 1950s, and in 1969, twelve years before his death, he completed his history of Atlanta University.[39]

By 1930, even the Kansas City School Board recognized the need for a replacement for Lincoln High School. The school was stretched well beyond its capabilities; in 1929, eleven hundred students were attending classes in a space designed for eight hundred. Many of them attended classes in wooden frame buildings attached to the main brick structure. By this time, the school board began considering

39. Clarence Bacote, *The Story of Atlanta University: A Century of Service, 1865–1965* (Princeton, N.J.: Princeton University Press, 1969). For discussions of Clarence Bacote's academic career, see *Kansas City Call*, August 30, 1929; Lewis, *W. E. B. Du Bois*, 215; and Meier and Rudwick, *Black History*, 129, 157.

the former Ridge estate, a nine-acre tract at Twenty-first and Woodland, as the site for a new black high school and in 1931 acquired the property. In 1936, students began attending the new Lincoln High School at 2111 Woodland. The new facility, which sat at the crest of a hill with a view of downtown, cost seven hundred thousand dollars to construct. It was designed to accommodate eleven hundred students, and the building housed two gymnasiums and a swimming pool. The new school—as Lincoln High School, Lincoln Academy, and Lincoln College Preparatory Academy—continued to serve generations of African American students through the twentieth century.[40]

The old school building at Nineteenth and Tracy was renovated, converted into a vocational and junior high school, and named in honor of Richard T. Coles, who had died in 1930. Earl Thomas, who would later be principal at Lincoln High School and Lincoln Junior College, was installed as the first principal. A copy of the *Coles Pilot*, the student newspaper, from 1938 shows the emphasis placed on the vocational arts in the school's early years. Although faculty members are listed for academic subjects such as English, mathematics, and social science, they are vastly outnumbered by teachers in food preparation, clothing, tailoring, home management, beauty culture, auto mechanics, shoe repair, electricity and printing, painting, woodwork, and building maintenance. The school's curriculum again followed the ideological principles of Richard T. Coles, who had emphasized industrial arts while serving as principal of the Garrison School.[41]

Religious Institutions

I know that this world is messed up and confused. I know that much of society stretches out like a gaping sore that refuses to be healed. I know that life is often heartless, as hard as pig iron. And yet, in the midst of all this I affirm my faith that God is love—whatever else He may be.

—HOWARD THURMAN, "BARREN OR FRUITFUL" (1932)

The first black churches in Kansas City, as they would in other urban areas of the North and South, grew out of the religious experiences of

40. *Kansas City Call*, September 13, 1929; *Kansas City American*, September 28, 1933; Young and Young, *Your Kansas City and Mine*, 156.

41. Gibson, *Mecca of the New Negro*, 133–34.

African Americans during slavery and developed in the context of a people seeking venues for self-expression and self-affirmation. In the first years of emancipation, African Americans quickly established separate religious institutions, with black ministers and leaders. The black church served as an indispensable and fundamental anchor for African American communities through the rest of the nineteenth century, and as Albert Raboteau notes, churches served as sources of both continuity and social change in the first half of the twentieth century when large-scale forces of migration and urbanization helped reshape black urban life.[42] In Kansas City, by the end of the 1920s, African Americans congregated in more than forty separate churches, with most of the churches adhering to either the Baptist or African Methodist Episcopal faith. The black churches in 1929 ranged from the mammoth (Allen Chapel AME and St. Stephen's Baptist) to the small gathering of like-minded individuals in rented or borrowed space in former residences or storefronts. Black churches supported and were sustained by the various institutions within the African American community.

Critics of the twentieth-century black church have pointed to its ubiquitous nature, its acceptance and enforcement of the status quo, its sometime emphasis on otherworldly salvation over present-day concerns, the occasional venality of its leaders, and its potential for manipulation and exploitation. Such criticisms, however, ignore the church's potential for social change. Within African American communities, that potential was often realized. Moreover, the church was an expression of communal identity, serving as a venue for the exchange of ideas and grievances and for the creation of social networks to attack the most pressing concerns. The black church was not a perfect institution, yet in the first half of the twentieth century it served specific needs in African American communities, including Kansas City's.

Sociologists St. Clair Drake and Horace R. Cayton, writing in the 1930s, lamented how black Chicago, as a prototype of black urban development, was "overchurched."[43] They undoubtedly would have made the same observation of black Kansas City by the end of World War II. At that time, the Kansas City Urban League counted 101 churches that served a black population of about forty-one thousand. Yet the number of religious institutions in Kansas City was more reflective of geographical

42. Albert J. Raboteau, *A Fire in the Bones: Reflections on African-American Religious History,* 103.

43. Drake and Cayton, *Black Metropolis,* 632–36.

Table 5.1.
African American Churches in Kansas City, about 1929

Church	Address	Year Founded
Allen Chapel	Tenth and Charlotte	1866
Antioch Baptist	1609 Michigan	1913
Bethel AME	24th and Flora	1912
Bethesda Baptist	5800 East Thirty-fifth Street Terrace	1926
Blue Valley Baptist	Twelfth and Crystal	1907
Cain Memorial AME	595 Tracy	1919
Centennial ME	Nineteenth and Woodland	1888
Central Baptist	Fourteenth and Spruce	1913
Clark Chapel ME	1644 Madison	before 1900
Ebenezer AME	Sixteenth and Lydia	1886
Friendship Baptist	Seventeenth and Tracy	1914
Gilbert Memorial AME	Thirty-seventh and Topping	1916
Grant Chapel AME	Eleventh and Crystal	1903
Greater Progressive Baptist	1416 Vine	1910
Greenwood Baptist	Eighteenth and Belleview	1892
Highland Avenue Baptist	1111 Highland	1894
Jamison Temple	Eighteenth and The Paseo	1897
Morning Star Baptist	2311 Vine	1895
New Hope Baptist	2938 Summit	1910
Park Avenue Baptist	Nineteenth and Park	1921
Pilgrim Rest Baptist	3400 Hardesty	about 1920
Pleasant Green Baptist	Fourteenth and Michigan	1884
Provident Missionary Baptist	2120 East Twelfth	1926
Second Baptist	Tenth and Charlotte	1865
Second Christian	Twenty-fourth and Woodland	about 1911
South Side Baptist	5400 Montgall	1906
St. Augustine's	Eleventh and Troost	1882
St. James AME Zion	Eighteenth and Woodland	1911
St. James Baptist	4043 Mill Street	1871
St. John's AME	1751 Belleview	1869
St. Luke's AME	Forty-third and Roanoke	1870
St. Matthew's AME Zion	Twenty-ninth and Mersington	1911
St. Monica's Catholic	Seventeenth and Lydia	1910
St. Peter's AME Zion	Nineteenth and Askew	1915
St. Stephen's Baptist	910 Harrison Street	1903
Sun Rise Baptist	2714 Bell	about 1918
Tabernacle Baptist	2611 Vine	1912
Turner Chapel	3007 Mercier	1920

Table 5.1. *(continued)*

Church	Address	Year Founded
Union Baptist	Twenty-first and Harrison	1916
Vine Street Baptist*	Twenty-fifth and The Paseo	1884
Ward Chapel AME	1120 Woodland	1904
Willis Chapel AME	5325 Bellefontaine	1912
Woodland Avenue Baptist	1015 Woodland	1891

*Vine Street Baptist became Paseo Baptist in 1931.

separation than of ideological schisms. African American communities through the interwar period, particularly those most isolated, tended to congregate around a church, however small it might be.

Second Baptist

The first black church in Kansas City, Missouri, was organized by a small group of African Americans in a small building near Tenth and Charlotte. The church was officially named Second Baptist Church, but it also was known as the Charlotte Street Church. Clark Moore was selected pastor.[44] We know nothing about Moore's background, but we do know that he fulfilled an important function in Kansas City's nascent African American community: marrying former slaves who had lived together as man and wife before the Civil War. Slave marriages were expressly forbidden in Missouri, though such unions, often recognized by the slave master, the slave community, or both, were not uncommon. After slavery officially ended in January 1865, black men and women sought the state's sanction for these unions; they also undoubtedly sought to legitimate their offspring in the eyes of the law. Annette Curtis's analysis of marriage records in Jackson County for "Americans of African descent" indicates that Moore officiated for at least sixty-eight "remarriages" between 1865, when slavery was abolished in the state of Missouri, and 1870.[45]

44. Hoggins, *Centenary History,* 153.

45. Curtis, *Jackson County, Missouri Marriage Record, American Citizens of African Descent, 1865–1881: An Abstract with Indexes and Commentary.* The Missouri legislature added a legal component to the desire of African Americans to legitimize their marriages. In February 1865, the legislature passed a bill requiring all former slaves living together as man and wife to appear before a justice of the peace or any other officer authorized to perform the ceremony of marriage. Slave couples were given twelve months to obtain legal sanction for their unions or face criminal prosecution.

By 1870, the congregation had purchased a nearby lot on the southwest corner of Tenth and Charlotte Streets and constructed a frame meetinghouse. The next year, Second Baptist welcomed a new pastor, Henry Roberson of Boonville, Missouri, and it was under Roberson's leadership that the church first blossomed and gained prominence in Kansas City's African American communities. Roberson, according to Olive Hoggins, was a former slave born in Charlottesville, Virginia, but according to the 1880 census, Roberson and his wife were both born in Pennsylvania. Regardless of his background, the thirty-three-year-old Roberson and his family became leaders of Second Baptist and black Baptists within the Kansas City area.[46]

Within a year, Roberson oversaw the completion of a five thousand–dollar church structure, and in 1881, Second Baptist claimed more than five hundred members. The growth of the African American community in Kansas City helped fuel the growth of the church, and soon the size of the congregation strained the limits of the recently completed building. As a result, Roberson led a ten-year effort to construct another larger edifice on the same site. The new facility, large enough to accommodate Second Baptist's one thousand members, was completed in 1893, and a year later, Roberson stepped down as pastor, to be replaced by Samuel W. Bacote, who was discussed earlier.[47]

Under Bacote, Second Baptist continued to prosper. Two years after Bacote's arrival, the Second Baptist congregation raised more than fourteen thousand dollars for the construction of a handsome two-story brick church. In 1898, dedication ceremonies were held for the new church, just months before the church played host to the national convention of black Baptists. By the start of the First World War, the church membership stood at more than three thousand. Throughout the 1920s, Second Baptist's auditorium (with a capacity of twenty-five hundred) was the site for various secular and religious functions. Black journalist William Monroe Trotter, a founding member of the Niagara Movement; East St. Louis doctor LeRoy Bundy; and U.S. representative L. C. Dyer of Missouri, proponent of an antilynching bill, graced the church's stage. Lucy Bacote, the pastor's wife, organized a chorus of 150 voices that performed at a variety of functions. The church occasionally served as host for the Sunday Forum, a gathering of African Americans to discuss issues affecting the African American communities. The auditorium's

46. Hoggins, *Centenary History;* U.S. Department of Commerce, Bureau of the Census, Tenth Census.

47. Hoggins, *Centenary History.*

size made it attractive to various organizations. In 1919, the auditorium was nearly full for a memorial service for former president Theodore Roosevelt. Second Baptist members Henley Cox, L. Amasa Knox, and Ida M. Becks were among the speakers to eulogize Roosevelt. A Knights of Pythias gathering the following year drew more than fifteen hundred delegates. The church auditorium also played host to one of the sessions of the NAACP national convention held in Kansas City in 1923.[48]

Second Baptist's place of prominence in the African American communities was threatened in 1926, when a fire gutted the structure. The congregation met in the Paseo YMCA while the structure was rebuilt, and in 1928, a new stone, brick, and terra-cotta building was erected. The fireproof building included an auditorium, a chapel, separate rooms for Sunday school, a study for the pastor, as well as a modern kitchen and dining area. Also included was a ten thousand–dollar pipe organ. The new church would remain a cornerstone of the Church Hill area through the interwar period. It would be rivaled in prominence by only one other Baptist church, James Wesley Hurse's St. Stephen's, and two churches of the African Methodist Episcopal denomination—Allen Chapel and Ebenezer.[49]

St. Stephen's Baptist

St. Stephen's Baptist originally relied on the charismatic personality of its pastor, James Wesley Hurse, for its development and to sustain its growth. The church's early years are a reflection of Hurse's early years as a pastor and as a leader in Kansas City's African American communities. St. Stephen's traces its roots to the old Pilgrim Baptist Church, where Hurse was called to take over as pastor in 1901. After several years of negotiations and debate, St. Stephen's was organized in a little chapel on a triangle where Admiral Boulevard and Sixth Street converged near Charlotte Street. By 1910, the church had constructed a new building at 604–606 Charlotte, where it remained for the next ten years. Early in the 1920s, with its congregation consisting of more than a thousand members, St. Stephen's purchased the property of the Central Presbyterian Church at 910 Harrison Street. By the end of the 1920s, when Olive Hoggins wrote her church histories, St. Stephen's was the largest church in the African American communities. Its membership

48. Ibid.; *Western Messenger,* January 24, February 2, 1919; April 2, May 13, 1920; *Kansas City Sun,* May 22, 29, July 3, 1920; June 25, 1921.

49. *Kansas City Post,* February 13, 1927.

had grown to thirty-five hundred, and its Sunday attendance often approached two thousand persons. Unlike the members of Second Baptist and Allen Chapel, practically all of St. Stephen's congregation appeared to be from the black working class. Dr. D. Madison Miller, who would serve as superintendent of General Hospital No. 2 in the 1930s, was one exception. Thomas McGrew, a deacon at St. Stephen's and head of the Building Laborers union, undertaker H. B. Moore, and business owner Eddie Verter were others, but the strength of the church lay in its numbers and Hurse's standing within the community. By the beginning of World War II, St. Stephen's had moved into a larger edifice at Fifteenth Street (now Truman Road) and Troost.[50]

Allen Chapel AME

Allen Chapel's roots also run back to the months following Emancipation. In 1866, Jane Shelby asked Second Baptist pastor Clark Moore to assist her in finding someone to organize a church for Kansas City's black Methodists. A Baptist minister from Leavenworth and a Methodist minister from Quindaro provided guidance until the AME assigned William B. Cushley as the parish's new pastor. A new structure was completed on the northeast corner of Tenth and Charlotte, and Cushley named the new church Allen Chapel, in honor of Richard Allen, the founder of the African Methodist Episcopal Church.[51]

Allen Chapel went through a succession of pastors over the next thirty years. H. B. Parks served as pastor early in the 1890s, and helped the church eliminate its outstanding debt. Rev. F. Jesse Peck succeeded Parks and led Allen Chapel on a fund-raising drive to finance the construction of a larger structure.[52] By the first decade of the twentieth century, Allen Chapel had gained primacy among the AME churches in Kansas City. Under a series of progressive pastors (William H. Thomas, 1914–1919; Felix Isaacs, 1919–1922; I. M. Wittenberg, 1922–1925; and C. S. Williams, 1925–1928), Allen Chapel eliminated church debt, expanded its physical structure, and built its membership to more than two thousand. Unlike Second Baptist, however, Allen Chapel claimed more than its share of black professionals and elites. In the 1920s, its membership rolls included brothers Nelson Crews and James Crews, music instructor R. G. Jackson, lawyers Charles H. Calloway and William

50. Hoggins, *Centenary History,* 150.

51. Ibid., 161; *Kansas City Sun,* July 2, 1921; September 2, 1922.

52. Peck would serve as president of Western University after World War I. Ibid., March 12, 1919.

C. Hueston, Dr. William J. Thompkins, YMCA executive secretary Frank A. Harris, and Dr. Thomas C. Unthank and his wife, Gertrude.[53]

Like Second Baptist, Allen Chapel drew some of the nation's most celebrated African Americans. For example, tenor Roland Hayes and pianist Lawrence Brown, noted for their interpretations of African American folk music as well as the classics, entertained a "select audience" at Allen Chapel in 1919. A year later, the enigmatic William Pickens (Yale graduate, Booker T. Washington disciple, and recent NAACP convert) appeared in the church's pulpit.[54] Allen Chapel AME also had a significant social outreach program. Before World War I, the church had opened a bathhouse, swimming pool, basketball court, gymnasium, library, and day-care center for the residents of the Church Hill area, and had established a nursery school in the East Bottoms to serve the children there. The church also contributed financially to the Douglass Hospital on the Kansas side.[55]

Ebenezer AME

Ebenezer AME grew out of a decision by nineteen members of Allen Chapel to form their own church. Led by B. W. Stewart, the group first began holding services in 1886 in a rented space at Independence Avenue and Harrison. After about six months, the group purchased an old dwelling at Third and Holmes and converted the structure into a church. By 1903, the church had purchased a lot at the corner of Admiral Boulevard and Holmes Street and begun construction on a new structure. The Holmes Street site would be the home of Ebenezer AME through the first decade of the twentieth century. The church's membership remained small at that point; Hoggins says only about sixty African Americans claimed it as their church home when Ebenezer purchased an old church, which had been used by a German Baptist congregation, at Seventeenth Street and Tracy Avenue. That facility also proved inadequate, and under a new pastor, W. C. Williams, Ebenezer AME purchased a lot at Sixteenth Street and Lydia Avenue, near the Lincoln School, and constructed a new stone church at a cost of thirty thousand dollars. The investment in a new structure spurred an increase

53. Hoggins, *Centenary History;* A. Martin, *Our Negro Population,* 186; *Kansas City Sun,* January 25, February 22, March 8, August 9, November 1, 1919; April 2, May 28, 1921.

54. *Kansas City Sun,* July 5, 1919; April 17, 1920.

55. David Thelen, *Paths of Resistance: Tradition and Democracy in Industrializing Missouri,* 144; *Kansas City Sun,* February 22, March 8, 22, 1919. Thelen incorrectly identifies Samuel Bacote, a Baptist, as the pastor at Allen Chapel in 1910.

in attendance, and by the time William T. Osborne was appointed pastor after World War I, the church counted more than one thousand members.[56]

Of all of Ebenezer's pre–World War II pastors, Osborne was probably the most celebrated. He was described by contemporaries as a powerful speaker, and his sermons regularly drew overflow crowds to the church sanctuary. Ona B. Wilson, an Ebenezer member, theology student at Western University, and frequent contributor to the *Kansas City Sun* in the early 1920s, on one occasion described Osborne's sermons as "practical" as well as "soul-stirring, invigorating and inspiring." Osborne also oversaw an expansion of the church balcony to increase seating, as well as a fund-raising drive to pay off the church debt. Like his counterparts at other black churches in the two Kansas Cities, Osborne opened up his church to discussions of secular issues and topics. One Sunday service was given over to Kansas City's NAACP branch; William C. Hueston was the featured speaker. On another occasion, before the Nineteenth Amendment was ratified, Ebenezer was the site for a debate on woman suffrage. In 1920, Ebenezer held "possibly the first celebration" of George Washington's birthday by Kansas City's African Americans. Western University professor Caswell Crews (nephew of Nelson and James) was the featured speaker for the benefit; proceeds were to go toward a scholarship for a theological student at Western. The same year, the Budding Genius Literary Club of Fire Company no. 11 presented a program at Ebenezer.[57]

Ebenezer, unlike many of its Baptist counterparts of the 1920s, defied gender conventions and recognized the spiritual, emotional, physical, and intellectual contributions of its female members. In 1919, the church held women's day on a Sunday in May. A woman preached the morning service; likely candidates would have included three recent graduates of the teaching program at Western University (Ona Wilson, Anna Roberts, and class valedictorian Olivia Moore). In addition, the women organized an elaborate all-day program, and women were asked to contribute five dollars for the church's programs.[58]

Osborne's wife, a noted stage director, produced a series of plays and entertainments, using local talent. In 1923, the "Osborne Players" gave a benefit performance at the Grand Theater, staging a production of the *Queen of Sheba* to raise funds for Western University in Kansas

56. Hoggins, *Centenary History,* 156.

57. Ibid.; *Kansas City Sun,* January 25, February 22, March 1, May 17, December 6, November 8, 1919; March 6, April 10, 1920.

58. *Kansas City Sun,* May 5, 1919.

City, Kansas. Pinkie Osborne's crowning achievement was a production of the play *Under the Shadow of a Crime,* in which she drew solely from the Ebenezer congregation for its cast. Seventeen hundred spectators were in attendance, and several hundred were turned away after the last seat was filled. Physician C. Lloyd Peebles, as the lead actor, displayed "a magnificent voice, a splendid stage presence and poise," one observer noted.[59] The Osbornes left Kansas City in late 1923, and W. H. Peck assumed the pastorate in 1924. In his four years at Ebenezer, a parish house was constructed and two nearby apartment houses were purchased to assist the church's community service. By the end of the 1920s, Ebenezer's membership stood at more than twelve hundred.[60]

The larger churches sustained and perpetuated whatever divisions of class might have existed in Kansas City's African American communities prior to World War II. African American professional and business men and women were more likely to attend Second Baptist, St. Stephen's Baptist, Allen Chapel, or Ebenezer AME church. Yet none of the churches—even Allen Chapel—could exist solely on the support of Kansas City's small black professional class. Working-class African Americans sustained these churches just as they did the countless other smaller congregations scattered around the Kansas City area. The smaller churches seldom claimed the attention of the NAACP branch or world-class singers. Instead, they served as the foundations for communities of African Americans that even by 1940 were still physically isolated from the Eighteenth and Vine corridor. It is worth our while to examine three of the smaller churches.

Greenwood Baptist

In 1892, the Reverend John King organized a church for African Americans in the West Bottoms and christened it First Baptist Church. Within months, the church had moved farther south to a lot at the corner of Twentieth and Madison Streets. Over the next fourteen years, the church, now called Greenwood Baptist, moved through a succession of homes before the Reverend J. J. Adams led the congregation in purchasing a four-room frame cottage in the 1800 block of Terrace Street. Adams left the church shortly afterward, and the new pastor, the Reverend George T. Moseby, led a drive in 1910 to finance the construction

59. Ibid., February 28, 1920; *Kansas City Call,* September 28, 1923.
60. Hoggins, *Centenary History,* 156.

of a new edifice on the site. In 1925, Greenwood Baptist purchased a new church home at Eighteenth and Belleview Streets, where it would remain through the interwar period. The church never claimed more than several hundred members, but it served as a locus of religious activities for black Baptists on the West Side. Even in 1940, a significant African American population remained in the area near Greenwood Baptist. An analysis of the 1940 census by the Kansas City Urban League showed that 4,568 African Americans (or about one-tenth of the city's black population) resided in the area between the state line and Troost and north of Twenty-fifth Street. In the census tracts just south of the Greenwood Baptist church (between Summit and Beardsley Road, Eighteenth to Twenty-fifth Streets), African Americans accounted for between 50 percent and 75 percent of the population. African Americans constituted as much as 10 percent of the population in the census tracts around the church.[61]

St. James Baptist

St. James Baptist Church, at the corner of Forty-third and Mill Streets, served a small enclave of African Americans around Westport. Many of the first black residents of the area were former slaves; the 1870 census counted 149 African Americans in Westport City and the area around it. Two former slaves from Kentucky, however, are credited with starting the Baptist church in the region. In late 1870, the families of Wallace E. Smith and Howard Smith arrived in Westport. By the spring of the next year, they had pulled together black Baptists for weekly prayer meetings; on occasion, they were led by Second Baptist pastor Henry Roberson. Shortly afterward, Westport's African American Baptists organized a church in temporary quarters at 4043 Mill Street just south of Westport Road. Wallace Smith served as the church's clerk.[62]

In 1885, under the leadership of pastor James W. Anderson, a cornerstone was laid for the church's first permanent home on Mill Street. Over the next thirty years, the church grew slowly under the leadership of a succession of pastors. In 1915, J. W. Wilson was called to be pastor, and he remained through the 1920s. Under Wilson, St. James continued to grow, and its activities reached out into the African American community of Westport. A "Martha Washington Party" raised more

61. Ibid., 160–61; KCULP, *Matter of Fact* 1:2 (August–September, 1945), box KCULP1, file 1.

62. Hoggins, *Centenary History,* 155.

than thirty-five dollars in 1919, and the church's annual bazaar reported a profit of more than one hundred dollars the following year. St. James also was the scene for cultural activities. A music recital, admission ten cents, was advertised in 1919. By 1920, the church's congregation drew African Americans from all walks of life.[63]

Sun Rise Baptist

Of all of the black churches in Kansas City, Sun Rise Baptist was among the least known and least recognized. Olive Hoggins did not include its genealogy in her otherwise all-encompassing history of Kansas City's churches. It did not attract or produce pastors of note, and its congregation probably was primarily working-class individuals. Sun Rise, however, is typical of the black churches that served as anchors of geographically distinct African American communities. During the interwar period, the church in the 2700 block of Bell (one block east of the state line) served a small cluster of African Americans living just north of Southwest Boulevard. In the 1920s, the community also included a small neighborhood grocery. The community and the church would survive through World War II but would eventually be displaced by the construction of Interstate 35.

The development of health care institutions for African Americans in the Kansas City area is an oft-repeated tale. Proprietary hospitals such as the John Lange Hospital (1902–1919), Perry's Sanitarium (later Wheatley-Provident, 1910–1968), and Douglass Hospital in Kansas City, Kansas (1898–1978), often proved inadequate to meet the demand of black medical needs. Although the University of Kansas medical center in Kansas City, Kansas, accepted black patients, many African Americans were leery of entering it, fearful of the type of treatment or lack of treatment they might receive. Their experiences with the city medical facilities in Kansas City justified many of those fears.

Prior to the First World War, people of color who entered the city hospital on Holmes received treatment on a segregated basis. Beds in the basement of the building were reserved for African Americans and Hispanics. In addition, black doctors were not allowed to practice in the city facility, and the nursing staff was entirely white. In 1903, when floodwaters raced through the West Bottoms, African American victims were taken to the Convention Hall for treatment. In the aftermath,

63. Ibid.; *Western Messenger,* February 28, 1919; February 13, 1920.

T. C. Unthank, a recent graduate of the Howard medical school, began pushing city officials to create a separate medical facility for African Americans, where black physicians and nurses could be trained. The city at first resisted, but in 1908 the city constructed a new facility for white patients and reserved the old hospital for African American and Hispanic patients. The new facility was christened General Hospital No. 1. The old facility was variously known as the Colored Division of Kansas City's General Hospital, the Old City Hospital, and the name by which it is most remembered, General Hospital No. 2.[64]

Between 1908 and 1911, the Old City Hospital was staffed solely by white physicians and nurses and had a white superintendent. In 1911, four African American doctors, including T. C. Unthank, were appointed to the staff; black nurses were accepted into the facility at the same time. In 1914, the first black superintendent, William J. Thompkins, was appointed. At that point, it became a unique entity in the United States: the only city-owned medical facility run by African Americans with a staff of black doctors and nurses.[65]

The Old City Hospital became a point of pride for many African Americans. Even in 1919, when the structure was forty years old, Nelson Crews felt confident in running a small front-page story in the *Sun* with the headline: "Conditions Are Ideal at Old City Hospital." Crews praised the physical condition of the structure ("The floors are wood and the walls painted plaster, [but] not a speck of dust or dirt was visible anywhere") and the staff ("Every one is busy and apparently satisfied"). Dr. William J. Thompkins, in his second term as the superintendent of the facility, noted the occasional difficulties in obtaining equipment but was generally pleased with the operation of the hospital five years after African Americans gained control.[66] The hospital provided one more venue for African American doctors and nurses to be trained and to practice. An undated flier from the mid-1920s described the operation of the facility.[67] The facility itself housed a general hospital, complete with a pathology laboratory, an X-ray laboratory, and an out-patient clinic. Separate wards were maintained for tuberculosis patients and

64. All three names were used interchangeably in the 1920s, until a new segregated facility opened in 1930.

65. Gamble, *Making a Place,* 70; Sidney L. Bates, "Medicine without Method: Kansas City, Missouri's General and Allied Hospitals under the Department of Health, 1870–1962," 45–48.

66. *Kansas City Sun,* October 25, 1919.

67. The flier, possibly a newspaper clipping, is found in Gibson, *Mecca of the New Negro,* 188.

those with other contagious diseases. Living quarters for the interns were provided, and a home for the nurses completed the facility. The staff at that time comprised forty-two black doctors and ten interns. The nurses' training school included twenty teachers, three supervisors, and a class of thirty-two student nurses. Not surprisingly, some of the medical interns would open their first practices in Kansas City after graduation; for example, J. O. Henley, an intern at the hospital after World War I, opened his practice at 1309 East Eighteenth Street in 1920 and was listed among the doctors practicing at the facility in the mid-1920s.[68]

In the hospital's early years, Thompkins put its unique status to good use. In 1920, the hospital gained permission from the Hospital and Health Board of Kansas City to establish an intensive training school in pathology and bacteriology. The school would be open to any African American doctor in the country, free of charge.[69] Thompkins and the hospital also turned the nurses' graduation ceremonies into an annual event for Kansas City's African American communities. The graduation in 1921 was one such special occasion. The Reverend Samuel Bacote gave the baccalaureate sermon to an overflow crowd at Second Baptist Church. The graduation itself was held in the auditorium of the Paseo YMCA, and eight hundred spectators attended. Musical selections were provided by an orchestra conducted by N. Clark Smith; pins were awarded by Albertine Felts, the supervisor of nurses; and *Kansas City Sun* editor Nelson Crews presented the diplomas. Speeches were made by Thompkins, the city's health commissioner, a black doctor from St. Louis, and Mrs. S. Joe Brown of Des Moines, Iowa, a member of the executive board of the National Federation of Colored Women's Clubs. Even more remarkable than the elaborate presentation, *none of the nine* graduates was from Kansas City. For members of Kansas City's African American communities, the graduation itself bespoke of the progress African Americans had made. The graduation ceremony would continue to be an important function in the African American community into the World War II era.[70]

African Americans would be less fond of the politics surrounding the appointment of the superintendent. By the 1920s, the position had become part of the city's patronage system, and when a new administration was elected in 1922, Thompkins, a Democrat, was removed from

68. *Kansas City Sun,* May 15, 1920; Gibson, *Mecca of the New Negro.*

69. *Kansas City Sun,* August 14, 1920.

70. Ibid., May 28, 1921; Gibson, *Mecca of the New Negro,* 188; *Kansas City Call,* May 16, 1930.

the post. The replacement was Dr. James F. Shannon, a former schoolteacher in Georgia who graduated from Meharry Medical School in Nashville, Tennessee. After serving as an intern with Dr. Middleton H. Lambright in 1898, Shannon opened his practice in Kansas City. His appointment revealed a fissure in Kansas City's African American communities. The *Sun*'s Nelson Crews, although a Republican, lauded the choice, noting that Shannon was "a stickler for discipline and integrity" who believed that "the poor, ignorant and needy should receive as much consideration as the man of superior intelligence and wealth." Chester Franklin, an ardent Republican, objected vehemently to the politics of the appointment, devoting three full columns of the front page of the *Kansas City Call* to the issue.[71]

Even more devastating than the political maneuvering was a fire that gutted the hospital in 1927. City leaders had been promising a new hospital for nonwhites since the early 1920s, but it was only after the fire that plans moved forward. There were obstacles, however; the site for the new facility became a point of conflict between city administrators and white Kansas Citians on the East Side. The city's first choice was a tract of land on Michigan Avenue between Twenty-sixth and Twenty-seventh Streets, just east of Spring Valley Park. The proposed site stood at the edge of black residential settlement, as African Americans who attempted to acquire homes south of Twenty-seventh Street in the Troost-Brooklyn corridor were rebuffed—sometimes violently—by white home owners. As soon as the city's plans for the new hospital became known, whites near the proposed site organized a protest. A delegation of whites visited city manager H. F. McElroy the day after the formal announcement, and in February 1927, members of the Linwood Improvement Association voiced the reasons for their position in a letter to the *Kansas City Star:*

> The location is in the extreme southeast corner of the district occupied by the people it is intended to serve; it is within one block of restricted homes of white families and it adjoins Spring Valley Park, which is used by these and other families.
>
> In view of the fact that there is 35,000 feet of vacant ground in the negro district, it seems there could be a fair choice of hospital sites and that one of them would be more convenient to patients than that selected. The hospital site was chosen by the city officials,

71. *Kansas City Sun*, June 10, 1922. The particular issue of the *Call* no longer exists, though Nelson Crews described "Ches's" indignation in detail. It is worth noting that in the midst of another furor over the appointment of the superintendent, Franklin described Shannon as "an outstanding doctor." *Kansas City Call*, August 29, 1930.

> regardless of the known agitation in this district resulting from the attempt to take over territory occupied by white families.[72]

Although McElroy first argued that by the Linwood home owners' logic, General Hospital No. 1 should be located in a white residential area, eventually city officials relented. A new site was chosen just west of General Hospital No. 1 on Twenty-second Street. On March 2, 1930, General Hospital No. 2 held its grand opening, and by April, the 250-bed facility was accepting patients. Chester Franklin of the *Call* described the new facility as the "most modern public hospital in the country." He noted that every bit of equipment in the seven-and-a-half-story, three hundred thousand–dollar brick structure was brand new, and floor by floor, he told the *Call*'s readers what to expect when they entered the facility. He graciously noted that city officials "have not only built a new hospital but they have built the very best hospital." He added, "They did not try to build something 'good enough for Negroes' but something as good as money could buy."[73] Although it would be troubled by political wrangling over the next two decades, General Hospital No. 2 and its staff provided a much-needed health care option for members of Kansas City's African American communities.

Bigger and better funded than Wheatley-Provident, and more accessible to most of the city's African American residents than the University of Kansas Medical Center or the all-black Douglass Hospital in Kansas City, Kansas, General Hospital No. 2 fulfilled, in the words of Chester Franklin, the "fondest dreams of public and physicians."[74] It would be the major medical facility in the African American community until 1957, when the city merged its two hospitals.

Health care also fell to a network of private and public institutions that tended to particular needs of the African American communities. All owed their existence to the activism of women and the philanthropy of both black and white.

Niles Home for Children

The Niles Home, although named for a white benefactor, owed its origin to the work and benevolence of an African American bricklayer,

72. *Kansas City Times*, January 12, 1927; *Kansas City Post*, January 13, 1927; *Kansas City Star*, February 10, 1927.
73. *Kansas City Call*, February 28, 1930.
74. Ibid.

Samuel Eason. Starting in the late 1880s, Eason rented a building to provide housing for homeless black children and elderly black women. Dwayne Martin describes Eason as a quiet, unassuming man who used his own savings to support the home. Eventually, Eason began to solicit support from outside sources, primarily white benefactors, to continue his work. After Eason's death, a number of individuals continued his work until 1924, when cigar manufacturer Frank C. Niles donated funds for a new home for the facility. The F. C. Niles Home, by then dedicated to the care of orphaned and neglected children, moved into a large, well-equipped home at 1911 East Twenty-third Street with room for a staff of nine full-time employees and forty children between the ages of six and twelve. Alice Grady was hired as the first superintendent, and she served the Niles Home until her death in 1949.[75]

Florence Crittenton Home

A year after the Niles Home for Children moved into its new quarters, activists began planning for the establishment of a home for unwed African American mothers. Led by Elizabeth Bruce Crogman, supporters purchased a residence at 2446 Michigan for the purpose of providing shelter and medical care for mothers and newborn infants. A year later, the maternity home received a charter from the Florence Crittenton Mission, a philanthropic organization. In 1930, the home moved into a three-story, colonial-style residence at 2228 Campbell Avenue.[76]

Big Sister Home for Negro Girls

In 1928, woman's activist Pearl M. Dabney, in collaboration with the Kansas City Urban League, began to investigate the possibilities of opening a home for neglected or homeless African American girls between the ages of twelve and eighteen. In 1934, the Big Sister Home for Negro Girls opened at 2326 Brooklyn Avenue. Fredericka Perry, wife of Dr. John E. Perry, was appointed superintendent, and Rosetta Walker Gibson became the first house mother. Gibson remained involved with

75. D. Martin, "Hidden Community," 150–51; Young and Young, *Your Kansas City and Mine,* 106.

76. Young and Young, *Your Kansas City and Mine,* 105.

the Big Sister Home until her death in 1944. She bequeathed her home at 2519 Park Avenue to the Big Sister Organization as a replacement for the Brooklyn Avenue facility.[77]

In 1927, alarmists within the Kansas City area charged that tuberculosis was increasing among African Americans and urged whites to distance themselves from black Kansas Citians as much as possible. Some even advocated eliminating African Americans from those jobs in which the two races came in close proximity. Such scares were not uncommon in early-twentieth-century America, and there is no evidence that white Kansas Citians took this scare seriously. Yet for years afterward, the black press trumpeted the fact that black deaths from tuberculosis actually were on the decline. An undated newspaper article found in Urban League records duly notes a coroner's report that African American deaths in Kansas City from respiratory causes were down for the year 1933, and that the majority of those twenty-two deaths were from pneumonia.[78]

One of the realities of early-twentieth-century life was the lack of modern plumbing within many residential units. Public baths were commonplace in America's cities, and in 1919, in recognition of the changing nature of the neighborhood, the Parks Board opened up a bathhouse at Seventeenth Street and The Paseo for the exclusive use of African Americans. The board's decision came at the prodding of Dr. William Thompkins, former superintendent of Old City Hospital.

The rededication of the facility was the cause for yet another gala celebration among Kansas City's elites. On a Sunday afternoon in June, representatives of the major black churches, labor organizations, fraternal societies, and civic and social clubs gathered for a parade and rededication ceremony. A community chorus under the direction of Clyde Leroy Glass performed, and addresses were made by Nelson Crews; R. T. Coles; the Reverends James Wesley Hurse and B. G. Dawson; L. Amasa Knox; Felix Payne; Mrs. A. E. Jenkins, representing the City Federation of Colored Women's Clubs; and Pearl Dabney, speaking on behalf of black children. Alderman William J. Scannell presented the symbolic key to the bathhouse to the African American community, and war veteran

77. Ibid., 106.

78. "Tuberculosis Declining in Negro Race," undated newspaper clipping (likely from *Kansas City American*), KCULP, box N1, file 1.

Homer Roberts accepted on behalf of black Kansas City. With that, African Americans in Kansas City claimed another small piece of the urban landscape for their own and continued their transformation of the area around Eighteenth and Vine. The "acquisition" of the bathhouse had practical ramifications. Many residences of African Americans lacked interior plumbing and sanitary facilities, and the demand was high for those homes that did. The Paseo bathhouse offered black Kansas Citians a chance for cleanliness, as well as swimming and recreational opportunities. The bathhouse then symbolized the continual assault of Kansas City's African Americans on race-based visions of cleanliness and health held by many white Americans.

The schools, churches, and medical facilities were vital institutions within Kansas City's African American communities. They were structures in which African Americans defined themselves and what was important to them. They built magnificent churches or congregated in storefronts or homes to practice their religion. Educational and medical facilities were segregated, and until the 1930s often in deplorable condition. But over time, Kansas City's African American pushed until they had institutions they could be proud of. That was one of the biggest lessons learned in the African American community in the interwar period.

Six

Play
Not without Laughter

Oh my, marvelous town. Clubs, clubs, clubs, clubs, clubs, clubs, clubs. As a matter of fact, I thought that was all Kansas City was made up of, was clubs at one time.

—WILLIAM "COUNT" BASIE, QUOTED IN *GOIN' TO KANSAS CITY*, BY NATHAN W. PEARSON

THE FIRST PART OF Count Basie's comment is typical of the recollections of Kansas City used by historian Nathan Pearson Jr. in his study of the city's jazz tradition. It also is typical of the popular perception of black life in Kansas City in the 1920s and 1930s; jazz—and baseball—are seen as the essence of the African American communities at the time. The second part of Basie's comments, however, suggests that contemporary and historical perceptions of Kansas City are actually misconceptions. Black life then was no more defined by sporting competition and musical interpretation than it is today. Granted, jazz and baseball provide a safe entry point for outside observers of Kansas City's African American world. Yet, by remaining at this entry point, by accepting black life as consisting solely of music and sports, the outside observer becomes a voyeur tantalized by perception rather than a visitor immersed in the reality of black life. One must recognize that Kansas City's jazz scene as well as its rich history in baseball were simply subcultures within Kansas City's African American communities. These subcultures coexisted in uneasy tension with that of the majority black culture—one driven by the sober, churchgoing, hardworking men and women of Allen Chapel, Second Baptist, St. Stephen's, Vine Street, and Paseo Baptist churches. It would be incredibly naive to assume that there was no overlap between the two cultures, but at least for public consumption, most African Americans in Kansas City of the time constructed a hard-and-fast line between the two.

Yet the importance of Kansas City's contributions to "America's classical music" (as trumpeter Wynton Marsalis styles it) cannot be overstated. First, Kansas City provided a setting for the grooming and maturation of some of the country's most important jazz voices. As Nathan Pearson and other scholars have argued, Kansas City's jazz scene prospered in the mid-1920s and 1930s because of the activities of "the corrupt but economically stimulating" Pendergast machine.[1] Particularly after the onset of the Great Depression, Pendergast fostered an open atmosphere that drew some of the finest musicians from throughout the Great Plains and Southwest. Pendergast's goal was to keep Kansas City working, and that applied to the jazz clubs that sprouted throughout the period along Twelfth and Eighteenth Streets on the East Side. In the 1930s, these clubs, which seemed to never close, offered jobs to musicians in a period when few other jobs existed. The jobs were low paying, but they paid enough to attract musicians the caliber of Count Basie, Lester Young, Ben Webster, Jimmy Rushing, and Jay McShann. Homegrown products Julia Lee, Mary Lou Williams, and (to a lesser degree) Charlie "Bird" Parker honed their skills in Kansas City's jazz scene. Second was the development of a distinctive Kansas City style of jazz, one epitomized by the sound of Basie, Young, and Williams. It was a sound that gave the city a jazz reputation exceeded only by that of New York City.

Kansas City jazz, the epitome of a midwestern musical style that flourished in the 1920s and 1930s, had its roots in a variety of sources developed within a geographical territory that included Texas, Oklahoma, eastern Kansas, and western Missouri. The musicians who developed Kansas City's distinctive jazz style in the mid-1920s and 1930s often grew up playing the ragtime music perfected and popularized by Scott Joplin, as well as brass band and popular dance music. Before 1925, they honed their skills, Pearson notes, playing on "village greens and in carnivals, minstrel shows, vaudeville theaters, and dance halls."[2]

1. Pearson, *Goin' to Kansas City,* xviii.
2. Ibid., 1.

Private music instructors, such as Charles Watts, and brass bands organized by black fraternal and social organizations helped tutor a generation of musicians who came of age in the years around World War I. For instance, the Kansas City chapters of both the Elks and the Knights of Pythias had organized bands in the early 1920s. Booker Washington, born in St. Charles, Missouri, but a graduate of Western University in Kansas City, Kansas, recalled playing for a twenty-piece brass band as a sideline in the 1920s. "We played all over Kansas City," Washington recalled.[3]

Lawrence Denton played with a town band in his hometown of Hartville, Missouri, as a youth and then arrived in Kansas City just before the outbreak of World War I. He first joined the Second Regiment Band organized by William Melford for the Knights of Pythias. "The lodges in them days, they had a drill team, they used to drill like soldiers. There was a drillmaster in our band that was an old army man.... They was very experienced in drilling. That's where they got the name, Second Regiment." Bands organized by the lodges also served a social function within the African American community. They were often asked to perform during the funerals and processions for deceased lodge members. "Oh, we used to be on the street pretty near every Sunday—all through June, July and August." Denton said. "We played marches, funeral marches, dirges." Denton later joined the Daniel Blackburn band as the first-clarinet player. Blackburn's band played regularly in parks within the African American communities, drawing large crowds on a regular basis. "Sometimes we played for three or four thousand, five thousand people would come out there to hear the band," Denton recalled. "A lot of white [people] would come [too]."[4]

Another source of employment and training for African American musicians was vaudeville and movie theaters, which in the early 1920s often were the same thing. Until the advent of talking pictures, theater bands provided the accompaniment as the dramatic picture played out on the screen. The Lincoln, Gem, Eblon, and Love Theaters all housed bands at one point in the 1920s and 1930s. Theater bands offered consistent employment, but because band members were expected to play a musical score provided by the filmmakers, the bands provided little chance for musical creativity. Those opportunities would come with the advent of dance bands during the period. Although Kansas City would attract a lengthy list of bands in this period, the most notable

3. Ibid., 17.
4. Ibid., 17–18.

were Walter Page's Blue Devils, Andy Kirk's Twelve Clouds of Joy, the George Lee Orchestra, and the Bennie Moten band that launched the career of Count Basie.

The Twelve Clouds of Joy

The Twelve Clouds of Joy was originally organized by T. Holder in 1925 in Dallas, Texas. Holder was an excellent musician who relied more on instinct than training to become proficient in his craft. Holder left the Alphonso Trent band early in the 1920s, and decided to form his own band. "I had done gotten a little older," Holder said, "and realized that I hadn't gotten much. . . . I just told everybody, well, 'I'm going to get up a band myself. We're just letting all this work go and we ain't doin' nuthin'.' "[5]

Holder, described by Pearson as a charismatic figure, recognized his strengths as a bandleader ("I was good at putting bands together and making it pay") but also acknowledged his shortcomings. Holder was neither a good manager nor reliable. When Holder took off from the band during a 1928 engagement in Tulsa, Oklahoma, to visit his girlfriend in Dallas, Texas, the band members came together and fired him. Andy Kirk, the tuba player, took over as bandleader. Claude "Fiddler" Williams, who joined the band a year or so before Holder's dismissal, said the Clouds of Joy selected Kirk because he "was just about the oldest, and he was more settled" than the rest of the members of the band. Kirk soon proved to be a wise choice. Under his leadership, the band enjoyed tremendous success up through World War II. Pearson notes that the Clouds of Joy had a string of hit recordings between 1936 and 1945.[6]

Life with the Cloud of Joys, whether under Holder's or Kirk's leadership, was rewarding both musically and financially. The band, like most of the territory bands of the period, lived a peripatetic existence, traveling from city to city, ballrooms to dance halls and back. The Clouds of Joy, under Holder's leadership, played primarily in Texas and Oklahoma, sandwiching engagements for as long as two months around one-nighters in nearby communities. The pay was lucrative, however. In a time when most African Americans in Kansas City were making

5. Ibid., 54–55.
6. Ibid., 56–59.

less than twenty dollars a week, the Clouds of Joy often received twenty dollars a night per man. Under Kirk, the band expanded its horizons, making appearances in Topeka, Texas, and Louisiana with occasional forays into Kansas City. It was at one of the Twelve Clouds of Joy's appearances in Kansas City that a young Bill Basie came under the influence of the group's piano player, Mary Lou Williams.[7]

Williams and her husband, saxophonist John Williams, came to the Twelve Clouds of Joy in 1929, a year after Holder's dismissal. In addition to being an outstanding pianist, Mary Lou Williams took over the arranging and the bulk of the composing for the group. She became an instant star and helped drive the Twelve Cloud of Joys to greater heights. "We played everything," Williams said, "and then we'd come back swinging. . . . We'd play sweet music until twelve o'clock then everybody'd start playing. They were afraid of losing the dancers." After leaving the Twelve Clouds of Joy, Williams enjoyed a successful career as a soloist and composer.[8]

Walter Page's Blue Devils

According to Nathan Pearson, the Blue Devils began in 1923 in Kansas City as a traveling vaudeville and carnival troupe known as Billy King's Road Show. The group lasted for two years before disbanding after a performance in Oklahoma City in 1925. Walter Page, the band's bass and saxophone player and its acknowledged musical leader, reformed the band on the spot, and renamed it Walter Page's Blue Devils. Page had spent a semester in the University of Kansas's music program (studying piano, voice, violin, saxophone, composition, and arranging) and soon turned the thirteen-piece group into one of the most energetic and prominent of the territorial bands in the mid-1920s, playing in various cities and venues from Kansas City through the Great Plains and into the Southwest. In their heyday, the Blue Devils included such jazz luminaries as saxophonist Lester Young, vocalist Jimmy Rushing, and for eight months pianist William Basie.[9]

Despite the high level of musical ability and popularity, the Blue Devils would survive less than a decade. Page, the titular head of the Blue

7. Ibid., 56–61. Basie says no piano player "was as great as Mary Lou [Williams] at that time. I think Mary Lou was number one."

8. Ibid., 61, 63.

9. Ibid., 64–65.

Devils, was not a strong manager. In addition, the Blue Devils suffered more than their share of misfortune. The result was a feeling of uncertainty within the group, a feeling that was intensified by raids on the Blue Devils' personnel by other orchestras. In particular, Bennie Moten raided the Blue Devils' roster, starting with Bill Basie in 1929 and adding Jimmy Rushing, Oran Page, Eddie Durham, and eventually Walter Page by 1931. The nucleus of the Blue Devils attempted to keep the group alive, but even the addition of saxophonist Lester Young (one of the most talented musicians in the interwar period) could not keep the band afloat. In 1933, the Blue Devils conceded defeat when they ran out of money while playing in West Virginia. Bennie Moten brought many of the band's members, including Young, to Kansas City, and they became core members of the Bennie Moten and Count Basie bands.[10]

The Bennie Moten Orchestra

The Twelve Clouds of Joy and the Blue Devils had strong connections to the Kansas City musical scene, but the most recognized orchestra of the period belonged to Bennie Moten. A strong leader and talented pianist, Moten led what is considered the first jazz orchestra in the city. Pearson argues that more than any other jazz group of the time, Moten's orchestra personified Kansas City's music and musical scene. Moten's orchestra attracted musicians from throughout the Midwest, the Great Plains, and the Southwest. The roster of musicians who passed through Moten's band reads like a Who's Who of the national jazz scene in pre–World War II America: pianist Count Basie, vocalist Jimmy Rushing, saxophone players Lester Young and Ben Webster, bassist Walter Page, and trumpet player Oran "Hot Lips" Page, among others.

Moten's first band, the B.B. and D. (for Bennie Moten, Bailey Hancock, and Dude Lankford), was a three-man group formed in the waning months of the First World War. The band played three nights a week at a ballroom on the second floor of the Labor Temple at Fourteenth Street and Woodland Avenue. Before the advent of the Urban League's community center, the Labor Temple was the scene for a variety of functions within the African American community, ranging from dances and benefit concerts staged by the Beau Brummels Club to fashion shows as fund-raisers for Wheatley-Provident Hospital. B.B. and

10. Ibid.

D. drew capacity crowds to the ballroom. On one night, Dude Lankford avers, the band drew more than twenty-three hundred dancers. The pay was generous; Lankford said at one point he and Moten were making one hundred dollars a night.[11]

After a year, Hancock and Lankford left the group, and Moten began organizing a five-man band under his name. By 1922, the Bennie Moten Orchestra was beginning to take shape, and in 1923, when the first jazz recordings were made, the distinctive sound of Moten (and Kansas City jazz) was committed to vinyl. Moten's band and his sound continued to evolve during the 1920s. In the middle of the decade, Moten organized Bennie Moten's Radio Orchestra, a five-man group with Moten on piano leading a drummer, trumpet player, trombone player, and clarinet player. Within a couple of years, the band had grown in size and sophistication. A photograph of Moten's group from around 1926 shows an eight-man orchestra. By this time, Moten had emerged as the leading bandleader among Kansas City's musicians. The addition of the Blue Devils' members in the late 1920s, though, was the catalyst for the band's greatest period: the six years between 1929 and Moten's death in 1935. "Bennie Moten had the best band [in Kansas City]," trumpeter Buck Clayton recalled. "It was a hit band all the time, but it was better when Basie and Lips [Oran Page] got into it. It just turned Bennie's band around. They played music; it was a nice band but it didn't swing like it did when Basie came."[12]

Bill Basie joined the Moten Orchestra in 1929, giving it much stronger presence on piano. Moten, who recognized his limitations as a pianist, had actively recruited Basie for some time, and he concentrated on his responsibilities as band leader more after Basie's arrival. Equally important to the rise of the Moten Orchestra was the addition of guitar player Eddie Durham, who took responsibility for the group's arrangements and compositions. At the behest of band members, Durham composed "Moten's Swing," which became the orchestra's signature piece. "We needed it for a show in Philadelphia," Durham said. "We took a lot of encores . . . so the band said, 'You got to get some more songs because we're playing the same things over and over.' So I took off and went downstairs to make 'Moten Swing.' I based it on 'You're Driving Me Crazy.'" By this time, the Moten band was recording and touring nationally. "When Bennie Moten took his band to New York, with Basie playing

11. Ibid., 122–24; *Kansas City Sun*, March 15, 1919; April 2, 1921.
12. Pearson, *Goin' to Kansas City*, 131.

piano, they took New York by storm. They'd never heard nothing like it, that Kansas City beat," booking agent Jimmy Jewell recalled.[13]

Moten's orchestra also reigned supreme among Kansas City's jazz bands. In the weekly battle of the bands sponsored by the Musicians' Protective Union Local 627 (the all-black musicians' union based at 1823 Highland) at the Paseo Dance Academy, Moten's band battled all comers. These games of musical upmanship usually came down to the orchestras of Moten and George Lee, with each group backed by its own outspoken followers. One observer notes that "Moten's Swing" often was the deciding blow; few bands had anything in their repertoire that could match it.

The onset of the Great Depression reduced traveling for the Moten band. It spent much of the five years between 1929 and 1935 performing in and around Kansas City. In December 1932, however, members of the Moten band boarded a bus and headed for Camden, New Jersey, for the band's seminal—and final—recordings. That session, according to Pearson, "produced a stream of spectacular recordings, among the first, and greatest version of 'Moten's Swing,' 'Prince of Wails,' 'Toby,' 'Lafayette,' and 'Milenburg Joys.'" The recordings represented "the apex of Moten's recording career and, for many, the height of Kansas City jazz.... These last recordings also clearly show that the roughness... was long gone. This was a superb, thoroughly polished swing band."[14] By this time, the lineup included Basie, Walter Page on trumpet, saxophonists Ben Webster on tenor and Eddie Barefield on alto, and guitarist Eddie Durham. Jazz historian Jack Tracy, in addition, argues that these recordings, particularly of "Moten's Swing," show Basie's emergence as leader of the ensemble. "The whole Basie style and approach are all here," Tracy asserts, "his Fats Waller–influenced piano, Walter Page's rock-steady walking bass; some firm, unobtrusive rhythm guitar; fiery soloists... and a simple, climactic shout chorus from the ensemble." It was, Tracy notes, "the nucleus of a style that for [forty-nine] years would serve Basie well as he led his own band."[15] While Basie literally set the tempo for the ensemble at this time, Moten remained the band's nominal leader. He brought in most of the remaining Blue Devils after that band's collapse in 1933, including saxophonist Lester Young, and for the next two years, he led the premier band in Kansas City. Unfortu-

13. Ibid., 130, 132.
14. Ibid., 133.
15. Jack Tracy, *Count Basie.*

nately for music fans, the Camden recordings, produced at the height of the Depression when few records were being made, were the last for the Moten band. No recordings of the band with Webster, Young, Basie, and Page were ever made.

The Count Basie Orchestra

In 1935, Bennie Moten, then thirty-nine years of age, entered Wheatley-Provident Hospital for a routine tonsillectomy. He died of heart failure during the surgery. With him, an era in Kansas City jazz ended. William "Count" Basie was ready to make his own contribution to the city's jazz history. After Moten's death, his nephew Buster attempted to keep the band going. Buster Moten, however, had neither the musical nor the leadership skills of his uncle, and although several members of the band followed Buster to a job at the Coconut Grove nightclub, most of the musicians followed Bill Basie and Buster Smith to a lower-paying but ultimately more lucrative job at the Reno Club. This band, originally known as the Barons of Rhythm, carried on the Bennie Moten tradition. Within months of its formation, the Barons of Rhythm was being heard on radio broadcasts from the tiny Reno Club. Record producer John Hammond heard one of these broadcasts in 1936 and came to Kansas City to hear the orchestra. Hammond helped Basie increase the group to a full big band and booked it on a tour headed toward New York and the record studios. By the first of 1937, when the band's initial recordings were made, Count Basie was a star and an entire nation was introduced to the Kansas City style of jazz.[16]

Over the next forty-eight years, until his death in 1984, Count Basie led jazz ensembles of all sizes and produced more than enough recordings to fill the average jazz library. All during this time, he kept some type of ensemble going—through the heyday of big-band music during the Second World War, its nadir during the 1950s and 1960s, and its revival of sorts in the 1970s and 1980s when the contributions of Basie and the other big-band masters to the world of jazz were again appreciated. Basie, however, was more than a bandleader; he was an outstanding, if sometimes underappreciated, pianist who played and recorded in duet, trio, and quartet settings. His sparse technique combined with a gentle wit and astute sense of the music's possibilities

16. Pearson, *Goin' to Kansas City,* 134–35.

made his sound one of the most recognized of any jazz pianist of his or subsequent generations. He continued to lead, develop, and record up until the last years of his life.

Jay McShann and Charlie Parker

Although Jay McShann and Charlie Parker made their most significant contributions to jazz after World War II (particularly Parker), it is worth noting their roots in Kansas City's jazz scene in the interwar period. McShann, an Oklahoma native, came to Kansas City in 1937 after several successful years leading bands throughout the Southwest. A year after arriving in Kansas City, McShann began leading a small group, but with the financial assistance of a local insurance executive, he enlarged his group to big-band size. On occasion for his Kansas City dates, McShann would use eighteen-year-old Charlie Parker on alto saxophone.[17]

By the time McShann hit Kansas City, Parker had been playing professionally for better than two years. Primarily self-taught, Parker had worked with his friend Lawrence Keyes, a pianist, in the Deans of Swing (a group of high school students who were students of Alonzo Lewis) and on gigs at Lincoln Hall; performed with Ernie Daniels on playing dates in Jefferson City; played weekly in Eldon, Missouri, with the Tommy Douglas septet; and had a brief playing engagement with Mary Kirk, a pianist. Mary Lou Williams heard Parker play, and recommended him to McShann. By the time he joined McShann, however, Parker was already displaying the personality flaws that plagued him the rest of his life. He was moody, forgetful, and unreliable and consistently tested McShann's patience. When Parker chose to move to Chicago in 1938, McShann was not altogether unhappy to see him go.[18]

Parker spent just a few weeks in Chicago before pawning his clarinet for bus fare to New York. He found it hard to gain work in New York, however, and he spent his first few months in the city scrubbing dishes at a restaurant. There was one side benefit to the dishwashing job; the house pianist was the legendary Art Tatum. Parker stayed at the restaurant just to be exposed to Tatum's mastery of his instrument. At the same time, Parker continued working on his own musical skills, and eventually he gained employment on a few minor playing dates. He

17. Ibid., 163.
18. Giddins, *Celebrating Bird*, is the best available biography of Parker.

also participated in the nightly jam sessions around New York, honing his skills while at the same time experimenting with the possibilities inherent in jazz music. His first big break in New York came when he was hired by Tadd Dameron, but Dameron quickly tired of Parker's immaturity and fired him after about a month. Undaunted, Parker returned to Kansas City and rejoined McShann's big band just as McShann was ready to make his first national appearance. In 1941, the McShann band hit New York, with Parker much bolder and much more confident. He looked at music differently than most of his bandmates and, indeed, most jazz musicians and fans. He absorbed popular music and took it in different directions than musicians had previously, inverting, extending, distorting traditional chord changes to produce a new music. Bebop was born, and although jazz fans were not appreciative at first, other musicians followed Parker's lead. Parker and collaborator Dizzy Gillespie led a jazz revolution. By the end of World War II, bebop had replaced swing as the dominant form of jazz. By the same time, Parker had cut all of his ties to Kansas City. Over the next decade, until his premature death in 1955, Parker was the dominant saxophone voice in the world of jazz. His music inspired four generations of jazz musicians, and his legacy was reflected throughout the world of music and popular culture for the rest of the twentieth century.[19]

The revolution in jazz led by Parker, Gillespie, and others played out on the stages and in the clubs of New York. Coincidentally, and perhaps fittingly, jazz in Kansas had faded. The demise of the Pendergast machine was accompanied by a "cleanup" of the clubs and dance halls that housed Kansas City's musicians in the interwar period. Some dance halls remained and jobs with better pay were available, but the region's strongest musicians had already left the scene by 1939. In addition, as Pearson points out, the new generation of jazz musicians that emerged from Kansas City in the late 1930s and early 1940s was more musically sophisticated. Kansas City jazz, which was rooted in the blues and made to swing, seemingly had little place in a jazz world dominated by innovators and improvisers. Admittedly, the Kansas City sound could still be heard in the music of Count Basie and a few others, but the state of jazz in Kansas City after 1941 can best be summed up in the oft-quoted letter from a frustrated musician to *Downbeat* magazine in 1939: "All the night clubs are dark, and most of our musicians are

19. Giddins, *Celebrating Bird.*

walking the streets. . . . [A]s far as jazz music goes Kay Cee, once the great fount-head of the 'beat and drive style'. . . is now a muted city."[20]

In the spring of 1920, the Paseo YMCA played host to an incredible meeting. The twelve men brought together that day were some of the most successful individuals at that time in the black athletic world. Summoned by Chicago's Andrew "Rube" Foster, the twelve men—eleven black and one white (Kansas City's J. L. Wilkinson)—endeavored to organize and promote a league of black baseball teams. All had been successful on their own; now they hoped to learn the advantages of cooperation. Out of that weekend grew the Negro National League (NNL), the most successful sporting endeavor in black America during the Jim Crow era.[21] The NNL provided opportunities for three generations of African American athletes. Players such as Josh Gibson, "Cool Papa" Bell, and Satchel Paige became as familiar and popular in black households as Babe Ruth, Ty Cobb, and Cy Young were with white baseball fans. In Kansas City's African American communities, the city's NNL franchise—the Kansas City Monarchs—became an example of black creativity, class, persistence, and excellence. The team's players were celebrities throughout the interwar period, and the Monarchs' considerable success on the field was a point of pride for every black man, woman, and child in the two Kansas Cities.

There had been black baseball players and teams in Kansas City prior to the organization of the Monarchs. Historian Janet Bruce notes that the first all-black team in Kansas City was organized in 1897 as the Wall's Laundry Grays by a Chinese laundryman, Quong Fong. Shortly after the organization of the Grays, J. W. Jenkins of the Jenkins Music Company organized another black baseball team. Jenkins, who was, according to Bruce, a strict Methodist, subsequently withdrew his support from the team when it began playing on Sundays. The team then was renamed the Monarchs, with Bill Hueston as manager. That Monarchs team played into the 1910s, but by World War I it had disappeared from the scene.[22]

20. Pearson, *Goin' to Kansas City,* 163, 185; the quote is from Young and Young, *Your Kansas City and Mine,* 135.

21. The incorporation papers were drawn up by a black Topeka lawyer, Elisha Scott. Scott and his sons, both also lawyers, did most of the preliminary legal work in the landmark *Brown v. Topeka Board of Education* suit that paved the way for the desegregation of public education in this country.

22. J. Bruce, *Kansas City Monarchs,* 17–19.

Although Wilkinson had not been involved with all-black teams before the historic meeting at the Paseo YMCA, he possessed several important qualifications. First, he had been involved in promoting semi-professional baseball for more than a decade. His All-Nations team, a conglomeration of whites, African Americans, Native Americans, and Asian Americans, had become well known throughout the Great Plains region in the years before World War I. In particular, Wilkinson had earned a reputation for treating all of his players well regardless of race. Second and equally important, Wilkinson had a lease agreement with American Association Park in Kansas City, and Rube Foster and other organizers believed it imperative to have a team in the new league that could take advantage of the city's growing black population. Although Foster and some other African Americans at the meeting reputedly were hesitant to have a white owner in the league, Wilkinson ultimately proved to be a wise addition to the NNL's ownership structure. Wilkinson's Kansas City Monarchs would emerge as one of the dominant franchises in black baseball over the next three decades, winning the Negro World Series two times and creating an enduring legacy that forever linked the Negro leagues and Kansas City in the popular imagination.

The Monarchs' success was a combination of talented players such as Satchel Paige, Hilton Smith, Newt Allen, Wilbur "Bullet Joe" Rogan, Ernie Banks, Elston Howard, Buck O'Neil, and, of course, Jackie Robinson, with astute business decisions by Wilkinson and the men he hired to operate the franchise. Although Wilkinson harbored no animosity toward African Americans, he was astute enough to recognize that other whites were not as progressively minded. In addition, Janet Bruce notes that Wilkinson was particularly shy and preferred to stay in the background, allowing others to accept the accolades. One of the first steps Wilkinson took in organizing the Monarchs was hiring a black businessman, Quincy Gilmore, as the team's traveling secretary. Gilmore, according to Bruce, served a variety of functions and became in some respects Wilkinson's alter ego. Gilmore, much more outspoken than Wilkinson, often represented the Monarchs at league functions and in dealings with the African American community. In what became an annual tradition—the Monarchs' opening-day parade—Gilmore often rode in the lead car, with Wilkinson riding in a car farther back in the procession. More important, Gilmore represented the team when the "etiquette of segregation" (as Janet Bruce terms it) required a black face to represent a black team. Yet what distinguished the Monarchs from many sports franchises was Wilkinson's ability to communicate with his players and command their loyalty and respect. Infielder Newt Allen, who joined the team in 1922 for a two-decade stay, described Wilkinson as "a considerate man" who knew people. "Your face could be black as tar; he treated everyone alike," Allen said years later.[23]

To fill the roster of his first team, Wilkinson first turned to the core of his All-Nations team, signing four players: pitcher John Donaldson of Glasgow, Missouri; pitcher and outfielder Bill Drake of Sedalia; infielder Frank Blukoi, a native of the Philippines; and pitcher Jose Mendez, a black Cuban. Mendez served as the Monarchs' manager for the first season. Wilkinson then signed five players from a former army team stationed in Arizona. From the Twenty-fifth Infantry Wreckers, Wilkinson acquired Wilbur Rogan, Dobie Moore, Oscar "Heavy" Johnson, Lemuel Hawkins, and Bob Fagin. All but Fagin would be key members of the 1924 Monarchs team that won the first Negro World Series.[24] To assist in the promotion of the team within Kansas City's African American communities, Wilkinson enlisted the services of three black men: Gilmore, Dr. Howard Smith, and Frank "Jewbaby" Floyd.

Gilmore's responsibilities as traveling secretary included running the team's headquarters at 1517 East Eighteenth Street. He came to Kansas City toward the end of the First World War and soon landed a position with the Watkins Brothers undertaking firm. Gilmore, a native of Colorado, is also given credit for reviving the Fraternal Order of the Elks within Kansas City's black communities and was instrumental in bringing the Elks' national convention to Kansas City in 1920. In the early 1920s, he engaged in a series of speculative business ventures before he began operating the Elks Rest nightclub. With Wilbur "Bullet Joe" Rogan, Gilmore also ran the Monarchs Billiard Room (affectionately known as the Monarchs' "official headquarters") across Eighteenth Street in the Street Hotel.[25] Also instrumental in the Monarchs' success was Howard Smith, who had been a member of Kansas City's African American communities for about a decade. Smith, a native of Baltimore, had practiced medicine in Philadelphia and Chicago before coming to Kansas City in 1911. Before 1919, Smith was appointed superintendent of Jackson County's home for elderly, indigent African American citizens.

23. University of Missouri–Kansas City: Joint Collection, Western Historical Manuscripts Collection and the State Historical Society of Missouri: Manuscripts: Kansas City Monarchs Oral History Collection: recorded interview with Newt Allen, in ibid., 19.

24. Ibid., 21, 133–35.

25. Ibid., 21–22; *Kansas City Sun*, July 24, 1920; February 19, 1921; May 20, June 3, 1922; Young and Young, *Your Kansas City and Mine*, 56; "Elks Rest Operator to Chicago and Hot Springs, Vacationing," undated news clipping in Gibson, *Mecca of the New Negro*, 210.

He also served on the steering committee for the county's proposed home for black youth and in 1926 began a five-year tenure as superintendent of the Old City Hospital.[26] Smith, a member of both the Masons and the Elks, had the social and political connections to generate support for the Monarchs and the new league. In fact, Janet Bruce asserts that Rube Foster may have first approached Smith about fielding a Kansas City team, but Smith's inability to acquire a lease for American Association Park proved too large an obstacle. Smith, however, had a demonstrated love for baseball. He annually accompanied Gilmore in the lead car for the Monarchs' season-opening parade, and in 1924 was chosen as one of the commissioners for the Negro World Series.

Frank "Jewbaby" Floyd was a former baseball scout and a licensed chiropractor who served as the Monarchs' trainer for thirty years. In addition to tending to the players' physical and emotional needs, Floyd supervised the locker room, and when Quincy Gilmore was away, Floyd tended the Monarchs' offices on Eighteenth Street. In the winter, he worked as a trainer for a minor-league hockey team.[27]

Equally important to the Monarchs' success within the African American communities were the team's accomplishments on the playing field. Wilkinson quickly put together a winning team, and in the early years of the Negro National League, the Monarchs were one of its most successful franchises. The team's triumphs received prominent display in all of Kansas City's black weekly newspapers. The newspapers also were the team's most ardent boosters. Readers of the *Sun*, the *Call*, and the *American* were encouraged to participate in the season-opening parade and to flock to American Association (and later Muehlebach) Park for the Monarchs' games. The season-opening ceremonies drew prominent African Americans from both sides of the state line as well as members of the major social clubs and fraternal orders. The games themselves were well attended. During the 1920s, it was not uncommon for the Monarchs' games to draw more than four or five thousand spectators. The crowds were racially integrated, and the Monarchs resisted any attempts by stadium management to enforce Jim Crow rules. The Monarchs' ability to attract black and white spectators also contributed to the team's legacy and its place of importance in Kansas City's historical memory.

The Monarchs represented one of the more stable franchises in the new league. Tensions over umpiring, scheduling, and player contracts

26. Kinsler, *Trip South; Kansas City Sun*, August 13, 1921.
27. J. Bruce, *Kansas City Monarchs*, 23.

were just some of the growing pains endured by the Negro National League in the 1920s. The league functioned well enough to promote the first Negro World Series in 1924. The Monarchs represented the NNL against Hilldale, champions of the rival Eastern Colored League (formed in 1922). The Monarchs won the ten-game series five wins to four (with one game called by darkness with the score tied). Three games of the series were played to capacity crowds at Muehlebach Park, a new fifteen thousand–seat ballpark at Twenty-second and Brooklyn that the Monarchs began using in 1923. The final game was played in Chicago, and pitcher-manager Jose Mendez hurled a two-hit shutout in a 5–0 Monarchs victory. The Monarchs were the "World's Colored Champions."[28]

The Monarchs also claimed the title of "Kansas City's Champions" in the 1920s. The team shared American Association Park and later Muehlebach Park with the Kansas City Blues, a minor-league baseball team. In 1921, the Monarchs challenged the Blues to a city championship series. The Blues won the series five games to three. A year later, the challenge was renewed, and the Monarchs easily won the series five games to one. Janet Bruce argues that the Monarchs' win in the 1922 series as well as a series of drubbings inflicted by other all-black teams on their white counterparts led Judge Kenesaw Mountain Landis, commissioner of the major leagues, to ban future series with black teams. As a result, the Monarchs' only chances to display their abilities to their white counterparts were in "all-star contests" or in winter barnstorming tours.

In addition to looking for talent in players, Wilkinson required that they be of high moral character. He instituted a dress code for travel; players were expected to wear suits. Fighting or possession of knives or dice was grounds for immediate dismissal. The Monarchs, according to Bruce, worked hard to be respectable representatives of black America. Of course, the players were not perfect. Because of the similarities in lifestyles, many of the players were friends with the jazz musicians who called Kansas City home. Both groups were celebrities in Kansas City's African American communities. Many of the players frequented the Street Hotel, as did many of the musicians. Both groups attracted large numbers of fans. Opportunities were plentiful for players to stray, but few apparently crossed the line as far as Wilkinson was concerned.

In the 1920s, the Monarchs' games at American Association Park and

28. For more details of the first Negro World Series and the politics involved, see J. Bruce, *Kansas City Monarchs*, 52–57.

later Muehlebach Park were the place to be for Kansas City's African Americans. Games often were fashion shows, with men and women shedding their work clothes and putting on their finery. The opening-day parade, organized by the Monarchs' booster club, drew thousands to watch team management and players, as well as bands from Lincoln High School and Western University, march through the East Side to the ballpark. The booster club, started by Quincy Gilmore and Howard Smith, drew the support of many of the prominent voices in the African American community: Chester Franklin, owner of the *Kansas City Call;* undertaker T. B. Watkins; businessman Felix Payne; Dr. John E. Perry; and most of the leading black ministers. White business owners in the black community also supported the team.

In addition to their NNL schedule, the Monarchs embarked on barnstorming tours during the spring, summer, and fall. In 1922, Janet Bruce notes, more than fifty communities wrote to Quincy Gilmore issuing challenges to the Monarchs. These games, played in the small communities of Kansas City's hinterlands, served a threefold purpose. First, they generated additional income that Wilkinson and the team desperately needed. From the league's inception, NNL teams struggled financially, with gate receipts from league games failing to cover the teams' expenses. These barnstorming games often drew two thousand to three thousand paying customers. Second, the tours increased the Monarchs' visibility in the Great Plains region and advertised the team and the league. Finally, the games gave Wilkinson and the Monarchs opportunities to scout players. Wilkinson and the Monarchs supported the Twilight League, a collection of black semipro and sandlot teams in Kansas City. The Twilight League, for instance, produced second baseman Newt Allen, who played for the Monarchs for twenty-eight years. Early in the decade, Wilkinson reorganized the All-Nations team and used it as a training ground for young players. The barnstorming tours allowed the Monarchs to identify some of the players who would be signed for the All-Nations team. Wilkinson also forged relationships with other semipro teams where he sometimes "stashed" players.

The Great Depression, however, dramatically changed the Monarchs' fortunes. Even before the economic crash of 1929, teams in the NNL had struggled. In fact, by that time, the NNL was a league in name only. Wilkinson elected to withdraw the Monarchs from the league after the 1930 season. For the next six seasons, the Monarchs thrived as an independent team, touring the country in their own private bus and playing to interracial crowds of three thousand to six thousand at Muehlebach Park. Although the economic downturn forced Wilkinson to reduce the Monarchs' roster, the team still played a schedule of eighty to one hundred games yearly. The key for the Monarchs was Wilkinson's purchase of a portable lighting system and generator in 1928. By towing the lighting system from town to town, the Monarchs increased their options for playing sites and times. They became the first professional team to play night games, which allowed the average worker to attend the games. Racial barriers also began to drop in many of the communities in which the Monarchs played. Though they sometimes faced other independent teams such as the All-Nations or the House of David (a team composed of members of a religious sect), the Monarchs often faced white minor-league teams in exhibition games. The Monarchs became the first black team to participate in a baseball tournament sponsored by a Denver newspaper. They traveled extensively, playing games throughout the South, Midwest, and West as well as in Canada and Mexico. Although the Monarchs sometimes relied on gimmicks, they relied more on their baseball skills to attract fans; they insisted on being portrayed as black professionals rather than as entertainers. Their demeanor on the field was matched by the way they carried themselves off the field. They took seriously their roles as representatives of African American society and culture. "You couldn't help but feel you were part of something special," said first baseman Buck O'Neil, who joined the Monarchs in 1938. "And not only when you were in Kansas City, either. We carried ourselves like Monarchs wherever we went, and to people all over, we were Monarchs."[29]

In the mid-1930s, the Negro National League was revived, and a year later, in 1937, the Monarchs joined the new Negro American League. Both of the new leagues struggled financially in the 1930s, as did the Monarchs, despite the presence of such stars as Hilton Smith, Newt Allen, Bullet Joe Rogan, and Buck O'Neil. It was not until 1941, when pitcher Satchel Paige (the most recognized player in black baseball) recovered from arm problems and joined the Monarchs that the Kansas City team regained a solid footing financially. A consummate showman and athlete, Paige had been pitching professionally for more than a decade when he signed with Wilkinson in 1939. While waiting for his arm to recover, Paige played with Wilkinson's All-Nations team for two years before joining Kansas City on almost a full-time basis in 1941. For the next decade, Paige was the dominant attraction in the Negro Leagues, and the Monarchs became the dominant team. The Monarchs

29. Ibid., 67–97. O'Neil, with Steve Wulf and David Conrads, *I Was Right on Time: My Journey from the Negro Leagues to the Majors,* 98.

won Negro American League championships in 1937, 1939, and 1940 and with the pitching tandem of Paige and Hilton Smith (considered by many to be a better pitcher than Paige) added league crowns in 1941, 1942, and 1950. In 1942, the Monarchs claimed their second Negro World Series championship. Despite wartime restrictions on travel and night baseball, the Monarchs averaged six thousand to seven thousand fans a game at Muehlebach Park. When Paige pitched, crowds approaching thirty thousand were not uncommon. The Monarchs' success on the field was rewarded with an increase in wages. Star players made as much as one thousand dollars a month (five to ten times more than an average black worker in Kansas City made); other players still made three hundred to five hundred dollars a month. Satchel Paige reputedly made thirty thousand to forty thousand dollars a year.

Yet the end of the Negro Leagues' ascendancy was nearly at hand. In 1945, a former All-American football player from the University of California at Los Angeles, Jackie Robinson, signed with the Monarchs as an infielder. At the same time, the end of the Second World War brought a renewed call by African Americans for the end of segregation in American life and black inclusion in the mainstream culture. African American newspaper editors and activists began to pressure team owners in the white major leagues to reopen their game to black players. Faced with dwindling attendance and increasing black presences in northern urban areas, the owners eventually acquiesced. In 1947, Brooklyn Dodgers owner Branch Rickey signed Robinson away from the Monarchs. Robinson became the first African American to wear a major-league uniform in more than fifty years, and he led a wave of black players into the majors. Satchel Paige, Ernie Banks, Elston Howard, and Buck O'Neil were some of the former Monarchs who moved on to major-league careers. With the integration of the major leagues, the Negro Leagues lost part of their reason for being. Support for the Negro League teams dwindled over the next decade, and by the 1960s, all but the most hardy of the franchises had folded. The Monarchs, champions of black baseball, played their last game in 1964.[30]

Other Amusements

> I'm awake. I'm away!
> I have jewels in trust,
> They are rights of the soul

30. J. Bruce, *Kansas City Monarchs*, 98–132.

That are holy and just;
There are deeds to be done,
There are goals to be won,
I am stripped for the race
In the glare of the sun
I am throbbing with faith
I can! And I must!
My forehead to God
My feet in the dust.
—Aaron Douglas,
"The Black Runner" (1926)

Although jazz and baseball often are considered the outstanding achievements and contributions of Kansas City's African American communities, in reality they represented just a fraction of the leisure activities available to the city's black residents. Activities sponsored by churches, the YMCA, YWCA, and Urban League were just as significant in the lives of Kansas City's African Americans. In addition, like other Americans, black residents of Kansas City were rapidly becoming enthralled with the new mediums of the radio and the talking motion picture. In the 1920s and 1930s, theaters within the black community continued the transition from stage productions to movies. New theaters such as the Love, Eblon, and Gem opened. African Americans also availed themselves of the entertainments offered by amusement parks.

In 1907, owners of the Heims Brewery near Brush Creek Boulevard and The Paseo opened Electric Park nearby. The "great white city" boasted one hundred thousand incandescent lightbulbs, which were used with great effect to showcase the scenes of castles and waterfalls throughout the park. Electric Park was built as a lure for Kansas City families to use the streetcar line, financed by the brewery, that ran from the city's core to the new Heims plant. Electric Park remained an amusement attraction into the 1920s, but the "great white city" remained that, as far as Kansas City's African American communities were concerned during the 1910s. People of color apparently were not welcome to visit Electric Park and to see its replica of a German village or to sail along its tunnel of love. It was therefore a matter of much significance when a group of African Americans leased Electric Park for the sole use of black Kansas Citians for three days in September 1922.[31]

31. Schirmer and McKinzie, *At the River's Bend,* 154; *Kansas City Sun,* September 2, 9, 1922.

The outing was organized by Don Hayden and members of some of the many fraternal orders in black Kansas City. An advertisement for the gala, run in the *Kansas City Sun,* offered that it would be the "greatest three-day event ever pulled off by" Kansas City's African American communities. Twenty cents would gain admission to the park, where all the attractions and all of the concessions would be made available. The organizers and the park's management also assured that "every protection" would be accorded the black patrons. For these three days, it is assumed, black Kansas Citians would be free from the segregated and discriminatory practices they faced in other amusement venues, and despite the reservations of "disgruntled and pessimistic persons" (as Nelson Crews styled them), the three-day carnival was deemed a success. Special children's activities were offered Tuesday afternoon, and "flappers" and members of the fraternal orders gathered on Wednesday night. The opening-night crowd on Monday was less than organizers had hoped for, but by Wednesday, the park was filled with enthusiastic black men and women. Many, Crews noted, were already planning for a repetition of the gala the following year.[32]

There is no record of a return of African Americans to Electric Park the following year or any subsequent year. Sherry Lamb Schirmer and Richard D. McKinzie note that even before the Great Depression, amusements such as Electric Park had fallen on hard times, the victims of the increasing sophistication of American tastes and the advent of talking movies and the radio as forms of entertainment. And it is impossible to ascertain the motives of the park's management in deciding to manipulate the community's less-than-rigid Jim Crow traditions. Was the decision completely altruistic, an attempt to bolster sagging revenues, or some pragmatic melding of the two? Or was it motivated by the opening of a new amusement facility, solely for the use of African Americans, near the Leeds district earlier that summer?[33]

Liberty Park, at Thirty-fourth Street and Raytown Road, was billed as the only amusement park in the United States for the exclusive use of African Americans. The Liberty Amusement Association was established by three Kansas City promoters, at least two of whom were white. Gilbert C. Lea, president of the Liberty Amusement Association, had worked for nineteen years for the Fern Laundry. Robert E. McBride, the association's vice president and general manager of the park, had more than twenty years' experience as a manager of entertainment

32. *Kansas City Sun,* September 2, 23, 1922.
33. Schirmer and McKinzie, *At the River's Bend,* 154.

enterprises, and J. B. Smith, the secretary-treasurer, had worked as a cashier for a Kansas City corporation for eighteen years.[34] Together they raised twenty-five thousand dollars to purchase about fifteen acres tucked in a valley on the west side of Raytown Road. Charles A. Astwood, a salesman for the Square Deal Realty Company, was hired to promote the park in Kansas City's African American communities. After purchasing the property early in 1922, the group immediately began seeking investors to help finance improvements to the park. A dance pavilion, advertised as the finest in Kansas City, was constructed, and George Lee's jazz orchestra, on at least one occasion, provided the musical entertainment.[35]

Liberty Park also offered picnic grounds, a baseball diamond, a grove of trees where religious services could be held, as well as boat rides and a variety of concessions. The park was to be open daily from morning to evening, and admission was half of that charged at Electric Park: ten cents for adults and just a nickel for children. The park was accessible by trolley; patrons were advised to take the Thirty-first Street car to the end of the line, from where it was a short walk to the park. On Sundays and holidays, arrangements had been made for buses to run from Eighteenth and Vine and Twelfth and Highland to the park. Nelson Crews saw the opening of the park as filling "a long-felt need" among Kansas City's African Americans. It is not surprising then that Crews was among the speakers for the grand opening on June 18. He was joined on the speakers' platform by Charles Astwood, lawyer Charles Calloway, Fred Dabney of the Square Deal Realty Company, as well as Harry Bennett Burton, the mayor of Kansas City, Kansas; Stewart McCoy, former mayor of Independence; and John C. Pew, a member of the city council.

The grand opening started a flurry of activity at Liberty Park through the summer of 1922. One Sunday in July drew thousands of patrons, lured by free motion pictures, the dance pavilion, and the chicken dinners served by Charles Fuller. On July 22, a picnic was held for the benefit of the Colored Orphans Home in Kansas City, Kansas. Later in the month, the Huntsmen Club gathered at Liberty Park for its annual cele-

34. Lea and McBride were identified as Caucasian in the 1920 census and the *Polk City Directory* for 1922. McBride is listed as manager of Liberty Park in the city directory. Smith's ethnicity could not be determined.

35. Pearson (*Goin' to Kansas City*, 148–49) describes Lee's little orchestra as the "major rival" to Bennie Moten's dance band for supremacy among Kansas City's black bands in the 1920s. The Lee band is best remembered for launching the career of George Lee's sister, Julia Lee, the preeminent female vocalist on the Kansas City jazz scene in the 1940s and 1950s. The Lee band also helped launch the career of bebop pioneer Charlie Parker. See also *Kansas City Sun*, June 17, July 1, 1922.

bration, and in August, black employees of the Kansas City Bolt and Nut Company as well as laundry workers held their annual summer picnics. On Labor Day, members of the Willing Workers Club, made up of the African American employees of the Montgomery Ward catalog center, spent the day at the park. Frank N. Lane, executive secretary of the Kansas City Urban League, was on hand to supervise the athletic activities that day, and the Knights of Pythias band "enlivened the throng."[36]

When the park reopened in May the following year, it had two new managers: Percy Lee and Roy Dorsey, two founding members of the Beau Brummels social club. Lee was a teacher at the Attucks School who had been involved with a number of professional and fraternal organizations in black Kansas City. He was vice president of the Negro Teachers' Convention, president of the Manual Training Teachers' Club, and chairman of the membership committee for the Allen Chapel choir. Dorsey, the proprietor and owner of the Rajah Tailoring and Cleaning Establishment, also had links with various activities in Kansas City's African American communities. He was the first president of the Community Twilight Baseball League, an amateur organization that had drawn twenty-five thousand spectators for the fifty games of its first season in 1922. Dorsey also was a charter member of the local Elks lodge and an organizer of the Musicians' Union.[37]

Lee and Dorsey assumed the leadership of a park that offered the full gamut of amusements. In addition to the activities it offered in 1922, by 1923 Liberty Park boasted a crazy house, a Ferris wheel, a penny arcade, a pool hall, a fun house, a miniature railroad, and an ice-cream parlor and soda fountain. Liberty Park would remain a popular site for black Kansas Citians throughout the 1920s. But like Electric Park, Liberty Park could not compete against the advent of movie theaters and other entertainment options, and by the end of the decade it had closed. The site of Liberty Park was eventually acquired by the Kansas City Parks Department, and in 1967 funds were obtained to convert the space into a traditional park setting, still bearing the name of the original amusement park. Today, a solitary baseball backstop is the only permanent structure on the fourteen-acre site, and a sole wooden sign marks the home of Liberty Park.

Social clubs such as the Beau Brummels, the Cheerio Boys Club, and the Ivanhoe Club were other opportunities for recreation and

36. *Kansas City Sun*, July 22, August 26, September 9, 1922.
37. Ibid., May 12, 1923.

self-expression for African Americans. Each of the clubs combined social activities with service to the community. The Beau Brummels, formed during World War I as the Bon Vivants, originally organized to provide recreational opportunities for African American military personnel who took weekend leave in Kansas City. After the war, members of the club agreed to continue their recreational function for the community, and the club's annual party was one of the social highlights for Kansas City's African American communities. The Cheerio Boys Club was organized in 1926 by a group led by Ivan McElroy as another avenue for providing social, recreational, and charitable opportunities for African American men. The club drew from a wide range of occupations and professions; government employees mingled with members of the working class. The Ivanhoe Club (formed in 1909) was considered the most elite of the social clubs of Kansas City's African American communities. Nathan Young and William Young describe places on the club's guest list for its social functions as most desired. For example, the Ivanhoe Club's annual Christmas party in 1919 drew more three hundred guests to the Labor Temple; partygoers came from ten states and were drawn from a "rigidly selected list" of guests. Noted pianist Clyde Glass provided the music, with vocal assistance from Anna Smith and Beatrice Lee.[38]

The men's social clubs had their women's counterparts as well. Although most of these groups were drawn together under the banner of the City Federation of Colored Women's Clubs, the most prominent was the Inter-City Dames, an aggregation of about forty black women from the two Kansas Cities who first came together early in the twentieth century.[39] The club's function was solely social; the members served as official hostesses for prominent visitors to Kansas City through the interwar period. Among the guests to be entertained by the club were singer Azalia Hackley and the wife of Booker T. Washington.[40]

When African Americans in the two Kansas Cities organized a benefit concert for the Paseo YWCA in 1919, they invited a promising

38. Young and Young, *Your Kansas City and Mine*, 74, 76; *Kansas City Sun*, January 4, 1919.

39. The date of origin of the Inter-City Dames is subject to dispute. Young and Young (*Your Kansas City and Mine*) put the founding in the early 1920s, an article by the *Kansas City Call* in 1959 cites an origin near the turn of the twentieth century, while an undated document in the Franklin Collection at the Mid-America Black Archives cites 1908 for the group's start.

40. Young and Young, *Your Kansas City and Mine*, 74; *Kansas City Call*, June 5, 1959; undated document, Franklin Collection, box BA4.FRA07, folder 0408.

young violinist, Clarence Cameron White, to be one of the featured performers. White would gain an international reputation for his work as a violinist and orchestra conductor as well as for his compositions based on African American and Haitian themes. For his appearance in Kansas City, White performed a diverse program of his own works as well as those of Dvorák and Samuel Coleridge-Taylor.[41]

In March 1919, a movie theater in downtown Kansas City canceled its scheduled showings of *Homesteader*, the work of pioneering black filmmaker Oscar Micheaux. The decision to cancel the movie, which had drawn overflow crowds, appears to have been a curious one until the peculiar dynamics of Kansas City's racial environment are factored in. According to Nelson Crews's *Kansas City Sun*, nine out of ten moviegoers for screenings of *Homesteader* were African American, and the movie theater had discovered that its lease prohibited the sale of tickets to black patrons. Thus, to keep white Kansas Citians from being tainted by the presence of black Americans, a profitable property had to be relinquished. It appears that even the profit motive sometimes was held hostage to the illogic of racism.[42]

Kansas City boasted about a dozen theaters in the 1920s, most of which were downtown. These facilities combined live music and variety shows with an increasing number of moving pictures. The advent of "movies that speak," with dialogue and music included along with the picture, led to a dramatic rise in the popularity of moving pictures with all Americans. The Midland, Newman, and Royal Theaters were the first to offer talking pictures to Kansas Citians. Even before the advent of talkies, however, African Americans patronized many of these houses, much to the dismay of some African American activists. Those theaters that catered to whites enforced segregated seating for African Americans. Blacks were often required to enter the building through a back door and then seated in the balcony. When the Famous Georgia Minstrels, a troupe of forty entertainers, played the Grand Theater, the theater advertised that "both balconies were reserved" for African Americans. While members of the black professional class, particularly editors Nelson Crews and Chester Franklin, would excoriate theater owners for their treatment of black patrons, other African Americans saw an entrepreneurial opportunity and took advantage of it. In the years immediately after World War I, two black-owned theaters opened

41. Woodson and Wesley, *Negro in Our History*, 702.
42. *Kansas City Sun*, March 8, 1919.

in the Kansas City area: Love's Theater and the Eblon Theater. In addition, the owners of both the Gem and Lincoln Theaters made the decision to cater exclusively to an African American clientele.[43]

Love's Theater opened December 11, 1918, at Twenty-fourth and Vine Streets. The owner and proprietor was George Williard Kirk Love, a native of Kansas City and a graduate of Lincoln High School. A veteran of the Spanish-American War, Love returned to Kansas City and obtained employment as a clerk in the city treasurer's office for the next six years. After a decade of running a variety of businesses, Love opened his theater to a waiting audience. He immediately made it clear he was an African American catering to an African American clientele. When showings of *Homesteader* were canceled by the downtown theater, Love stepped in and obtained the movie for the remainder of its Kansas City run. When Love's Theater offered a screening of Douglas Fairbanks in *The Three Musketeers,* the advertisement in the *Sun* astutely pointed out that the movie was an adaptation of a novel by Alexander Dumas, "the world's Greatest Negro Writer." Love's appeal to African Americans was a success, at least in the first year. On one night in 1919, more than three hundred people were turned away because the theater was full for each of three shows. The *Sun* also noted that thirty-four automobiles were lined up outside that same night. Yet the luster quickly faded from the "Theater Beautiful" (as Love himself styled it). Although Nelson Crews lauded Love for making it possible for African Americans in Kansas City "to see any worthwhile motion picture without being Jim Crowed," Love was unable to sustain his early success. Competition from other theaters and a recession in the 1920s likely hurt business. In addition, Love was unable to consistently market movies catering particularly to African Americans. His showings mirrored those offered by downtown movie theaters and came after the films had already been run elsewhere in Kansas City. Thus, his offerings in the early 1920s included *Tarzan of the Apes,* William Hart in *Iron Test No. 6,* Charlie Chaplin in *Tillie's Punctured Romance,* Theda Bara in *The Forbidden Path,* and Ethel Barrymore in *Divorce.* The result was a serious decline in business in the winter of 1921–1922. That problem, coupled with a dispute between the black Masonic chapter, of which he served as royal grand patron, and the greater Masonic family, led to his premature death in 1922 at age forty-one.[44]

43. Undated advertisement in Gibson, *Mecca of the New Negro,* 251.

44. *Kansas City Sun,* February 8, March 8, 15, 29, October 4, 1919; December 11, 1920; February 11, April 8, 1922.

The next new theater to cater specifically to African Americans was the Lincoln Theater, which opened in 1920 at Eighteenth and Lydia. Morris Eisen, who also operated the Panama Theater on Twelfth Street, owned the Lincoln along with Morris Spicer, who operated a pawnshop and a theater near McGee Street and Independence Avenue. The first manager of the Lincoln Theater was Lawrence Goldman. The Lincoln was billed as "America's Finest Colored Theatre." It had room for fifteen hundred patrons and was equipped "with the latest and most costly projecting apparatus made." Like many theaters in the early 1920s, the Lincoln's program was a mixture of movies (silents and later talkies) with live performances. Opening day for the theater included a screening of Charles Ray in *The Egg-Crate Wallop.* All of the leading movie stars of the interwar period eventually graced the screen of the Lincoln Theater. Wednesdays, for instance, were "William Hart nights" at the Lincoln in 1920. The Lincoln also offered works by Oscar Micheaux and live shows on the Theater Owners Booking Association (TOBA) circuit. Rector's Knickerbocker Girls and George E. Glasgow's Red Hot Players were among the acts appearing in 1923. It also offered the first Kansas City production of Eubie Blake's *Shuffle Along,* the first Broadway musical production written and produced by African Americans. The theater owners also sponsored the Lincoln Players, a drama group of African Americans, in the 1920s. The Lincoln Orchestra, mentioned above, provided musical accompaniment, and indeed, the Lincoln was one of the consistent opportunities for employment for musicians throughout the 1920s and 1930s. In 1929, the Lincoln became the first theater catering to African Americans west of the Mississippi to offer talking pictures. At a cost of thirty thousand dollars, the Lincoln's owners installed equipment that offered a large segment of Kansas City's African American communities a chance to experience one of the technological wonders of the interwar period.[45]

A year after George Love's death, a second theater owned by African Americans opened on Vine Street. The Eblon Theater, at 1824 Vine, was owned and operated by Homer "Jap" Eblon. The sixty thousand–dollar "pleasure palace," which in some ways replicated the architecture of the Country Club Plaza, had room for one thousand patrons, and everything was designed with the customers' comfort in mind. An automatic ticket-taking machine greeted customers in the spacious lobby. Inside the theater, nattily attired ushers led patrons to the plush, wide

45. Ibid., February 14, 21 (advertisement), March 6, April 3, 1920; April 28, 1923 (advertisement); "Talking Pictures at Lincoln Theater," *Kansas City Call,* February 15, June 24, 1929.

seats. A specially designed cooling system kept temperatures comfortable. An orchestra, originally just five pieces, provided musical accompaniment for the movies and entertainment between features. A restroom for female patrons and a children's play area were among the other amenities the Eblon offered. In 1930, a few months after the Lincoln began offering talking movies, the Eblon acquired the new technology as well.[46]

Competition for the Lincoln and Eblon Theaters in the 1920s came from a variety of other places in and around the East Side. The Gem Theater on Eighteenth Street originally opened in 1909 but was remodeled in 1923–1924 for the new moviegoing public. Among the stars to appear on-screen at the Gem in 1924 were western stars Tom Mix and Hoot Gibson and Lon Chaney and Jackie Coogan. The Gayety offered early in the 1920s some of the finest acts on the TOBA circuit, including Sonny Thompson's Seven Colored Entertainers in 1923, Liza and Her Shufflin' Band, and Dave "Snuffy" Marion with Leona Williams (America's foremost syncopated star).[47] As the facilities were identified primarily with African Americans, seating was on a nonsegregated basis. Activists in the African American community, including Nelson Crews and Chester Franklin, urged black theatergoers to patronize these East Side establishments rather than subject themselves to the indignities of Jim Crow that were common in most of the downtown facilities. By the end of the interwar period, then, theaters such as the Gem, Lincoln, and Eblon had a monopoly on African American patrons. They would continue to provide entertainment to the black community for years after World War II.

Late in the nineteenth century, a black visitor to Kansas City remarked on the lack of horizontal divisions within its African American communities. "The ones who constitute society here," the visitor told the *American Citizen*, "are the common every day People and cannot be called high-toned or above anyone; everyone appears to be on an equality here."[48]

Historian Willard B. Gatewood, who examined the development of class divisions withn the African American communities in most of the nation's major cities before World War I, scoffed at the visitor's com-

46. Advertisement, *Kansas City Call*, October 26, 1923; "Theatre Is Only One Owned by Colored People," ibid.; Gibson, *Mecca of the New Negro*, 98.

47. Advertisement, *Kansas City Call*, September 28, 1923; undated advertisement in Gibson, *Mecca of the New Negro*, 126–29.

48. *Kansas City American Citizen*, January 15, 1897.

ment and blamed it on the visitor's "casual" knowledge of the community. Yet, in many respects, the visitor's remark is more on target than Gatewood allows. Even by 1920, Kansas City did not have a well-defined "black aristocracy." It had a privileged class, but with just a few exceptions, members of that class did not maintain lives separate from those of the city's black working class. The residences of members of a certain profession might cluster on one city block (for example, teachers), but their neighbors were as likely to be janitors or street laborers as they would be other professionals. Even on so-called Negro Quality Hill (Twenty-fourth and The Paseo), working-class men and women mingled with doctors, teachers, and businessmen. Professionals or working class, black men and women supported the same churches and institutions, attended the same events, and sent their children to the same schools.

Two preconditions for the development of a black elite class, cited by Gatewood, did not exist in Kansas City.[49] In cities with a definable black aristocracy, Gatewood notes that most had a sizable free black population before the Civil War. Not only did Kansas City not have a large population of free blacks before 1860, it also lacked a black community of any discernible size. There also is no indication that mixed-race individuals (mulattos) gained any particular advantage in Kansas City's black communities. Although Samuel Bacote and Hugh and Myrtle Foster Cook, for example, appear to have been fair-complected, Nelson Crews, James Wesley Hurse, and Josephine Silone Yates were dark-skinned individuals. The final factor in the development of this almost egalitarian community was provided by Kansas City's reputation as a frontier city, sitting as the "Gateway to the West." Black men and women who came to Kansas City after 1865 were looking for economic and social opportunities. Many of them would describe themselves as self-made individuals who had gained their status in the community not through family wealth or connections but through their own hard work. The largest division in Kansas City's black community before World War II was between those who strove for success and those who did not.

Although Roy Wilkins would later argue that a small group of elites in the Ivanhoe Club dominated black society in Kansas City in the 1920s, the guest list of an elaborate party thrown in 1920 best illustrates just how egalitarian the African American community could be. In October of that year, B. B. Francis and his wife, of 1412 Vine Street,

49. Gatewood, *Aristocrats of Color,* 7–38.

organized a party in honor of their son, Nicholas P. Francis, and his wife. The younger Francises were returning to the Kansas City area for a visit, along with a friend, Charles Frazier of Grand Canyon, Arizona. The guest list at the Francis home consisted of 150 people, including a number of young single women. Also in attendance were two physicians, J. E. Dibble and E. C. Bunch, and their wives, along with Samuel Hopkins and his wife. Hopkins was the owner of Square Deal Realty and Square Deal Oil and Gas. They were joined by the Reverend Felix Isaacs, the new pastor at Allen Chapel AME Church, and his wife, and Theo Clay, a postal carrier, and his wife. As far as can be determined using city directories and census data, the bulk of the guest list, however, was made up of members of Kansas City's black working class and their spouses. Aaron Fox, of 1304 Highland, was a porter; Pompey Scott, of 2126 Highland, was a porter for the Firestone Company; Richard Gaines was a porter for the Greenlease Motor Company; Louis Collins, of 2001 Highland, was listed as an employee of the Fidelity Safe Deposit Company; and Robert J. Armstrong of Kansas City, Kansas, was a messenger for Gate City National Bank. William McKnight was listed as a laborer in the 1920 city directory, but he also had worked as a waiter. G. A. Page, Charles Fields (1331 Vine Street), W. B. Garrett (2218 Flora), W. H. Hubbel (2628 Highland), and Steve Burnett (2018 Bales) were all listed as laborers. The class divisions apparently were not always as great as Wilkins and Gatewood would have us believe.[50]

Class distinctions were also masked within the memberships of the various fraternal orders and social clubs that existed within Kansas City's African American communities. These organizations provided opportunities for the janitors, laborers, and domestics to shed their work clothes and to mingle with teachers, businessmen, lawyers, and doctors. Class tensions within these clubs undoubtedly existed, but they proved ultimately irrelevant to the dynamics of race. In 1912, Asa Martin identified thirteen men's and women's fraternal orders and auxiliaries among Kansas City's African Americans. The Masons, Knights of Pythias, and Elks all drew from the ranks of both the professional and the working classes. According to Martin, the men's and women's fraternal orders and auxiliaries claimed more than eight thousand members combined. He did note that many African Americans held memberships in more than one of the groups.[51] One fraternal

50. A list of some of the guests appeared in the *Kansas City Sun*, October 23, 1920.
51. A. Martin, *Our Negro Population*, 140–43.

order not mentioned by Martin was the Elks, which had become moribund. The attention and agitation of Quincy Gilmore helped revive the order, and in the summer of 1920, Gilmore arranged for the black Elks to hold their national convention in Kansas City.

The arrival of the ten thousand African American visitors was a milestone in the history of the Kansas City chapter. The convention also confirmed the web of connections between the African American communities on both sides of the state line as well as the limits on black life in the early 1920s. Black men and women from both Kansas Cities were required to transport, house, and on occasion feed the visitors, as there were not enough hotels and restaurants to accommodate such an influx of African Americans. Gilmore, who by then was serving as exalted grand ruler of Midwest Lodge no. 233, was credited with making the convention a success, along with the efforts of lawyer L. Amasa Knox and undertaker Theron B. Watkins.[52]

To escape the heat of summer, those black Kansas Citians who could afford it headed to cooler environs.[53] In the 1920s, for example, Garrison School principal Richard T. Coles and his wife spent the summers with other black professionals in the woods of Idlewild, Michigan. Later in the 1920s, African Americans in Kansas City began seeking refuge at Lake Placid in the foothills of the Ozark Mountains, making the 115-mile drive for fishing and relaxation. Dr. Perry C. Turner, superintendent at General Hospital No. 2 from 1933 to 1945, took credit for finding and naming the area. As chairman of a committee for the Chi Delta Mu medical fraternity early in the 1930s, Turner sought a recreational area near the lake for the use of his peers. The committee finally found a suitable site near a man-made dam. Turner described the lake as smooth as a mirror and commented, "This is Lake Placid." The name stuck, and well into the twentieth century, Lake Placid remained a haven for African Americans.[54]

Movies were just one of the entertainment options for African Americans during the interwar period, though by the end of the 1930s they had surpassed other traditional entertainments in popularity.

52. *Kansas City Sun*, July 24, September 4, 1920.

53. Historians are just beginning to investigate the leisure activities of black Americans during the first half of the twentieth century. See, for example, Myra B. Young Armstead, *"Lord, Please Don't Take Me in August": African Americans in Newport and Saratoga Springs, 1870–1930*.

54. For Turner's quote, see Young and Young, *Your Kansas City and Mine*, 58.

Intellectual forums, held at the leading churches and at Lincoln High School, had become outdated. Outings to Liberty Park, however, remained popular with African American consumers as did dances and socials at the Community Center, the Labor Temple, Lincoln Hall, and other venues. Although segregation often shaped the possible choices, African Americans in Kansas City kept themselves entertained and distracted from the rigors of everyday life. The impact of segregation on African Americans, particularly at home, is what we shall explore next.

Seven

Housing

The other morning as I lay in bed, I heard an explosion, the second in six weeks' time—Kansas City was at work on its housing problem.

—CHESTER A. FRANKLIN,
"AMERICA'S ADVENTURE IN BROTHERHOOD" (1926)

An ef anyone come ast you
Who were it wrote dis heah song
Ah's a pore nigger in worn-out duckins
Alookin' fo' a home
Jes alookin' fo' a home.

—UNNAMED WORK SONG, QUOTED IN
"NEGRO SONGS OF PROTEST: NORTH AND
SOUTH CAROLINA AND GEORGIA," BY LAWRENCE GELLERT

AFRICAN AMERICANS IN Kansas City lived in numerous discrete districts during the interwar period. Of course, the transformation of the Eighteenth and Vine district into the heart of the black community had already begun, but the rigid geographical demarcation of a singular, solitary black community would not occur until after World War II. Sociologists Douglas S. Massey and Nancy A. Denton, using Stanley Lieberson's ward-level census data, computed the spatial segregation by race of fifteen "northern" cities, including St. Louis and Kansas City. Massey and Denton's analysis determined that, compared with

1900, African Americans in Kansas City were more than twice as likely in 1930 to live in an all-black neighborhood. Their computations, however, indicate that more than two-thirds of black Kansas City still lived in racially diverse neighborhoods in 1930. In fact, Massey and Denton reveal that while racial segregation increased in Kansas City between 1900 and 1930, it increased at a slower pace than in most of the other northern cities studied. In 1910, when its black population stood at 23,556, Kansas City had the highest rate of spatial segregation of any of the fifteen cities. Twenty years later, five cities—Chicago, Cincinnati, Cleveland, New York, and St. Louis—had surpassed Kansas City, and a sixth, Detroit, was almost statistically even.[1]

Black spatial isolation in parts of the Troost-Vine corridor was offset by African Americans living in scattered pockets on the West Side, in the Church Hill area, and elsewhere. These longtime pockets of black residency apparently countered little opposition. It was only when African Americans attempted to expand the boundaries of the East Side that they encountered acts of violence.

Dynamite seemed to the weapon of choice of whites who opposed black spatial expansion. As early as 1911, African American home owners were met by homemade bombs when they settled in certain parts of the city. In some cases, it appears violence was meted out only when the percentage of black residents on a block or within a neighborhood surpassed some undefined but critical limit. For instance, in 1911, the NAACP's national office reported receiving this correspondence from a black resident of Kansas City:

> We desire to place before the legal department of the N.A.A.C.P. the case of a group of Negroes of Kansas City, Mo., who have suffered repeated attempts to destroy their property by an organization of white men who have demanded that they leave the neighborhood. There are nine Negro families in one block and twelve in the next who have purchased or are in progress of buying their homes, ranging in price from $1,500 to $4,000. In the block in which I live five explosions of dynamite have occurred in the past year, causing considerable damage to our homes and much mental uneasiness on the part of our families. The last of these, which

1. Douglas S. Massey and Nancy A. Denton, *American Apartheid: Segregation and the Making of the Underclass*, 23. See also Massey and Denton, "The Dimensions of Residential Segregation." Sociologist Robert L. Boyd ("Racial Segregation and Insurance Enterprise among Black Americans in Northern Cities") uses Massey and Denton's computations to examine the relationship of spatial segregation and black entrepeneurship, particularly in the insurance industry.

Table 7.1.
Black Spatial Isolation in Fifteen Northern Cities, 1900–1930

City	1900	1910	1920	1930
Boston	6.4	11.3	15.2	19.2
Buffalo	4.4	5.7	10.2	24.2
Chicago	10.4	15.1	38.1	70.4
Cincinnati	10.1	13.2	26.9	44.6
Cleveland	7.5	7.9	23.9	51.0
Detroit	6.4	6.8	14.7	31.2
Indianapolis	15.1	18.5	23.4	26.2
Kansas City	13.2	21.7	23.7	31.6
Milwaukee	2.4	1.9	4.1	16.4
Minneapolis	1.6	1.7	2.1	1.7
Newark	5.5	5.4	7.0	22.8
New York	5.0	6.7	20.5	41.8
Pittsburgh	12.0	12.0	16.5	26.8
St. Louis	12.6	17.2	29.5	46.6
Means	8.6	10.7	18.4	32.1

Black spatial isolation (BI) is "the extent to which blacks live in neighborhoods that are predominantly black." A BI value of 100 indicates that all blacks live in neighborhoods that are 100 percent black; a value less than 50 indicates that, on average, blacks live in neighborhoods that are less than 50 percent black, meaning blacks are more likely to have whites than blacks as neighbors.

Source: Douglas S. Massey and Nancy A. Denton, *American Apartheid: Segregation and the Making of the Underclass,* 23.

happened November 11, was by far the most destructive of them all, completely wrecking the home of Mr. Hezekiah Walden. At that time, Mr. Walden was in Salt Lake City[,] and his wife with two small children were alone in the house.

We have again and again appealed to the mayor and the chief of police to give us protection from these crimes, but the detectives have been of no help either in running the perpetrators to earth or in checking further threats and outrages. We feel that we have a clear case against the city, inasmuch as we have faithfully discharged our duties as citizens, and we are about to retain eminent legal counsel to defend our cause. In addition to this, we beg that we may have the assistance of some member of the legal department of the N.A.A.C.P., who will join us in vigorously prosecuting the case.[2]

2. "Second Annual Report, N.A.A.C.P.," quoted in Herbert Aptheker, *A Documentary History of the Negro People in the United States,* 3:37–38.

The case of Hezekiah Walden involved the transformation of the 2400 block of Montgall. Sometime in 1910 or 1911, Walden and his family attempted to move into a home at 2442 Montgall, one block east of Prospect. Walden is listed in the 1910 city directory as a teacher at Lincoln High School, and he would have been joining several of his colleagues at Lincoln who had bought homes on Montgall, including Anna Jones and Hugh O. Cook, vice principal of the school.[3] By 1911, violence against black residents had begun. It would not deter any of the African Americans who had chosen to live there. Jones maintained her home on the block until she retired in 1919 and moved to California. Cook and his wife, Myrtle Foster Cook, remained in their home. It may have taken several months for the Waldens to repair the damage and return to their home on Montgall. They are not listed in the 1911 city directory, but the family is listed in the 1912 city directory and lived at the residence at least through 1917.

To pursue action against the bombers, the NAACP legal department contacted white attorneys in Kansas City but gained no information on the matter and promised to continue to investigate. It apparently did not matter; dynamite greeted the first black families on some blocks in Kansas City into the 1930s. In 1919, dynamite was used on the home of Samuel and Lucy Bacote in the 2200 block of Kansas Avenue (three blocks east of Prospect); the Bacotes had lived on the block for twelve years before their residence was attacked. Three years later, the home of Dr. W. H. Bruce in the 1200 block of East Twenty-sixth Street was bombed three times in one summer. The same year, the home of two sisters, Sadie Collins and Ida Williams, in the 2200 block of East Twenty-first Street, was dynamited a month after the women moved in.[4]

When violence was not an option, white Kansas Citians used other means to limit the expansion of African American settlement. Fear of African Americans living nearby led whites in the area around Twenty-seventh and Woodland to petition the city for the creation of a park overlapping Twenty-seventh Street. Spring Valley Park was to serve as a buffer between black and white residential settlement.

The homes attacked by white vigilantes were some of the most attractive owned by African Americans in Kansas City. Few pictures or real descriptions of black-owned homes from the interwar period exist,

3. The 1910 city directory lists five other schoolteachers living on that block, including two more from Lincoln High School.

4. *Kansas City Sun*, September 13, 1919; May 13, August 12, 1922.

though the homes of some of the black professional class were described by contemporaries as tastefully furnished or attractively decorated.

Shortly after World War I, an African American entrepreneur encouraged readers of the *Kansas City Sun* to show their visiting friends the sights of Kansas City. Among those places deemed worthy of viewing were the homes of Dr. John E. Perry, Hugh O. Cook, and Anna Jones on Montgall; the home of James Dallas Bowser at Twenty-fourth and The Paseo; N. Clark Smith's home on Tracy; the Highland Avenue residences of Dr. D. Madison Miller, Nelson Crews, and James Holbert; and the "beautiful homes" occupied by African Americans on Michigan, Euclid, and Garfield Streets. These homes were to be seen in the same light as the Paseo YMCA as well as the magnificent apartment buildings on Linwood, Armour, and Benton Boulevards; the Country Club development; the elaborate homes on Sunset Hill and Swope Park; and the zoo. Though doubtlessly some of the comparisons are exaggerated, the tour guide's pride in the dwellings owned and maintained by a select group of African Americans is self-evident. Included among these attractive homes was that of Homer Roberts's two-story shirtwaist residence sitting atop the hill in the 2400 block of The Paseo. Few, if any of those homes, however, could match the Twelfth Street residence owned by Sarah Rector, Kansas City's first female millionaire, and her husband, Kenneth Campbell.

Sarah Rector, born in 1902 near Taft in Indian Territory (the northeastern part of present-day Oklahoma), gained her fortune through her status as a member of the Creek Nation. A year before Sarah's birth, the black descendants of slaves and former slaves who came west with the Creeks in the 1830s were declared citizens of the Creek Nation and entitled to land allotments of 160 acres. In 1916, oil deposits were found on Sarah's allotment, and through leasing agreements, she became a wealthy young woman. Before the end of World War I, Sarah and her family moved to Kansas City and settled on the West Side. In 1921, at the age of nineteen, Rector purchased a two-story brick home at 2000 East Twelfth Street. A year later, she married Kenneth Campbell (soon to be a partner in Homer Roberts's automobile dealership).[5]

According to contemporaries, Rector flaunted her wealth throughout the 1920s. In addition to her home, she purchased a number of expensive automobiles. She was a frequent customer of a downtown jeweler.

5. See Geraldlyn Sanders, "The Life of Sarah Rector," in *An Extraordinary Man*, by Restuccia, Gibson, and Sanders, 107–11.

On occasion, her three children rode to school in a chauffeur-driven limousine. She was also known to flout the Jim Crow conventions of downtown clothing stores. Rector was one of the few and possibly the only African American woman who was allowed to try on clothing before purchasing it. Her biography concluded that she used her wealth, at least in the 1920s, to overcome obstacles facing other African Americans in Kansas City at the time.[6]

Although not all of the homes of black Kansas Citians were as ostentatious as that of Sarah Rector or of the black professionals, affordable single-family dwellings were available in limited numbers to members of the black working class—at least through the early 1920s. In fact, in the years immediately after the First World War, at least two housing additions for African American home buyers were advertised in the pages of the *Kansas City Sun.* The Holly Addition, at Thirty-sixth and Topping in the Leeds district, was advertised for "Colored People, Exclusively." For as little as $1,450 ($50 down and $16 a month), African American home buyers could purchase a three-room bungalow (complete with closets). Within six months, most of the one hundred homes in the addition had been sold. Among the purchasers were Art Hackley, head barber at the Kansas City Athletic Club who bought a five-room bungalow for $1,800; Frank Sims, another employee of the Kansas City Athletic Club; and Susie Lewis, who also bought a five-room bungalow. Two years later, new homes for African Americans were built in the College Hill Addition around Garfield and Twenty-second and Twenty-third Streets. These homes, however, were at the edge of black settlement on the East Side, and the developer and home buyers met resistance from some whites in the area. At one point during the construction, a bomb inflicted minor damage on two of the houses, but homes in the addition were ready for occupancy by the end of 1922.[7]

The competition for new housing was intense and magnified, one contemporary observed, by the arrival of newcomers from the South "with money." A random survey of housing advertised in the *Kansas City Sun* and the *Kansas City Call* reveals a range of housing options for African Americans "with money." A cursory look also reveals that despite competition for the available housing stock, prices remained

6. Ibid. Rector lost most of her money by the 1930s, either as the result of the stock-market crash in 1929, poor investing, or the spending of her husband. A settlement she received after World War II from the oil companies allowed her to purchase a small farm in western Kansas City, Kansas.

7. *Kansas City Sun,* January 17, July 17, 1920; October 21, 1922.

relatively stable, allowing packinghouse worker John X. Brown and a janitor-turned-butcher, Robert Rose, to purchase homes during this period. Statistics compiled by the U.S. Bureau of the Census reveal the range in price ranges for African American home buyers. Of the more than 11,000 African American families in Kansas City in 1930, 16 percent (1,825 families) owned their own homes. Most (1,441 families) owned homes valued at less than $4,500. The largest portion of these 1,825 families (677, or 37.1 percent), however, owned homes valued between $3,000 and $4,499. In addition, 11 African Americans owned homes valued at more than $15,000 each, including seven worth $20,000 each. This range of prices is in direct opposition to conditions on the Kansas side. Although African Americans in Kansas City, Kansas, were more likely to be home owners than their neighbors in Missouri (51 percent to 16 percent), most of the homes owned by the Kansas City, Kansas, families were in the lower price ranges; more than 60 percent of black homes on the Kansas side were valued at less than $2,000 in 1930.

But much of the housing stock available to African Americans had not improved since Hugh O. Cook, working under the direction of the city's Department of House Inspection, surveyed the housing available in the Eighteenth and Vine district in 1912. Asa Martin, in his 1913 study, *Our Negro Population*, quotes a portion of Cook's report, and it is worth reproducing here:

> In all, the work covered 282 single houses and 59 apartments or tenements containing 2,463 rooms, of which 334 were without sufficient sunlight and 843 without sufficient ventilation. Of the total number, 1,251 were sleeping-rooms (more than 50 percent), of which 173, or 14 per cent, had less than 400 cubic feet of space for each occupant. This becomes serious when we take into account the unwillingness of many of those who live in such an unsanitary and congested neighborhood to give correct returns of all those who sleep under their roof. Of the total number of houses, 151 had city water in the yard and 126 had water in the house, leaving 64, or 18.7 per cent, without, except in a few cases where an old well or cistern furnished a limited and dangerous supply.
>
> There were 212 privy vaults, none of which had any water connection, and 52 of which had no sewer connection whatever; these latter, even with attention, cannot be anything but a menace to the health and comfort of the surrounding tenants.
>
> The question of cleanliness is so near to morality that I wish to call special attention to the lack of washing and bathing facilities. There are 267 sinks in the district, nearly half of the families being

> without, and but 99 bathtubs—1 tub to every 22 persons; but when you take into account that most of the apartments have a sink and bath for each apartment, you may readily see that the great majority of the 2,192 persons have neither.
>
> Two notable examples of this condition can be seen in the Hadley Flats at Nineteenth and Woodland and the Tait Flats on Nineteenth near Euclid. The former has 48 rooms, with a rear apartment of 20 rooms, and the latter 36 rooms, with a rear apartment of 10 rooms, all divided into two-room suites, with neither sink nor bath for more than 150 persons. The conscience of some owners ought to be aroused, if the city will not compel them to give these tenants a chance to be clean as well as to enrich some owner. These conditions are duplicated on Lydia Avenue near the Belt Line and at 1913–15–17–19 East Nineteenth Street.[8]

Housing conditions were not much changed in the 1920s and 1930s. They might be particularly brutal for the almost nine out of ten black families that rented homes or apartments. Some paid a little more than $20 a month (one week's wage) for a minimum amount of space in apartment buildings or converted residences.[9] Yet, according to Census Bureau figures, almost half of the city's African American families paid $20 to $50 in monthly rent. Despite those prices, black families found it hard to acquire adequate living space with a modicum of privacy. One-quarter of all black families renting rooms or apartments in 1930 took in unrelated lodgers. The economic crash of 1929 exacerbated the problem. George J. noted that his uncle had refused to take in roomers prior to 1929 but in the spring of 1930 was forced to accept lodgers. George's mother remarried in 1930; she, her new spouse, and George moved into a large apartment in the 1300 block of The Paseo. The apartment had been cut up, George recalled, into twelve rooms. The family lived in one room; they rented out the other eleven rooms. "Sometimes," George said, "we rented out the hallway. People were packed in like lambs going to slaughter. There were whole families sleeping in one room. All these people shared one bath."[10]

Overcrowded conditions taxed whatever sanitation systems were available and exacerbated health issues in the African American communities. Frayser T. Lane, executive secretary of the Kansas City Urban

8. Cook to L. A. Halbert, superintendent of the Board of Public Welfare, in A. Martin, *Our Negro Population*, 102–3.

9. The median monthly rent for African American families (N = 9,044) in 1930 was $20.47.

10. Page, *George*, 48–49.

League, though not the first to do so, made the important linkage between disease and poor housing conditions early in the 1920s. Lane's observations, drawn from a report he and his staff conducted for the Missouri Industrial Commission, are worth noting at length:

> On 4th Street near Troost Avenue there are four houses in which there have been three deaths from tuberculosis in four months. In the West Bottoms, the average is nearly one per month. The unsanitary and unhealthy conditions of these places is the cause. They are seldom, if ever, renovated. At 1832 Lydia there are no windows in the bed room, the toilet opens into the kitchen and there is no way to ventilate it. 1912 Tracy has not been papered in twelve years. Many houses have leaky roofs, rotten window sills and dead rats between the walls.
>
> Much evidence of this sort can be produced to prove that much of the property for which Negroes pay high rent is a culture media for tuberculosis germs.
>
> There is a very definite and close relation between the death rate among Negroes and the unsanitary houses in which they live.
>
> There is no housing code to regulate the type of buildings. Sanitary laws are not enforced in Negro districts, notwithstanding the fact that a large number of them are engaged in personal service as cooks, waiters, chauffeurs and laundresses. A few acts of prevention may save the expense of an epidemic and eradicate many evils.[11]

African Americans and concerned whites would continue to decry the condition of and constraints upon housing on the East Side throughout the interwar period and beyond. As more and more African Americans abandoned the West Side (as John X. Brown and his wife did) and moved into the East Side, conditions only intensified. More and more African Americans, aside from the Sarah Rectors and black professionals, found housing at a premium. More and more African Americans crowded into a rigidly defined geographic space. Yet the transition was not always instantaneous. An examination of two different neighborhoods on the East Side demonstrates some of the economic and social forces at work in Kansas City during the interwar period.

The intersection of Twelfth and Vine Streets was immortalized in song, yet it was another intersection—that of Eighteenth and Vine Streets—that came to symbolize Kansas City's African American community in the first half of the twentieth century. The intersection

11. *Kansas City Sun*, June 25, 1921.

represented the hub of African American entrepreneurship and African American culture as it was expressed in Kansas City. The Shannon Building, on the northwest corner, housed the Urban League office and its Community Center through the 1920s. The Lincoln Building, which opened in 1921, was the home of black doctors and lawyers. The Roberts Building complex, the site of Homer Roberts's automobile dealership, was just south of the intersection. The Street Hotel was just to the west. The Paseo YMCA and the YWCA were only blocks away. And within walking distance of the intersection were the homes of African Americans of all walks of life. Lawyer L. Amasa Knox made his home at 1825 Paseo, a mere two blocks away, until his death in 1945. His neighbors included porters at pool halls and hotels, a maid, a waiter, a laborer for the city, and a truck driver. A Pullman porter, an engineer, a butcher at a packinghouse, and a seamstress lived nearby. The Eighteenth and Vine area thus represented a microcosm of black life in Kansas City before World War II. An examination of the neighborhood, taken from the 1920 census, and of a neighborhood farther south reveals some of the dynamics of community formation within black Kansas City at the time.

Current perceptions of the Eighteenth and Vine area contain two popular misconceptions. One is the essential character of the neighborhood. Although the area is best remembered as a black business district, up until World War II, the Eighteenth and Vine area (for the purposes of this study, Seventeenth to Nineteenth Streets, The Paseo to Highland) was of mixed character. Retail and commercial usage was mixed with single-family and multifamily dwellings. Many business spaces also often included residential space, for owners, proprietors, or tenants. The second misconception is the extent and historical depth of black business development around Eighteenth and Vine. A significant proportion of the commercial and retail operations of the district up and through World War II were white owned, and most of these businesses had extended connections to the area. These businesses would help shape the nature and character of the development of Eighteenth and Vine as much as some of their storied black counterparts.

Life around Eighteenth and Vine

A visitor to the Eighteenth and Vine district in 1920 would have been struck first of all by the sheer density of the area, by the number of African Americans who claimed Eighteenth and Vine as their homes. He or she might also have been surprised to encounter the white Kansas

Citians native to the area. Some single-family dwellings remained in the area, but most of the residents lived in apartments or rooms adjacent to or above one of the many businesses around Eighteenth and Vine.

Let's start at Eighteenth Street and Highland and walk our way back toward Vine Street on the south side of the block. First we encounter a dwelling with two established households. One belonged to a native-born white from New York of Italian descent, a thirty-two-year-old female working in a laundry. The residence also included Mark Miller, a forty-two-year-old Pullman porter, and a thirty-seven-year-old woman, who is identified as Miller's "helper" in the manuscript census. Miller's household also included three male lodgers: a musician at a theater, a packinghouse butcher, and a seventeen year old working as a porter in a pool hall.

The next two residences housed the families of two single black women who worked as hair stylists. Samuella Lainge, a thirty-five-year-old divorced woman from Oklahoma, lived with her fifteen-year-old son. Stella Haughton, forty-six, had two lodgers living in her home, including a seventy-five-year-old Kentucky native who worked for a trucking firm. The census indicates that both Lainge and Haughton owned their own shops; it does not indicate if their residences also were their places of business.

Julius Jones, an engineer at a packinghouse, lived at the next address, with two male lodgers and a female lodger who worked as a laundress. A young married couple came next. Richard Young, twenty-two, worked as a truck driver for a coal company. His twenty-eight-year-old wife worked as a maid.

Next door was the family grocery owned by Henry Solomon. Solomon had been born in Canada of Russian-émigré parents. He and his parents entered the United States when Henry was five and apparently settled in Minnesota, where Henry met his wife. Both of their children, ages ten and six in 1920, were born in Minnesota as well. The Solomons shared the building with an African American family, a thirty-three-year-old widow and her five children.

Let's turn south on Vine now. In one dwelling we encounter Eunice Brown, a forty-two-year-old seamstress working out of her own home. Nearby was the home of John and Mabel Smith; John worked as a laborer for an auto company. Mary Nickels, a forty-year-old maid, lived nearby with thirty-year-old Maggie Smith and her two children. Eugene Carter, a sixty-three-year-old teamster for the city, also lived nearby. On the other side of the street, seventy-two-year-old Willie Brown, a cook, lived with his seventy-year-old wife and two lodgers, ages sixty-eight and seventy. A fifty-year-old woman lived farther south, with an adult daughter and a thirteen-year-old son; they shared the residence with a sixty-year-old teamster for the city and his wife. One more example is illustrative: farther south on Vine, we find the home of Mary Busbee, a sixty-four-year-old widow from Germany. Busbee's parents brought her to the United States shortly after her birth; she shared her home with her daughter and son-in-law.

The examples cited above are brief samples of the range and complexity of life around Eighteenth and Vine shortly after World War I. Black men and women of various ages, with various life experiences, had come to claim the area as home. In limited numbers, some white Kansas Citians were added to the mix. Few, if any, were native-born whites. In addition to the descendants of Russian and German immigrants mentioned above, Italian- and Scottish-born individuals were also scattered throughout the area in 1920. Many undoubtedly operated businesses within the region. Over time, however, the number of whites living in the area dwindled to none; some would continue to own their businesses around Eighteenth and Vine, but they would claim other parts of the city as their home.

Business Development around Eighteenth and Vine

One of the most prominent features in the area was the Lincoln Building at 1601 East Eighteenth Street. On its second floor sat the offices of six dentists and doctors: S. S. Hill, W. H. Bruce, Walter Maddux, McQueen Carrion, J. R. Williams, and J. Edgar Dibble. An advertisement from 1922 notes some of the other prominent tenants in the area: Highland Gardens, "Kansas City's Finest Outdoor Theatre for Colored People," sat at Eighteenth and Highland. The Public Drug Store, with W. P. Taylor as manager, sat on the northeast corner of Eighteenth and The Paseo; J. Matlaw, "Men's High Grade Furnishings," which just opened in 1919, stood at Eighteenth and Vine; and the Royal Barber Shop, Billy Bass proprietor, stood at 1616 East Eighteenth. On Vine Street south of Eighteenth, Ingram's Cafe, "The Home of Good Things to Eat," was at 1803; next door at 1805 Vine was Mrs. Stella Hubbard's "Fine Millinery."[12] These advertisements, of course, provided just a

12. The advertisements, likely taken from the *Kansas City Call*, appear in Gibson, *Mecca of the New Negro*.

partial representation of business development in the area. A more complete picture emerges two decades later.

A study conducted by the Urban League in 1946 illustrated the growth and limits of black businesses around Eighteenth and Vine. It did not delineate that particular area; instead, it examined business development on five major thoroughfares through the African American communities: Eighteenth Street, Vine Street from Twelfth to Twenty-fourth Street, Prospect from Eighteenth to Twenty-fourth, Brooklyn Avenue from Tenth to Twenty-eighth Street, and Twelfth Street. By drawing from the survey's conclusions, we can make some broad comments about the nature of business development in and around the Eighteenth and Vine area.

By the end of World War II, the study found 183 businesses operating on Eighteenth Street from Charlotte to Prospect (a twenty-two-block span). The study found another 55 businesses on Vine Street. Of these 238, 94 were owned by whites and 144 were owned by African Americans. White businesses on Eighteenth Street tended to have a longer tenure; the 83 white-owned establishments' average length of operation was sixteen and a half years, meaning many were established before the Great Depression. The average length of operation for the 100 black-owned businesses on Eighteenth Street was just seven years; many had started since the outbreak of World War II. Businesses on Vine Street tended to have about the same length of tenure (nine years for white owned and eleven years for black owned), and many apparently had started during and survived through the Depression. From these few statistics and surviving anecdotal evidence, we can advance a few conclusions: Business development along Eighteenth Street was an ongoing process from the end of World War I until and through World War II. White business owners on this east-west thoroughfare had claimed their niche in the African American community earlier than many of their black counterparts. Businesses on Vine Street tended to have been formed later in the period, probably as a survival tactic for individuals and families as opportunities for wage labor disappeared. These businesses tended to be small operations, with family members composing most if not all of the businesses' employees. The 209 black-owned businesses enumerated in the Urban League's study employed just 435 individuals, or slightly more than 2 employees per business. The majority of the employees were engaged in service occupations: 61 drove taxis, 56 were waitresses, 41 were beauticians, and 32 were barbers. The survey, in other words, demonstrates how limited African

American entrepreneurial efforts were in the first half of the twentieth century. Hampered by limited capitalization and the relative poverty of their target audience, black businesses in the Eighteenth and Vine area struggled to survive through the first four decades of the twentieth century. Some, through a combination of sound business judgment and plain luck, emerged into the postwar period. Many were not so fortunate.

Rapid Transition of a Neighborhood

Few neighborhoods in the African American communities better reveal how rapidly the process of community transformation can occur than did a two-block span of Forest Street (one block east of Troost). In a span of less than twenty years, the 2100 and 2200 blocks of Forest went from the home of native-born and immigrant white families to a community that was virtually all black. Oral traditions in the African American community have related the nature of this transition. An advertisement for Samuel R. Hopkins's Square Deal Realty Company stated that in the summer of 1923 all of the properties in the 2100 block of Forest (and on the adjoining block of Twenty-first Street west of Forest) were owned and occupied by whites, but by November all but two of the households had been replaced by African American families.[13] Hopkins's advertisement clearly overstated the case, but by using the sociological concepts of *persistence* and *precedence* we can offer an empirical look at how quickly the transformation occurred and some of its characteristics.[14]

The 1910 census identified forty-five different households living in the 2100 and 2200 blocks of Forest. Of that number, thirty-one (69 percent) of the households were headed by native-born whites. Thirteen (29 percent) were headed by foreign-born whites, including three each by Irish- and Russian-born immigrants. The two blocks also contained

13. *Kansas City Call*, November 23, 1923.

14. *Persistence* is defined as the percentage of individuals or families within a given geographical space who remain in the space after a given period of time. *Precedence* approaches the question from the opposite direction: It asks what percentage of individuals or families in that defined geographical space were present at a *previous* point in time. These percentages would be identical, of course, if the population of an area remained constant. Populations, however, are seldom—if ever—so obliging; the density of any area changes over time. That would be the case for the two blocks on Forest Avenue. By using manuscript census records and city directories, it is possible to trace the evolution of this two-block stretch over the twenty-year span.

one African American household. The war years then produced one of the dramatic transformations the two blocks experienced. By 1920, all but three of the households had moved out of their homes on Forest. All of the households headed by native-born whites in 1910 had disappeared by 1920. Other native-born whites had moved into the two-block span, but most of the new households were headed either by foreign-born whites (33 percent of the households) or African Americans (50 percent). By 1925, most of the newcomer whites had moved on, most to addresses outside of the burgeoning African American community. to be replaced by African American households. It is worth noting, however, that as quickly as the neighborhood transformed by 1925, it was as quickly stabilized by 1930. Almost half of the households identified by the city directory in 1925 remained in the neighborhood in 1930.

Even when African Americans obtained suitable housing, obstacles thrown up by hostile whites and negligent city officials could arise. In the fall of 1923, a garbage station was installed along the railroad right-of-way at Twentieth Street and Woodland Avenue, in the heart of a black residential district. The location of the site, in which garbage from all over the city was collected before it was transferred to the city dump along the Missouri River, violated a recently approved city ordinance, a fact that Chester Franklin of the *Kansas City Call* noted regularly over the next two months.[15] The headquarters of the Cosmopolitan Club, an organization of young black elite males, was just on the other side of Woodland from the offensive site.

The Attucks School, at Nineteenth and Brooklyn, and Western Baptist Bible College were within walking distance of the transfer site, and members of the congregation at Centennial Methodist Episcopal Church were met by the stench from the site at every service they attended. Franklin, in his typical no-nonsense style, attacked city officials for their seeming lack of concern. Why, the *Call* asked, had the city acted so promptly to remove a similar site from the West Bottoms, near the viaduct over the Kaw River that connected the two Kansas Cities? "If garbage is a nuisance along the Inter-City viaduct, it is nothing less than that in the midst of a residential section," the *Call*'s article said in a brief editorial aside in a front-page article. The headline for the article read "GARBAGE WITH THEIR MEALS!" and in it Franklin (or his new protégé, Roy Wilkins) described at great length the nature of the nuisance:

15. *Kansas City Call*, November 2, 9, 16, 30, December 21, 1923.

> Trickling rivers of filth, running leaky swill containers, swarms of flies, heaps of stable manure, rumbling trucks and shouting drivers, these are the civic center maintained in the choice of a residential district. . . . All day long to this one spot from all over the city trucks make a procession with their evil-smelling contents, there to be transferred, to other, larger containers and hauled away, all except that which is spilled on the ground in the transfer. . . . On all sides live respectable families, many of them owning their own homes. They cannot move, and these institutions cannot move. And the swill moves, and moves—in an unending circle through their very midst.[16]

In front-page articles through November and December, the *Call* reminded its readers of the offensive site. The headlines, however, were a challenge to city officials to rectify the situation: "GARBAGE WITH THEIR SERMON!" "GARBAGE WITH THEIR STUDIES: Twenty-four Hour a Day Smell May Force Western Baptist to Move, Says President," "Garbage with Their Games! Children at Attucks School Get Odors of Swill, Not Fresh Air, on Playground," and finally: "GARBAGE FOR XMAS PRESENT: Kansas City Will Send Greetings to Residents from Its Swill Station"[17]

The impact of the *Call*'s campaign cannot be ascertained with any certainty, but by 1925 the dump had been removed. It hardly matters; Sherry Lamb Schirmer points out that another garbage facility opened at Twenty-first and Woodland (still within the African American community) later in the decade.

Life in Leeds

The Leeds district, on Kansas City's eastern edge, was a distinct community for much of the interwar period. Its residents were attracted to the area, historian Gary Kremer notes, by its semirural nature. Many of its early residents were migrants from the South, and they wished to carry on the agricultural traditions with which they were familiar. The community developed its own institutions—churches, businesses, and an elementary school—and lived a life fairly separate from that of the more urban African Americans around Eighteenth and Vine. During

16. Ibid., November 2, 1923.
17. Ibid., November 2, 9, 16, 30, December 21, 1923.

World War II, male members of the community would find work at nearby industrial plants, and after the war, many gained work at the Chevrolet plant in the district or at a nearby railroad-tie plant.[18]

The Threat of Lynching

This is no Excelsior Springs.

—*KANSAS CITY CALL*, SEPTEMBER 4, 1925

On the first weekend of September 1925, readers of the *Kansas City Call* were regaled with a front-page story of a near lynching and the "bloodless race riot" it precipitated in the Eighteenth and Vine area. The tale contained all of the elements with which the *Call*'s African American readers were familiar: the alleged sexual assault of a white female by a black male, white vigilantes following bloodhounds straining at their leashes, the identification of a black suspect, and the immediate and imminent threat of vigilante justice. The *Call*'s story also contained additional elements: the intervention of one gallant African American hero followed by a surge of armed black men to protect the "hero" and the criminal suspect. Eventually, the suspect is deemed innocent, and white and black combatants fade back into their respective worlds and historical anonymity. In many respects, the tale is too good to be true. Yet the story of the near lynching is a valuable tool to assess the mind-set of the African Americans of Kansas City and the surrounding community.[19]

Although the incidents were separated by time and distance, residents of Kansas City's African American communities had no trouble recalling instances of legal and extralegal violence against black bodies. The race riots in East St. Louis and Tulsa would have been easily recalled, as would the outbreaks of racial violence in Omaha, Nebraska (1919), and Helena, Arkansas (1923). African Americans would also have noted extreme cases of police brutality in Kansas City, which were not uncommon in the early 1920s; a week before the near lynching occurred, two white police officers were cleared in the shooting death of a black Kansas City youth. Some of the older residents could recall the valiant stand in Kansas City, Kansas, by black veterans of the Spanish-

18. Kremer, "'Just Like the Garden of Eden.'"
19. "Near Lynching Brings Crowd to No. 6 Station," *Kansas City Call*, September 4, 1925.

American War to protect an African American high school student from a lynch mob. Some could likely recall that black veterans in Tulsa had attempted to frustrate a lynch mob as well. The most searing memory for Kansas City's African Americans was of more immediate vintage: the lynching of an African American male just three weeks previously in Excelsior Springs, a small Clay County town about thirty miles northeast of downtown Kansas City.

Unlike the tale of the near lynching, the lynching of thirty-three-year-old Walter Mitchell was well documented. At least two of the city's four daily newspapers gave the lynching and its aftermath front-page coverage, and the *Call*, a weekly, devoted significant portions of its front page in successive weeks to the story. *Opportunity*, the official journal of the National Urban League, ran a photograph of Mitchell's body hanging from a tree limb surrounded by white onlookers. The lynching, however, has received little attention from scholars, in part because on the surface it lacks unusual circumstances. Mitchell was accused of sexually assaulting a white woman, arrested, taken despite resistance by African Americans and white law enforcement agents from the county jail in Liberty, and dragged back to the "scene of the crime," where he was hung. Even the underlying "facts of the case," as ascertained by Chester Franklin and an investigator for the *Call*, lack any particular significance for most modern researchers.[20] Mitchell, according to the *Call*, was acquainted with the alleged victim. She was the girlfriend of one of Mitchell's white partners in a cattle-stealing gang that operated in Clay and Platte Counties in the mid-1920s. The assault allegation, the *Call* asserted, was the result of a falling out among thieves. Mitchell was guilty of a crime, the *Call* agreed, but not the one for which he was hung.[21]

For the two weeks after the Mitchell lynching, Chester Franklin and the *Call* kept its African American readers apprised of the few developments in the case—most of which involved various Clay County officials decrying the lynching (after the fact) and attempting to shift the blame

20. Most historians now acknowledge that most black lynch victims in the United States were not guilty of sexual assaults, as was portrayed at the time. Many lynching victims were not accused of such offenses until after the fact. Most rationales for lynching masked tensions between economic competitors, or in the Mitchell case, tension between black and white individuals. Little has been written, however, on how some whites could use lynchings or the *threat* of lynchings to control African American behavior.

21. "Innocent Man Lynched by Excelsior Springs Mob," *Kansas City Call*, August 14, 1925. See also *Kansas City Call*, August 21, 1925; *Kansas City Star*, August 7, 8, 9, 1925; *Kansas City Times*, August 8, 10, 1925; and *Opportunity*, 2:9 (September 1925).

onto others. In fact, the first subsequent issue not to mention Mitchell's lynching contained the story of the near lynching. Thus, the tale of the near lynching would have greatly resonated with residents of Kansas City's African American communities.

The near lynching occurred on what would have been an ordinary Friday afternoon and evening in the Eighteenth and Vine neighborhood.[22] The calm was shattered by the invasion of a group of whites from the Twenty-first and Montgall area, some on foot following bloodhounds and others in automobiles. The bloodhounds paused in front of the Yellow Front nightclub at Eighteenth Street and Forest Avenue and were encouraged by the whites to enter the building. There the bloodhounds paused in front of an African American man, identified by the *Call* only as Charles. Members of the white posse then began to lead Charles away and toward one of the waiting automobiles. According to the newspaper's account, there was very little if any conversation between the white vigilantes and the accused. Suddenly, a hero intervened. Oliver "Blue" Moore asked the white men what their intentions were toward the suspect. One responded that they were tracking a suspect in the sexual assault of a white girl in their neighborhood, while some of the whites began muttering about a lynching. At this point, Moore grabbed the steering wheel of the car into which Charles had been thrust and began to demand that the police be called if the whites suspected Charles of a crime. In response, one of the whites pointed a gun toward Moore, who steadfastly held onto the steering wheel. Suddenly, another black patron of the poolroom pulled a weapon, and an armed standoff began, with Charles squeezed into an auto, Moore clenching the steering wheel, and white and black men with guns drawn. The standoff ended with a summons to the police, and when law enforcement officials decided to take Charles in for questioning, blacks and whites followed. Meanwhile, word of the situation had quickly spread, and it was here that Franklin or the *Call* reporter was at his dramatic best: "About that time somebody did a Paul Revere, and roused the countryside. Never in the history of Kansas City have so many men, quiet, determined men gathered and they were [indecipherable] while doing it, and the cry was 'This is not Excelsior Springs.' Red lights against traffic at 18th and Paseo were not even observed. It was like the dash of the taxi cabs of Paris against the Germans at the first battle of the Marne." For Franklin's readers, there was no explanation necessary.

22. *Kansas City Call*, September 4, 1925.

Black Missourians had failed to protect Walter Mitchell in Excelsior Springs; they were not going to fail Charles now.

The dramatic standoff outside the Eighteenth Street poolroom proved to be the climactic moment of our tale. The victim of the alleged assault was allowed to view the suspect and bluntly said Charles was not the assailant. Police officials elected not to release Charles immediately, but his black protectors announced that they would stay at the station until he was released. With that, Charles was released and the whole episode was over. Yet any good tale must have a moral: besides the merits of dramatic, assertive group resistance, the story, Franklin argued, demonstrated the value of relying on the police department to fulfill its lawful responsibilities and maintaining constant vigilance.

The Great Depression exacerbated housing woes for most of Kansas City's African American communities. The outbreak of World War II and the resulting increase in industrial production in Kansas City and other urban areas drove the problem to the breaking point. Two studies conducted by the Kansas City Urban League in the 1940s illustrate the problem. A breakdown of the 1940 census by the KCUL revealed the increasing racial segregation of housing that confined African Americans to the east of Troost and to the north of Thirty-first Street. The same study also shows that significant clusters of African Americans remained on the West Side and in the Leeds area.[23]

The study shows that 29,497 of the city's 41,514 African American residents (71 percent) lived in the area bounded by Troost and Jackson, Independence Avenue on the north, and Thirty-first Street on the south. In three of the nineteenth census tracts in the area, African Americans made up more than 75 percent of the residents. In three others, black residents composed more than half of the population.[24]

In those areas outside of the Troost-Cleveland corridor, African Americans tended to cluster in significant numbers. The census tracts containing the Church Hill area remained more than 50 percent black. Two tracts on the southern edge of the West Bottoms had black populations of more than 50 percent. The study also demonstrated the resilience of the African American communities in Westport around St. James Church, in the Leeds district, and in the East Bottoms.[25]

23. KCULP, "A Matter of Fact," 1:2 (August–September 1945), box KCULP1, file 1.
24. Ibid.
25. Ibid.

The concentration of African Americans on the East Side coincided with the aging of most of the housing stock in the area. Another study, conducted by the Community War Services in 1943, noted that much of the black settlement on the East Side was in "deteriorating neighborhoods."[26] According to the confidential report, only fifty new dwelling units had been built for African Americans in the area in the previous twenty years. The report stated that most of the dwellings occupied by African Americans were in need of major repair or had no private bathing facilities. Most rents ranged from ten dollars to twenty-four dollars a month. The higher rents did not necessarily result in better facilities or increased privacy. About one-fifth of all of the dwellings surveyed averaged three people for every two rooms in the building. The study also noted, without drawing the obvious conclusion, that the greatest crowding was in those areas with the lowest percentages of rental property. Black home owners, it is apparent, often needed the extra income provided by boarders and lodgers in order to afford the housing they could obtain.[27]

The report made clear, as indicated above, that African Americans had begun to move into areas south of Twenty-seventh Street. "They are, however, merely taking over older and deteriorating neighborhoods," according to the report, "a logical development in view of the increasing population and dearth of new construction."[28]

The challenge to find decent, livable housing was the most daunting African Americans faced in Kansas City in the 1920s. A privileged few were able to acquire attractive homes and raise their families without the intrusion of lodgers or relatives. It is important to note, however, that not even the black professionals were immune to the overcrowded conditions. Some of their households included members of their extended families. Other professionals sought to escape the crowded conditions. Herman Kinsler, a self-described real-estate baron, owned an apartment building on Michigan. He found it necessary and possibly financially prudent to live in the same building as his tenants.

Although the housing situation appeared intractable, it did not destroy African Americans' sense of community. While dealing with the blatant discrimination enforced in the housing market as well as inequities in

26. KCULP, Community War Services, "Report on Negro In-Migration in the Greater Kansas City Area," 4–5, box H1, file 6.

27. Ibid.

28. Ibid., 6.

the educational and political processes, the residents of Kansas City's African American communities created a world of stable institutions in the churches and schools, social and fraternal organizations, and many of their businesses. Nostalgia often makes this world seem more perfect than it was, but it is equally misleading to concentrate on the harsh realities of black life. Life for African Americans in Kansas City in the interwar period was a mixture of the two, shaped by both impersonal forces and the personalities of the men and women involved.

Eight

The Challenges of the Great Depression, 1930–1939

The sensible thing for all is to realize that the old days of "rugged individualism" are succeeded by a new conception of social relations. The Negro worker must be placed in somewhere. What could be more logical than that he make his entry where his needs create the work?

—CHESTER FRANKLIN, *KANSAS CITY CALL*, NOVEMBER 19, 1937

AMONG TOM PENDERGAST'S enduring legacies to Kansas City was his ability to keep the city working through the worst of ten years of economic depression. Pendergast and his cronies in the city administration pushed through an ambitious set of civic improvements—the Ten-Year Plan—with three goals in mind: provide the city with much-needed changes in its infrastructure, keep able-bodied men off the relief rolls, and line the pockets of Pendergast and his associates. Historians have noted how well Pendergast achieved all three objectives before he was deposed in 1939. In this ten-year span, Kansas City constructed a new city hall and a new Jackson County courthouse downtown. The elegant Municipal Auditorium replaced Convention Hall as the site for artistic and cultural events. The zoo, the Downtown Airport, and the Municipal Hospital were expanded. Kansas City, in the midst of the greatest economic crisis the country has ever faced, seemed to be booming. And men were finding work. Pendergast had decreed, or so the story goes, that actual manpower—not machine power—would fuel this building binge. The number of men working on city projects escalated to as many six thousand a week. They did the work that machines could do more easily or faster, but that was not the issue. They were working, while much of the country sat idle. They were also helping make Pendergast and members of the machine rich. Much of the concrete used to line Brush Creek, for the runways at the Downtown Airport, and for the new municipal facilities came from Pendergast-controlled companies. It was a winning situation for almost everyone.

Their glee could be seen in Kansas City's burgeoning club scene. Pendergast's associates in the criminal underworld continued to operate their jazz joints along Twelfth and Eighteenth Streets throughout the Great Depression. The clubs provided diversions of all kinds—legal and illegal—to those with money to spend. And they provided jobs, particularly for musicians and especially black musicians, when few entertainment jobs were available elsewhere in the country. Most of Kansas City's jazz legends—Count Basie, Bennie Moten, and others—benefited from Kansas City's thriving music scene of the 1930s.

Yet historians are beginning to uncover just how much of a facade the Pendergast legacy was. Underneath the booming municipal construction sat a stagnant economy. Construction on projects that were not part of the Ten-Year Plan was almost nonexistent. As in other parts of the country, the construction of new housing was almost at a standstill. Other segments of the Kansas City economy also reflected the troubled times. The railroad industry had been in trouble *before* the stock market crash of October 1929. Two other vital components of the region's economy—the stockyards and lumber industry—were in dire straits as well. Jobs in those industries began to disappear, and those hit hardest were those on the bottom rungs of the job ladder, particularly African Americans. The blue-collar jobs in the railroads, stockyards, packinghouses, and stone quarries—the jobs that had sustained the African American communities through the 1920s—had all but disappeared after the first year of the Depression. And Tom Pendergast's economic miracle notwithstanding, African Americans would be hard-pressed during the 1930s to find suitable replacement work. Many would be hard-pressed to find work at all.[1]

1. Two major sources document the structural changes within the job market for African Americans. First is the statistical summary from the 1930 census. The numbers compiled by the census bureau's statisticians reflect a major—and negative—change in the range of work opportunities for Kansas City's African Americans. The second source are the records

Part of the Pendergast legend was the machine's use of small material gifts to influence Jackson County voters through the 1930s. How many African American families were offered or accepted these offers of aid is subject to debate.[2] It is apparent, however, that many African Americans in Kansas City were jobless or working too erratically to adequately support their families. They sought the assistance of a variety of agencies, but more often than not they ultimately ended up turning to the Urban League. For example, on numerous occasions, African Americans seeking aid from the Provident Association, one of Kansas City's oldest charitable organizations, were directed to the Urban League office. The Missouri Employment Service often was unable—or unwilling—to help black job seekers. They also were directed to the Urban League.

Within a few months of the onset of the Depression, African American workers—particularly black men—saw fewer job openings than they had ten years previously. They also found a racialized ceiling on what little work they would be able to obtain. In 1920, about 61 percent of the African Americans in Kansas City were involved in wage labor. Eight out of ten black males were working, while four of ten black females were listed in the census as wage laborers that year. A decade later, the percentages had changed perceptibly. The percentage of wage laborers in the black population fell a little more than two percentage points to 59 percent. While an increase in the black birthrate or an in-migration of young children into Kansas City could explain the slight change in the percentage of African Americans working, an analysis of the job market by gender indicates that the changes were more within the world of work than in the African American community itself. The percentage decrease among African American men working was precipitous. Whereas in 1920 80.5 percent of the black male population in Kansas City was in the job market, in 1930 just 72.7 percent of black males were wage earners. Even more indicative of the changed nature

---

of the Kansas City Urban League. The Urban League offices were the major arbiters between Kansas City's African Americans and the vagaries of the economic downturn, particularly after the state eliminated direct relief payments in Jackson County in 1932.

2. Larry Grothaus ("Kansas City Blacks, Harry Truman and the Pendergast Machine"), writing in the 1970s, argued that the Pendergast organization's ability to provide concrete assistance to African Americans—along with the increasingingly callous indifference of white Republicans—helps account for the swing of the city's black voters into the Democratic camp in the early 1930s. More recently, Lawrence H. Larsen and Nancy J. Hulston (*Pendergast!* 103–5) have documented that much of the Democrats' success in predominantly black wards was due to blatant voter fraud.

Table 8.1.
Distribution of African American Workers, 1930

All Occupations	Male	Female	Total
Agriculture, forestry, animal husbandry	63	6	69
Clerical occupations	158	101	259
Domestic and personal service	4,857	7,740	12,597
Extraction of minerals	130	—	130
Manufacturing and mechanical industries	4,365	289	4,654
Professional service	483	400	883
Public service	216	5	221
Trade	1,525	114	1,639
Transportation	2,370	26	2,396
Totals	14,167	8,681	22,848

Source: Kansas City Urban League, "The Negro Worker in Kansas City," box KCULP3, file 1, 53.

of black work, the percentage of black women in the job market increased by four percentage points (from 42 percent in 1920 to 46 percent a decade later). It is obvious, then, that black men were finding fewer work opportunities and that more black women were being forced to move into the workplace in order to sustain their families.

An analysis of occupational categories also reveals the changes in black work. In absolute terms, the number of African Americans employed in the stockyards and packinghouses declined dramatically between 1920 and 1930. Although changes in the statistical summaries of the census make direct comparisons difficult, it is safe to say that more than half of the sixteen hundred jobs in the stockyards and packinghouses held by black males from Kansas City, Missouri, in 1920 no longer existed or were held by native whites or foreign-born whites in 1930. The result was a mixed bag of occupational change. Inexplicably, the number of African American men engaged in professional pursuits almost doubled, though their numbers still made up just a fraction of the black male working population (3.4 percent). The other dramatic increase was less surprising: the number of black men involved in domestic and personal service (working as chauffeurs, barbers, porters, servants, and waiters) increased by almost one-third to more than forty-eight hundred.

Coinciding with the slide of black males back into the low-skilled and low-paying jobs was a similar decline in the occupational opportunities for African American women. The number of African American women working in 1930 increased by about twenty-two hundred from 1920; the number of black women working in personal service increased by almost twenty-one hundred. Clearly, the only job opportunities expanding for African American women in the first years of the Depression were as laundresses, waitresses, private nurses, and domestics. Even these jobs were not secure. Historians Carter Woodson and Lorenzo Greene, citing a 1929 article by the *Baltimore Afro-American*, note that a major Kansas City drugstore fired all of its black waitresses and replaced them with white women. As the Depression deepened, even those job opportunities would be limited, and black families began to rely more and more on outside agencies for support.[3]

Since its birth in 1920, the Kansas City Urban League had attempted to match African American workers with the needs of local industry. Unlike, for example, in Detroit, where the Urban League office served as a conduit between one major industry with a tremendous demand for labor (auto manufacturing) and recent migrants from the South, the Kansas City Urban League faced a much broader and in some ways much more demanding task.[4] The KCUL sought to break down racial barriers in employment and by persuasion open the doors to jobs long denied to Kansas City's African American workers. The KCUL, despite its connections with white businessmen who supported the league, could claim few even minor successes in this regard prior to 1929. For instance, the 1920 census lists 7 African Americans working in semiskilled positions in automobile factories (presumably at the Ford plant that opened in eastern Kansas City in 1912). By 1930, the number of African Americans employed in automobile factories, garages, and repair work had grown to 170 (many of them residents of the Leeds district near the new Chevrolet plant that opened in 1928 and the Fisher body plant that opened in 1929), but that represented just 8 percent of all Kansas City males so employed.[5] And according to the author of *The Spirit of Freedom*, just one black man was employed on

3. According to the Office of Housing and Community Development (*Spirit of Freedom*), almost a quarter of black families in Kansas City were on public relief by 1935. See also *The Baltimore Afro-American*, June 1, 1929, as quoted in Greene and Woodson, *The Negro Wage Earner*, 232. The same *Afro-American* article reported that African American bus boys were fired and replaced by "Filipinos."

4. For a discussion of the Detroit Urban League's employment services, see Richard Thomas, *Life for Us Is What We Make It: Building Black Community in Detroit, 1915–1945*.

5. A decade later, a tour of the automobile industry showed just 165 workers among the 4,600 men employed in Kansas City's three plants. Office of Housing and Community Development, *Spirit of Freedom*, 18–19.

the assembly line. Despite the KCUL's best efforts, most Kansas City employers consistently maintained barriers to black employment.

After 1929, the KCUL's employment focus changed dramatically. Over the next two years, the demand on the league's employment service was such that by early 1932, as state and county sources of relief dried up, the league chose to hire a full-time industrial secretary. The man chosen was Thomas A. Webster, who had been working with the KCUL as an agent of the Department of Labor.[6]

By 1932, the Urban League was reporting that the employment situation in Kansas City was becoming acute, particularly for African Americans. According to a study for the first six months of the year, the league's office received just 257 orders for workers. On the other hand, more than 5,000 men and women came to the Urban League looking for work. Only 234 applicants were referred to jobs. Most of the applicants reported that they were heads of families who had been laid off because of a reduction in the workforce by their employers. Many of the unemployed had first turned to the Provident Association, but by 1932, the KCUL's board of directors was noting a disparity in the benefits handled by that charity. Charles Guild, a member of the KCUL's Social Science Committee, noted that the Provident Association had secured employment for between 30 and 40 African Americans out of 2,200 black families with which it worked. Guild then compared that to the association's success rate for white families: 650 jobs for 4,000 families.[7]

The first priority for Webster and the KCUL was to continue pressuring city and state officials to include African Americans on the public works projects around Kansas City. They were joined in this effort by other leaders in the African American communities. Chester Franklin and columnist Roy Wilkins of the *Kansas City Call* were among the most outspoken voices. Fred McGuire, secretary in the Water Department, assured Franklin in February 1932 that a crew of African Americans would be hired among the 2,000 workers needed for the construction of a new million-dollar water-main system. Yet by July of that year, the situation had not only not improved but even gotten worse. At a meeting with Judge Casimir Welch (a Democratic ward boss), Mayor

6. KCULP, "Minutes, Industrial Committee, March 8, 1932," Urban League Minutes, Board of Directors, box M1, file 1; "Minutes, Board of Directors, December 20, 1932," Urban League Minutes, Board of Directors, box M1, file 1.

7. KCULP, "Urban League Report Shows Jobs Are Few," unattributed newspaper clipping, box N1, file 1; "Minutes—February 16, 1932," Urban League Minutes, Board of Directors, box M1, file 1.

Bryce Smith, and Mathew Murray, director of public works, KCUL executive secretary W. Robert Smalls was told that of approximately 5,400 men working on various projects, no more than 100 were African American. Six months later, Wilkins noted that of the 6,000 workmen on public works projects around Kansas City, just 120 of them were black workers. Two years later, the KCUL's board of directors attempted to lobby city officials for the inclusion of black workers on the construction of Municipal Auditorium.[8]

In an editorial likely written around the same time, titled "We Have Had Little Public Work," Chester Franklin argued that both white employers and black workers had been negligent in ensuring African Americans were represented on public works projects. Franklin noted that under city manager H. F. McElroy, a number of city improvement projects had begun, employing as many as 4,000 workers in one week. "Yet the high point of our employment by the city was only 135," Franklin noted. The same situation existed on state projects. "We repeat what we have said before," Franklin exclaimed. "Missouri has spent a hundred million dollars on modern roads. . . . Yet so backward have we been in insisting our rights to work, that this ocean of money has not meant a single drop of comfort to us." Therein lay the rub, Franklin said. African Americans could not sit back and wait for jobs to come to them "like manna from heaven." Black workers needed to demand their rightful share of jobs, and most important, they needed to be prepared to assume the skilled and semiskilled jobs that paid more than the "very small amount" African American workers were accustomed to receiving.[9]

The Community Garden: An Experiment in Self-Help

The shortcomings of both federal and state relief efforts during the Hoover administration had become readily apparent by the spring and summer of 1932. Sources of financial aid for all but those in the most dire straits had dried up, and social service agencies began looking

8. "To Hire Negro Labor on Water Main Job," *Kansas City Call*, February 13, 1932; Roy Wilkins, "Talking It Over," ibid., April 7, 1933, both in KCULP, box N1, file 1; KCULP, "Minutes, Executive Committee, July 7, 1932," box M1, file 1; "Minutes: June (1934) meeting—board of directors," Urban League Minutes, Board of Directors, box M1, file 1.

9. "We Have Had Little Public Work," undated editorial from the *Kansas City Call* (likely written around 1933), in KCULP, box N1, file 2.

toward innovative strategies to assist the needy. One innovation was the creation of community gardens, where the donation of a few seeds and a little garden, combined with the labor of clients, could provide sustenance for destitute families. In many communities, the gardens tapped rural skills in an urban setting. Such was the case with Kansas City's Community Garden, at Twenty-fifth Street and Brooklyn.

W. Robert Smalls, the Urban League's executive secretary, first broached the idea of a community garden in March 1932. Much of the legwork involved in getting the project started then fell to Thomas A. Webster, at the time a special agent for the Department of Labor attached to the Urban League's Kansas City branch.[10] The idea was far from novel when Webster began pursuing it in 1932, and he thus was able to draw from the experiences of communities as diverse as Pittsburgh, Pennsylvania, and Muskogee, Oklahoma. Webster saw the garden as a way to ease the burden on charity organizations as well as boost the morale of the unemployed, particularly poor African Americans.

The league's plan certainly seemed ambitious. It hoped to establish a garden large enough to produce a sufficient yield that each family contributing labor to the project could take home enough produce to sustain itself during the summer and fall and have enough left over to preserve for consumption during the winter months.[11]

The first step was to obtain a site for the garden, and by the end of 1932, Webster had negotiated with the trustees of the former St. Peter and Paul Cemetery for the use of an eleven-acre tract on the southwest corner of Twenty-fifth and Brooklyn. The cemetery had been abandoned years previous, and all but two graves had been moved when negotiations between Webster and the trustees began.

The site itself could have been better. The soil on much of the acreage had been compromised. The tract had been filled in with subsoil, and in some places cinders and other materials had been dumped. An analysis of the soil led H. W. Guengerich, the Jackson County horticultural agent, to gloomily predict that few garden crops could be grown on the site. Guengerich, however, suggested that the application of leaf compost as well as manure (undesirable because of the proximity of homes) might improve the physical condition of the soil.[12] Before the site could

10. KCULP, "Minutes, Industrial Committee, March 8, 1932," Urban League Minutes, Board of Directors, box M1, vol. 1.

11. KCULP, Industrial Department, "Subsistence Garden Project," undated two-page document in box PPC1, file 1.

12. KCULP, Guengerich to Webster, March 8, 1933, box PPC1, file 1.

be prepared for cultivation, however, it had to be cleared. The Board of Park Commissioners offered the use of a tractor, plow, harrow, and disk along with a three-man crew, who worked for five days removing tree stumps, clearing underbrush, and hauling away rocks and gravestones. The city crew was assisted by at least two area residents who would benefit from the garden. Lewis Neal of 2000 Howard hauled rocks, removed stumps, and moved leaves for almost forty hours that week. Nathaniel Atkins, of 2410 East Twenty-second, spent twenty-three hours spreading leaf compost over the site.[13]

By the time the league's Subsistence Garden Committee met on March 22, most of the preparatory work had been completed. Earl Beck, chairman of the committee, donated several thousand tomato and cabbage plants that had been cultured in the greenhouses at Swope Park. Other individuals and institutions donated seed, and by the end of March, the community gardeners had begun planting their crops. The community garden was actually two types of gardens: One portion was designed as a large-unit garden, which was planted, tended, and harvested communally. The crops from this garden would be divided based on the amount of work each gardener contributed. The rest of the acreage was divided into individual plots, which the residents of streets immediately adjoining the project had requested.[14] Attempts were made to ration the individual plots according to need, and those with the larger plots received more of the seeds and plants. Some residents obtained seeds from other sources. All of the space was under seed by the middle of March.

Who were the community gardeners, and what were their needs? Many were unemployed men who had sought assistance from the Provident Association. The Provident Association, its resources strained like all other agencies, directed many of the African American applicants to the Urban League and, in particular, to the gardening project. Of sixty-six individuals listed as working on the communal garden, almost two-thirds (forty-two) were described as clients of or referrals from the Provident Association. The sixty-six gardeners (at least one was a teenage boy) provided for, on average, between three and four individuals. Some of the gardeners, however, had large families that were counting on sustenance from the project. Moses Allen, of 2423 Woodland (about

13. KCULP, Subsistence Garden Committee, undated minutes, box PPC1, file 1; "Work History: Atkins, Nathaniel," undated, box PPC1, file 1; "Work History: Neal, Lewis," undated, box PPC1, file 1.

14. KCULP, Subsistence Garden Committee, box PPC1, file 1.

four blocks from the garden), listed eleven members in his family. Vic Rucker, of 1015 East Nineteenth Street (about a mile away), had ten mouths to feed, including his own.[15]

There was no correlation between size of family and amount of time spent on the communal garden. Some of the gardeners contributed no more than an hour or two to the project; others treated the communal garden as a part-time job. Lewis Neal and Nathaniel Atkins, mentioned earlier, were two of the five men who contributed at least one hundred hours each to the garden from the middle of March until the crops were harvested that summer.[16] The men's skills, as well as those of the rest of the communal gardeners, were put to a variety of tasks. The Jenkins Music Company contributed three piano cases that were converted into a storage shed. Both Lewis and Atkins worked on this project, and Atkins installed the lock. The Urban League had no funds to pay a watchman for the site, so the gardeners volunteered to split up those duties. But the most arduous task was carrying water to the garden. There were no water lines on the acreage, and the gardeners were required to ferry buckets of water from hydrants on nearby streets. A prolonged drought that spring made this chore even more difficult—and more necessary. Finally, the city permitted the all-black crew of Fire Station no. 11 to spray water on the communal garden and individual plots for two hours one day.[17]

How beneficial was the communal garden project? How many families survived because of the produce harvested from the garden? There is no real empirical method to determine the answer to either of these questions. Anecdotal evidence compiled by the Urban League after the harvest describes the various experiences and outcomes of some of the gardeners who worked the communal garden as well as individual plots.[18]

Eugene Sage, a fifteen-year-old high school student, raised enough vegetables to supply his family weekly with fresh foods. He worked daily before and after school and estimated his garden produced ten dollars' worth of vegetables.

Racy Clardy, a thirty-eight-year-old father of three children, was an unemployed plasterer who had sought assistance from the Provident

15. Ibid., "Work History."

16. Neal was credited with 163 hours and Atkins 148. The others: John Beasley, with 163; Louis Lay, with 162; and Kirby Harrison, with 116. "Work History," ibid.

17. Ibid.; KCULP, Subsistence Garden Committee, box PPC1, file 1.

18. KCULP, "Individual Gardener's Report," undated, box PPC1, file 1.

Association. In addition to the seeds provided by the Urban League, Clardy planted beans, peppers, and other vegetables. He was credited with forty-seven hours of labor on the communal garden, though Urban League records indicate members of his family also worked with him.

Ollie Hunter, forty-five, joined the project later than the other gardeners, but with their help was able to harvest fresh vegetables for his four dependents weekly. Hunter, a seasonal worker in the building trades, was credited with just eight hours' work on the communal garden.

Steve Thompson was a veteran of World War I and had worked as a janitor until his building was sold. Thompson, forty-five, had a plot on the side of a hill that required constant cultivation. He was up to the task and produced more than twenty dollars' worth of produce. Thompson, who lived at Twentieth and Holmes, also had one of the longest commutes to the garden.

Fannie Conner, a widow with a small boy, lived at 2006 East Twenty-fifth Street, adjacent to the communal garden. She planted tomato and cabbage plants, as well as rutabaga seeds, in a plot next to her preexisting flower garden.

Another widow, with the aid of her brother, planted late crops of sweet potatoes, cucumbers, turnips, and beans. She estimated the value of her crop at twenty-eight dollars.

William Moody was credited with just eight hours of work on the communal garden, but as a nearby resident he undoubtedly had a separate plot of his own. Moody had one and a half acres of crops under cultivation, including watermelons, beans, peppers, cucumbers, potatoes, sweet potatoes, carrots, and tomatoes. He credited the garden, along with odd jobs he was able to obtain, with enabling him and the other four members of his family to survive in 1933.

Charles Elam, of the 2600 block of Euclid, was entitled to an individual plot on the site, but he spent most of his time working on the communal garden. He was credited with fifteen hours of labor on the project.

By June 8, 1933, eight bushels of spinach, nine bushels of mustard, more than three bushels of onions, six pecks of radishes, and five bushels of peas had been harvested.[19] Those who had put the most time into the garden—such as Lewis Neal and Nathaniel Atkins—likely received a healthy ration of vegetables for their families' consumption that year. Others apparently were not as fortunate.

19. KCULP, "Garden History: Crops Harvested," box PPC1, file 1.

What was the fate of the communal garden? There are no references to the garden in subsequent years in surviving Urban League documents. More than likely it was believed to be redundant in light of the expanding federal role in relief efforts from Franklin D. Roosevelt's New Deal programs. For at least one summer, however, it provided sustenance to a segment of Kansas City's needy.

The election of Franklin Delano Roosevelt and the implementation of his New Deal policies altered the role of the Urban League in the Kansas City job market. From 1934 through 1939, the Urban League served as the main job broker in the African American communities. On a steady basis through this six-year span, African Americans visited the Urban League offices and checked the job openings. Surviving Urban League records detail most of this traffic flow.[20]

Between January 1934, the date of the first surviving monthly report, and December 1939, the Urban League's industrial secretary and staff handled the cases of at least 50 individuals a month. Few applicants made just one appearance at the Urban League offices; after January 1935, when the industrial secretary began counting each appearance as a separate job application, the total number of monthly appearances ranged from just above 200 to almost 550. The number of appearances varied widely and followed no discernible pattern. The only con-

20. Not all of the monthly statistics on job seekers, job openings, and placements have survived. In addition, the record-keeping standards varied through the period. For instance, in some months early in the period and for the final two years of this study, the Urban League office differentiated between new job seekers and those who were making second, third or more appearances in the month. In addition, for 1934 and most of 1935, the monthly statistics do not break placements down into temporary and permanent placements, an important distinction in the chaotic economy of the 1930s. The monthly reports, beyond providing a basic breakdown by gender, also do not indicate who received what jobs. How many African American men and women went through a succession of temporary jobs until finding permanent work is impossible to determine from these reports. The reports also do not indicate how many so-called permanent jobs became temporary ones, throwing African American workers back into the ranks of the jobless. These limitations notwithstanding, we can make some important points about the Urban League's employment activities and the job market as it pertained to African Americans during this period. In addition, many of the monthly reports contain summaries of the work of the industrial secretary. Thomas Webster and staff members who handled employment service duties after Webster was appointed executive secretary of the KCUL discussed in monthly summaries the problems facing African Americans in the job market. In addition, the summaries discuss "unusual" placements by the Urban League during this period. With a judicious use of the monthly reports and summaries, we can draw some first tentative conclusions about work for African Americans in Kansas City during the 1930s. All of the monthly reports from January 1934 to December 1939, inclusive, are contained in KCULP, box M1, Files 1, 2 and 3.

stant is that it appears there always were more job applicants than the jobs available.[21] This allowed the industrial secretary to record a fair amount of success in job placements. For the forty-five months for which statistics are available, the KCUL received 2,557 job offers. The KCUL successfully filled 2,007 of them (78.5 percent). The KCUL's success rate was remarkably consistent over the six years. It ranged from 75.5 percent in 1935 (when 391 of 518 jobs were filled over a nine-month period) to 82.2 percent in 1938 (when 198 of 241 jobs were filled in a five-month period). In 1939, the only year in which statistics for all twelve months survive, the Urban League filled 365 of 455 jobs (80.2 percent). The success rate did not vary greatly regardless of the volume of jobs and job activity. On only two occasions did the success rate fall below 60 percent for a month. Even when the KCUL had 90 to more than 100 jobs listed, it still successfully filled 80 to 90 percent of them. Clearly during this period, employers and would-be employees realized the KCUL was the venue for filling their respective needs. For African American job seekers (and Webster and the KCUL staff), however, the question sometimes was not how much work but what kind of work. The summaries of the Industrial Department's activities between 1934 and 1939 demonstrate the issues facing black workers in Kansas City during the Depression.

Paramount of these issues was the low wages offered to African Americans in many settings in Kansas City. Staff members in the Industrial Department reported in March 1936 that the "small wages" offered by some of the jobs listed made them difficult to fill. The same sentiment was expressed about 19 of the 106 job requests the KCUL received in April of that year. At the same time, another curtailment of direct public relief meant an increase in the number of job seekers visiting the offices. That increase continued through the summer, though in September and October, the KCUL staff reported an upward trend in wages for many of the jobs offered.[22]

Wages continued to climb in January of the next year, though some jobs still went unfilled because of the low wages offered or because of the inadequate living quarters offered as a condition of employment. Even worse, some job seekers reported that some employers were refusing to pay even when the work was done. When a group of African

21. In most months, "new applicants" also outnumbered job offers.

22. KCULP, "Monthly Report, March 1936"; "Administrative Report, April (1936)"; "Monthly Report, September, 1936"; "Monthly Report, October, 1936," all in Urban League Minutes, Board of Directors, box M1, vol. 1.

American workers successfully struck for a three-cent-an-hour wage increase in 1934, they soon learned that their hours were to be cut by 20 percent.[23]

In early 1936, the Jones Store, a major department store, hired a new manager, who immediately dismissed eight porters, five of them African Americans. The Urban League's Industrial Relations staff visited with the manager, who consented to rehire the porters and then posted openings for ten more porters. The manager also agreed to raise wages for the African American elevator operators in the store.[24]

In March 1937, the KCUL made two "unusual" placements. One African American man was hired as a refrigerator salesman for the Jones Store, and another was hired by the Continental Baking Company as a demonstrator to conduct bread tests in stores within the African American communities. In 1936, KCUL staffers placed several men with the Union Pacific Railroad, and in 1938, Webster placed four workers in temporary jobs with the Skelly Oil Company.[25]

In 1936, city officials drafted an ordinance to regulate hours and sanitary conditions for the countless barber shops. African American barbers, fearful that the proposed ordinance was designed to eliminate them as competition to white barbers, reorganized the Negro Barbers Association, with the help of KCUL staff members. By October 1936, the barbers' association had fifty-two members. By 1938, the organization was meeting regularly at the Urban League offices. The barbers were working to bring all black barbers into conformity with regulations regarding sanitation and hours. One of their goals was to eliminate the so-called bootleg barber.[26]

One of the major employment efforts of the Urban League in 1937 was to induce Kansas City's utility companies to hire African Americans. The first step was to gather information from other municipalities about their utilities' hiring practices. The first African American to break the

23. KCULP, "January Report (1937)," Urban League Minutes, Board of Directors, box M1, vol. 2; "Monthly Report, September, 1934," Urban League Minutes, Board of Directors, box M1, vol. 1.

24. KCULP, "Monthly Report, March 1937," Urban League Minutes, Board of Directors, box M1, vol. 1.

25. KCULP, "Monthly Report, March 1936," Urban League Minutes, Board of Directors, box M1, vol. 1; "Administrative Report, January, 1938," Urban League Minutes, Board of Directors, box M1, vol. 2.

26. KCULP, "Monthly Report, September 1936," Urban League Minutes, Board of Directors, box M1, vol. 1; "Monthly Report, October 1936," Urban League Minutes, Board of Directors, box M1, vol. 1; "January Report (1937)," Urban League Minutes, Board of Directors, box M1, vol. 2; "Urban League Activities for the Month of July 1938," Urban League Minutes, Board of Directors, box M1, vol. 2.

color barrier with Kansas City's utility companies was the Reverend Preston Allen, the pastor of Macedonia Baptist Church. Allen was hired in the fall of 1937 to read water meters on the East Side. Allen, who lived in the 2400 block of Forest, had been pastor at Macedonia Baptist for fourteen years when he was hired by the water company.[27]

Many industries were obstinate in their refusal to hire African American workers, despite the entreaties of Webster and his staff. In April 1936, the KCUL launched an investigation into two incidents involving "attitudes toward Negro workmen," but the KCUL staff was unable to resolve the issues to the satisfaction of the African American workers.[28]

In 1938, Webster's successor as industrial secretary, H. T. Kealing, sought to encourage the nine brewing companies in Kansas City to increase the percentage of African Americans they employed. Kealing argued that only "a few" African Americans worked in the industry because of the refusal of the major unions to admit black workers. Kealing hoped to pressure the brewing companies, starting with the Muehlbach Company, to either force the unions to eliminate the color bar or take matters into their own hands and hire African Americans. Kealing also hoped to ensure spots for African American workers on the various municipal projects funded by the Public Works Administration.[29]

One of Webster's first successes as industrial secretary came in the fall of 1932, when he successfully placed five African Americans with the Fuller Brush Company. The new salesmen were undoubtedly given sales territories in the African American communities, and their wages, as they were for most traveling salesmen of the period, were likely tied to the amount of sales they generated. Nevertheless, Webster's work in landing these jobs was lauded by the Urban League staff and board. Throughout the rest of the decade, Webster successfully orchestrated job placements for African Americans in positions not open to them earlier in the interwar period. In 1935, for example, he placed African Americans as "solicitors" for a major bakery and a laundry. In both cases, the workers were responsible for representing the company in African American neighborhoods. Although Webster and his successor, Kealing, made a number of "unusual" placements in the 1930s, they

27. KCULP, "Monthly Report, March 1937," Urban League Minutes, Board of Directors, box M1, vol. 2; "Rev. P. Allen is Appointed to City Post," *Kansas City Call*, October 22, 1937, in KCULP, box N1, file 2.

28. KCULP, "Administrative Report, April (1936)," Urban League Minutes, Board of Directors, box M1, vol. 1.

29. KCULP, "Urban League Activities for the Month of July 1938," Urban League Minutes, Board of Directors, box M1, vol. 2.

were unable to make a massive breakthrough in any particular occupation or industry. Those breakthroughs came only with the outbreak of World War II.[30]

An outbreak of labor unrest in the winter of 1936–1937 put African Americans in a squeeze. Most of the labor unions affiliated with the American Federation of Labor still refused to admit black workers. Thus, it was not surprising that African Americans employed by the Gordon Brothers Company did not participate in a strike by garment workers. On the other hand, African American workers joined the work stoppage at the Ford plant in Leeds, and when the CIO-affiliated Packing House Workers went on strike in 1938, African American workers at the Armour and Swift plants followed their union brothers out of the shops. A citywide strike in the produce industry in 1938 also left many African Americans without work: they either left their jobs when their employer refused to accede to the union's demands or found themselves displaced in those shops where union members had returned to work.[31] In February 1938, twenty-eight black workers at the Sheffield Steel Plant walked off the job; they returned to work only after Kealing's intervention.[32]

Throughout 1938 and 1939, Webster and Kealing continued their efforts for "unusual placements." Labor unions, particularly those affiliated with the American Federation of Labor, remained obstinate in their refusal to accept African American workers. In October 1939, Thomas Webster began lobbying with several serum manufacturing plants for the placement of a recent college graduate who had "special training in handling animals and in preparing cultures and slides." Despite follow-up telephone calls and personal visits, Webster was repeatedly rebuffed in his bid to find employment for the graduate, though he deemed several employers as being "sympathetic" to his overtures.[33]

Success was obtained on other fronts in October. After resuming efforts initiated in February, Webster placed six workers with the Ford automobile plant, though the surviving documents do not detail in what

30. KCULP, "Minutes, Board of Directors, December 20, 1932," Urban League Minutes, Board of Directors, box M1, vol. 1; "Monthly Report, March 1935," Urban League Minutes, Board of Directors, box M1, vol. 1.

31. KCULP, "Monthly Report, March 1937," Urban League Minutes, Board of Directors, box M1, vol. 2; "Administrative Report, January, 1938," Urban League Minutes, Board of Directors, box M1, vol. 2; "Monthly Report, October, 1938," Urban League Minutes, Board of Directors, box M1, vol. 2.

32. KCULP, "Minutes, Board of Directors, February 18, 1938," Urban League Minutes, Board of Directors, box M1, vol. 2.

33. KCULP, "October Report—1939," Urban League Minutes, Board of Directors, box M1, vol. 3.

capacity the African American laborers were hired. Urban League records do indicate, however, that Webster's appeals led to the hiring of thirty African Americans in custodial work in the new federal building at Ninth and Grand.[34]

Urban League records for late 1939 indicate the obstacles that Webster and Kealing faced in placing African Americans, particularly African American women. An analysis of job openings not filled by the league in November showed almost half (seven of sixteen) remained vacant because the wages were too low or wages were not offered at all. Two referrals were for work outside of Kansas City, and in another, the employer chose to hire a white worker to live on the premises instead. Just three of the sixteen referrals (18.8 percent) went unfilled because of the tardiness of the workers in responding. In short, most African Americans who came to the Urban League actively wanted work. Only in the most dire situations would they reject it.[35]

The return of direct relief programs in the late 1930s did little to ameliorate the conditions facing African American families. In fact, Thomas Webster went so far as to call the crisis "a very serious situation" facing Kansas City's African American communities. Direct relief, Webster concluded after an admittedly cursory study, was unable to meet the needs of African Americans. Many of the relief clients Webster interviewed, many of them unskilled laborers, had not worked for two or three years. The monthly relief allotment of eleven dollars did nothing to meet the needs of the families in the direst of straits.[36]

New Deal programs originally offered little solace to African American workers. Administrators in the National Recovery Administration programs bowed to pressures by organized labor and restricted access for black workers. The Civil Works Administration also offered few opportunities to African Americans in Kansas City until federal officials threatened to cut off funding to projects in Missouri unless racial restrictions on the projects in Jackson County were lifted. Once African Americans were admitted to these work programs, it was natural that the KCUL, with former federal employee Thomas Webster as its head, should assume some oversight responsibilities.[37]

The first National Youth Administration (NYA) project in Jackson County began at the Thomas H. Swope Settlement House in the 1600

34. Ibid.

35. KCULP, "November Report—1939," Urban League Minutes, Board of Directors, box M1, vol. 3.

36. "Administrative Report, January 1938."

37. Office of Housing and Community Development, *Spirit of Freedom*, 20.

block of Campbell. Young men and women between the ages of sixteen and twenty-five whose families were on relief were eligible for the program, and NYA administrators hoped to enlist thirty-nine young women and twenty-one young men to contribute their talents and skills on a part-time basis to the expansion of recreational and vocational programs at ten Kansas City community centers, including the Urban League center at Eighteenth and Vine. Participants in the project were to work a maximum of forty-three and a half hours a month for a minimum monthly wage of fifteen dollars. The KCUL also received an NYA grant to hire students to recondition toys for the use of African American children in hospitals and other institutions.[38]

By the middle of the decade, the KCUL was supervising seven New Deal programs in its offices. Early in 1936, the league offered space to federal personnel studying the training and employment of African Americans in white-collar and skilled labor. The league also supervised that spring a National Youth Administration recreational program that employed fifty black youths.[39] Adult education programs under the Works Progress Administration also proved popular. The night school sessions, under the guidance of J. Ernest Brown, drew fifteen hundred students in the fall of 1935.[40]

The Urban League was also called to protect the rights of African American men in various New Deal programs. In July 1937, four black enrollees at the Civilian Conservation Corps (CCC) camp at Lone Star, Kansas, near Lawrence, complained of the discriminatory practices of the camp's commander. The most serious of the complaints arose from incidents that resulted in jail sentences for three black youths. All three received discharges from the program and were turned over to Douglas County authorities. An inquiry by Thomas Webster resulted in a formal complaint to the CCC district office in Omaha. Two months later, Webster reported that conditions had improved for African Americans enrolled in the program.[41]

In 1936, NYA workers were used to paint the inside of the Garrison Field House; the scaffolding for the work was provided by the Parks

38. KCULP, "A New NYA Allotment," undated news clipping, box N1, file 2; "First NYA Jobs to 60," undated news clipping, box N1, file 2.

39. KCULP, "Monthly Report, March 1936," Urban League Minutes, Board of Directors, box M1, vol. 2.

40. KCULP, "Classes for Adults Now in Session," *Kansas City* Call, box N1, file 2.

41. KCULP, "Monthly Report, July 1937," Urban League Minutes, Board of Directors, box M1, vol. 2; "Minutes, September 16, 1937, Board of Directors," Urban League Minutes, Board of Directors, box M1, vol. 2; "Protest Jailing of CCC Camp Enrollees [1937]," undated news clipping, box N1, file 2.

Board.[42] Among the activities sponsored by the league through the NYA program was a metal-handcraft workshop. Metal used in the project came from illicit alcohol-brewing devices ("stills" in the parlance of the day) confiscated by the Kansas City Police Department.[43]

African Americans in the two Kansas Cities received some assistance in the early years of the Depression. In 1932, the charities bureau of the Chamber of Commerce set the quota of African Americans on a federal reforestation project on the basis of the percentage of African American men seeking aid through the Provident Association. As a result, more than eighty African American men were hired on the crew of four hundred, rather than the forty jobs that would have been made available had the bureau based the assignment on percentage of the total population (10 percent).[44] On the Kansas side, black workers were used on the construction of a new bridge across the Missouri River from the Fairfax industrial district into Platte County, Missouri. One hundred black men, part of a crew of two hundred, were used in cement mixing and materials handling work.[45]

"More Jobs for Negroes" Campaign

Throughout the Depression, African Americans in many urban areas organized in attempts to create more jobs within their communities. Many of them followed the "Don't Buy Where You Can't Work" campaigns developed in New York during the 1930s. A similar effort was orchestrated in Kansas City, when a group known as the Community League attempted to organize a "More Jobs for Negroes" campaign. Little is known about the Community League, but one member was Nathaniel Spencer Adkins, supreme clerk of the American Woodman's Fraternal Life Insurance Company of Camp Five.[46]

About the same time, Chester Franklin and the *Kansas City Call* lobbied for the employment of African Americans on the newly developed bus system in Kansas City. The objective was to have black drivers for

42. KCULP, "Monthly Report, March 1936," Urban League Minutes, Board of Directors, box M1, vol. 1.

43. Ibid.

44. KCULP, "Negro Quota in Forestry Jobs to 80," undated newspaper clipping, although likely 1933, in box N1, file 1.

45. KCULP, "100 Workers on Fairfax Bridge Job," undated newspaper clipping, although likely 1933, in box N1, file 2.

46. KCULP, "Monthly Report, October, 1938," Urban League Minutes, Board of Directors, box M1, vol. 2.

the one bus line that would go through the African American community on the near East Side. Although African Americans had not been employed on the city's trolley lines, Franklin argued that there existed several rationales for opening the door to black bus drivers. Experienced drivers were plentiful, needing just the little specialized training required to maneuver a bus through the city streets. Second, Franklin noted, the precedent had already been set elsewhere: other cities, notably New York, Detroit, and Tulsa, had hired African Americans as bus drivers. The only reason for Kansas City to exclude black bus drivers, Franklin saw, was that it had never been done. That reason was insufficient and outdated. In addition, he noted, the primary customers for the route—black men and women—would be more likely to patronize the bus if they saw one of their own behind the steering wheel. Despite Franklin's insistence, public transportation in Kansas City would not employ black drivers until after World War II.[47]

Kansas City's African Americans, with the help of the Urban League, tried a variety of strategies to combat the Great Depression. The community garden and the work programs sponsored by the KCUL offered some assistance to a fortunate few, but in general black Kansas Citians struggled throughout the decade of the 1930s. Like many Americans, and particularly black Americans, they would have to wait until the economic turnaround produced by the Second World War before enjoying any level of prosperity.

47. KCULP, "Work, a Worthy Objective," *Kansas City Call,* November 19, 1937, box N1, file 2.

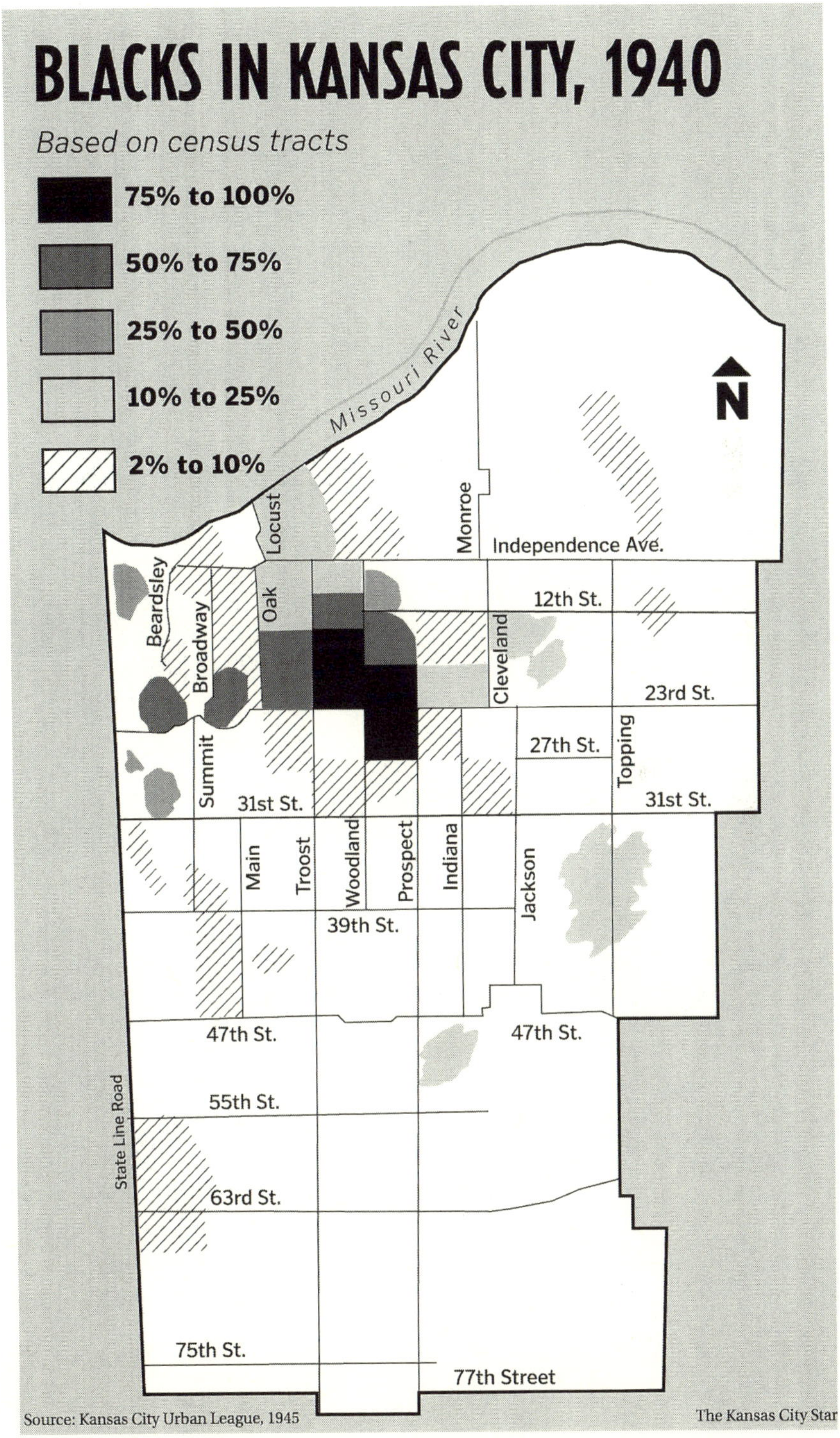
BLACKS IN KANSAS CITY, 1940
Based on census tracts
75% to 100%
50% to 75%
25% to 50%
10% to 25%
2% to 10%
Missouri River
N
Locust
Monroe
Independence Ave.
Beardsley
Broadway
Oak
12th St.
Cleveland
23rd St.
27th St.
Topping
Summit
31st St.
31st St.
Main
Troost
Woodland
Prospect
Indiana
Jackson
39th St.
47th St.
47th St.
55th St.
State Line Road
63rd St.
75th St.
77th Street
Source: Kansas City Urban League, 1945
The Kansas City Star

Nine

Coda
"The Weary Blues"

This nation once tried to live part slave and part free. It failed. It is now trying to live part white and part black. It has long since united all its white elements. The Negro alone remains segregated. Separated in schools, he is expected to become equally proficient; proscribed in industry, he is expected to carry a man's burden in a great democracy. Confined to a Negro district, he is expected to attain culture; limited in the law itself, he is expected to be a patriot.

—CHESTER A. FRANKLIN,
"AMERICA'S ADVENTURE IN BROTHERHOOD:
A DISCUSSION IN RACE RELATIONS" (1926)

WE BEGAN OUR investigation of Kansas City's African American community with a celebration; we shall end it with a celebration. In 1939, Kansas City's Music Hall was the scene for a festival marking the seventy-sixth anniversary of the Emancipation Proclamation. The program was less ambitious than that of the festival of twenty years previous, and the crowd was significantly smaller (about eight hundred spectators). Yet in much the same way as the celebration in 1919, the gala in 1939 offers a view of how Kansas City's African Americans, particularly the city's black professionals, saw themselves.

The program, sponsored by the Kansas City Community League and the Missouri Baptist Convention, started with a rendition of "Precious Lord" by a boys choir of three hundred directed by Wyatt L. Logan, music instructor at Lincoln High School, and Mrs. D. A. Holmes, music director of Paseo Baptist. Clement Richardson, president of Western Baptist seminary, and the Reverend D. A. Holmes of Paseo Baptist were among the speakers that day. Reverend Samuel Bacote of Second Baptist offered the opening prayer, but the featured address came from businessman Nathaniel S. Adkins. The first forty-five minutes of the jubilee were broadcast live by KCMO radio, and most of the airtime was devoted to the musical numbers. Thus, much of Kansas City missed Adkins's radical assessment of the state of black Kansas City.

Adkins took as his subject of the day "the business of being a Negro." In no uncertain terms, Adkins reminded his listeners at the Music Hall that the business of being black was often an unpleasant one. But he was not content in just mouthing generalities. Echoing the grievances articulated by the National Negro Constitutional Conservation League of America and the National Race Congress in the months following World War I, grievances repeated through the intervening years by representatives of the NAACP and the Urban League, Adkins set out a specific agenda for the improvement of the business of being black.

"The Negroes of Kansas City," Adkins said, "ask the white citizens of our city to allow us to join the labor unions. We ask to be permitted equal rights for employment. We ask our city manager to let the Negro become an employee of the city on the basis of merit." Finally, Adkins demanded "real opportunities for social justice" must be created, not only in Kansas City but throughout the country as well.[1]

How did Kansas City respond to Adkins's address? Like the petitions of the NNCCLA and the National Race Congress, his appeals apparently fell on deaf ears. Conditions for Kansas City's African Americans would remain unchanged through the 1930s; it would take another world war, the momentous Supreme Court ruling in *Brown v. Topeka Board of Education,* and the civil rights movement before the business of being black would drastically change in Kansas City.

That is not to say that change had not occurred in Kansas City's African American communities in the twenty years between the end of one world war and the beginning of another. For one, the "communities" were rapidly becoming one community. Although pockets of African Americans would remain on the West Side and in the Leeds

1. Undated news clipping in Gibson, *Mecca of the New Negro,* 73.

area, by 1940 most of the city's black population was crowded east of Troost and north of Thirty-first Street. The segregation of African Americans into the Troost corridor ironically would boost black businesses and the development of the Eighteenth and Vine area. At the same time, it created overcrowded living conditions, with all of the related problems. The institutions that Kansas City's African Americans would recall fondly in the 1980s and 1990s had taken firm hold by 1939. The construction in 1930 of General Hospital No. 2, by any measure, was a remarkable moment in the history of Kansas City. General Hospital No. 2, though at times still the subject of political intrigue, combined with Wheatley-Provident Hospital to provide a quality of health care for African Americans unmatched in many parts of the country. The Paseo YMCA and the YWCA continued to offer programs for the benefit of the area's black youth.

A new Lincoln High School had been built, and the "Castle on the Hill" would provide the foundation for many of the worthwhile causes and ventures generated by the African American community. At the same time, Lincoln's role as a regional black school exacerbated the overcrowding, and conditions at Lincoln and at the all-black grade schools would remain a source of contention for much of the century. A multimillion-dollar desegregation effort, an empty city, and a school system in disrepair were just part of segregation's legacy in the field of education.

Employment opportunities for African Americans remained limited in 1939. The Urban League would engage in a decadelong struggle to find work for black men and women, particularly with the city's utilities. It would take the Second World War and the accompanying manpower shortage for African Americans to break out of their "traditional" jobs in Kansas City. The opening of employment possibilities coincided with a rise in political power. The dismantling of the Pendergast machine and the effort to "clean up" Kansas City politics helped open the door to black political aspirations. White flight to the suburbs, a response to the growing black presence within the city and the threat of school desegregation, helped make black political participation a reality. The creation of Freedom, Inc., a black political club, and the election of African Americans to the city council and ultimately into the mayor's chair marked the ascendance of black political power in Kansas City.

That would all be in the future. Few sitting in the Music Hall or listening at home that Sunday afternoon could envision the world ahead of them. The years past had produced enough changes.

By 1939, many of the old settlers—James Dallas Bowser, Nelson Crews, Josephine Silone Yates, Thomas C. Unthank, T. H. Ewing, and Richard Coles—had died. John R. E. Lee had gone off and joined the Urban League's offices in Baltimore. Homer Roberts had moved his automobile dealership to Chicago. Dr. John E. Perry had retired—and unretired—from medicine. They had been replaced by a new generation, but one equally dedicated: men and women like T. B. Watkins, L. Amasa Knox, N. S. Adkins, Chester Franklin, Lucile Bluford, and the Reverend D. A. Holmes, who continued the fight for community advancement and against the tide of segregation and discrimination. Bound by the vagaries of kinship and nativity and the necessities of race, African Americans in Kansas City continued to develop their parallel world. Not until the 1960s and 1970s, when the concomitant forces of desegregation and suburbanization began to hold sway, did the threads of the mosaic of Kansas City African American communities begin to unravel.

Appendix A

G. A. Gregg's Description of the Tulsa Race Riot, May 30–June 2, 1921

LEAVING TULSA AS I did on on May 26th, 1921, to be present at the graduation of my two daughters, Ruth and Eunice, the latter from the Eighth grade, May 27th, and the former from Western University, June 2nd, found me away from Tulsa on the dates of the riots, May 31 and aurn [*sic*] June 5th.

But the Tulsa that I left and the Tulsa that I found on my return.

I left Tulsa throbbing with life and high hopes, people who were happy[,] people who in the main were prosperous, a wide awake, alert, active forwardlooking folk. Some who had come in the early day when it aried [*sic*] men's souls, and now were resting and beginning to enjoy the fruits of their years of toil. People who were singing the praises of Tulsa, prosperous.

No man, be he millionaire or pauper, had more pride in Tulsa than her upstanding, forwardlooking colored looking citizens. None clamored harder against the overbearing police system and the evils of the underworld.

Ten months in Tulsa, ten active, constructive months of human hopes and aspirations, ten months of a vision of a better day and then one platform and in press the phrase "The Dawn of a New Day" was in actual use. This is Tulsa colored.

Tulsa's colored citizens settled in the north end of the city, separating themselves at right angles to the Tulsa white.

Standpipe hill jutted out into the colored section like the state of Florida extends into the ocean. This hill is owned by a white man. From it one can get a panoramic view of Tulsa and the surrounding country. The white people would not buy it and the colored people could not, although they lived on three sides of it.

The good people of color were building magnificent church structures. One, Mt. Zion Baptist, had merged into completion at a cost of $85.000 [*sic*]—hard earned and frugally kept. It was a consolation to the old members, who had labored many years and now, in a home comfortable, were ready to worship God and patiently serve until He called them home.

Paradise Baptist church was a cozy brick building situated on the north side of standpipe hill, while Mt. Zion was on the south side of it. The members of the church were building on the pay-as-you-go plan. It was completed with the exception of interior furnishings. The Methodist Episcopal church and African Methodist Episcopal churches had their first story completed and money in the bank for the superstructure.

There were four well equipped drug stores, many grocery stores, Elliott & Hooker, men's and women's furnishing store carried as high a grade of goods as any in the city; two fine hotels accomodated [*sic*] the traveling public; Welcome grocery was a model, modern barber shops and two shoe shops with up-to-date machinery. Dreamland theatre catered to the pleasure and entertainment of the people. The physicians were equipping themselves with all the modern apparatus required to alleviate suffering. Young men as dentists had invested heavily in preparing to take care of the distressed in their line. Women had invested in beauty parlors and dressmaking establishments. Cafes were prepared to feed satisfactorily the many patrons. In fact the people were so industrious and put in so much time at work that they did not prepare their food at home but patronized the cafes. Four upholstered jitney busses carried the people from their homes to their work. An undertaking establishment equipped with caskets ranging from $50 to $1000, all for the accomodation [*sic*] of the colored people. A $10,000 limousine for the accomodation [*sic*] of the bereaved families was the latest addition.

The Tulsa colored people in every sense of the word were building a modern, up-to-date business city.

They were constantly handicapped as to public utilities, which were managed and controlled by the white man. They constantly prayed him to extend and furnish the same. Procrastination, political pramisese [*sic*] and hope deferred was the final result. The colored section of Tulsa was insufficiently lighted. And if evil did hold sway and the bad

Negro did exist he had the cover of a neglected city darkness in which to ply his evil trade. [Nonsensical line of type.] They have cried "Let there be light" and there was no light. The kerosene lamp, the tallow dip or darnkenss prevailed in their city. In Tulsa white[,] night had been turned into day.

The unsanitary condition, the surface tub-toilets, the stanch there from increased the wonder that the health of the community was as good as it was.

The colored man of Tulsa built his home not upon sand, but upon an exceedingly great faith, for when fire does break out all he can do is to stand by and see all his earthly possessions go down in ashes. Water protection was insufficient.

In spite of all physical and mental handicaps he has wrought well, and though a part of his city lies in ashes, the carpenter's hammer is heard and new lumber in the form of a home flares up in every direction. The Tulsa attitude of the black man is to build and rebuild.

The Young Men's Christian Association was the latest addition to civic betterment. This is an inspiring chapter in the city's history.

Conscious of the unwholesome moral trend of the life of the young people, a few acive wide awake, progressive citizens, on their own initiative and the friendly counsel and co-operation of that fine Christian gentleman, Mr. CM. Buckner, general secretary of the Tulsa "Y," set about the organization of the Hunton Branch Y.M.C.A.

They raised their own budget of $3,012 for the first year's work. The central association stood ready to furnish $1,000 of it, but the board of managers[,] led on by that prince of men, Mr. S. D. Hooker, raised the full amount themselves. The membership was more than 500 men and boys.

In like manner they raised the budget for the next year's work not withstanding the tightness of the times they increased the budget to $5,207 and the pleasure on Tuesday evening before the Tuesday of the riot of rejoicing over the fact that the entire amount had been pledged.

Shortly before that a community institute was held. For the first time in the history of the University Division, consisting of seven white men and women, experts in their line, carried on a three-day session in the colored community of Tulsa. They touched and stimulated the church, school, civic and home life of the people in a most encouraging manner. It gave our people a new hold on the cheering possibilities of life. The workers were pleasantly informed as to the inner life and cravings of the colored people. The [latter] did not know that white people could be kind, helpful and interested in their personal problems. The institute cost $1000. The people thought it worth many times the cost.

These are some of the new evidences of the attitude of mind developing in Tulsa's colored citizens.

Just another fact showing the desire for civic improvements, wholesome ideals, and better things for Tulsa.

Just a week before the riot, the board of managers of Hunton Branch Y.M.CA., together with the mayor and city commissioners invited President King of the Republic of Liberia to be Tulsa's guest. President King accepted.

This would have heartened the colored citizens of Oklahoma to make more their opportunities. The $1,000 cost to the colored citizens of Tulsa for this visit of President King and his party was delivered.

The houses of Tulsa's colored citizens ranged from the temporary floorless box house to modern equipped ones of the latest and best interior and exterior furnishings.

This, in brief, and in brief only, for much can be said of the high hopes and aims of the colored citizens of Tulsa. This is the Tulsa that I lft on the night of the 26th of May 1921.

And the Tulsa that I found on my return the 4th of June. What a contrast!

Tulsa had turned a page to run parallel with the Huns and Goths—vandals of Europe or the Indians in Custers [*sic*] last charge.

An awkward colored boy steps on the toe of a white elevator girl—she stops him—a retort discourteous on his part—arrested on the charge of assault and battery—newspaper omits "and battery"—public thinks rape—threatening groups of whites gather about [jail]—colored men fearing the usual happening, gather to prevent a lynching—a careless, reckless shot—and the restraints of civilization are thrown aside and men became brutish beasts.

The boy ought to have apologized. The girl ought to have recognized the accident. The paper ought [not] to have garbled the story with false emphasis White men ought not to have gathered about the jail. They should be willing to let the law have the right of way. The colored men ought to have trusted those whose sworn duty it was to protect the prisoner.

A cordon of police could have surrounded the first groups, white and black. But these are sad words "It might have been." But nothing that happened can [justify] the driving of twelve thousand innocent sleeping colored people clad in their night clothes out into the streets, marched to convention hall and elsewhere, then loot, rob and steal the hard, laborious earnings of a struggling people, handicapped at best.

I have worked two months with these people. I have had a deep sympathy for them in their struggle against great odds.

Loot—they backed auto trucks up to the vacated [by force] Negro homes and loaded everything movable and of value. One colored woman went to eleven different white homes and in each recovered portions of her household goods.

Rob—every bit of money found on their persons was taken. Masonic rings were removed from their fingers, watches and chains from their persons. In fast everything of a material nature, etc., preparatory to the cruel initiation which has not yet ended was taken from them. And so in their penniless, destitute condition they were coralled [*sic*] first one place and then another.

Thanks to the good people who took them into their homes, fed and clothed them, housed them until the cruel police order compelled even the white people to give up and send to the fair grounds those whom they had befriended. Kind offers were thwarted by the police regulation.

With homes looted, homes and stores burned, to ashes, with the sick, aged and enfeebled carried out or left to perish in the flames, mothers giving birth to children in the open, herded, coralled [*sic*] and guarded like prisoners of war, and before the smoke of a thousand homes had blown away the trembling, homeless learn that the city fathers have passed an ordinance making it forever impossible for them in this destitute condition to go back and rebuild on their own home place.

While their hearts are bleeding, their homes and all the relics that make the memory of life's past sustaining with shocking realization that their families are broken and scattered and fearing that they may be slain by the cruel bullet of the mob, with trembly, weak, tired, hungry and hungerless bodies compelled to be in the stalls of the fair grounds under heavy guard, cruel guard of home guards—guards who great them with harsh orders and vular language—while suffering all this and more the mayor and commissioners, the Real Estate Exchange, the Welfare Board are like them who crucified Christ, casting lots for the Negro's hard-earned land.

Ah, if they would stop and think how long it required those poor struggling people to own that little portion of earth.

Yet by every method known and being discovered by the combined trained minds of the best legal talent that the city and state affords, not one loop hole is being left through which or by means of which the colored citizens can ever again rebuild on his own land.

We appeal to the conscience and good judgement of the American people, where is the line seperating [*sic*] the lower element that cleared [the] way and [the] higher element that sat at noon luncheon under the cool of the electric fans and judiciously planned that this "never again [could] be a Negro section."

And immediately proceeds to publish without the owner's consent or offering a cent.

"Wanted. Wholesale Hauses [*sic*] in Tulsa."

"New Welfare committee in active campaign to Better City."

"Through the reconstruction committee appointed by the mayor and city commissioners Tuesday [June 14] Tulsa extends a welcoming hand to wholesale houses and industrial plants are to be located on the trackage property in Little Africa swept by fire and which is now within the city fire limits restricted to the erection of fire-resistant buildings. The committee also expressed a sentiment in favor of using a part of the burned area for a union station whenever such a project by the railroads entering Tulsa"—Tulsa World, June 15, 1921.

Think of it! A union station where the races of men pass through built upon the blood stained soil of the Negroes' property. What an approach to Tulsa! What a gateway to the "Magic City of the Great Southwest." A symbol of greed and blood.

And added to that anguish of soul comes quick and fast the police regulation that all Negroes to have the freedom of Tulsa's streets must wear a green tag stating age, residence, name and name of employer, who must be white. Men who did business for themselves had to find a white man to sign their cards. If not employed, a red card must be worn. This reads: "If the bearer is on the streets after 7 o'clock he will be arrested and taken to the fairground"—By some called the "bull-pen."

The guards are placed at all roads entering the colored section. Men, women, boys and girls are held up by these guards, many of whom are rough, rude and discourteous.

Every step from the suddening awakening by the firing of guns and the buzzing of aeroplanes to the present moment evidences in increasing humiliation Those who were privileged to return to their homes found their contents gone or mutilated. Everything from a shoe, a piano, to an automobile was found in the homes of white folks.

I left a happy, hopeful, progressive people. I found a crushed, humiliated, discouraged humanity. I felt [left?] a praying people; I found them wondering if God is just. I left a Young Men's Christian Association with bright and promising prospects just ready to jump into a $150,000 building campaign. I found a budget destroyed, resources consumed[,] a board of managers in despair.

Tulsa has destroyed the homes, taken the lives and maimed the bodies of the best friends the white man has in America, yea, the world.

There is no man in the world that has [stood] by [and] will stand by the white man like the Negro.

There is no justification for the wholesale destruction of property and resources of the thousands of innocent, law abiding, home building Negroes. We do not condone the wrong deeds of the bad Negro. We deplore his existence. We pray the co-operative influences of all people to help reform or restrain as his co-partners in white. We find it difficult to reach him. They clash You and we are thrown into a whirlpool of human rage. We who emerge with bloody bruised bodies and the savings and buildings of a life-time smouldering in ashes must face each other and realize how trivial and avoidable the cause and how deplorable and lasting the results.

Is the spirit of America dead? Shall the color of a man's skin be the symbol for adverse sentiment?

Mine is a Christian program. Am thoroughly convinced that an active wide awake Christianity will cure this human ill.

There comes times in a Christian program when it becomes necessary to drive out the money changers and land grafters.

Unhappily Tulsa has worked into that stage.

Tulsa is not all bad. There are good citizens in Tulsa. They, as much as any, deplore the plot that will not out.

We need a nearer approach to the principles and teachings of the Golden Rule. The hammer and claw pistol and gun create hate. And hate hurries us ont to destruction.

There is no place in a Christian program for hate.

Let's make America safe for her own citizens and courteous to others.

G. A. Gregg, Executive Secretary
Hunton Branch Young Men's Christian Association

Appendix B

Graduates of the First Janitor Training School Conducted by the Kansas City Urban League

NAMES AS PROVIDED in news release, whether found in city directories for 1932, 1933, or 1938; occupations and home addresses listed (h)

Name	1932 Occupation	1933 Occupation	1938 Occupation
Moses Allen	Y janitor Urban League (h) 2423 East Twenty-third	Y janitor Urban League same	Y janitor Urban League 2106 East Twenty-fourth Terrace
James A. Anderson	NA	NA	NA
William Bell	NA	NA	NA
Arthur Bennett	NA	Y not listed	Y janitor Raineer Apts (h) 1113 Troost
Roscoe Bohanon	Y waiter (h) 2211 Olive	Y waiter (h) 2418 Olive	Y waiter same
Fred Cheeks	NA	NA	NA
Eddie Davis	NA	NA	NA
Sherman Dawson	Y porter Bostonian shoe store (h) 815 Euclid	Y porter same same	Y porter same same

Name	1932 Occupation	1933 Occupation	1938 Occupation
Ottaway Doyle	NA	NA	Y deliveryman Dolan Bros. Pharmacy (h) 1325 East Thirteenth
George Faulkner	Y janitor 1113 East Seventeenth	Y janitor same	Y janitor 1712 Forest
Ruben Gardner	NA	NA	Y deliveryman (h) 2501 Brooklyn
Gus Goff	Y janitor Meyer Building (h) 1007 Vine	Y laborer operator same	Y elevator same
LeRoy Grant	Y not listed (h) 3035 Holly	Y laborer same	Y pastor 2938 Belleview
Arthur Hamilton	NA	NA	NA
Sylvester Hamilton	NA	NA	NA
R. O. Harris	Y laborer 2605 Euclid	Y packinghouse 1805 Brooklyn	Y laborer same
Zeldon Harris	NA	NA	Y laborer 1109 Campbell
Eugene Hatcher	NA	Y janitor 2627 East Twenty-ninth	Y janitor 2504–06 Troost (basement)
Noah Hayden	NA	NA	NA
Alce Hicks	NA	NA	Y porter furniture company 1329 Michigan
Edward Holmes	NA	Y janitor 1020A Lydia	NA
Daniel C. Houston	Y janitor Monmouth Apartments 32 Linwood Terrace	Y janitor same	Y meat cutter 1008 Virginia
Emmett Hughes	Y not listed Montgomery Ward 2437 Prospect	Y not listed same 3130 Garfield	NA
Harold W. Johnson	NA	NA	NA

Name	1932 Occupation	1933 Occupation	1938 Occupation
Harrison Johnson	NA	Y laborer 570 Troost	NA
A. F. Joplin	NA	NA	NA
Louis Lay	NA	Y not listed 2423 Euclid	Y laborer same
Edward Madison	Y Pullman porter 2302 Park	Y laborer same	Y laborer 2502 East Twenty-fourth
James Mallory	NA	Y laborer 1521 Virginia	NA
Grant Mason	Y laborer 3536 Drury	Y not listed same	Y janitor 1214 Garfield (basement)
A. J. Matthews	NA	Y laborer 1706 East Twenty-seventh	NA
Leo McClelland	NA	NA	Y laborer 822 East Twenty-fourth
Albert Miller	NA	NA	NA
Edward Miller	NA	NA	NA
William N. Milton	Y janitor 1525 Virginia	Y laborer 1425 Campbell	NA
Simon Mitchem	NA	NA	Y laborer 1826 East Twenty-sixth
Harry Morris	NA	Y laborer 2422 East Thirteenth	NA
William Myree	NA	Y janitor 2436 Tracy	NA
William Nelson	NA	Y janitor 1219 The Paseo	NA
John Patterson	Y laborer 2512 Woodland	Y not listed same	NA
Clarence Peniston	Y janitor Beebe Apartments	Y janitor same	NA

Name	1932 Occupation	1933 Occupation	1938 Occupation
Carter Perry	Y not listed 2455 Michigan	NA	Y janitor 1124 The Paseo
Fred Phillips	Y laborer 724 East Ninth	NA	NA
John Ragsdale	NA	NA	NA
Oliver Ray	NA	Y janitor Valencia Apartments 408 West Forty-sixth	NA
Charles T. Ricketts	Y porter Ferguson and Allison 1007 Woodland	NA same	Y porter Muehlebach Brewing
James B. Rose	NA	Y laborer 2414 East Twenty-third	Y butcher 2323 Olive
Robert R. Rose	NA	Y laborer 2414 East Twenty-third	Y butcher 2325 Olive
M. W. Ruffin	Y sales agent 2326 Brooklyn	Y sales agent 2453 Wabash	Y salesman 2215 Lydia
Vernon Scott	NA	Y janitor Stafford Arms Hotel 3220 Harrison	Y janitor 1327 Troost
Boss Spears	Y sales agent Pyramid Life 914 West Twenty-first	Y laborer Doyle Bros. Funeral 1710 Tracy	Y helper
Jesse Stephens	NA	Y janitor 1204 The Paseo (basement)	NA
H. L. Stewart	NA	NA	NA
William L. Stewart	NA	Y laborer 1702 East Twenty-seventh	Y janitor 2711 East Twenty-third
Harvey Thompson	Y laborer 2416 Charlotte	Y laborer same	Y laborer 3825 East Ninth
Willard Tolson	NA	NA	NA

Name	1932 Occupation	1933 Occupation	1938 Occupation
Hubert Tyson	Y laborer 2207 Olive	Y janitor 2904 Park	Y laborer 1718 Park
Manuel Vanzant	Y cook 2123 Vine	Y laborer same	Y janitor Broadway Apartments 3425 Broadway (basement)
Walter L. Walker	Y not listed 1320 Brooklyn	Y not listed 1010 East Twenty-seventh	NA
Warren H. Walker	Y not listed 1715 Euclid	Y not listed same	Y laborer 1820 East Seventeenth
Matthew Williams	Y laborer 2817 Highland	Y not listed same	Y janitor 4114–16 The Paseo (basement)

Bibliography

Newspapers

Crisis: A Journal of and for the Darker Races (NAACP)
Kansas City American Citizen
Kansas City Call
Kansas City Journal-Post
Kansas City Post
Kansas City Rising Sun
Kansas City Star
Kansas City Sun
Kansas City Times
Labor Herald (Kansas City, Mo.)
Opportunity (National Urban League)
Pilot (Kansas City Urban League)
Topeka Plaindealer
Western Messenger

Archival Collections

Benson, Arthur. Papers. Western Historical Manuscripts, University of Missouri–Kansas City.

Franklin, Chester A., Collection. Black Archives of Mid-America.

Kansas City Urban League. Records, 1919–1995. Missouri State Archives Local Records Preservation Program, microfilm, four reels, M330–M333, Jefferson City.

Naysmith Collection. Western Historical Manuscripts, University of Missouri–Kansas City.

Vernon, Bishop William Tecumseh. Papers. University of Kansas Libraries, Lawrence.

Washington, Booker T. Papers. University of Illinois Press, online edition.

Government Documents

U.S. Department of Commerce. *Negroes in the United States, 1920–1932* Washington, DC: Government Printing Office, 1935. Reprint, New York: Arno Press, 1969.

U.S. Department of Commerce, Bureau of the Census. Eighth Census of the United States (1860). Washington, DC: GPO, 1861.

———. Ninth Census of the United States (1870). Washington, DC: Government Printing Office, 1871.

———. Tenth Census of the United States (1880). Washington, DC: Government Printing Office, 1881.

———. Twelfth Census of the United States (1900). Washington, DC: Government Printing Office, 1901.

———. Thirteenth Census of the United States (1910). Washington, DC: Government Printing Office, 1911.

———. Fourteenth Census of the United States (1920). Washington, DC: Government Printing Office, 1921.

———. *The Social and Economic Status of the Black Population in the United States: An Historical View, 1790–1978.* Washington, DC: Government Printing Office, 1979.

———. *Statistical Abstract of the Census of the United States, 1910.* Washington, DC: Government Printing Office, 1911.

———. *Statistical Abstract of the Census of the United States, 1920.* Washington, DC: Government Printing Office, 1921.

———. *Statistical Abstract of the Census of the United States, 1930.* Washington, DC: Government Printing Office, 1931.

U.S. Department of Labor. *The Negro and Work during the World War and Reconstruction.* By George E. Haynes. Washington, DC: Government Printing Office, 1921.

Other Sources

Allen, Theodore. *The Invention of the White Race.* Vol. 1, *Racial Oppression and Social Control.* London: Verso, 1994.

Ambrose, Stephen E. *Undaunted Courage: Meriwether Lewis, Thomas*

Jefferson, and the Opening of the American West. New York: Simon and Schuster, 1996.

Anderson, Benedict. *Imagined Communities.* Rev. ed. 1983. Reprint, New York: Verso, 1996.

Anderson, James D. *The Education of Blacks in the South, 1860–1935.* Chapel Hill: University of North Carolina Press, 1988.

Anderson, Jervis. *A. Philip Randolph: A Biographical Portrait.* New York: Harcourt Brace Jovanovich, 1972.

Aptheker, Herbert. *A Documentary History of the Negro People in the United States.* 7 vols. 1973. Reprint, New York: First Carol Publishing Group, 1990.

Armstead, Myra B. Young. *"Lord, Please Don't Take Me in August": African Americans in Newport and Saratoga Springs, 1870–1930.* Urbana: University of Illinois Press, 1999.

Arnesen, Eric. *Brotherhoods of Color: Black Railroad Workers and the Struggle for Equality.* Cambridge, MA: Harvard University Press, 2001.

———. *Waterfront Workers of New Orleans: Race, Class and Politics, 1863–1923.* New York: Oxford University Press, 1991.

Arnesen, Eric, Julie Greene, and Bruce Laurie. *Labor Histories: Class, Politics and the Working-Class Experience.* Urbana: University of Illinois Press, 1998.

Athearn, Robert. *In Search of Canaan: Black Migration to Kansas, 1879–1880.* Lawrence: Regents Press of Kansas, 1978.

Bacote, Samuel William. *Who's Who among the Colored Baptists of the United States.* Kansas City: Franklin Hudson, 1913. Reprint, New York: Arno Press, 1980.

Baldwin, Peter C. *Domesticating the Street: The Reform of Public Space in Hartford, 1870–1930.* Columbus: Ohio State University Press, 1999.

Banks, William M. *Black Intellectuals: Race and Responsibility in American Life.* New York: W. W. Norton, 1996.

Bates, Beth Tompkins. *Pullman Porters and the Rise of Protest Politics in Black America, 1925–1945.* Chapel Hill: University of North Carolina Press, 2001.

Bates, Sidney L. "Medicine without Method: Kansas City, Missouri's General and Allied Hospitals under the Department of Health, 1870–1962." Master's thesis, University of Missouri–Kansas City, 1972.

Batterson, Jack A. *Blind Boone: Missouri's Ragtime Pioneer.* Columbia: University of Missouri Press, 1998.

Berland, Oscar. "The Emergence of the Communist Perspective on the 'Negro Question' in America, 1919–1931." Pts. 1 and 2. *Science and Society* 63:4 (Winter 2000): 411–32; 64:2 (Summer 2000): 194–217.

Berlanstein, Lenard R., ed. *Rethinking Labor History: Essays on Discourse and Class Analysis.* Urbana: University of Illinois Press, 1993.

Berlin, Ira. *Many Thousands Gone: The First Two Centuries of Slavery in North America.* Cambridge, MA: Harvard University, Belknap Press, 1998.

Berlin, Ira, Barbara J. Fields, Thavolia Glymph, Joseph P. Reidy, and Leslie S. Rowland, eds. *Free at Last: A Documentary History of Slavery, Freedom and the Civil War.* New York: New Press, 1992.

Bernard, Emily, ed. *Remember Me to Harlem: The Letters of Langston Hughes and Carl Van Vechten.* New York: Alfred A. Knopf, 2001.

Bernhard, Virginia, Betty Brandon, Elizabeth Fox-Genovese, Theda Perdue, and Elizabeth H. Turner, eds. *Hidden Histories of Women in the New South.* Columbia: University of Missouri Press, 1994.

Berwanger, Eugene. "Hardin and Langston: Western Black Spokesmen of the Reconstruction Era." *Journal of Negro History* 64:2 (Spring 1979): 101–14.

Bethel, Elizabeth Raue. *The Roots of African-American Identity: Memory and History in Antebellum Free Communities.* New York: St. Martin's Press, 1997.

Blee, Kathleen. *Women of the Klan: Racism and Gender in the 1920s.* Berkeley and Los Angeles: University of California Press, 1991.

Blumer, Herbert. *Symbolic Interactionism: Perspective and Method.* Berkeley and Los Angeles: University of California Press, 1969.

Bonner, Marita. *Frye Street and Environs.* Edited by Joyce Flynn and Joyce Occomy Stricklin. Boston: Beacon Press, 1987.

Bourdieu, Pierre, and Loic J. D. Wacquant. *An Invitation to Reflexive Sociology.* Chicago: University of Chicago Press, 1992.

Bowser, James Dallas, et al. *Negro Men, Women and Affairs of Greater Kansas City.* Kansas City: Burton Publishing, 1915. Only an incomplete fragment of this work is known to exist.

Boyd, Robert L. "Racial Segregation and Insurance Enterprise among Black Americans in Northern Cities." *Sociological Quarterly* 39:2 (Spring 1998): 337–49.

Brady, Marilyn Dell. "Kansas Federation of Colored Women's Clubs, 1900–1930." *Kansas History* 9:1 (Spring 1986): 19–30.

Braudel, Fernand. *Afterthoughts on Material Civilization and Capitalism.* Translated by Patricia M. Ranum. Baltimore: Johns Hopkins University Press, 1977.

Brinkley, Alan. *The End of Reform: New Deal Liberalism in Recession and War.* New York: Vintage Books, 1995.

Brophy, Albert. *Reconstructing the Dreamland: The Tulsa Race Riot of 1921.* Oxford: Oxford University Press, 2001.

Brown, A. Theodore, and Lyle W. Dorsett. *K.C.: A History of Kansas City, Missouri.* Boulder: Pruett Publishing, 1978.

Brown, Hallie Q. *Homespun Heroines and Other Women of Distinction.* Reprint, New York: Oxford University Press, 1988.

Bruce, H. C. *The New Man: Twenty-nine Years a Slave, Twenty-nine Years a Free Man; Recollections of H. C. Bruce.* Blacks in the American West Series. Lincoln: University of Nebraska, 1996.

Bruce, Janet. *The Kansas City Monarchs: Champions of Black Baseball.* Lawrence: University Press of Kansas, 1985.

Canaan, Gareth. "'Part of the Loaf': Economic Conditions of Chicago's African American Working Class during the 1920s." *Journal of Social History* 35:1 (Fall 2001): 147–74.

Carper, James C. "The Popular Ideology of Segregated Schooling: Attitudes toward the Education of Blacks in Kansas, 1854–1900." *Kansas History* 1:4 (Winter 1978): 254–65.

Carter, Dan T. *Scottsboro: A Tragedy of the American South.* 1969. Reprint, Baton Rouge: Louisiana State University Press, 1979.

Cecelski, David S., and Timothy B. Tyson, eds. *Democracy Betrayed: The Wilmington Race Riot of 1898 and Its Legacy.* Chapel Hill: University of North Carolina Press, 1998.

Cell, John. *The Highest Stage of White Supremacy: The Origins of Segregation in South Africa and the American South.* 1982. Reprint, Cambridge: Cambridge University Press, 1992.

Chafe, William H. "The Negro and Populism: A Kansas Case Study." *Journal of Southern History* 34:3 (August 1968): 402–19.

Charras, Françoise. "Landings: Robert Hayden's and Kamau Brathwaite's Poetic Renderings of the Middle Passage in Comparative Perspective." In *Black Imagination and the Middle Passage,* edited by Maria Diedrich, Henry Louis Gates Jr., and Carl Pedersen, 57–69. New York: Oxford University Press, 1999.

Chaudhuri, Nupur. "'We All Seem Like Brothers and Sisters': The African American Community in Manhattan, Kansas, 1865–1940." In *"We Specialize in the Wholly Impossible": A Reader in Black Women's History,* edited by Darlene Clark Hine, Wilma King, and Linda Reed, 543–60. Brooklyn: Carlson Publishing, 1995.

Cheek, William, and Aimee Lee Cheek. *John Mercer Langston and the*

Fight for Black Freedom, 1829–65. Blacks in the New World Series. Urbana: University of Illinois Press, 1989.

Clark-Lewis, Elizabeth. *Living In, Living Out: African American Domestics in Washington, D.C., 1910–1940.* Washington, DC: Smithsonian Institution, 1994.

Cohen, Anthony P. *The Symbolic Construction of Community.* Key Ideas Series. 1985. Reprint, London and New York: Routledge, 1993.

Cohen, Lizabeth. *Making a New Deal: Industrial Workers in Chicago, 1919–1939.* Cambridge: Cambridge University Press, 1990.

Cohen, Warren I. *Empire without Tears: America's Foreign Relations, 1921–1933.* Philadelphia: Temple University Press, 1987.

Cooper, Anna Julia. *A Voice from the South.* Schomberg Library of Nineteenth-Century Black Women Writers. New York: Oxford University Press, 1988.

Cooper, Frederick, Thomas C. Holt, and Rebecca J. Scott. *Beyond Slavery: Explorations of Race, Labor, and Citizenship in Postemancipation Societies.* Chapel Hill: University of North Carolina Press, 2000.

Cooper, Wayne. *Claude McKay: Rebel Sojourner in the Harlem Renaissance.* Baton Rouge: Louisiana State University Press, 1987.

Cornish, Dudley Taylor. *The Sable Arm: Black Troops in the Union Army, 1861–1865.* Lawrence: University Press of Kansas, 1987.

Costiglia, Frank. *Awkward Dominion: American Political, Economic and Cultural Relations with Europe, 1919–1933.* Ithaca, NY: Cornell University Press, 1984.

Cott, Nancy, ed. *No Small Courage: A History of Women in the United States.* Oxford: Oxford University Press, 2000.

Coulter, Charles E. "The Two Josephines: Josephine St. Pierre Ruffin and Josephine Silone Yates." Unpublished paper.

Couto, Richard A. *Ain't Gonna Let Nobody Turn Me Around: The Pursuit of Racial Justice in the Rural South.* Philadelphia: Temple University Press, 1991.

Cox, Thomas C. *Blacks in Topeka, Kansas, 1865–1915: A Social History.* Baton Rouge: Louisiana State University Press, 1982.

Crockett, Norman L. *The Black Towns.* Lawrence: Regents Press of Kansas, 1979.

Cronon, William. *Nature's Metropolis: Chicago and the Great West.* New York: W. W. Norton, 1991.

Cullen, Jim. *The Art of Democracy: A Concise History of Popular Culture.* New York: Monthly Review Press, 1996.

Cunard, Nancy, and Hugh Ford, eds. *Negro: An Anthology.* 1970. Reprint, New York: Continuum, 1996.

Curtis, Annette W. *Jackson County, Missouri, Marriage Record: American Citizens of African Descent, 1865–1881; An Abstract with Indexes and Commentary.* N.p., 1992.

Davis, Angela. *Blues Legacies and Black Feminism: Gertrude "Ma" Rainey, Bessie Smith, and Billie Holiday.* New York: Pantheon Books, 1998.

———. *Women, Race and Class.* 1981. Reprint, New York: Random House, 1982.

Davis, Elizabeth Lindsay. *Lifting as They Climb.* 1933. Reprint, New York: G. K. Hall, 1996.

Denning, Michael. *The Cultural Front: The Laboring of American Culture in the Twentieth Century.* New York: Verso, 1996.

DeVoto, Bernard, ed. *The Journals of Lewis and Clark.* Boston: Houghton Mifflin, 1953.

Diedrich, Maria, Henry Louis Gates Jr., and Carl Pedersen, eds. *Black Imagination and the Middle Passage.* New York: Oxford University Press, 1999.

Donham, Donald L. *History, Power and Ideology: Central Issues in Marxism and Anthropology.* Berkeley and Los Angeles: University of California Press, 1999.

Drake, St. Clair, and Horace R. Cayton. *Black Metropolis: A Study of Negro Life in a Northern City.* 1945. Reprint, Chicago: University of Chicago Press, 1993.

Du Bois, William Edward Burghardt. *Black Reconstruction in America, 1860–1880.* 1935. Reprint, New York: Atheneum, 1992.

———. *Darkwater: Voices from within the Veil.* 1921. Reprint, Millwood, NY: Kraus-Thompson Organization, 1975.

———. *Dusk of Dawn: An Essay toward an Autobiography of a Race Concept.* 1940. Reprint, New York: Schocken, 1968.

———. *The Gift of Black Folk: The Negroes in the Making of America.* 1924. Reprint, New York: Washington Square Press, 1970.

———. *The Philadelphia Negro: A Social Study.* 1899. Reprint, Philadelphia: University of Pennsylvania Press, 1996.

———. *The Souls of Black Folk.* 1903. Reprint, New York: New American Library, 1969.

Dumenil, Lynn. *Modern Temper: American Culture and Society in the 1920s.* New York: Hill and Wang, 1995.

Durkheim, Emile. *The Division of Labor in Society.* Translated by W. D. Halls. New York: Free Press, 1984.

———. *The Rules of Sociological Method and Selected Texts on Sociology and Its Method.* Translated by W. D. Halls. New York: Free Press, 1982.

Early, Gerald, ed. *"Ain't but a Place": An Anthology of African American Writings about St. Louis.* St. Louis: Missouri Historical Society Press, 1998.

Elias, Norbert. *On Civilization, Power and Knowledge: Selected Writings.* Edited by Stephen Mennell and Johan Goudsblom. Chicago: University of Chicago Press, 1998.

Ellison, Ralph. *Going to the Territory.* New York: Vintage Books, 1986.

———. *Shadow and Act.* 1953. Reprint, New York: Vintage Books, 1964.

Ellsworth, Scott. *Death in a Promised Land: The Tulsa Race Riot of 1921.* Baton Rouge: Louisiana State University Press, 1982.

Farnsworth, Robert M., ed. *Caviar and Cabbage: Selected Columns by Melvin B. Tolson from the "Washington Tribune," 1937–1944.* Columbia: University of Missouri Press, 1982.

———, ed. *Melvin Tolson, 1898–1966: Plain Talk and Poetic Prophecy.* Columbia: University of Missouri Press, 1984.

Fass, Paula. *The Damned and the Beautiful: American Youth in the 1920s.* New York: Oxford University Press, 1977.

Feldman, Lynne B. *A Sense of Place: Birmingham's Black Middle Class Community, 1890–1930.* Tuscaloosa: University of Alabama Press, 1999.

Fernandes, Leela. *Producing Workers: The Politics of Gender, Class, and Culture in the Calcutta Jute Mills.* Philadelphia: University of Pennsylvania Press, 1997.

Ferrer, Ada. *Insurgent Cuba: Race, Nation and Revolution, 1868–1898.* Chapel Hill: University of North Carolina Press, 1999.

Fink, Deborah. *Agrarian Women: Wives and Mothers in Rural Nebraska, 1880–1940.* Chapel Hill: University of North Carolina Press, 1992.

Fink, Leon. *Workingmen's Democracy: The Knights of Labor and American Politics.* Urbana: University of Illinois Press, 1985.

Flanning, Douglas. *Bound for Freedom: Black Los Angeles in Jim Crow America.* Berkeley and Los Angeles: University of California Press, 2005.

Fluker, Walter Earl, and Catherine Tumber, eds. *A Strange Freedom: The Best of Howard Thurman on Religious Experience and Public Life.* Boston: Beacon Press, 1998.

Flynn, Jane Fifield. *Kansas City Women of Independent Minds.* Kansas City: Fifield Publishing, 1992.

Fogel, Walter. *The Negro in the Meat Industry.* Vol. 12. Philadelphia: University of Pennsylvania Press, 1970.

Folsom, Franklin. *Impatient Armies of the Poor: The Story of Collective Action of the Unemployed, 1808–1942.* Boulder: University of Colorado Press, 1991.

Foner, Eric. *Freedom's Lawmakers: A Directory of Black Officeholders during Reconstruction.* Rev. ed. Baton Rouge: Louisiana State University, 1996.

———. *Free Soil, Free Labor, Free Men: The Ideology of the Republican Party before the Civil War.* Oxford: Oxford University Press, 1970.

———. *Nothing but Freedom: Emancipation and Its Legacy.* Baton Rouge: Louisiana State University Press, 1983.

———. *Reconstruction: America's Unfinished Revolution, 1863–1877.* New York: Harper and Row, 1988.

Foner, Philip S., ed. *Black Socialist Preacher: The Teachings of Reverend George Washington Woodbey and His Disciple Reverend George W. Slater Jr.* San Francisco: Synthesis Publications, 1983.

Foner, Philip S., and Robert James Branham, eds. *Lift Every Voice: African American Oratory, 1787–1900.* Tuscaloosa: University of Alabama Press, 1998.

Foner, Philip S., and Ronald L. Lewis, eds. *Black Workers: A Documentary History from Colonial Times to the Present.* Philadelphia: Temple University Press, 1989.

Foucault, Michel. *The Archaeology of Knowledge.* New York: Pantheon Books, 1972.

Franklin, Buck Colbert. *My Life and an Era: The Autobiography of Buck Colbert Franklin.* Edited by John Hope Franklin and John Whittington Franklin. Baton Rouge: Louisiana State University Press, 1997.

Franklin, Jimmie Lewis. *Journey toward Hope: A History of Blacks in Oklahoma.* Norman: University of Oklahoma Press, 1982.

Franklin, John Hope. *The Free Negro in North Carolina, 1790–1880.* 1943. Reprint, Chapel Hill: University of North Carolina Press, 1995.

———. *Race and History: Selected Essays, 1938–1988.* Baton Rouge: Louisiana State University Press, 1989.

———. *Reconstruction: After the Civil War.* Chicago: University of Chicago Press, 1961.

Franklin, John Hope, and Alfred A. Moss Jr. *From Slavery to Freedom: A History of African Americans.* 7th ed. New York: Alfred A. Knopf, 1994.

Frazier, E. Franklin. *The Negro Family in the United States.* 1938. Reprint, Chicago: University of Chicago Press, 1966.

Gamble, Vanessa Northington. *Making a Place for Ourselves: The Black Hospital Movement, 1920–1945.* New York: Oxford University Press, 1995.

Gaspar, David Barry, and Darlene Clark Hine, eds. *More than Chattel:*

Black Women and Slavery in the Americas. Bloomington: Indiana University Press, 1996.

Gate City Directory. Vols. 1–15. Kansas City: Gate City Publishing, 1925–1939.

Gatewood, Willard B. *Aristocrats of Color: The Black Elite, 1880–1920.* Bloomington: Indiana University Press, 1990.

———. *Black Americans and the White Man's Burden, 1898–1903.* Urbana: University of Illinois Press, 1973.

Geertz, Clifford. *The Interpretation of Cultures: Selected Essays.* New York: Basic Books, 1973.

Gellert, Lawrence. "Negro Songs of Protest: North and South Carolina and Georgia." In *Negro: An Anthology,* edited by Nancy Cunard and Hugh Ford, 226–37. Reprint, New York: Continuum, 1996.

Gerber, David. *Black Ohio and the Color Line, 1860–1915.* Urbana: University of Illinois Press, 1976.

Gibson, Elvis. *Kansas City: Mecca of the New Negro.* Kansas City, 1997.

Giddings, Paula. *When and Where I Enter: The Impact of Black Women on Race and Sex in America.* New York: Bantam Books, 1984.

Giddins, Gary. *Celebrating Bird: The Triumph of Charlie Parker.* New York: Beech Tree Books, 1987.

Gilmore, Glenda. *Gender and Jim Crow: Women and the Politics of White Supremacy in North Carolina, 1896–1920.* Chapel Hill: University of North Carolina Press, 1996.

Gilroy, Paul. *The Black Atlantic: Modernity and Double Consciousness.* Cambridge, MA: Harvard University Press, 1995.

Goings, Kenneth W., and Raymond A. Mohl, eds. *The New African American Urban History.* Thousand Oaks, CA: Sage Publications, 1996.

Goldberg, Michael Lewis. *An Army of Women: Gender and Politics in Gilded Age Kansas.* Baltimore: Johns Hopkins University Press, 1997.

Goodman, James. *Stories of Scottsboro.* New York: Vintage Books, 1994.

Gordon, Jacob U. *Narratives of African Americans in Kansas, 1870–1992: Beyond the Exodust Movement.* Lewiston, NY: Edwin Mellen Press, 1993.

Gordon, Linda. "Black and White Visions of Welfare: Women's Welfare Activism, 1890–1945." In *"We Specialize in the Wholly Impossible": A Reader in Black Women's History,* edited by Darlene Clark Hine, Wilma King, and Linda Reed, 449–85. Brooklyn: Carlson Publishing, 1995.

Gosnell, Harold F. *Negro Politicians: The Rise of Negro Politics in Chicago.* Chicago: University of Chicago Press, 1967.

Gottlieb, Peter. *Making Their Own Way: Southern Blacks' Migration to Pittsburgh, 1916–1930*. Urbana: University of Illinois Press, 1987.

Green, Dan S., and Edwin D. Driver, eds. *W. E. B. Du Bois on Sociology and the Black Community*. Chicago: University of Chicago Press, 1978.

Green, James R. *The World of the Worker: Labor in Twentieth-Century America*. Urbana: University of Illinois Press, 1998.

Greenbaum, Susan O. *The Afro-American Community in Kansas City, Kansas: A History*. Kansas City: City of Kansas City, Kansas, 1982.

Greenberg, Cheryl Lynn. *Or Does It Explode? Black Harlem in the Great Depression*. New York: Oxford University Press, 1991.

Greene, Lorenzo J. *The Negro in Colonial New England*. New York: Columbia University Press, 1942.

Greene, Lorenzo J., Gary R. Kremer, and Antonio F. Holland. *Missouri's Black Heritage*. Rev. ed. Columbia: University of Missouri Press, 1993.

Greene, Lorenzo J., and Carter G. Woodson. *The Negro Wage Earner*. 1930. Reprint, New York: AMS Press, 1970.

Greenwood, Janette Thomas. *Bittersweet Legacy: The Black and White "Better Classes" in Charlotte, 1850–1910*. Chapel Hill: University of North Carolina Press, 1994.

Gregson, Mary Eschelbach. "Population Dynamics in Rural Missouri, 1860–1880." *Social Science History* 21:1 (Spring 1997): 85–110.

Grossman, James R. *Land of Hope: Chicago, Black Southerners, and the Great Migration*. Chicago: University of Chicago Press, 1989.

Grothaus, Larry. "Kansas City Blacks, Harry Truman and the Pendergast Machine." *Missouri Historical Review* 69:1 (October 1974): 65–82.

Grover, Kathryn. *Make a Way Somehow: African-American Life in a Northern Community, 1790–1965*. Syracuse, NY: Syracuse University Press, 1994.

Gutman, Herbert. *The Black Family in Slavery and Freedom, 1750–1925*. New York: Vintage Books, 1976.

Hale, Grace Elizabeth. *Making Whiteness: The Culture of Segregation in the South, 1890–1940*. New York: Pantheon Books, 1998.

Hall, Jacqueline Dowd, James Leloudis, Robert Korstad, Mary Murphy, LuAnn Jones, and Christopher B. Daly. *Like a Family: The Making of a Southern Cotton Mill World*. New York: W. W. Norton, 1987.

Halpern, Rick, and Roger Horowitz. *Meatpackers: An Oral History of Black Packinghouse Workers and Their Struggle for Racial and Economic Equality*. Oral History Series. New York: Twayne Publishers, 1996.

Hamilton, Kenneth W. *Black Towns and Profit: Promotion and Development in the Trans-Appalachian West, 1877–1915*. Urbana: University of Illinois Press, 1991.

Harris, Abram L. "The Negro Population in Minneapolis: A Study in Race Relations." Minneapolis: Minneapolis Urban League and Phyllis Wheatley Settlement House, 1926.

———. *Race, Radicalism and Reform: Selected Papers*. Edited by William Darity Jr. New Brunswick, NJ: Transaction Publishers, 1989.

Hartman, Saidiya V. *Scenes of Subjection: Terror, Slavery and Self-Making in Nineteenth-Century America*. New York: Oxford University Press, 1997.

Harvey, David. *The Urban Experience*. Baltimore: Johns Hopkins University Press, 1989.

Hawley, Ellis. *The Great War and the Search for a Modern Order*. New York: St. Martin's Press, 1979.

———. "Herbert Hoover, the Commerce Secretariat, and the Vision of an 'Associative State,' 1921–1928." *Journal of American History* 61:2 (June 1974): 116–40.

Henderson, Alexa Benson, and Janice Sumler-Edmond. *Freedom's Odyssey: African American History Essays from Phylon*. Atlanta: Clark Atlanta University Press, 1999.

Herskovits, Melvin. *The Myth of the Negro Past*. 1941. Reprint, Boston: Beacon Press, 1990.

Higginbotham, Evelyn Brooks. *Righteous Discontent: The Women's Movement in the Black Baptist Church, 1880–1920*. Cambridge, MA: Harvard University Press, 1993.

Higham, John. *Strangers in the Land: Patterns of American Nativism, 1860–1925*. New York: Atheneum, 1973.

Hine, Darlene Clark. "Black Professionals and Race Consciousness: Origins of the Civil Rights Movement, 1890–1950." *Journal of American History* 89:4 (March 2003): 1279–94.

———. *Black Women in White: Racial Conflict and Cooperation in the Nursing Profession, 1890–1950*. Bloomington: Indiana University Press, 1989.

———. *Hine Sight: Black Women and the Re-construction of American History*. Brooklyn: Carlson Publishing, 1994.

———, ed. *The State of Afro-American History*. Baton Rouge: Louisiana State University Press, 1986.

Hine, Darlene Clark, Wilma King, and Linda Reed, eds. *"We Specialize in the Wholly Impossible": A Reader in Black Women's History*. Brooklyn: Carlson Publishing, 1995.

Hine, Darlene Clark, and Kathleen Thompson. *A Shining Thread of Hope: The History of Black Women in America.* New York: Broadway Books, 1998.

Holt, Thomas C. "Marking: Race, Race-Making and the Writing of History." *American Historical Review* 100:1 (February 1995): 1–20.

———. *The Problem of Freedom: Race, Labor and Politics in Jamaica and Britain, 1832–1938.* Baltimore: Johns Hopkins University Press, 1992.

Honey, Michael K. *Southern Labor and Black Civil Rights.* Urbana: University of Illinois Press, 1993.

hooks, bell. *Killing Rage: Ending Racism.* New York: Henry Holt, 1995.

Hoyes City Directory. Vols. 8–37. Kansas City: Hoyes Publishing, 1895–1924.

Huber, Patrick J., and Gary R. Kremer. "Nathaniel C. Bruce, Black Education and the 'Tuskegee of the Midwest.'" *Missouri Historical Review* 86:1 (October 1991): 37–54.

Huggins, Nathan. *Harlem Renaissance.* New York: Oxford University Press, 1971.

Hughes, Langston. *The Big Sea: An Autobiography of Langston Hughes.* New York: Alfred A. Knopf, 1940.

———. *Good Morning Revolution: Uncollected Writings of Social Protest.* Edited by Faith Berry. New York: Carol Publishing, 1973.

———. *The Panther and the Lash: Poems of Our Time.* New York: Vintage Books, 1992.

———. *The Ways of White Folks.* 1934. Reprint, New York: Vintage Books, 1962.

Hunter, Tera W. *To 'Joy My Freedom: Southern Black Women's Lives and Labors after the Civil War.* Cambridge, MA: Harvard University Press, 1997.

Hurt, R. Douglas. *Agriculture and Slavery in Missouri's Little Dixie.* Columbia: University of Missouri Press, 1992.

Ignatiev, Noel. *How the Irish Became White.* New York: Routledge, 1995.

Jackson, Kenneth T. *The Ku Klux Klan in the City, 1915–1930.* 1967. Reprint, Chicago: Ivan R. Dee, 1992.

Jackson, Lawrence. *Ralph Ellison: Emergence of Genius.* New York: John Wiley and Sons, 2002.

Jacobson, Matthew Frye. *Whiteness of a Different Color: European Immigrants and the Alchemy of Race.* Cambridge, MA: Harvard University Press, 1998.

James, C. L. R. *Black Jacobins: Toussaint L'Ouverture and the San Domingo Revolution.* 1938. Reprint, New York: Vintage Books, 1962.

Jaynes, Gerald David. *Branches without Roots: Genesis of the Black Working Class in the American South, 1862–1882.* New York: Oxford University Press, 1986.

Jenkins, Keith, ed. *The Postmodern History Reader.* New York: Routledge, 1997.

Johnson, Alonzo, and Paul Jersild, eds. *Ain't Gonna Lay My 'Ligion Down: African American Religion in the South.* Columbia: University of South Carolina Press, 1996.

Johnson, James Weldon. *The Autobiography of an Ex-Coloured Man.* 1912. Reprint, New York: Penguin Books, 1990.

Johnson, Paul, ed. *African-American Christianity.* Berkeley and Los Angeles: University of California Press, 1994.

Jones, Anna H. "The American Colored Woman." *Voice of the Negro* 2:10 (October 1905): 692–94.

———. "A Century's Progress for the American Colored Woman." *Voice of the Negro* 2:9 (September 1905): 631–33.

Jones, Jacqueline. *American Work: Four Centuries of Black and White Labor.* New York: W. W. Norton, 1998.

———. *Labor of Love, Labor of Sorrow: Black Women, Work and the Family, from Slavery to the Present.* New York: Vintage Books, 1985.

———. "Reverend Daniel Arthur Holmes." Unpublished paper.

Kalberg, Stephen. *Max Weber's Comparative Historical Sociology.* Chicago: University of Chicago Press, 1994.

Kanigel, Robert. *The One Best Way: Frederick Winslow Taylor and the Enigma of Efficiency.* New York: Penguin Books, 1997.

Kansas Department of Education. *The WPA Guide to 1930s Kansas.* 1939. Reprint, Lawrence: University Press of Kansas, 1984.

Kasper, Shirl. "The *Kansas City Call,* 1929–1930." Unpublished paper.

Katz, Michael B., and Thomas J. Sugrue, eds. *W. E. B. Du Bois, Race, and the City: "The Philadelphia Negro" and Its Legacy.* Philadelphia: University of Pennsylvania Press, 1998.

Katznelson, Ira. *Marxism and the City.* Oxford: Oxford University Press, 1992.

Katznelson, Ira, and Aristide R. Zolberg, eds. *Working-Class Formation: Nineteenth-Century Patterns in Western Europe and the United States.* Princeton, NJ: Princeton University Press, 1986.

Kelley, Robin D. G. *Hammer and Hoe: Alabama Communists during the Great Depression.* Chapel Hill: University of North Carolina Press, 1990.

———. *Race Rebels: Culture, Politics and the Black Working Class.* New York: Free Press, 1994.

———. "'We Are Not What We Seem': Re-thinking Black Working-Class Opposition in the Jim Crow South." *Journal of American History* 80:1 (June 1993): 75–112.

Kenan, Malik. "The Mirror of Race: Postmodernism and the Celebration of Difference." In *In Defense of History: Marxism and the Postmodern Agenda,* edited by Ellen Meiksins Wood and John Bellamy Foster, 113–34. New York: Monthly Review Press, 1997.

Kennedy, Florynce. *Color Me Flo: My Hard Life and Good Times.* New York: Prentice-Hall, 1976.

Kerber, Linda K., Alice Kessler-Harris, and Kathryn Kish Sklar, eds. *U.S. History as Women's History: New Feminist Essays.* Chapel Hill: University of North Carolina Press, 1995.

Kessler-Harris, Alice. *Out to Work: A History of Wage-Earning Women in the United States.* Oxford: Oxford University Press, 1982.

Kester, Howard. *Revolt among the Sharecroppers.* Knoxville: University of Tennessee Press, 1997.

Kinsler, Herman. *The Biography of Kansas City's Negro Business and Professional Men and the Trip South.* Kansas City, 1920.

Kirkschke, Amy Helen. *Aaron Douglas: Art, Race and the Harlem Renaissance.* Jackson: University Press of Mississippi, 1995.

Klugler, Richard. *Simple Justice: The History of "Brown v. Board of Education" and Black America's Struggle for Equality.* New York: Alfred A. Knopf, 1976.

Knock, Thomas J. *To End All Wars: Woodrow Wilson and the Quest for a New World Order.* Princeton, NJ: Princeton University Press, 1992.

Knupfer, Anne Meis. *Toward a Tenderer Humanity and a Nobler Womanhood: African American Women's Clubs in Turn-of-the-Century Chicago.* New York: New York University Press, 1996.

Kornweibel, Theodore, Jr. *In Search of the Promised Land: Essays in Black Urban History.* Port Washington, NY: Kennikat Press, 1981.

Kremer, Gary R., ed. *George Washington Carver in His Own Words.* Columbia: University of Missouri Press, 1987.

———. *James Milton Turner and the Promise of America: The Public Life of a Post-Civil War Black Leader.* Columbia: University of Missouri Press, 1991.

———. "'Just Like the Garden of Eden': African-American Community Life in Kansas City's Leeds." *Missouri Historical Review* 98:2 (January 2004): 121–44.

Kremer, Gary R., and Cindy M. Mackey. "'Yours for the Race': The Life and Work of Josephine Silone Yates." *Missouri Historical Review* 90:2 (January 1996): 199–215.

Kremer, Gary R., and Evan P. Orr. "Lake Placid: 'A Recreational Center for Colored People in the Missouri Ozarks.'" *Missouri Historical Review* 95:1 (October 2001): 68–83.

Kusmer, Kenneth L. *A Ghetto Takes Shape: Black Cleveland, 1870–1930.* Urbana: University of Illinois Press, 1976.

Lane, Ann J. *The Brownsville Affair: National Crisis and Black Reaction.* Port Washington, NY: Kennikat Press, 1971.

Lane, Roger. *Roots of Violence in Black Philadelphia, 1869–1900.* Cambridge, MA: Harvard University Press, 1986.

———. *William Dorsey's Philadelphia and Ours.* New York: Oxford University Press, 1991.

Larsen, Lawrence H., and Nancy J. Hulston. *Pendergast!* Columbia: University of Missouri Press, 1997.

———. "Through the Eyes of a Medical Student: A Window on Frontier Life in Kansas City." *Missouri Historical Review* 88:4 (July 1994): 430–45.

Larsen, Nella. *Passing.* New York: Modern Library, 2000.

Lasch-Quinn, Elizabeth. *Black Neighbors: Race and the Limits of Reform in the American Settlement House Movement, 1890–1945.* Chapel Hill: University of North Carolina Press, 1993.

Laurie, Bruce. *Artisans into Workers: Labor in Nineteenth-Century America.* Urbana: University of Illinois Press, 1997.

Lemelle, Sidney, and Robin D. G. Kelley, eds. *Imagining Home: Class, Culture and Nationalism in the African Diaspora.* New York: Verso Press, 1994.

Lerner, Gerda. *Black Women in White America: A Documentary History.* New York: Vintage, 1973.

Letwin, Daniel. *The Challenge of Interracial Unionism: Alabama Coal Miners, 1878–1921.* Chapel Hill: University of North Carolina Press, 1998.

Levine, Lawrence W. *Black Culture and Black Consciousness: Afro-American Thought from Slavery to Freedom.* Oxford: Oxford University Press, 1977.

Lewis, David Levering. *W. E. B. Du Bois: Biography of a Race, 1868–1919.* Vol. 1. New York: Henry Holt, 1993.

———. *W. E. B. Du Bois: The Fight for Equality and the American Century, 1919–1963.* Vol. 2. New York: Henry Holt, 1993.

———. *W. E. B. Du Bois: A Reader.* New York: Henry Holt, 1995.

Lewis, Earl. *In Their Own Interests: Race, Class, and Power in Twentieth-Century Norfolk, Virginia.* Berkeley and Los Angeles: University of California Press, 1991.

———. "Invoking Concepts, Problematizing Identities: The Life of Charles N. Hunter and the Implications for the Study of Gender and Labor." *Labor History* 34:2–3 (Spring–Summer 1993): 292–308.

Lincoln, C. Eric, and Lawrence H. Mamiya. *The Black Church in the African American Experience.* Durham, NC: Duke University Press, 1990.

Litwack, Leon. *Trouble in Mind: Black Southerners in the Age of Jim Crow.* New York: Alfred A. Knopf, 1998.

Locke, Alain. *The New Negro: Voices of the Harlem Renaissance.* 1925. Reprint, New York: Atheneum, 1992.

Logan, Rayford. *The Betrayal of the Negro: From Rutherford B. Hayes to Woodrow Wilson.* 1954. Reprint, New York: Collier Books, 1965.

———. *The Negro in American Life and Thought: The Nadir, 1877–1901.* New York: Dial Press, 1954.

Lutz, Tom, and Susanna Ashton, eds. *These "Colored" United States: African American Essays from the 1920s.* New Brunswick, NJ: Rutgers University Press, 1996.

Majors, Monroe A. *Noted Negro Women: Their Triumphs and Activities.* 1893. Reprint, Chicago: Donohue and Hennebery, 1971.

Maloney, Thomas N. "Degrees of Inequality: The Advance of Black Male Workers in the Northern Meat Packing and Steel Industries before World War II." *Social Science History* 19:1 (Spring 1995): 31–62.

Marable, Manning. *Beyond Black and White: Transforming African-American Politics.* London and New York: Verso Press, 1996.

———. *Black Leadership.* New York: Columbia University Press, 1998.

———. *Speaking Truth to Power: Essays on Race, Resistance and Radicalism.* Boulder, CO: Westview Press, 1996.

Marable, Manning, and Leith Mullings, eds. *Let Nobody Turn Us Around: Voices of Resistance, Reform, and Renewal; An African American Anthology.* Boulder, CO, and New York: Rowman and Littlefield, 2000.

Marks, Carole. *Farewell, We're Good and Gone: The Great Black Migration.* Bloomington: Indiana University Press, 1989.

Martin, Asa. *Our Negro Population: A Sociological Study of the Negroes of Kansas City, Missouri.* Kansas City, MO: Franklin Hudson, 1913.

Martin, Dwayne. "The Hidden Community: The Black Community of Kansas City, Missouri, during the 1870s and 1880s." Master's thesis, University of Missouri–Kansas City, 1982.

Massey, Douglas S., and Nancy A. Denton. *American Apartheid: Segregation and the Making of the Underclass.* Cambridge, MA: Harvard University Press, 1993.

———. "The Dimensions of Residential Segregation." *Social Forces* 67: 2 (December 1988): 281–315.

McGovern, James R. *Anatomy of a Lynching: The Killing of Claude Neal.* Baton Rouge: Louisiana State University Press, 1982.

McKiven, Henry M. *Iron and Steel: Class, Race, and Community in Birmingham, Alabama, 1875–1920.* Chapel Hill: University of North Carolina Press, 1995.

McLagan, Elizabeth. *A Peculiar Paradise: A History of Blacks in Oregon, 1788–1940.* Portland, OR: Georgian Press, 1980.

McLaurin, Melton A. *Celia, a Slave.* Athens: University of Georgia Press, 1991.

———. "Divine Convictions: The Tale of an African American Trickster in Victorian Britain." *Gateway Heritage* 15:3 (Winter 1994–1995): 5–17.

McLemee, Scott, ed. *C. L. R. James on the "Negro Question."* Jackson: University Press of Mississippi, 1996.

McMillan, Neil R. *Dark Journey: Black Mississippians in the Age of Jim Crow.* Urbana: University of Illinois Press, 1990.

McMurry, Linda O. *To Keep the Waters Troubled: The Life of Ida B. Wells.* New York: Oxford University Press, 1998.

Meier, August. *Negro Thought in America, 1880–1915: Racial Ideologies in the Age of Booker T. Washington.* Ann Arbor: University of Michigan Press, 1968.

Meier, August, and Elliott Rudwick. *Black History and the Historical Profession, 1915–1980.* Urbana: University of Illinois Press, 1986.

Missouri State Highway Department. *Missouri: The WPA Guide to the "Show Me" State.* 1941. Reprint, Jefferson City: Missouri State Historical Society Press, 1998.

Montgomery, David. *The Fall of the House of Labor: The Workplace, the State, and American Labor Activism, 1865–1925.* 1987. Reprint, Cambridge: Cambridge University Press, 1991.

Montgomery, Rick, and Shirl Kasper. *Kansas City: An American Story.* Kansas City, MO: Kansas City Star Books, 1999.

Moore, Shirley Ann Wilson. *To Place Our Deeds: The African American Community in Richmond, Calif., 1910–1963.* Berkeley and Los Angeles: University of California Press, 2000.

Morris, Ann. *North Webster: A Photographic History of a Black Community.* Webster Groves, MO: Webster Groves Historical Society, 1993.

Moses, Wilson Jeremiah. *Alexander Crummell: A Study of Civilization and Discontent.* Amherst: University of Massachusetts Press, 1989.

———. *The Golden Age of Black Nationalism.* New York: Oxford University Press, 1978.

Moss, Alfred A. *The American Negro Academy: Voice of the Talented Tenth.* Baton Rouge: Louisiana State University Press, 1981.

Mullen, Bill. *Revolutionary Tales: African American Women's Short Stories from the First Story to the Present.* New York: Laurel, 1995.

Murphy, John W., and Jung Min Choi. *Postmodernism, Unraveling Racism and Democratic Institutions.* Westport, CT: Praeger Publishers, 1997.

Nash, Roderick. *The Nervous Generation: American Thought, 1917–1930.* 1970. Reprint, Chicago: Ivan R. Dee Publishers, 1990.

Nathan, Daniel A. "Bearing Witness to Blackball: Buck O'Neil, the Negro Leagues and the Politics of the Past." *Journal of American Studies* 35:3 (Fall 2001): 453–69.

Neckerman, Kathryn M. "Divided Households: Extended Kin in Working Class Chicago, 1924." *Social Science History* 19:3 (Fall 1995): 371–98.

Nelson, Bruce. *Divided We Stand: American Workers and the Struggle for Black Equality.* Princeton, NJ: Princeton University Press, 2001.

Neverdon-Morton, Cynthia. *Afro-American Women of the South and the Advancement of the Race, 1895–1925.* Knoxville: University of Tennessee Press, 1989.

Office of Housing and Community Development. *The Spirit of Freedom: A Profile of the History of Blacks in Kansas City, Missouri.* N.p., 1978.

Oldfield, J. R., ed. *Civilization and Black Progress: Selected Writings of Alexander Crummell on the South.* Charlottesville: University Press of Virginia, 1995.

O'Neil, Buck, with Steve Wulf and David Conrads. *I Was Right on Time: My Journey from the Negro Leagues to the Majors.* New York: Simon and Schuster, 2001.

Ovington, Mary White. *Black and White Sat Down Together: The Reminiscences of an NAACP Founder.* New York: Feminist Press, 1995.

———. "The National Association for the Advancement of Colored People." *Journal of Negro History* 9:2 (April 1924): 107–16.

Page, Georgette Stanley. *George: A Divided Soul . . . and a Divided City, 1913–1992.* Kansas City, 1992.

Painter, Nell Irvin. *The Exodusters: Black Migration to Kansas after Reconstruction.* New York: Alfred A. Knopf, 1976.

Pascoe, Peggy. "Miscegenation Law, Court Cases, and Ideologies of 'Race' in Twentieth-Century America." *Journal of American History* 83:2 (June 1996): 44–69.

Payne, Josephine A., ed. *Second Baptist Church, 1863–1983.* Kansas City, 1983.

Pearson, Nathan W. *Goin' to Kansas City.* 1987. Reprint, Chicago: University of Chicago Press, 1994.

Perata, David D. *Those Pullman Blues: An Oral History of the African American Railroad Attendant.* New York: Twayne Publishers, 1996.

Phillips, Kimberly. *Alabama North: African-American Migrants, Community and Working-Class Activism in Cleveland, 1915–45.* Urbana: University of Illinois Press, 1999.

Ploski, Harry A., and Earnest Kaiser, eds. *The Negro Almanac: The Black Experience in America.* New York: Bellwether, 1971.

Polk City Directory. Kansas City, n.p.

Potts, Louis W., and George F. W. Hauck. "Frontier Bridge Building: The Hannibal Bridge at Kansas City, 1867–1869." *Missouri Historical Review* 89:2 (January 1995): 139–61.

Preston, William, Jr. *Aliens and Dissenters: Federal Suppression of Radicals, 1903–1933.* 2d ed. Urbana: University of Illinois Press, 1994.

Rabinowitz, Howard N., ed. *Southern Black Leaders of the Reconstruction Era.* Urbana: University of Illinois Press, 1982.

Rachleff, Peter J. *Black Labor in the South: Richmond, Virginia, 1865–1890.* Philadelphia: University of Pennsylvania Press, 1984.

Rampersand, Arnold. *The Art and Imagination of W. E. B. Du Bois.* 1976. Reprint, New York: Schocken Books, 1990.

———. *The Life of Langston Hughes: I, Too, Sing America, 1902–1941.* Vol. 1. New York: Oxford University Press, 1986.

Rawick, George P., ed. *The American Slave: A Composite Autobiography.* Vol. 16. Westport, CT: Greenwood Publishing, 1972.

Reddig, William M. *Tom's Town: Kansas City and the Pendergast Legend.* Columbia: University of Missouri Press, 1986.

Reid, John B. "'A Career to Build, a People to Serve, a Purpose to Accomplish': Race, Class, Gender and Detroit's First Black Women Teachers, 1865–1916." In *"We Specialize in the Wholly Impossible": A Reader in Black Women's History,* edited by Darlene Clark Hine, Wilma King, and Linda Reed, 303–20. Brooklyn: Carlson Publishing, 1995.

Restuccia, B. S., E. Edward Gibson, and Geraldlyn Sanders. *An Extraordinary Man: Homer B. Roberts, 1885–1952.* Ann Arbor, MI: Rustic Enterprise, 2001.

Robinson, Cedric J. *Black Marxism: The Making of the Black Radical Tradition.* 1983. Reprint, Chapel Hill: University of North Carolina Press, 2000.

Rodgers, Samuel U. "Kansas City General Hospital No. 2: An Historical Summary." *Journal of the National Medical Association* 54:5 (September 1962): 525–44.

Roediger, David. *Towards the Abolition of Whiteness: Essays on Race, Politics and Working Class History.* New York: Verso, 1994.

———. *The Wages of Whiteness: Race and the Making of the American Working Class.* New York: Verso, 1991.

Rowley, Hazel. *Richard Wright: His Life and Work.* New York: Henry Holt, 2001.

Rudwick, Elliott. *Race Riot in East St. Louis, July 2, 1917.* 1964. Reprint, Urbana: University of Illinois Press, 1982.

Salem, Dorothy. *To Better Our World: Black Women in Organized Reform, 1890–1920.* Brooklyn: Carlson Publishing, 1990.

Savage, W. Sherman. "The Legal Provisions for Negro Schools in Missouri from 1865 to 1890." *Journal of Negro History* 16:4 (July 1931): 309–21.

Schirmer, Sherry Lamb. *A City Divided: The Racial Landscape of Kansas City, 1900–1960.* Columbia: University of Missouri Press, 2002.

———. "Landscape of Denial: Space, Status and Gender in the Construction of Racial Perceptions among White Kansas Citians, 1900–1958." PhD diss., University of Kansas, 1995.

Schirmer, Sherry Lamb, and Richard D. McKinzie. *At the River's Bend: An Illustrated History of Kansas City, Independence and Jackson County.* Woodland Hills, CA: Windsor Publications, 1982.

Schweninger, Loren. *Black Property Owners in the South, 1790–1915.* Urbana: University of Illinois Press, 1990.

Scott, Joan Wallach. *Gender and the Politics of History.* New York: Columbia University Press, 1988.

———. *Only Paradoxes to Offer: French Feminists and the Rights of Men.* Cambridge, MA: Harvard University Press, 1996.

Shaw, Stephanie. "Black Club Women and the Creation of the National Association of Colored Women." In *"We Specialize in the Wholly Impossible": A Reader in Black Women's History,* edited by Darlene Clark Hine, Wilma King, and Linda Reed, 433–47. Brooklyn: Carlson Publishing, 1995.

———. *What a Woman Ought to Be and to Do: Black Professional Women Workers during the Jim Crow Era.* Chicago: University of Chicago Press, 1996.

Sheridan, Richard B., ed. *Freedom's Crucible: The Underground Railroad in Lawrence and Douglas County, Kansas, 1854–1865; A Reader.* Lawrence: University Press of Kansas, 1998.

Sitkoff, Harvard. *A New Deal for Blacks: The Emergence of Civil Rights as a National Issue: The Depression Decade.* New York: Oxford University Press, 1978.

Skocpol, Theda, ed. *Vision and Method in Historical Sociology.* 1984. Reprint, New York: Cambridge University Press, 1995.

Snell, Darryn. "Struggling against Defeat: Race, Class and Biracial Unionization among Kansas City, Kan., Packinghouse Workers." Master's thesis, University of Missouri–Kansas City, 1993.

Southern, Eileen. *The Music of Black Americans: A History.* 3d ed. New York: W. W. Norton, 1997.

Spear, Allan H. *Black Chicago: The Making of a Negro Ghetto, 1880–1920.* Chicago: University of Chicago Press, 1967.

Spero, Sterling D., and Abram L. Harris. *The Black Worker: The Negro and the Labor Movement.* 1931. Reprint, New York: Atheneum, 1968.

Stack, Carol B. *All Our Kin: Strategies for Survival in a Black Community.* New York: Harper and Row, 1974.

———. "The Kindred of Viola Jackson: Residence and Family Organization of an Urban Black American Family." In *Afro-American Anthropology: Contemporary Perspectives,* edited by Norman E. Whitten Jr. and John F. Swzed, 303–12. New York: Free Press, 1973.

Stein, Judith. *The World of Marcus Garvey: Race and Class in Modern Society.* Baton Rouge: Louisiana State University Press, 1986.

Stimpson, Eddie, Jr. *My Remembers: A Black Sharecropper's Recollections of the Depression.* 1996. Reprint, Denton: University of North Texas, 1999.

Stockley, Grif. *Blood in Their Eyes: The Elaine Race Massacres of 1919.* Fayetteville: University of Arkansas Press, 2001.

Susman, Warren I. *Culture as History: The Transformation of American Society in the Twentieth Century.* New York: Pantheon Books, 1984.

Taylor, Quintard. *The Forging of a Black Community: Seattle's Central District from 1870 through the Civil Rights Era.* Seattle: University of Washington Press, 1994.

———. *In Search of the Racial Frontier: African Americans in the West, 1528–1990.* New York: W. W. Norton, 1998.

Thelen, David. *Paths of Resistance: Tradition and Democracy in Industrializing Missouri.* 1986. Reprint, Columbia: University of Missouri Press, 1991.

Thomas, Richard. *Life for Us Is What We Make It: Building Black Community in Detroit, 1915–1945.* Bloomington: Indiana University Press, 1992.

Thomas, William B., and Kevin J. Moran. "The Illusions of Aristocracy: Intra-racial Divisions in a Racist Labour Market, 1910–1930." In *Racism and the Labour Market: Historical Studies,* edited by Marcel Van Der Linden and Jan Lucassen, 237–62. Bern: Peter Lang, 1995.

Thompson, Edward P. *Making History: Writings on History and Culture.* New York: New Press, 1994.

———. *The Making of the English Working Class.* 1963. Reprint, New York: Alfred A. Knopf, 1967.

———. *The Poverty of Theory.* 1978. Reprint, London: Merlin Press, 1995.

Toomer, Jean. *Cane.* New York: Liveright, 1975.

Tracy, Jack. *Count Basie.* Philadelphia: Institute of Jazz Studies, 1985.

Trotter, Joe William, Jr. "African American Workers: New Directions in U.S. Labor Historiography." *Labor History* 35:4 (Fall 1994): 495–523.

———. *Black Milwaukee: The Making of an Industrial Proletariat.* Urbana: University of Illinois Press, 1988.

———, ed. *The Great Migration in Historical Perspective: New Dimensions of Race, Class and Gender.* Bloomington: Indiana University Press, 1991.

———. *River Jordan: African American Urban Life in the Ohio Valley.* Lexington: University Press of Kentucky, 1998.

Trotter, Joe William, Jr., and Earl Lewis, eds. *African Americans in the Industrial Age: A Documentary History, 1915–1945.* Boston: Northeastern University Press, 1996.

Trotter, Joe William, Jr., and Eric Ledell Smith, eds. *African Americans in Pennsylvania: Shifting Historical Perspectives.* State College: Pennsylvania State University Press, 1997.

Turner, W. Burghardt, and Joyce Moore Turner, ed. *Richard B. Moore: Caribbean Militant in Harlem, Collected Writings, 1920–1972.* Bloomington: Indiana University Press, 1988.

Tuttle, William. *Race Riot: Chicago in the Red Summer of 1919.* New York: Atheneum, 1975.

Urban League of Kansas City. "The Negro Worker of Kansas City: A Study of Trade Union and Organized Labor Relations." Kansas City, MO: Urban League of Kansas City, 1939.

Urquhart, Brian. *Ralph Bunche: An American Life.* New York: W. W. Norton, 1993.

Wadelington, Charles W., and Richard F. Knapp. *Charlotte Hawkins Brown and Palmer Memorial Institute: What One Young African American Woman Could Do.* Chapel Hill: University of North Carolina Press, 1999.

Walker, Clarence E. *Deromanticizing Black History: Critical Essays and Reappraisals.* Knoxville: University of Tennessee Press, 1991.

Ward, Andrew. *Dark Midnight When I Rise: The Story of the Jubilee Singers Who Introduced the World to the Music of Black America.* New York: Farrar, Strauss, and Giroux, 2000.

Ware, Susan. *Holding Their Own: American Women in the 1930s.* Boston: G. K. Hall, 1982.

Weber, Max. *Sociological Writings.* Edited by Wolf Heydebrand. German Library, vol. 60. New York: Continuum, 1994.

Wedin, Carolyn. *Inheritors of the Spirit: Mary White Ovington and the Founding of the NAACP.* New York: John Wiley and Sons, 1999.

Weems, Robert E., Jr. *Black Business in the Black Metropolis: The Chicago Metropolitan Assurance Company, 1925–1985.* Bloomington: Indiana University Press, 1996.

Weisbrot, Robert. *Father Divine: The Utopian Evangelist of the Depression Era Who Became an American Legend.* Boston: Beacon Press, 1983.

Wells, Ida B. *The Memphis Diary of Ida B. Wells: An Intimate Portrait of the Activist as a Young Woman.* Edited by Miriam DeCosta-Willis. Boston: Beacon Press, 1995.

Wells, Ida B., et al. *The Reason Why the Colored American Is Not in the World's Columbian Exposition.* Edited by Robert W. Rydell. Urbana: University of Illinois Press, 1999.

White, Deborah Gray. *Ar'n't I a Woman? Female Slaves in the Plantation South.* New York: W. W. Norton, 1985.

———. *Too Heavy a Load: Black Women in Defense of Themselves, 1894–1994.* New York: W. W. Norton, 1999.

Whitten, Norman E., Jr., and John F. Swzed, eds. *Afro-American Anthropology: Contemporary Perspectives.* New York: Free Press, 1970.

Wiebe, Robert H. *The Search for Order, 1877–1920.* Making of America Series. New York: Hill and Wang, 1967.

Wilkins, Roy. *Standing Fast: The Autobiography of Roy Wilkins.* New York: Da Capo Press, 1994.

Williams, Eric. *Capitalism and Slavery.* 1944. Reprint, Chapel Hill: University of North Carolina Press, 1994.

Wilson, Sondra Kathryn, ed. *The "Crisis" Reader: Stories, Poetry, and Essays from the N.A.A.C.P.'s "Crisis" Magazine.* New York: Random House, 1999.

———, ed. *The "Messenger" Reader: Stories, Poetry and Essays from the "Messenger" Magazine.* New York: Random House, 2000.

———, ed. *The Selected Writings of James Weldon Johnson.* Vol. 1, *The New York Age Editorials (1914–1923).* New York: Oxford University Press, 1995.

———, ed. *The Selected Writings of James Weldon Johnson.* Vol. 2, *Social, Political, and Literary Essays.* New York: Oxford University Press, 1995.

Wilson, Thomas D. "Chester A. Franklin and Harry S. Truman: An African-American Conservative and the 'Conversion' of the Future President." *Missouri Historical Review* 88:1 (October 1993): 48–77.

Wilson, William Julius. *The Declining Significance of Race.* Chicago: University of Chicago Press, 1980.

Winslow, Calvin, ed. *Waterfront Workers: New Perspectives on Race and Class.* Urbana: University of Illinois Press, 1997.

Wolcott, Victoria W. *Remaking Respectability: African American Women in Interwar Detroit.* Chapel Hill: University of North Carolina Press, 2000.

Wood, Ellen Meiksins, and John Bellamy Foster. *In Defense of History: Marxism and the Postmodern Agenda.* New York: Monthly Review Press, 1997.

Woods, Randall Bennett. *A Black Odyssey: John Lewis Waller and the Promise of American Life, 1878–1900.* Lawrence: Regents Press of Kansas, 1981.

Woodson, Carter G., and Charles H. Wesley. *The Negro in Our History.* 10th ed. 1923. Reprint, Washington, DC: Associated Publishers, 1962.

Woodward, C. Vann. *The Strange Career of Jim Crow.* 3d ed. New York: Oxford University Press, 1974.

———. *Tom Watson: Agrarian Rebel.* 1938. Reprint, New York: Oxford University Press, 1972.

Wright, George C. *Life behind a Veil: Blacks in Louisville, 1865–1930.* Baton Rouge: Louisiana State University Press, 1991.

Yates, Josephine Silone. "The Equipment of the Teacher." *Voice of the Negro* 1:6 (1904): 248–52.

Yellin, Jean Fagan, and Cynthia D. Bond, eds. *The Pen Is Ours: A Listing of Writings by and about African American Women before 1910 with Secondary Bibliography to the Present.* New York: Oxford University Press, 1991.

Young, Nathan B., and William H. Young. *Your Kansas City and Mine.* 1950. Reprint, Kansas City, MO: Midwest Afro-American Genealogy Interest Coalition, 1997.

Zamir, Shamoon. *Dark Voices: W. E. B. Du Bois and American Thought, 1888–1903*. Chicago: University of Chicago Press, 1995.

Zwick, Jim. "'The White Man's Burden' and Its Critics." http://www.boondocksnet.com/kipling/. In *Anti-Imperialism in the United States, 1898–1935,* edited by Jim Zwick. http://www.boondocksnet.com/ail98-35.html.

Index

About the Author

Charles E. Coulter is a retired teacher of African American Studies and a retired journalist. Among his accomplishments, he provided most of the text for the permanent exhibit at the Black Archives of Mid-America in Kansas City's historic 18th and Vine district.

He and his wife live in the historic Northeast area of Kansas City, Missouri.